Correlation Risk Modelling and Management

Correlation Risk Modelling and Management
Second Edition

Gunter Meissner

Risk Books is a trading name of Infopro Digital Risk Limited
© Infopro Digital Risk (IP) Limited 2018
All rights reserved.

Infopro Digital
Haymarket House 28–29 Haymarket
London SW1Y 4RX
Tel: +44(0) 20 7316 9000
Sites: www.riskbooks.com

© 2018 Infopro Digital Risk Limited

ISBN 978-1-78272-405-6

The first edition of this book was published by John Wiley & Sons, Inc. 2014.

British Library Cataloguing in Publication Data
A catalogue record for this book is available from the British Library

Publisher: Nick Carver
Commissioning Editor: Emma Glass
Managing Editor: Lewis O'Sullivan
Designer: Lisa Ling
Copyeditor: MFE Editorial Services

Typeset by Mark Heslington Ltd, Scarborough, North Yorkshire
Printed and bound in the UK by PrintonDemand-Worldwide

Conditions of sale
All rights reserved. No part of this publication may be reproduced in any material form whether by photocopying or storing in any medium by electronic means whether or not transiently or incidentally to some other use for this publication without the prior written consent of the copyright owner except in accordance with the provisions of the Copyright, Designs and Patents Act 1988 or under the terms of a licence issued by the Copyright Licensing Agency Limited of Saffron House, 6–10 Kirby Street, London EC1N 8TS, UK.

Warning: the doing of any unauthorised act in relation to this work may result in both civil and criminal liability.

Every effort has been made to ensure the accuracy of the text at the time of publication, this includes efforts to contact each author to ensure the accuracy of their details at publication is correct. However, no responsibility for loss occasioned to any person acting or refraining from acting as a result of the material contained in this publication will be accepted by the copyright owner, the editor, the authors or Infopro Digital.

Many of the product names contained in this publication are registered trade marks, and Risk Books has made every effort to print them with the capitalisation and punctuation used by the trademark owner. For reasons of textual clarity, it is not our house style to use symbols such as TM, ®, etc. However, the absence of such symbols should not be taken to indicate absence of trademark protection; anyone wishing to use product names in the public domain should first clear such use with the product owner.

While best efforts have been intended for the preparation of this book, neither the publisher, the editor nor any of the potentially implicitly affiliated organisations accept responsibility for any errors, mistakes and or omissions it may provide or for any losses howsoever arising from or in reliance upon its information, meanings and interpretations by any parties.

Contents

About the Author		vii
Acknowledgements		ix
Glossary		xi
	Introduction	1
1	Correlation Basics: Definitions, Applications, and Terminology	7
2	Empirical Properties of Correlation: How do Correlations Behave in the real World?	51
3	The Pearson Correlation Model – Work of the Devil?	65
4	Cointegration – A Superior Concept to Correlation?	105
5	Financial Correlation Modelling – Bottom-up Approaches	121
6	Valuing CDOs with the Gaussian Copula – What Went Wrong?	149
7	The One-Factor Gaussian Copula Model – Too Simplistic?	167
8	Financial Correlation Models – Top-Down Approaches	193
9	Stochastic Correlation Models	207
10	Quantifying Market Correlation Risk	231
11	Quantifying Credit Correlation Risk	251
12	Hedging Correlation Risk	285
13	Correlation Trading Strategies – Opportunities and Limitations	301

14	Credit Value at Risk under Basel III – Too Simplistic?	331
15	Basel III and XVAs	349
16	Fundamental Review of the Trading Book	371
17	The Future of Correlation Modelling	385
	Answers to Questions	413

About the Author

After a lectureship in mathematics and statistics at the Economic Academy Kiel, Gunter Meissner PhD joined Deutsche Bank in 1990, trading interest-rate futures, swaps and options in Frankfurt and New York. He became head of product development in 1994, responsible for originating algorithms for new derivatives products, which at the time were Index amortising swaps, Lookback Options, and Quanto Options and Bermuda Swaptions.

In 1995–6, Meissner was head of options at Deutsche Bank, Tokyo. From 1997 to 2007, he was professor of finance at Hawaii Pacific University and, from 2008 to 2013, director of the financial-engineering programme at the University of Hawaii. Currently, he is president of derivatives software (www.dersoft.com), and adjunct professor of mathematical finance at Columbia University and NYU.

Meissner has published numerous papers on derivatives and is a frequent speaker at conferences and seminars. He is the author of five books, including the first edition of this title, published in 2014: *Correlation Risk Modeling and Management – An Applied Guide including the Basel III Correlation Framework*. He can be reached at gunter@dersoft.com.

Acknowledgements

Many of my students, colleagues and friends have significantly contributed in writing this book. I would like to thank the MFE classes of 2012 and 2013 at the Shidler College of Business at the University of Hawaii for detailed discussions and number crunching on the first edition. In particular, Martin Chang, Zhen Chen, Clint Davis, Charles Demarest, Barrett Gady, Susan Globokar, Ziyan Jiang, Thuy Le, Stefan Mayr, Dongfang Nie, Amirarsalan Pakravan, Babak Saadat, Alex Schnurrer, Jun Sheng, Wenjing Tang, Manogaran Thanabalan, Ryuichi Umeda, Jeremy Whitley, Eugene Wong, Amir Yousefi and Elke Zeller contributed strongly.

I would like to thank Ranjan Bhaduri and Edgar Lobachevskiy for discussions on mathematical issues. Seth Rooder programmed two of the models, which are referenced in the book. King Burch, Sidy Danioko, Brendan Lane Larson, Stefan Mayr, Eric Mills, Jason Mills, Rudolf Meissner and Pedro Villarreal did an excellent job proofreading the book, finding errors and suggesting improvements. Pedro Villarreal also helped to solve small and big computer problems and derived complex graphics.

A special thanks goes to Jeremy Whitley for number crunching for the second edition and Raul Diego, Kai Nolte and Hector Silva for a thorough proofreading of the second edition.

"Do we have to understand this?" (Jasmine 12, Jake 8)
Well, while my kids struggle with the content of this book, I hope that the reader enjoys the book and learns from it. I am happy to receive feedback, so please email me at gunter@dersoft.com.

There is an errata page at www.dersoft.com/errata.docx. If you find an error, please inform me. Naturally, all mistakes are my own.

Glossary

Accrued interest: The accumulated interest of an investment from the last payment date.

Algorithmic trading: The application of computers, which execute buy and sell order via pre-programmed mathematical algorithms.

American-style option: Option that can be exercised at any time before or at the option maturity date.

Antithetic variable technique: A method to reduce computations when simulating trials (as in the Monte Carlo method) by changing the sign of the random sample.

Arbitrage: A risk-free profit, achieved by simultaneously buying and selling equivalent securities on different markets. In trading practice, often defined more widely as a strategy used when trying to exploit price differences.

Asset swap: A swap based on the fixed rate of an asset. Typically, that fixed rate is swapped into LIBOR plus a spread.

Asset swap spread: Spread over LIBOR that is paid in an asset swap. Reflects the credit quality of the issuer.

Association: A measure of association is a fairly new statistical term synonymous with measure of dependence (*see also* dependence).

Attachment point: The number or the amount of defaults necessary to trigger a payoff in a basket default swap or a tranche of a CDO.

Autocorrelation: The degree of which a variable is correlated to its past values.

Back-testing: Testing how well current value-at-risk (VaR), credit value-at-risk (CVaR), or other methods would have performed in the past.

Bank for International Settlements (BIS): An international organisation that fosters cooperation among central banks and other agencies in pursuit of monetary and financial stability.

Banking book: Constitutes the account where a bank's conventional transactions such as loans, bonds and deposits are recorded. These transactions are typically not marked to market (*compare* trading book).

Bankruptcy: Refers to a party not honouring its obligations to its creditors and whose assets are therefore administered by a trustee.

Barrier option: A type of option that can be knocked in or knocked out, depending on whether the underlying asset has reached a predetermined price. A barrier option is cheaper than a standard option.

Basel Committee on Banking Supervision (BCBS): Committee of the BIS, established in 1975. It functions as a supervisory authority, establishing the regulatory framework for financial institutions.

Basel III: A set of guidelines developed after the global financial crisis of 2007 to 2009 to strengthen the global financial system and make it more shock-resilient.

Basis: The difference between the spot price and the futures price of a security. In the credit default swap market, the difference between the credit default swap premium and the asset swap spread.

Basis point: One-hundredth of one percentage point (ie, 0.01%).

Basis risk: The risk of the basis changing.

Basket option: An option in which the option buyer receives a basket of assets if the value of the basket is higher than the strike price. Basket options have a positive Cora, ie, their value increases for increasing correlation between the assets in the basket.

Bid: The highest price a buyer is willing to pay for a security.

Binomial correlation measure: Measures the correlation between two variables with binomial outcomes such as default or no default. It is a limiting case of the Pearson correlation model.

Binomial model: A model in which the price of a security can move only two (bi) ways, typically up or down.

BIS: *See* Bank for International Settlements (BIS).

Black–Scholes–Merton model: A mathematical model suggested by Fischer Black and Myron Scholes and separately by Robert Merton in 1973 to find a theoretical price for European-style options on an underlying security that pays no dividends.

Bottom-up correlation model: A model that derives correlations on an individual level and aggregates them to an overall correlation measure (*compare* top-down correlation model).

Brady bonds: Bonds issued by emerging countries in the early 1990s, which were guaranteed by US Treasury bonds.

Calibration: The process of finding values for the input parameters of a model so that the model's output matches market values.

Call on the maximum of two: An option in which the buyer receives asset 1 or asset 2 if the any of those assets has a higher price than the strike price.

Call option: The right but not the obligation to buy an underlying asset at the strike price on a certain date (European style) or during a certain period (American style).

Cancellable credit default swap: A swap in which one or both parties have the right to terminate the swap.

Cap: A contract that gives the cap owner the right to pay a fixed interest rate (strike) and receive a LIBOR rate.

Capital adequacy: Capital requirements set by the Basel Committee on Banking Supervision of the BIS for different types of risk.

Capital asset pricing model (CAPM): A model that demonstrates the relationship between risk and return.

Cash settlement: Type of settlement of derivatives where a cash amount is paid to the profiteer (*see also* physical settlement).

CDO: *See* collateralised debt obligation (CDO).

CDS: *See* Credit default swap (CDS).

Characteristic equation: In calculus, an equation upon which the solution of a differential or difference equation depends.

CID correlation model: *See* Conditionally independent default (CID) correlation model.

Cointegration: A measure of association. If two or more time series (eg, two stock prices in time) are individually integrated, but some linear combination (a portfolio) of them has a lower order of integration, then the two series are said to be cointegrated.

Collateral: An asset pledged by a debtor as a guarantee for repayment.

Collateralised debt obligation (CDO): A tranched debt structure in with the credit risk of an underlying portfolio is transferred from the CDO seller (originator) to the CDO investor.

Collateralised mortgage obligation: A pool of mortgages, typically tranched, which investors can buy. Defaults of mortgagers lead to losses for the investors, the junior tranche bearing the first losses.

Collateralised value adjustment (ColVA): An adjustment for the cost of funding the collateral in a derivatives transaction or the related hedge.

Common market factor: A factor that impacts all assets in a portfolio. An example would be the general state of the economy.

Concentration risk: The risk of financial loss due to a concentrated exposure to a particular group of counterparties.

Conditionally independent default (CID) correlation model: A model that does not derive the correlation between variables directly, but indirectly by conditioning on a common (market) factor.

Continuously compounded interest rate: An interest rate where interest is compounded in infinitesimally short time units (*see also* instantaneous interest rate).

Control variate technique: A method to reduce computations when simulating trials (as in the Monte Carlo method) for two similar derivatives.

Convertible: A bond issued by a company that can be converted into shares of that company during the life of the bond.

Convertible arbitrage: A long position in a convertible security and a short position in the underlying stock.

Convexity: The second (partial) derivative of a function. Measures the curvature of the function.

Copula: A function that joins multiple univariate distribution functions to form a single multivariate distribution function.

Cora: A measure of how much a dependent variable changes if the correlation between two or more independent variables changes by an infinitesimally small amount.

Correlation: Used quite broadly in practice, referring to the comovement of assets. Defined more narrowly in statistics, referring to the linear strength of a relationship derived in the Pearson correlation framework.

Correlation coefficient: A standardised statistical measure in the Pearson correlation framework that measures the strength of a linear relationship. Takes values between −1 and +1. Defined as the covariance divided by the product of the standard deviations of the two variables.

Correlation desk: A term for an area where traders sit who perform correlation trading.

Correlation risk: The risk of financial loss due to the adverse movement in correlation between two or more variables.

Correlation swaps: In a correlation swap, one party pays a fixed correlation rate in exchange for a realised, stochastic correlation rate. The fixed-rate payer is "buying correlation", since they benefit from an increase in correlation.

Correlation trading: The attempt to generate a profit by anticipating the change in the correlation between two or more variables.

Counterparty: A partner in a financial transaction.

Counterparty risk: The risk of the counterparty not honouring its obligation.

Covariance: A statistical measure within the Pearson correlation framework that measures the linear strength between two variables.

Covered call writing: A short call option position and a long position in the underlying security.

Credit correlation risk: The risk that credit quality correlations between two or more counterparties change unfavourably.

Credit default swap (CDS): A financial product in which the credit risk of an underlying asset is transferred from the CDS buyer to the CDS seller.

Credit default swap premium: Price of a credit default swap. Also termed credit default swap spread, fee, or fixed rate.

Credit derivative: A future, swap, or option that transfers credit risk from one counterparty to another.

Credit event: The ISDA 1999 documentation defines six credit events: bankruptcy, failure to pay, obligation acceleration, obligation default, repudiation/moratorium, and restructuring.

CreditMetrics: A transition-matrix-based model developed by JPMorgan to value portfolio credit risk.

Credit rating: An assessment of the credit quality of a debtor, expressed in categories from AAA to D.

Credit risk: The risk of a financial loss due to an adverse change in the credit quality of a debtor. Consists of credit migration risk and default risk.

Credit Risk +: An actuarially based model developed by Credit Suisse Financial Products to value portfolio credit risk.

Credit risk premium: *See* credit spread.

Credit spread: Also referred to as credit risk premium. The excess in yield of a security with credit risk over a comparable security without credit risk.

Credit triangle: An approximate relationship of the credit default swap premium s, the default probability λ and the recovery rate R (*see* Equation 6.6).

Credit value adjustment (CVA): An adjustment to address counterparty credit risk. Typically applied to derivative transactions.

Credit value-at-risk (CVaR): The maximum loss of a portfolio due to credit risk with a certain probability for a certain time frame. Also called credit at risk or worst-case default rate (WCDR).

CVA: Credit value adjustment (CVA).

CVaR: *See* credit value-at-risk (CVaR).

Debt value adjustment (DVA): Allows an entity to adjust the value of its portfolio by taking its own default probability into consideration.

Default: Occurs when a party has not honoured its legal obligation to its creditors.

Default correlation: A measure of joint default probability of two or more entities within a short time frame.

Default intensity: The probability of default for a short period of time conditional on no earlier default. Identical with hazard rate.

Default probability: The likelihood that a debt instrument or counterparty will default within a certain time. *See also* default intensity.

Default risk: The risk that a debtor may be unable to honour its financial obligation.

Delta: The change in the value of a derivative for an infinitesimally small change in the price (or rate) of the underlying security.

Dependence: Two events are statistically dependent if the occurrence of one affects the outcome of another.

Dickey–Fuller test: A test whether an autoregressive process is integrated to the order 1, I(1).

Derivative: A security whose value is at least in part derived by the price of an underlying asset.

Discount factor: The number that a cashflow occurring at a future date is multiplied by, to bring it to its present value.

Discount rate: The interest rate that is used in the discount factor.

Dispersion trading: A long dispersion trade is buying index-component volatility and selling index volatility (for example by buying straddles on the index-components and selling straddles on the index). A short dispersion trade is buying index volatility and selling index-components volatility (for example by buying straddles on the index and selling straddles on index components).

Distance to default: A term derived by Moody's KMV displaying the difference between the value of assets and the value of liabilities at a certain future point in time. Mathematically identical with the risk-neutral d_2 in the Merton model.

Double default approach: An approach by the Basel Committee to calculate the capital charge for double defaults. Results typically in a lower capital charge than the substitution approach (*see also* substitution approach)

Drift rate: The average change of a variable in a stochastic process.

Duration: A measure of the relative change in the value of a bond with respect to a change in its yield to maturity. Also measures the average time that an investor has to wait to get the investment back.

DVA: *See* Debt value adjustment (DVA).

Economic capital: Capital to protect against loss; often measured by value-at-risk.

EDF: *See* Expected default frequency (EDF).

Efficient market hypothesis: A hypothesis that asset prices include all relevant information. If correct, above market gains are not possible.

Empirical correlation trading: The utilisation of empirical market correlations; for example, the positive correlation between international markets.

Equity tranche: The riskiest tranche of a CDO. The investors in the equity tranche absorb the first losses from defaults.

European-style option: An option that can be exercised only on the maturity date.

Excess yield: The difference between the yield of a risky bond and the yield of a risk-free bond.

Exchange option: An option to exchange one asset for another.

Exotic option: An option whose payoff, evaluation and hedging are different from, and typically more complex, than those of standard options.

Expected default frequency (EDF): A term from Moody's KMV's model for the probability of default. Real-world representation of the risk-neutral $N(-d_2)$ in the Merton model.

Expected shortfall: The loss in excess of VaR (value-at-risk).

Exposure at default: The capital that is lost when the debtor defaults. The outstanding loan amount in case of a standard loan.

Finite difference method: A method to solve differential equations by transferring the differential equations into difference equations and solving these iteratively.

First passage time model: A type of structural model. In first passage time models, bankruptcy occurs when the asset value drops below a predefined, usually exogenous barrier, allowing for bankruptcy before the maturity of the debt.

Floating rate: An interest rate that periodically changes according a certain reference rate such as LIBOR.

Floor: Opposite of a cap. A contract that gives the floor owner the right to receive a fixed interest rate (strike) and pay a LIBOR rate.

Forward contract: A transaction in which the price is fixed today, but settlement takes place at a future date.

Fundamental review of the trading book: A new framework by the Basel Committee, proposing major changes to capital requirements for market risk.

Funded transaction: A transaction in which the buyer pays an upfront premium to buy a security (*compare* unfunded transaction).

Funding value adjustment (FVA): An adjustment to the price of a transaction due to the cost of funding for the transaction or the related hedge.

Future contract: A standardised forward contract that trades on an exchange. Standardised are the notional, price, maturity quality, deliverability, type of settlement, trading hours and so forth.

FVA: *See* Funding value adjustment (FVA).

Gamma: Second partial derivative of the option function with respect to the underlying price. A measure for the curvature of the option function. Gamma is the change in the delta of an option for an infinitesimally small change in the price of the underlying.

General wrong-way risk (WWR): *See* Wrong-way risk (WWR).

Generalised Wiener process: A process in which a variable has a constant, expected growth rate. Superimposed on this growth rate is a stochastic volatility term.

Geometric Brownian motion: A process in which the relative change of a variable follows a generalised Wiener process (*see* Equation 5.1).

Gora: Second partial derivative of a function with respect to correlation. A measure of how much Cora changes if the correlation between two or more independent variables changes by an infinitesimally small amount.

Granger causality: A concept that tries to find the causality between variables. Assumptions of Granger causality are (1) the cause happens before the effect and (2) the cause has unique information about the future values of its effect.

Haircut: A discount to the value of securities held as collateral, reflecting the price uncertainty of the security.

Hazard rate: *See* default intensity.

Hedging: Reducing risk. More precisely, entering into a second trade to reduce the risk of an original trade.

Heston 1993 model: One of the most rigorous and useful correlation models for finance. Correlates the Brownian motions of two or more variables.

Heteroscedasticity: Heteroscedasticity exists if the error terms ε_i in the regression Y(X) are not constant but have a different dispersion in X.

High-frequency trading: A type of algorithmic trading. Computers process information and execute buy and sell orders in milliseconds.

IMA: *See* Internal model approach (IMA).

IMM: *See* Internal model method (IMM).

Implied volatility: Volatility that is implied by observed option prices.

In arrears: Refers to a later date at which a payment is made.

Index-option-implied volatility: The implied volatility at which the index trades.

Instantaneous interest rate: An interest rate that is applied to an infinitesimally short period of time (*see also* continuously compounded interest rate).

Integrated to the order d: A time series is integrated to the order d, $I(d)$, if taking repeated differences d times results in a stationary process.

Interest-rate swap: An exchange of interest-rate payments on a predetermined notional amount and in reference to predetermined interest-rate indexes.

Internal model approach (IMA): *See* internal model method (MM).

Internal model method (IMM): Also called internal model approach (IMA). Allows banks to derive their own models to calculate capital requirements. Banks need regulatory approval to apply the IMM.

Internal-rating-based approach (IRB): An approach that allows banks to estimate certain risk parameters for calculating regulatory capital themselves. It is applied by large, sophisticated banks (*compare* standardised approach).

Intrinsic value: The payoff when the option is exercised. For a call, the intrinsic value is the maximum of the spot price minus the strike price and zero. For a put, the intrinsic value is the maximum of the strike price minus the spot price and zero.

Investment grade bond: A bond with a rating of BBB or higher.

Junior tranche: A tranche in a CDO with moderate default risk. The junior tranche is protected by the equity tranche, which absorbs the first losses from defaults.

Junk bond: A high-yield bond with a rating lower than BBB.

Kurtosis: Fourth moment of a distribution; a measure of the fatness of the tails of the distribution.

Large homogeneous portfolio (LHP): A portfolio of assets with similar default probability, default correlation, maturity and coupon, possibly from the same sector. The LHP is underlying the one-factor Gaussian copula model.

Latent variable: Also called frailty variable. A variable that is not directly observable. In credit models, typically the lower the latent variable, the earlier the default.

LHP: *See* Large homogeneous portfolio (LHP).

LIBOR: London Interbank Offered Rate (LIBOR).

LIBOR market model (LMM): A term structure model in which interest rates are conveniently expressed as discrete forward rates.

Liquidity premium: A premium that lowers an asset price due to asset illiquidity.

LMM: *See* LIBOR market model (LMM)

Lognormal distribution: A distribution with a fat right tail. A variable follows a lognormal distribution if the logarithm of the variable is normal. Often applied to model stock price behaviour, as in the Black-Scholes-Merton model.

London Interbank Offered Rate (LIBOR): An interest rate paid by highly rated borrowers; fixed daily in London.

Long position: A trading position that generates a profit if the underlying instrument increases in price (opposite of a short position).

Margin-value adjustment: An adjustment for the cost of an initial margin and a variation margin for non-centrally cleared derivatives.

Market price of risk: *See* Sharpe ratio.

Market risk: The risk of financial loss due to an unfavourable change in the price of a financial security.

Marking to market: The evaluation of a transaction, or account value, to reflect current market variables.

Markov process: A stochastic, memoryless process. Hence only present information, not past information, is relevant.

Markowitz implied volatility (MIV): The MIV is the theoretical value, based on implied component volatility and historical correlation, at which the index volatility σ_I should trade.

Martingale process: A stochastic process with a zero drift rate. Hence the expected future value of a variable is the current value.

Maturity: The date on which a transaction or a financial instrument is due to end.

Maturity adjustment: An adjustment for the length of a transaction, required by the Basel Committee to calculate the required capital for credit risk.

Mean reversion: The tendency for a price or a rate to revert back towards its long-term mean.

Migration probability: The probability of a firm's credit rating moving to another rating state.

Migration risk: The risk that the credit rating changes unfavourably.

MIV: *See* Markowitz implied volatility (MIV)

Monte Carlo simulation: A technique for approximating the price of a derivative by randomly sampling the evolution of the underlying security.

Multicollinearity: Multicollinearity refers to two or more regressors (ie, independent or explanatory variables) to be linearly associated.

Netting: Offsetting contracts with positive and negative values with another counterparty.

Nonsense correlation: A correlation between two or more variables, which are not causally related.

Normal distribution: Also called Gaussian distribution or bell curve. A standard, popular probability distribution forming a symmetrical curve. Suffers from the inability to replicate fat tails found in financial practice.

Notional amount: Also called principal amount. Dollar amount of a security or transaction.

Numeraire: The price of a security in which other securities are measured.

Numerical finance: Attempts to solve financial problems with numerical methods (such as Monte Carlo simulation), without the need for mathematical solvency.

Off balance sheet: Refers to a transaction that does not have to be included on the balance sheet of the party in question.

One-factor Gaussian copula (OFGC): A model to derive correlated credit risk of a portfolio. The simplistic assumptions that (1) all entities have the same default probability and (2) all assets have the same pairwise correlation, are made.

Operational risk: The risk of direct or indirect loss resulting from inadequate or failed internal processes, people and systems or from external events [BIS definition].

Option on the better of two: An option in which the buyer receives the asset with the higher price at option maturity.

Option on the worse of two: An option in which the buyer receives the asset with the lower price at option maturity.

Ornstein–Uhlenbeck process: A process with a drift term (average growth rate) and a stochastic volatility term. The drift term includes mean reversion. The model is also called Vasicek (1977) model.

Over the counter (OTC): Refers to a transaction traded directly between counterparties, hence not traded on an exchange.

Pairs trading: Pairs trading finds two stocks, whose prices are highly correlated. Once the price correlation weakens, the stock that has increased is shorted and the stock which has declined is bought. Presumably, the spread will narrow again and a profit is realised.

Pearson correlation model: Measures the strength of a linear dependence. It is the most popular correlation model in statistics and is also widely applied in finance but suffers from a variety of problems (*see* Chapter 3).

Percentile: Value of a distribution under which the percentile value falls. For example, the 95th percentile is the value under which 95% of values in the distribution are found.

Physical settlement: Type of settlement of derivatives in which physical delivery and payment of the underlying asset take place (*see also* cash settlement).

Premium: The price of a financial transaction (*see also* credit spread).

Present value: Current value of discounted future cashflows.

Principal component analysis: A method trying to find the critical factors (components) that explain the variation of a large number of possibly correlated variables.

Put option: The right but not the obligation to sell an underlying asset at the strike price on a certain date (European style) or during a certain period (American style).

Quantile: An integer, indicating certain essentially equally sized intervals of a cumulative distribution function. For example, the 2-quantile is the median, and the 100-quantiles are the percentiles (*see also* percentile).

Quanto option: An option that allows buyers to exchange their payoff in a foreign currency into their home currency at a fixed exchange rate.

Random variable: A variable that can take a set of different values, each associated with a probability.

Random walk: A term expressing the process of a random variable. The randomness is often generated by a drawing from a standard normal distribution.

Recovery rate: The percentage of the notional amount that a creditor receives in case of default.

Reduced form model: A type of model that does not include the asset-liability structure of the firm to generate default probabilities. Rather, reduced form models use bonds and credit default swaps (CDSs) as main inputs to model the bankruptcy process.

Reference asset: Also called reference obligation or reference entity. Typically has the form of a bond or a note. The default risk of the reference asset can be insured with a credit derivative, often a credit default swap.

Reference obligation: *See* reference asset.

Regulatory capital adjustment (KVA): An adjustment for holding regulatory capital during the life of the derivative.

Repo: Repurchase agreement. A securitised loan; in a repo, a security is sold with a guarantee that it will be repurchased at a later date at a fixed, typically higher, price.

Risk-averse: An attitude toward risk that causes an investor to prefer an investment with a certain expected return to an investment with the same expected return but greater uncertainty.

Risk category: The Basel Committee defines five risk categories, each comprising certain risk factors and their subsets' risk factor variables, for different liquidity horizons.

Risk factor: The Basel Committee on Banking Supervision defines five risk factors that are relevant to derive market risk: (1) equity risk, (2) interest-rate risk, (3) credit-spread risk, (4) FX risk and (5) commodity risk.

Risk factor variables: A criterion of a risk factor, such as risk-factor volatility or high yield versus investment-grade credit risk.

Risk-free rate: An interest rate that can be achieved without risk. Typically the interest rate for securities issued by an AAA-rated government or firm.

Risk management: The process of identifying, quantifying and, if desired, reducing risk.

Risk-neutral: An attitude toward risk that leads an investor to be indifferent between investment A with a certain expected return and investment B with the same expected return but higher uncertainty.

Senior tranche: A tranche of a CDO with relatively low default risk. The senior tranche is protected by the equity and junior tranches, which absorb losses from defaults first.

Sharpe ratio: Also termed market price of risk; return of a risky asset minus the return of the risk-free asset, divided by the standard deviation of the risky asset.

Short position: A trading position that generates a profit if the underlying instrument decreases in price (opposite of long position).

Short selling: Selling a security that is borrowed, in anticipation of a decline of that security.

Short squeeze: A term for traders buying a security to increase the price since they know the security has to be bought back by (short) sellers.

Skewness: Third moment of a distribution function. Measure of the asymmetry of a distribution.

Smile effect: A term referring to the higher implied volatilities of out-of-the-money options and in-the-money options compared to at-the-money options.

Special-purpose corporation (SPC): *See* special-purpose vehicle (SPV).

Special-purpose entity (SPE): *See* special purpose vehicle (SPV).

Special-purpose vehicle (SPV): Legal entity, separate from the parent entity, typically highly rated. Often functions as an intermediary in structured financial transactions.

Specific wrong-way risk (WWR): *See* Wrong-way risk (WWR).

Spot price: The price of a security for immediate (in practice often two days) delivery.

Spread option: An option in which the option buyer received the difference in price between two assets, if the difference is higher than the strike price.

SPV: *See* Special-purpose vehicle (SPV).

Spurious correlation: Spurious correlations occur when the absolute values of variables show no pairwise correlation, even though the relative values show a non-zero correlation.

Spurious relationship: Another term for nonsense correlation.

Standardised approach: An approach that applies external parameters to calculate regulatory risk charges. It is applied by smaller, less sophisticated banks (*compare* internal-rating-based approach).

Stationary process: A process where mean and variance are constant in time (weak stationary), or all moments (strict stationary) are constant in time.

Stochastic process: A process with an unknown outcome.

Stress testing: Testing how a portfolio behaves under extreme market movements.

Strike price: For a call option, the price at which the underlying security may be bought; for a put option, the price at which the underlying security may be sold.

Structural model: A type of model that derives the probability of default by analysing the capital structure of a firm, especially the value of the firm's assets compared with the value of the firm's debt.

Subadditivity: Exists, when the risk of a portfolio R is smaller than or equal to the risk of the individual positions, ie, $R(A + B) \leq R(A) + R(B)$. It can be shown that VaR (value-at-risk) does not necessarily satisfy subadditivity. However, ES (expected shortfall) satisfies subadditivity.

Substitution approach: An approach by the Basel Committee to calculate the capital charge for double defaults. The credit quality of the guarantor can be substituted for the credit quality of the obligor (*see also* double default approach)

Swap: The agreement between two parties to exchange a series of cashflows.

Swaption: Also called swap option; an option on a swap. A payer swaption allows the owner to pay a fixed swap rate and to receive a floating rate. A receiver swaption allows the owner to receive a fixed swap rate and to pay a floating rate.

Synthetic structure: A financial structure in which exposure is assumed synthetically. For example, in a synthetic CDO, the SPV assumes credit risk by selling CDSs.

Systematic risk: Also called market risk or common risk. Risk associated with the movement of a market or market segment as opposed to risk associated with a specific security. Systematic risk cannot be diversified away.

Systemic risk: The risk of a financial market or an entire financial system collapsing.

Term structure model: A stochastic, binomial or multinomial discrete or continuous model, generating the process of short-term interest rates.

Theta: The change in price of a derivative for an infinitesimally small change in time.

Time value: The portion of an option's premium that is attributed to uncertainty. Time value equals the option price minus the intrinsic value.

Top-down correlation model: A model that abstracts from individual correlations, but rather models correlations on an aggregate level (*compare* bottom-up correlation model).

Trading book: Comprises instruments that are explicitly held with trading intent or in order to hedge other positions (*compare* banking book).

Tranches: Segments of deals or structures, typically with different risk levels.

Transition matrix: A matrix showing the probability of a firm moving to other rating categories within a certain time frame.

Underlying: The security that a derivative is based on and that at least in part determines the price of the derivative.

Unexpected loss: A loss amount exceeding VaR (value-at-risk) or CVaR (credit value-at-risk).

Unfunded transaction: A transaction in which the buyer does not pay an upfront premium as in a swap or a futures contract.

Unit root: A linear stochastic process has a unit root if 1 is a root of the process's characteristic equation. A stochastic process with a unit root is not stationary.

Unsystematic risk: Also called idiosyncratic risk or specific risk. Risk that can be largely eliminated by diversification.

Value-at-risk (VaR): The maximum loss in a certain time frame, with a certain probability, due to a certain type of risk.

Variance swap: In a long variance swap the variance (ie, the square of volatility) of index components is received and the variance of the index is paid. The advantage of a variance swap is that no delta, gamma or vega risk exists.

Vega: First partial derivative of the option function with respect to implied volatility. A measurement of the sensitivity of the value of an option to changes in implied volatility.

Volatility: The standard deviation of percentage price changes (ie, returns)

Vulnerable option: An option whose price includes the possibility of default of the option seller.

Wiener process: A process in which the movement of a variable for a certain time interval is determined by a random drawing from a standard normal distribution, multiplied by the square root of the time interval.

Wrong-way risk (WWR): Two types exist: general wrong-way risk exists when the probability of default of counterparties is positively correlated with general market risk factors; specific wrong-way risk exists when the exposure to a specific counterparty is positively correlated with the counterparty's probability of default due to the nature of the transaction with the counterparty [BIS definitions].

Yield curve: Shows the relationship between yields and their maturities.

Introduction

Correlation risk is the risk that the correlation between two or more financial variables changes unfavourably. Correlation risk was highlighted in the global financial crisis in 2007 to 2009, when correlations between many financial variables, such as return correlation between equities, the default correlation between debtors or the default correlation between a debtor and an insurer, increased dramatically. This led to huge unexpected losses for many financial institutions, which in part triggered the global financial crisis.

This book is the first to address financial correlation risk in detail. In Chapter 1, we introduce the basic properties of correlation risk, before we show how correlations behave in the real world in Chapter 2, which contains 45 years of correlation data from 1972 to 2017. In Chapter 3, we discuss the most widely applied correlation approach in finance, the Pearson correlation model, and evaluate if it is a suitable model for finance. Chapter 4 is a new chapter in this second edition, assessing the Nobel-prise-rewarded Cointegration model. We address specific financial correlation measures in Chapter 5 and discuss whether the Copula correlation model is appropriate to measure financial correlations in Chapter 6. Often, as in the Basel III framework, a shortcut to the Gaussian copula is applied, such as the one-factor Gaussian copula (OFGC) model. This approach, which is utilised in the Basel framework to derive credit risk, is discussed in Chapter 7. In Chapter 8, we address a fairly new correlation family: the elegant, but somewhat coarse top-down correlation models. In chapter 9, we discuss stochastic correlation models, which are a new and promising way to model financial correlations. In Chapters 10 and 11, we introduce new concepts to quantify market and credit correlation risk. In chapter 12, we address the challenging task of hedging correlation risk.

Figure I.1 Main statistical and financial correlation models

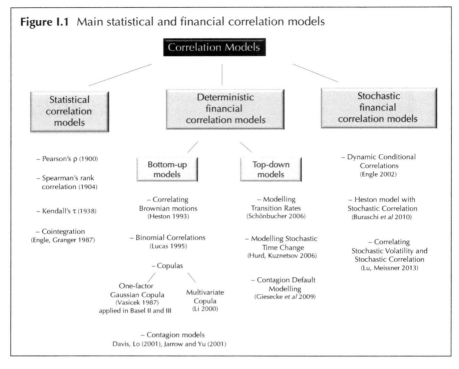

Chapter 13 is a new chapter in this second edition on the popular topic of Correlation Trading. Chapters 14 to 16 deal with new Basel III Correlation modelling (see below for details). Chapter 17 concludes with the future of correlation modelling, which may include neural networks, fuzzy logic, genetic algorithms, chaos theory, and combinations of these concepts.

Figure I.1 gives an overview of the main correlation models, which will be explained in this book. We will discuss the conceptual, mathematical and computational properties of the models and evaluate their benefits and limitations for finance.

BASEL III

This second edition includes three chapters on the Basel III accord. Chapter 14 explains the Basel accords' methodology to calculate CVaR (credit value-at-risk), which derives correlated credit risk for standard debt portfolios such as bonds and loans. Basel III applies an extension of the somewhat simplistic one-factor Gaussian copula, or OFGC, discussed in Chapter 7, to derive CVaR. Chapter

15 addresses CVA (credit value adjustment), which derives correlated credit risk for derivatives. We also discuss CVA's numerous extensions, termed XVAs. Chapter 16 explains the Fundamental Review of the Trading Book (*FRTB*), ie, the Basel III accord's new requirements to derive correlated market risk.

TARGET AUDIENCE

This book should be valuable to students of finance and anyone who is exposed to financial correlations and financial correlation risk. So it should be of interest to the upper management, risk managers, analysts, traders, compliance departments, model validation groups, controllers, reporting groups and brokers. The book contains questions and problems at the end of each chapter, which should facilitate using the book in a classroom. The answers to the problems are available in a section at the back of this book.

DOWNLOADS[1]

This book comes with 39 supporting models, spreadsheets and documents. The links are referenced below and can be downloaded for free. In addition, PowerPoint slides on the chapters are available for instructors by emailing gunter@dersoft.com with proof of purchase of this book.

For a general refresher on the basics of mathematical finance, see www.dersoft.com/mathrefresher.docx (comes with questions and problems; answers available for instructors).

Chapter 1
www.dersoft.com/2assetVaR.xlsx
www.dersoft.com/matrixprimer.xlsx
www.dersoft.com/exchangeoption.xlsm
www.dersoft.com/quanto.xls
www.dersoft.com/dependenceandcorrelation.xlsm
www.dersoft.com/logreturns.xlsx

Chapter 2
www.dersoft.com/correlationfitting.docx

Chapter 3
www.dersoft.com/matrixprimer.xlsx

www.dersoft.com/Anscombe.xlsx
www.dersoft.com/Pearsontimesensitivity.xlsx
www.dersoft.com/epsilon.xlsx
www.dersoft.com/xigraphicallydisplayed.xlsx

Chapter 4
www.dersoft.com/epsilon.xlsx
www.dersoft.com/cointegrationstationarytest.xlsx
www.dersoft.com/cointegration.xlsx

Chapter 5
www.dersoft.com/gbmwithconditionaljumps.xlsm
www.dersoft.com/2assetdefaulttimecopula.xlsm

Chapter 6
www.dersoft.com/CDOGausseducational.xlsm

Chapter 7
www.dersoft.com/ofgceducational.xlsm
www.dersoft.com/basecorrelationgeneration.xlsm

Chapter 8
www.dersoft.com/basecorrelationgeneration.xlsm

Chapter 9
www.dersoft.com/gbmwithconditionaljumps.xlsm
www.dersoft.com/stochasticcorrelation.xlsx

Chapter 10
www.dersoft.com/vareducational.xlsm
www.dersoft.com/varnassetcoragora.xlsm
www.dersoft.com/exchangeoptioncora.docx

Chapter 11
www.dersoft.com/cdswithdefaultcorrelation.xlsm
www.dersoft.com/cdsthreecorrelatedentitiespricingcode.docx

Chapter 12
www.dersoft.com/cdswithdefaultcorrelation.xlsm

www.dersoft.com/optiononthebetteroftwo.xlsm
www.dersoft.com/correlationswap.xlsx
www.dersoft.com/interestrateswap.xls

Chapter 13
www.dersoft.com/meanreversioncalculation.xlsx
www.dersoft.com/Dispersion.xlsx

Chapter 14
www.dersoft.com/epsilon.xlsx
www.dersoft.com/CVaR.xlsm
www.dersoft.com/Baseldoubledefault.xlsm

Chapter 16
www.dersoft.com/VaRESconversion.xlsx
www.dersoft.com/ESinFRTB.xlsm
www.dersoft.com/CVAcapitalcharge.xlsx

Chapter 17
www.dersoft.com/distance.xlsx

---

1 Under no circumstances shall the publisher have any liability to the reader for any loss or damage of any kind incurred as a result of clicking through these links and downloading these files. The files belong to, and are maintained by, the author and are hosted on servers over which the publisher has no control. Accordingly, any use of the files and information contained in them is at the sole risk of the reader.

1

Correlation Basics: Definitions, Applications, and Terminology

"Behold the fool saith, 'Put not all thine eggs in the one basket'"
— Mark Twain

In this introductory chapter, we define correlation and correlation risk, and show that correlations are critical in many areas of finance such as investments, trading, and risk management, as well as in financial crises and in financial regulation. We also show how correlation risk relates to other risks in finance such as market risk, credit risk, systemic risk, and concentration risk. Before we do, let's see how it all started.

A SHORT HISTORY OF CORRELATION

As with many groundbreaking discoveries, there is a bit of a controversy as to who the creator of the concept of correlation is. Foundations on the behaviour of error terms were laid in 1846 by the French mathematician Auguste Bravais, who essentially derived what is today termed the "regression line". However, Helen Walker (1929) describes Bravais nicely as "a kind of Columbus, discovering correlation without fully realising that he had done so". Further significant theoretical and empirical work on correlation was done by Sir Walter Galton in 1886, who created a simple linear regression and interestingly also discovered the statistical property of "Regression to Mediocrity", which today we call "Mean-Reversion".

A student of Walter Galton, Karl Pearson, whose work on relativity, antimatter and the fourth dimension inspired Albert Einstein, expanded the theory of correlation significantly. Starting in 1900, Pearson defined the correlation coefficient as a product moment coefficient, introduced the method of moments and principal component analysis, and founded the concept of statistical hypothesis testing, applying P-Values and Chi-squared distances. Please see Chapter 3, "The Pearson Correlation Model – Work of the Devil?", for details.

WHAT ARE FINANCIAL CORRELATIONS?

Heuristically (meaning non-mathematically), we can define two types of financial correlations, static and dynamic:

(a) Definition: static financial correlations measure how two or more financial assets are associated at a certain point in time or within a certain time period.

Examples are:

1. Correlating bond prices and their respective yields at a certain point in time, which will result in a negative association.
2. The classic VaR (value-at-risk) model, which answers the question: what is the maximum loss of correlated assets in a portfolio with a certain probability for a given time period (see "Risk management and correlation" below and Chapter 10 for details).
3. The copula approach for CDOs (collateralised debt obligations). It measures the default correlations between all assets in the CDO, typically 125, for a certain time period (see chapter 6 for details).
4. The binomial default correlation model of Lucas (1995), which is a special case of the Pearson correlation model. It measures the probability of two assets defaulting together within a short time period (see Chapter 5 for details).

Besides the static correlation concept, there are dynamic correlations:

(b) Definition: dynamic financial correlations measure how two or more financial assets move together in time.

Examples are:

1. In practice, "pairs trading" – where one asset is purchased and another is sold – is performed. Let's assume that the asset returns x and y have moved highly correlated in time. If now asset X performs poorly with respect to Y, then asset X is bought and asset Y is sold with the expectation that the gap will narrow.
2. Within the deterministic correlation approaches, the Heston model (1993) correlates the Brownian motions dz_1 and dz_2 of assets 1 and 2. The core equation is $dz_1(t) = \rho dz_2(t) + \sqrt{(1-p^2)} dz_3(t)$ where dz_1 and dz_2 are correlated in time with correlation parameter p. Please see chapter 5 for details.
3. Correlations behave random and unpredictable. Therefore, it is a good idea to model them as a stochastic process. Stochastic correlation processes are by construction time-dependent and can replicate correlation properties well. See Chapter 9 for details.

"Suddenly everything was highly correlated"
Financial Times, April 2009

WHAT IS FINANCIAL CORRELATION RISK?

Financial correlation risk is defined as the risk of financial loss due to adverse movements in correlation between two or more variables. These variables can comprise any financial variables. For example, the positive correlation between Mexican bonds and Greek bonds can hurt Mexican bond investors, if Greek bond prices decrease, which happened in 2012 during the Greek crisis. Or the negative correlation between commodity prices and interest rates can hurt commodity investors if interest rates rise. A further example is the correlation between a bond issuer and a bond insurer, which can hurt the bond investor (see the example displayed in Figure 1.1).

Correlation risk is especially critical in risk management. An increase in the correlation of asset returns increases the risk of financial loss, which is often measured by the VaR concept. For details see "Risk management and correlation" below. An increase in correlation is typical in a severe, systemic crisis. For example, during the great recession from 2007 to 2009, financial assets and financial markets worldwide became highly correlated. Risk managers who had negatively or low correlated assets in their portfolio suddenly witnessed many of them decline together, hence asset correlations increased sharply. For more on systemic risk, see "The global financial crises 2007 to 2009 and correlation" below as well as Chapter 2, which displays empirical findings of correlations.

Correlation risk can also involve variables that are non-financial as economic or political events. For example, the correlation between the increasing sovereign debt and currency value can hurt an exporter, as in Europe in 2012, where a decreasing euro hurt US exporters. Geopolitical tensions, as for example in the Middle East, can hurt airline companies due to the increasing oil price, or a slowing GDP in the US can hurt Asian and European exporters and investors, since economies and financial markets are correlated worldwide.

Let's look at correlation risk via an example of a credit default swap (CDS). A CDS is a financial product in which the credit risk is transferred from the investor (or CDS buyer) to a counterparty

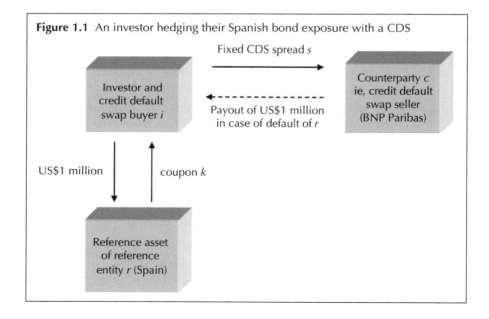

Figure 1.1 An investor hedging their Spanish bond exposure with a CDS

CORRELATION BASICS: DEFINITIONS, APPLICATIONS, AND TERMINOLOGY

(CDS seller). Let's assume an investor has bought US$1 million in a bond from Spain. They are now worried about Spain defaulting and have purchased a CDS from a French bank, BNP Paribas. Graphically this is displayed in Figure 1.1.

The investor is protected against a default from Spain since, in case of default, the counterparty BNP Paribas will pay the originally invested US$1 million to the investor. For simplicity, let's assume the recovery rate and accrued interest are zero.

The value of the CDS, ie, the fixed CDS spread s,[1] is mainly determined by the default probability of the reference entity Spain. However, the spread s is also determined by the joint default correlation of BNP Paribas and Spain. If the correlation between Spain and BNP Paribas increases, the present value of the CDS for the investor will decrease and they will suffer a paper loss. Worst-case scenario is the joint default of Spain and BNP Paribas, in which case the investor will lose their entire investment in the Spanish bond of US$1 million.

In other words, the investor is exposed to default correlation risk between the reference asset r (Spain) and the counterparty c (BNP Paribas). Since both Spain and BNP Paribas are in Europe, let's assume that there is a positive default correlation between the two. In this case, the investor has "Wrong-Way Correlation Risk" or, for short, "Wrong-Way Risk" (WWR). Let's assume the default probabilities of Spain and BNP Paribas both increase. This means that the credit exposure to the reference entity Spain increases (since the CDS has a higher present value for the investor) *and* the credit risk increases, since it is more unlikely that the counterparty BNP Paribas can pay the default insurance. We will discuss WWR, which is a key term in the Basel II and III accord, in Chapter 14.

The magnitude of the correlation risk is expressed graphically in Figure 1.2.

From Figure 1.2, we observe that for a correlation of −0.3 and higher, the higher the correlation, the lower is the CDS spread. This is because an increasing ρ means a higher probability of the reference asset and the counterparty defaulting together. In the extreme case of a perfect correlation of 1, the CDS is worthless. This is because, if Spain defaults, so will the insurance seller BNP Paribas.

We also observe from Figure 1.2 that, for a correlation from about −0.3 to −1, the CDS spread decreases slightly. This seems

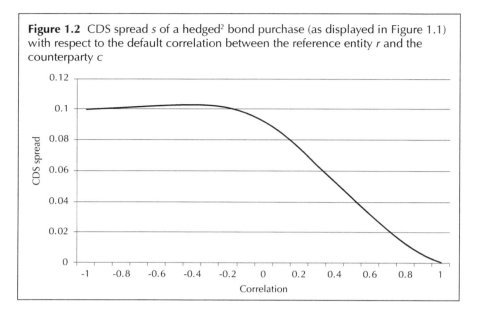

Figure 1.2 CDS spread s of a hedged[2] bond purchase (as displayed in Figure 1.1) with respect to the default correlation between the reference entity r and the counterparty c

counterintuitive at first. However, an increase in the negative correlation means a higher probability of either Spain *or* BNP Paribas defaulting. Hence we have two scenarios: (a) in the case of Spain defaulting (and BNP Paribas surviving) the CDS buyer will get compensated by BNP Paribas; (b) if the insurance seller BNP Paribas defaults (and Spain survives), the CDS buyer will lose his insurance and will have to repurchase it. This may have to be done at a higher cost. The cost will be higher if the credit quality of Spain has decreased since inception of the original CDS. For example, the CDS spread may have been 3% in the original CDS, but may have increased to 6% due to a credit deterioration of Spain. The scenarios (a) and (b) combined lead to a slight decrease of the CDS spread. For more details on pricing CDSs with counterparty risk and the reference asset – counterparty correlation – see Chapter 11, as well as Kettunen and Meissner (2006).

We observe from Figure 1.2 that the dependencies between a variable (here the CDS spread) and correlation may be non-monotonic, ie, the CDS spread sometimes increases and sometime decreases if correlation increases. We will also encounter this non-monotonic feature of correlation when we discuss the mezzanine tranche of a CDO in Chapter 6.

MOTIVATION: CORRELATIONS AND CORRELATION RISK ARE EVERYWHERE IN FINANCE

Why study financial correlations? That's an easy one. Financial correlations appear in many areas in finance. We will briefly discuss five areas: (1) investments, (2) trading, (3) risk management, (4) the global financial crisis and (5) regulation. Naturally, if an entity is exposed to correlation, this means that the entity has correlation risk, ie, the risk of a change in the correlation.

Investments and correlation

From our studies of the Nobel Prize-rewarded Capital Asset Pricing Model (Markowitz (1952), Sharpe (1964)), we remember that an increase in diversification increases the return/risk ratio. Importantly, high diversification is related to low correlation. Let's show this in an example. Let's assume we have a portfolio of two assets, X and Y. They have performed as in Table 1.1.

Table 1.1 Performance of a portfolio with two assets

Year	Asset X	Asset Y	Return of asset X	Return of asset Y
2013	100	200		
2014	120	230	20.00%	15.00%
2015	108	460	−10.00%	100.00%
2016	190	410	75.93%	−10.87%
2017	160	480	−15.79%	17.07%
2018	280	380	75.00%	−20.83%
		Average	29.03%	20.07%

Let's define the return of asset X at time t as x_t, and the return of asset Y at time t as y_t. A return is calculated as a percentage change, $(S_t - S_{t-1})/S_{t-1}$, where S is a price or a rate. The average return of asset X for the timeframe 2014 to 2018 is $\mu_X = 29.03\%$; for asset Y the average return is $\mu_Y = 20.07\%$. If we assign a weight to asset X, w_X, and a weight to asset Y, w_Y, the portfolio return is:

$$\mu_P = w_X \mu_X + w_Y \mu_Y \tag{1.1}$$

where $w_X + w_Y = 1$

The standard deviation of returns, called *volatility*, is derived for asset X with equation:

$$\sigma_X = \sqrt{\frac{1}{n-1}\sum_{t=1}^{n}(x_t - \mu_X)^2} \qquad (1.2)$$

where x_t is the return of asset X at time t and n is the number of observed points in time. The volatility of asset Y is derived accordingly. Equation 1.2 can be computed with = stdev in Excel and std in MATLAB. From our example in Table 1.1, we find that σ_X = 44.51% and σ_Y = 47.58%.

Let's now look at the covariance. The covariance measures how two variables "co-vary", ie, move together. More precisely, the covariance measures the strength of the linear relationship between two variables. The covariance of returns for assets X and Y is derived with equation:

$$COV_{XY} = \frac{1}{n-1}\sum_{t=1}^{n}(x_t - \mu_X)(y_t - \mu_Y). \qquad (1.3)$$

For our example in Table 1.1 we derive COV_{XY} = –0.1567. Equation (1.3) is = Covariance.S in Excel and cov in MATLAB. The covariance is not easy to interpret, since it takes values between –∞ and +∞. Therefore, it is more convenient to use the Pearson correlation coefficient ρ_{XY}, which is a standardised covariance, ie, it takes values between –1 and +1. The Pearson correlation coefficient is:

$$\rho_{XY} = \frac{COV_{XY}}{\sigma_X \sigma_Y} \qquad (1.4)$$

For our example in Table 1, ρ_{XY} = –0.7403, showing that the returns of assets X and Y are highly negatively correlated. Equation (1.4) is "correl" in Excel and "corrcoef" in MATLAB. For the derivation of the numerical examples of equations (1.2) to (1.4) and more information on the covariances see the appendix of chapter 1 and www.dersoft.com/matrixprimer.xlsx, sheet "Covariance Matrix".

We can calculate the standard deviation for our two-asset portfolio P as:

$$\sigma_P = \sqrt{w_X^2 \sigma_X^2 + w_Y^2 \sigma_Y^2 + 2w_X w_Y COV_{XY}} \qquad (1.5)$$

With equal weights, ie, $w_X = w_Y = 0.5$, the example in Table 1.1 results in σ_P = 16.66%.

Importantly, the standard deviation (or its square, the variance) is interpreted in finance as risk. The higher the standard deviation,

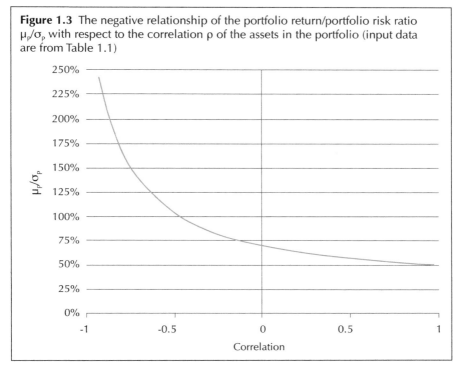

Figure 1.3 The negative relationship of the portfolio return/portfolio risk ratio μ_p/σ_p with respect to the correlation ρ of the assets in the portfolio (input data are from Table 1.1)

the higher the risk of an asset or a portfolio. Is standard deviation a good measure of risk? The answer is: it's not great, but it's one of the best there are. A high standard deviation may mean high upside potential of the asset in question! So it penalises possible profits! But high standard deviation naturally also means high downside risk. In particular, risk-averse investors will not like a high standard deviation, ie, high fluctuation of their returns.

An informative performance measure of an asset or a portfolio is the risk-adjusted return, ie, the return/risk ratio. For a portfolio it is μ_p/σ_p, which we derived in Equations (1.1) and (1.5). In Figure 1.3 we observe one of the few "free lunches" in finance: the lower (preferably negative) the correlation of the assets in a portfolio, the higher the return/risk ratio. For a rigorous proof, see Markowitz (1952) and Sharpe (1964).

Figure 1.3 shows the high impact of correlation on the portfolio return/risk ratio. A high negative correlation results in a return/risk ratio of close to 250%, whereas a high positive correlation results in a 50% ratio. The equations (1.1) to (1.5) are derived within the framework of the Pearson correlation approach. We will discuss the limitations of this approach in Chapter 3.

> "Only by great risks can great results be achieved"
> Xerxes

TRADING AND CORRELATION

In finance every risk is also an opportunity. Therefore, at every major investment bank and hedge fund, correlation desks exist. The traders try to forecast changes in correlation and try to financially gain from these changes in correlation. We already mentioned the correlation strategy "pairs trading" above. Generally, correlation trading means trading assets, whose price is determined at least in part by the co-movement of one asset or more in time. Many types of correlation assets exist.

Multi-asset options, also termed rainbow options or mountain range options. Many different types are traded. The most popular ones are listed below. S_1 is the price of asset 1 and S_2 is the price of asset 2 at option maturity, K is the strike price, ie, the price determined at option start at which the underlying asset can be bought in case of a call or the price at which the underlying asset can be sold in case of a put.

- Option on the better of two. Payoff = max (S_1, S_2).
- Option on the worse of two. Payoff = min (S_1, S_2).
- Call on the maximum of two. Payoff = max $[0, \max(S_1, S_2) - K]$.
- Exchange option (such as a convertible bond). Payoff = max $(0, S_2 - S_1)$.
- Spread call option. Payoff = max $[0, (S_2 - S_1) - K]$.
- Option on the better of two or cash. Payoff = max (S_1, S_2, cash).
- Dual strike call option. Payoff = max $(0, S_1 - K_1, S_2 - K_2)$.
- Basket option.

$$\left[\sum_{i=1}^{n} n_i S_i - K, 0\right]$$

where n_i is the weight of assets i.

Importantly, the price of these correlation options is highly sensitive to the correlation between the asset prices S_1 and S_2. In the list above, except for the option on the worse of two, and the basket

CORRELATION BASICS: DEFINITIONS, APPLICATIONS, AND TERMINOLOGY

option, the lower the correlation, the higher is the option price. This makes sense since a low, preferably negative correlation means that, if one asset decreases (on average), the other increases. So one of the two assets is likely to result in a high price and therefore in a high payoff. Multi-asset options can be conveniently priced analytically with extensions of the Black–Scholes–Merton option model (1973) – see Chapter 10 for details.

Let's look at the evaluation of an exchange option with a payoff of max(0, $S_2 - S_1$). The payoff shows that the option buyer has the right to give away Asset 1 and receive Asset 2 at option maturity. Hence, the option buyer will exercise their right, if $S_2 > S_1$. The price of the exchange option can be easily derived. We first rewrite the payoff equation max(0, $S_2 - S_1$) as: S_1 max(0, $(S_2/S_1) - 1$). We then input the covariance between asset S_1 and S_2 into the implied volatility function of the exchange option using a variation of equation (1.5):

$$\sigma_E = \sqrt{\sigma_A^2 + \sigma_B^2 - 2COV_{AB}} \tag{1.5a}$$

where σ_E is the implied volatility of S_2/S_1, which is input into the standard Black–Scholes–Merton option pricing model (1973). For an exchange option pricing model and further discussion, see Chapter 10, and the model at www.dersoft.com/exchangeoption.xlsm.

Importantly, the exchange option price is highly sensitive to the correlation between the asset prices S_1 and S_2, as seen in Figure 1.4.

From Figure 1.4 we observe the strong impact of the correlation on the exchange option price. The price is close to 0 for high correlation and US$15.08 for a negative correlation of –1. As in Figures 1.2 and 1.3, the correlation approach underlying Figure 1.4 is the Pearson correlation model. We will discuss the limitations of the Pearson correlation model in Chapter 3.

Another interesting correlation option is the quanto option. This is an option that allows a domestic investor to exchange their potential option payoff in a foreign currency back into their home currency at a fixed exchange rate. A quanto option therefore protects an investor against currency risk. Let's assume an American believes the Nikkei will increase, but they are worried about a decreasing yen, which would reduce or eliminate her profits from the Nikkei call option. The investor can buy a quanto

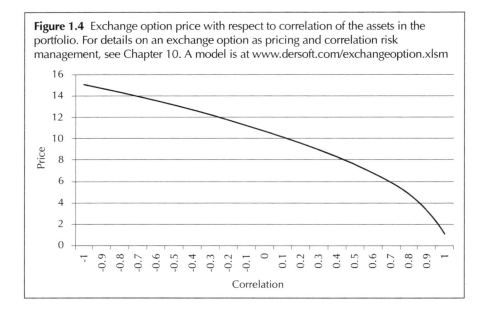

Figure 1.4 Exchange option price with respect to correlation of the assets in the portfolio. For details on an exchange option as pricing and correlation risk management, see Chapter 10. A model is at www.dersoft.com/exchangeoption.xlsm

call on the Nikkei, with the yen payoff being converted into dollars at a fixed (usually the spot) exchange rate.

Originally, the term quanto comes from the word "quantity", meaning that the amount that is re-exchanged to the home currency is unknown, because it depends on the future payoff of the option. Therefore the financial institution that sells a quanto call, does not know two things:

1. How deep will the call be in the money at option maturity, ie, which yen amount has to be converted into dollars?
2. What is the exchange rate at option maturity at which the stochastic yen payoff will be converted into dollars?

The correlation between (1) and (2), ie, the price of the underlying S' and the exchange rate X, significantly influences the quanto call option price. Let's consider a call on the Nikkei S' and an exchange rate X defined as domestic currency per unit foreign currency (so US$/1 yen for a domestic American) at maturity.

If the correlation is positive, an increasing Nikkei will also mean an increasing yen. That is in favour of the call seller. They have to settle the payoff, but need only a small yen amount to achieve the

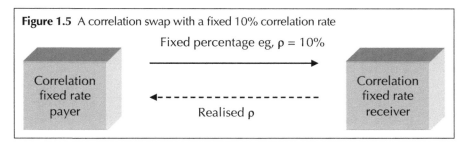

Figure 1.5 A correlation swap with a fixed 10% correlation rate

dollar payment. Therefore, the more positive the correlation coefficient, the lower is the price for the quanto option. If the correlation coefficient is negative, the opposite applies: if the Nikkei increases, the yen decreases in value. Therefore more yen are needed to meet the dollar payment. As a consequence, the lower the correlation coefficient, the more expensive is the quanto option. Hence we have a similar negative relationship between the option price and correlation, as in Figure 1.4.

Quanto options can be conveniently priced analytically with an extension of the Black–Scholes–Merton model (1973). For a pricing model and a more detailed discussion on a quanto option, see www.dersoft.com/quanto.xls.

The correlation between assets can also be traded directly with a correlation swap. In a correlation swap, a fixed (ie, known) correlation is exchanged with the correlation that will actually occur, called realised or stochastic (ie, unknown) correlation, as seen in Figure 1.5.

Paying a fixed rate in a correlation swap is also called "buying correlation". This is because the present value of the correlation swap will increase for the correlation buyer if the realised correlation increases. Naturally the fixed-rate receiver is "selling correlation".

The realised correlation ρ in Figure 1.5 is the correlation between the assets that actually occur during the time of the swap. It is calculated as:

$$\rho_{realised} = \frac{2}{n^2 - n} \sum_{i>j} \rho_{i,j} \qquad (1.6)$$

where $\rho_{i,j}$ is the Pearson correlation between asset i and j, and n is the number of assets in the portfolio. The payoff of a correlation swap for the correlation fixed rate payer at maturity is:

$$N\left(\rho_{realised} - \rho_{fixed}\right) \qquad (1.7)$$

where N is the notional amount. Let's look at an example of a correlation swap.

Example 1.1: What is the payoff of a correlation swap with three assets, a fixed rate of 10%, a notional amount of US$1,000,000 and a 1-year maturity?

First, the daily log-returns $\ln(S_t/S_{t-1})$ of the three assets are calculated for one year.[3] Let's assume the realised pairwise correlations of the log-returns at maturity are as displayed in Table 1.2.

Table 1.2 Pairwise Pearson correlation coefficient at swap maturity

	$S_{j=1}$	$S_{j=2}$	$S_{j=3}$
$S_{i=1}$	1	0.5	0.1
$S_{i=2}$	0.5	1	0.3
$S_{i=3}$	0.1	0.3	1

The average correlation between the three assets is derived by equation (1.6). We only apply the correlations in the shaded area from Table 1.2, since these satisfy $i > j$. Hence we have

$$\rho_{realised} = \frac{2}{3^2 - 3}(0.5 + 0.3 + 0.1) = 0.3.$$

Following equation (1.7), the payoff for the correlation fixed-rate payer at swap maturity is US$1,000,000 X (0.3 − 0.1) = US$200,000.

Correlation swaps can indirectly protect against decreasing stock prices. As we will see in this chapter in "How does correlation risk fit into the broader picture of risks in finance?", Figure 1.8, as well as in Chapter 2, when stock prices decrease, typically the correlation between the stocks increases. Hence a fixed correlation payer protects themselves indirectly against a stock market decline.

At the time of writing there is no industry-standard valuation model for correlation swaps. Traders often use historical data to anticipate $\rho_{realised}$. To apply swap valuation techniques, we require a term structure of correlation in time. However, no correlation term structure currently exists. We can also apply stochastic correlation models to value a correlation swap. Stochastic correlation models are currently emerging and will be discussed in Chapter 9.

Another way of buying correlation (ie, benefiting from an increase in correlation) is to buy put options on an index such as the Dow Jones Industrial Average (Dow) and sell put options on individual stock of the Dow. As we will see in Chapter 2, there is a positive relationship between correlation and volatility. Therefore, if the correlation between the stocks of the Dow increases, for example in a market downturn, so will the implied volatility[4] of the put on the Dow. This increase is expected to outperform the potential loss from the increase in the short put positions on the individual stocks. For details of this Dispersion trade see Chapter 13.

Creating exposure on an index and hedging with exposure on individual components is exactly what the "London whale", JP Morgan's London trader Bruno Iksil, did in 2012. Iksil was called the London whale because of his enormous positions in CDSs.[5] He had sold CDSs on an index of bonds, the CDX.NA.IG.9, and "hedged" it with buying CDSs on individual bonds. In a recovering economy this is a promising trade: volatility and correlation typically decrease in a recovering economy. Therefore, the sold CDSs on the index should outperform (decrease more than) the losses on the CDSs of the individual bonds.

But what can be a good trade in the medium and long terms can be disastrous in the short term. The positions of the London whale were so large, that hedge funds "short squeezed" Iksil: they started to aggressively buy the CDS index CDX.NA.IG.9. This increased the CDS values in the index and created a huge (paper) loss for the whale. JP Morgan was forced to buy back the CDS index positions at a loss of over US$2 billion.

Risk management and correlation
Since the global financial crises of 2007 to 2009, financial markets have become more risk-averse. Commercial banks and investment banks as well as nonfinancial institutions have increased their risk-management efforts. As in the investment and trading environment, correlation plays a vital part in risk management. Let's first clarify what risk management means in finance.

Definition: Financial risk management is the process of identifying, quantifying and, if desired, reducing financial risk.

The main types of financial risk are:

1. market risk;
2. credit risk; and
3. operational risk.

Additional types of risk may include systemic risk, liquidity risk, volatility risk and – the topic of this book – correlation risk. We will concentrate in this introductory chapter on market risk. Market risk consists of four types of risk: (1) equity risk, (2) interest-rate risk, (3) currency risk and (4) commodity risk.

There are several concepts to measure the market risk of a portfolio such as VaR, expected shortfall (ES), enterprise risk management (ERM) and more. VaR is currently (year 2018) the most widely applied risk-management measure. Let's show the impact of asset correlation on VaR.[6]

First, what is value-at-risk (VaR)? VaR measures the maximum loss of a portfolio with respect to market risk for a certain probability level and for a certain time frame. The equation for VaR is:

$$VaR_P = \sigma_P \alpha \sqrt{x} \qquad (1.8)$$

where VaR_P is the value-at-risk for portfolio P, and

α: Abscise value of a standard normal distribution, corresponding to a certain confidence level. It can be derived as = norms inv(confidence level) in Excel or norminv(confidence level) in MATLAB; α takes the values $-\infty < \alpha < +\infty$;

x: Time horizon for the VaR, typically measured in days;

σ_P: Volatility of the portfolio P, which includes the correlation between the assets in the portfolio. We calculate σ_P via:

$$\sigma_P = \sqrt{\beta_h C \beta_v} \qquad (1.9)$$

where β_h is the horizontal β vector of invested amounts (price time quantity); β_v is the vertical β vector of invested amounts (also price time quantity);[7] C is the covariance matrix of the returns of the assets.

Let's calculate VaR for a two-asset portfolio and then analyse the impact of different correlations between the two assets on VaR.

Example 1.2: What is the 10-day VaR for a two-asset portfolio with a correlation coefficient of 0.7, daily standard deviation of returns of asset 1 of 2%, asset 2 of 1%, and US$10 million invested in asset 1 and US$5 million invested in asset 2, on a 99% confidence level?

First, we derive the covariances Cov:

$$\text{Cov}_{11} = \rho_{11}\, \sigma_1\, \sigma_1 = 1 \times 0.02 \times 0.02 = 0.0004^8 \qquad (1.10)$$

$$\text{Cov}_{12} = \rho_{12}\, \sigma_1\, \sigma_2 = 0.7 \times 0.02 \times 0.01 = 0.00014$$

$$\text{Cov}_{21} = \rho_{21}\, \sigma_2\, \sigma_1 = 0.7 \times 0.01 \times 0.02 = 0.00014$$

$$\text{Cov}_{22} = \rho_{22}\, \sigma_2\, \sigma_2 = 1 \times 0.01 \times 0.01 = 0.0001$$

Hence our covariance matrix is

$$C = \begin{pmatrix} 0.0004 & 0.00014 \\ 0.00014 & 0.0001 \end{pmatrix}$$

Let's calculate σ_p following equation (1.9). We first derive $\beta_h\, C$

$$\begin{pmatrix} 10 & 5 \end{pmatrix} \begin{pmatrix} 0.0004 & 0.00014 \\ 0.00014 & 0.0001 \end{pmatrix}$$

$$= \begin{pmatrix} 10 \times 0.0004 + 5 \times 0.0004 & 10 \times 0.00014 + 5 \times 0.0001 \end{pmatrix}$$

$$= \begin{pmatrix} 0.0047 & 0.0019 \end{pmatrix}$$

and then

$$(\beta_h C)\beta_v = \begin{pmatrix} 0.0047 & 0.0019 \end{pmatrix} \begin{pmatrix} 10 \\ 5 \end{pmatrix} = 10 \times 0.0047 + 5 \times 0.0019 = 5.65\%$$

Hence we have

$$\sigma_p = \sqrt{\beta_h C \beta_v} = \sqrt{5.65\%} = 23.77\%.$$

We find the value for α in equation (1.8) from Excel as =normsinv(0.99) = 2.3264, or MATLAB as norminv(0.99) = 2.3264.

Following equation (1.8), we now calculate the VaR$_p$ as $0.2377 \times 2.3264 \times \sqrt{10} = 1.7486$.[9]

Interpretation: We are 99% certain that we will not lose more than US$1.7486 million in the next 10 days due to correlated market price changes of asset 1 and 2.

The number US$1.7486 million is the 10-day VaR on a 99% confidence level. This means that on average once in a hundred 10-day periods (so once every 1,000 days), this VaR number of US$1.7486

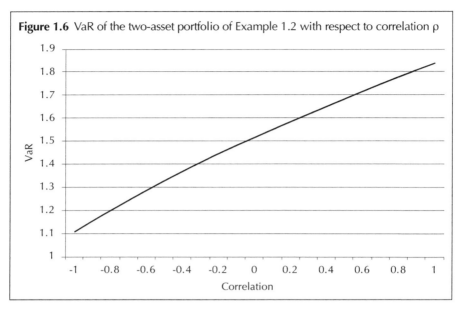

Figure 1.6 VaR of the two-asset portfolio of Example 1.2 with respect to correlation ρ

million will be exceeded. If we have roughly 250 trading days in a year, the company is expected to exceed the VaR about once every four years.

Let's now analyse the impact of different correlations between the asset 1 and asset 2 on VaR. Figure 1.6 shows the impact.

As expected, we observe from Figure 1.6 that the lower the correlation, the lower is the risk, measured by VaR. Preferably the correlation is negative. In this case, if one asset decreases, the other asset on average increases, hence reducing the overall risk. The impact of correlation on VaR is strong: for a perfect negative correlation of −1, VaR is US$1.1 million; for a perfect positive correlation, VaR is close to US$1.9 million. A spreadsheet for calculating two-asset VaRs can be found at www.dersoft.com/2assetVaR.xlsx (case-sensitive).

"There are no toxic assets, just toxic people."

The global financial crises 2007 to 2009 and correlation

Currently, in 2018, the global financial crisis of 2007 to 2009 seems like a distant memory. The Dow Jones Industrial Average has recovered from its low in March 2009 of 6,547 points and has almost quadrupled to over 25,000 as of October 2018. World economic growth is at a moderate 2.5%. The US unemployment rate as of October 2018 is historically low at 3.7%. However, to fight the crisis, governments engaged in huge stimulus packages to revive their faltering economies. As a result, enormous sovereign deficits are plaguing the world economy. The US debt is also far from benign with a total gross-debt-to-GDP ratio of about 107%. One of the few nations that are enjoying these enormous debt levels is China, which is happy buying the debt and taking in the proceeds.

A crisis that brought the financial and economic system worldwide to a standstill is naturally not mono-causal, but has many reasons. Here are the main ones.

(a) An extremely benign economic and risk environment from 2003 to 2006 with record low credit spreads, low volatility and low interest rates.
(b) Increasing risk-taking and speculation of traders and investors who tried to benefit in these presumably calm times. This led to a bubble in virtually every market segment like the housing market, the mortgage market (especially the subprime mortgage market), the stock market and the commodity market. In 2007, US investors had borrowed 470% of the US national income to invest and speculate in the real-estate, financial and commodity markets.
(c) A new class of structured investment products such as CDOs, CDO squared, CPDOs (constant-proportion debt obligations) and CPPI (constant proportion portfolio insurance), as well as new products such as options on CDSs, credit indices etc.
(d) The new copula correlation model, which was trusted naïvely by many investors and which could presumably correlate the $n(n-1)/2$ assets in a structured product. Most CDOs contained 125 assets. Hence there are $125(125-1)/2 = 7,750$ asset correlation pairs to be quantified and managed. For details see Chapters 6 and 7.
(e) A moral hazard of rating agencies, who were paid by the same companies whose assets they rated. As a consequence, many structured products received AAA ratings and gave the illusion of low price and default risk.
(f) Risk managers and regulators who lowered their standards

in light of the greed and profit frenzy. We recommend an excellent – anonymous – paper in *The Economist*: "Confessions of a Risk Manager".

The topic of this book is correlation risk, so let's concentrate on the correlation aspect of the crisis. Around 2003, two years after the Internet bubble burst, the risk appetite of the financial markets increased and investment banks, hedge funds, and private investors began to speculate and invest in the stock markets, commodities and especially in the real-estate market.

In particular, residential mortgages became an investment object. The mortgages were packaged in CDOs (see Chapter 6 for a detailed discussion), and then sold off to investors locally and globally. The CDOs typically consist of several tranches, ie, the investor can choose a particular degree of default risk. The equity tranche holder is exposed to the first 3% of mortgage defaults, the mezzanine tranche holder is exposed to the 3–7% of defaults and so on. The new copula correlation model, derived by Abe Sklar in 1959 and transferred to finance by David Li in 2000, could presumably manage the default correlations in the CDOs (see Chapter 6 for details).

A first correlation-related crisis, which was a forerunner of the major one to come in 2007 to 2009, occurred in May 2005. General Motors was downgraded to BB and Ford was downgraded to BB+, so both companies were now in "junk status". A downgrade to junk typically leads to a sharp bond price decline, since many mutual funds and pension funds are not allowed to hold junk bonds.

Importantly, the correlation of the bonds in CDOs (which originally were only investment-grade bonds) decreased, since bonds of different credit qualities are typically lower-correlated. This led to huge losses of hedge funds, which had put on a strategy where they were long the equity tranche of the CDO and short the mezzanine tranche of the CDO. Figure 1.7 shows the dilemma. Hedge funds had invested in the equity tranche[10] (0% to 3% in Figure 1.7) to collect the high-equity tranche spread. They had then presumably hedged[11] the risk by going short the mezzanine tranche[12] (3% to 7% in Figure 1.7). However, as we can see from Figure 1.7, this "hedge" is flawed.

CORRELATION BASICS: DEFINITIONS, APPLICATIONS, AND TERMINOLOGY

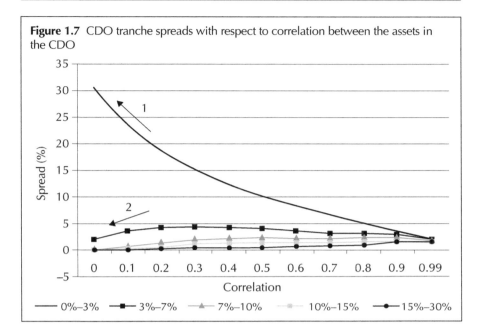

Figure 1.7 CDO tranche spreads with respect to correlation between the assets in the CDO

When the correlations between the assets in the CDO decreased, the hedge funds lost on both positions.

1. The equity tranche spread increased sharply (see Arrow 1). Hence the spread that the hedge fund received in the original transaction was now significantly lower than the current market spread, resulting in a paper loss.
2. In addition, the hedge funds lost on their short mezzanine tranche position, since a lower correlation lowers the mezzanine tranche spread (see Arrow 2). Hence the spread that the hedge fund paid in the original transactions was now higher than the market spread, resulting in another paper loss.

As a result of the huge losses, several hedge funds such as Marin Capital, Aman Capital and Baily Coates Cromwell filed for bankruptcy. It is important to point out that the losses resulted from a lack of understanding of the correlation properties of the tranches in the CDO. The CDOs themselves can hardly be blamed or called toxic for their correlation properties.

From 2003 to 2006 the CDO market, mainly referencing residential mortgages, had exploded and increased from US$64 billion to

US$455 billion. To fuel the CDOs, more and more questionable subprime mortgages were given, named NINJA loans, standing for "no income, no job or assets". When housing prices started levelling off in 2006, the first mortgages started to default. In 2007 more and more mortgages defaulted, finally leading to a real-estate market collapse. With it the huge CDO market collapsed, leading to the stock market and commodity market crash and a freeze in the credit markets. The financial crisis spread to the world economies, creating a global severe recession now called the "great recession".

In a systemic crash like this, naturally many types of correlations increase; see also Figure 1.8. From 2007 to 2009, default correlations between the mortgages in the CDOs increased. This actually helped equity tranche investors, as we can see from Figure 1.7. If default correlations between the assets in the CDO increase, the equity tranche spread decreases, leading to an increase in the value of the equity tranche. However, this increase was overcompensated by a strong increase in default probability of the mortgages; as a consequence, tranche spreads increased sharply, resulting in a huge loss of the equity tranche investors as well investors in the other tranches.

Correlations between the tranches of the CDOs also increased during the crisis. This had a devastating effect on the super-senior tranches. In normal times, these tranches were considered extremely safe since (a) there were AAA-rated and (b) they were protected by the lower tranches. But, with the increased tranche correlation and the generally deteriorating credit market, these super-senior tranches were suddenly considered risky and lost up to 20% of their value.

To make things worse, many investors had leveraged the super-senior tranches, termed LSS (leveraged super-senior tranche) to receive a higher spread. This leverage was typically 10 or 20 times, meaning an investor paid US$10,000,000 but had risk exposure of US$100,000,000 or US$200,000,000. What made things technically even worse, was that these LSSs came with an option for the investors to unwind the super-senior tranche if the spread had widened (increased). So many investors started to sell the LSS at low prices, realising a loss and increasing the LSS tranche spread even further.

In addition to the overinvestment in CDOs, the CDS market also exploded from its beginnings in the mid-1990s from about US$8 trillion in 2004 to almost US$60 trillion in 2007. CDSs are typically used as insurance to protect against default of a debtor, as we discussed in Figure 1.1. No one will argue that an insurance contract is toxic. On the contrary, it is the principle of insurance to spread the risk to a wider audience and hence reduce individual risk, as we can see from health insurance or life insurance contracts.

CDSs, though, can also be used as a speculative instrument. For example, the CDS seller (ie, the insurance seller) hopes that the insured event (eg, default or credit deterioration of the company) will not occur. In this case, the CDS seller keeps the CDS spread (ie, the insurance premium), as income as AIG tried to do in the crisis. A CDS buyer, when they do not own the underlying asset, speculates on the credit deterioration of the underlying asset, just like a naked put option holder speculates on the decline of the underlying asset.

So who can we blame for the 2007–09 global financial crises? The quants, who created the new products such as CDSs and CDOs and the models to value them? The upper management and the traders, who authorised and conducted the overinvesting and extreme risk-taking? The rating agencies, who gave an AAA rating to many CDOs? The regulators, who approved the overinvestments? The risk managers, who allowed the excessive risk taking?

The answer is: All of them. The whole global financial crisis can be summed up in one word: greed! It was the upper management, the traders and investors who engaged in excessive trading and irresponsible risk taking to receive high returns, huge salaries and generous bonuses. And most risk managers and regulators turned a blind eye.

For example, the London unit of the insurance company AIG had sold close to US$500 billion in CDSs without much reinsurance! Their main hedging strategy seemed to have been: pray that the insured contracts don't deteriorate. The investment banks of Iceland, a small country in Northern Europe, had borrowed 10 times Iceland's national GDP and invested it. With this leverage, Iceland naturally went *de facto* into bankruptcy in 2008, when the credit markets deteriorated. Lehman Brothers, before filing for bankruptcy in September 2008, reported a leverage of 30.7, ie,

US$691 billion in assets and only US$22 billion in stockholders' equity. The true leverage was even higher, since Lehman tried to hide their leverage with materially misleading repo transactions.[13] In addition, Lehman had 1.5 million derivatives transactions with 8,000 different counterparties on their books.

Did the upper management and traders of hedge funds and investment banks admit to their irresponsible leverage, excessive trading and risk taking? No. Instead they created the myth of the "toxic asset", which is absurd. It is like a murderer saying: "I did not shoot that person – it was my gun!" Toxic are not the financial products, but humans and their greed.

Most traders were well aware of the risks that they were taking. In the few cases where traders did not understand the risks, the asset itself cannot be blamed, rather the incompetence of the trader is the reason for the loss. While it is ethically disappointing that the investors and traders did not admit to their wrongdoing, at the same time it is understandable. If they would admit to irresponsible trading and risk taking, they would immediately be prosecuted.

Naturally risk managers and regulators have to take part of the blame to allow the irresponsible risk taking. The moral hazard of the rating agencies, being paid by the same companies whose assets they rate, needs to also be addressed.

Regulation and correlation

Correlations are critical inputs in regulatory frameworks such as the Basel accords, especially in regulations for market risk and credit risk. We will discuss the correlation approaches of the Basel accords in this book. First, let's clarify.

What are Basel I, II and III?
Basel I, implemented in 1988, Basel II, implemented in 2006, and Basel III, which is currently being developed and implemented until 2019, are regulatory guidelines to ensure the stability of the banking system.

The term Basel comes from the beautiful city of Basel in Switzerland, where the honourable regulators meet. None of the Basel accords has legal authority. However, most countries (about 100 for Basel II) have created legislation to enforce the Basel accords for their banks.

Why Basel I, II and III?
The objective of the Basel accords is to provide incentives for banks to enhance their risk measurement and management systems and to contribute to a higher level of safety and soundness in the banking system. In particular, Basel III addresses the deficiencies of the banking system during the financial crisis 2007 to 2009. Basel III introduces many new ratios to ensure liquidity and adequate leverage of banks. In addition, new correlation models are implemented that deal with double defaults in insured risk transactions as displayed in Figure 1.1. Correlated defaults in a multi-asset portfolio quantified with the Gaussian copula, correlations in derivatives transactions termed credit value adjustment (CVA) and correlations in what is called "wrong-way risk" (WWR) have been proposed. We will devote Chapters 14 to 16 to addressing the benefits and limitations of these correlation approaches in Basel III.

HOW DOES CORRELATION RISK FIT INTO THE BROADER PICTURE OF RISKS IN FINANCE?

As already mentioned, we differentiate three main types of risks in finance: market risk, credit risk and operational risk. Additional types of risk may include systemic risk, concentration risk, liquidity risk, volatility risk, legal risk, reputational risk and more. Correlation risk plays an important part in market risk and credit risk and is closely related to systemic risk and concentration risk. Let's discuss it.

Correlation risk and market risk
Correlation risk is an integral part of market risk. Market risk comprises equity risk, interest-rate risk, currency risk and commodity risk. Market risk is typically measured with the VaR concept. Since VaR has a covariance matrix of the assets in the portfolio as an input, VaR implicitly incorporates correlation risk, ie, the risk that the correlations in the covariance matrix change. We have already studied the impact of different correlations on VaR in "Risk management and correlation" above.

Market risk is also quantified with expected shortfall (ES), also termed "conditional VaR" or "tail risk". Expected shortfall measures market risk for extreme events, typically for the worst 0.1%, 1% or 5% of possible future scenarios. A rigorous valuation of expected shortfall naturally includes the correlation between the asset returns in the portfolio, as VaR does. We discuss expected shortfall in detail in Chapter 16.[14]

Correlation risk and credit risk
Correlation risk is also a critical part of credit risk. Credit risk comprises (a) migration risk and (b) default risk. Migration risk is the risk that the credit quality of a debtor decreases, ie, migrates to a lower credit state. A lower credit state typically results in a lower asset price, so a paper loss for the creditor occurs. We already studied the effect of correlation risk of an investor, who has hedged their bond exposure with a CDS earlier in the section titled, "What is financial correlation risk?". We derived that the investor is exposed to changes in the correlation between the reference asset and the counterparty, ie, the CDS seller. The higher the default correlation, the higher is the CDS paper loss for the investor and, importantly, the higher is the probability of a total loss of their investment.

The degree to which defaults occur together (ie, default correlation) is critical for financial lenders such as commercial banks, credit unions, mortgage lenders and trusts, which give many types of loans to companies and individuals. Default correlations are also critical for insurance companies, which are exposed to credit risk of numerous debtors. Naturally, a low default correlation of debtors is desired to diversify the credit risk. Table 1.3 shows the default correlation from 1981 to 2001 of 6,907 companies, of which 674 defaulted.

The default correlations in Table 1.3 are one-year default correlations averaged over the time period 1981 to 2001. For example, the number 3.8% in the upper left corner means that, if a certain bond in the auto industry defaulted, there is a 3.8% probability that another bond in the auto industry will default. The number −2.5% in the column named "Fin" in the fourth row means that, if a bond in the energy sector defaulted, this actually decreases the probability that a bond in the financial sector defaults by 2.5% and vice versa.

From Table 1.3 we also observe that default correlations between industries are mostly positive, with the exception of the energy sector. This sector is typically viewed as a recession-resistant, stable

Table 1.3 Default correlation of 674 defaulted companies by industry

	Auto	Cons	Ener	Fin	Build	Chem	HiTec	Insur	Leis	Tele	Trans	Util
Auto	3.8%	1.3%	1.2%	0.4%	1.1%	1.6%	2.8%	-0.5%	1.0%	3.9%	1.3%	0.5%
Cons	1.3%	2.8%	-1.4%	1.2%	2.8%	1.6%	1.8%	1.1%	1.3%	3.2%	2.7%	1.9%
Ener	1.2%	-1.4%	**6.4%**	-2.5%	-0.5%	0.4%	-0.1%	-1.6%	-1.0%	-1.4%	-0.1%	0.7%
Fin	0.4%	1.2%	-2.5%	**5.2%**	2.6%	0.1%	0.4%	3.0%	1.6%	3.7%	1.5%	4.5%
Build	1.1%	2.8%	-0.5%	2.6%	**6.1%**	1.2%	2.3%	1.8%	2.3%	**6.5%**	4.2%	1.3%
Chem	1.6%	1.6%	0.4%	0.1%	1.2%	3.2%	1.4%	-1.1%	1.1%	2.8%	1.1%	1.0%
HiTec	2.8%	1.8%	-0.1%	0.4%	2.3%	1.4%	3.3%	0.0%	1.4%	4.7%	1.9%	1.0%
Insur	-0.5%	1.1%	-1.6%	3.0%	1.8%	-1.1%	0.0%	**5.6%**	1.2%	-2.6%	2.3%	1.4%
Leis	1.0%	1.3%	-1.0%	1.6%	2.3%	1.1%	1.4%	1.2%	2.3%	4.0%	2.3%	0.6%
Tele	3.9%	3.2%	-1.4%	3.7%	**6.5%**	2.8%	4.7%	-2.6%	4.0%	**10.7%**	3.2%	0.8%
Trans	1.3%	2.7%	-0.1%	1.5%	4.2%	1.1%	1.9%	2.3%	2.3%	3.2%	4.3%	0.2%
Util	0.5%	1.9%	0.7%	4.5%	1.3%	1.0%	1.0%	1.4%	0.6%	-0.8%	-0.2%	**9.4%**

Correlations above 5% are in bold.
Note: One year US default correlations – non-investment grade bonds 1981–2001.

Table 1.4 Term structure of default probabilities for an A-rated bond and a CC-rated bond in 2002

	Year									
	1	2	3	4	5	6	7	8	9	10
A	0.02%	0.07%	0.13%	0.14%	0.15%	0.17%	0.18%	0.21%	0.24%	0.25%
CC	23.83%	13.29%	10.31%	7.62%	5.04%	5.13%	4.04%	4.62%	2.62%	2.04%

Source: Moody's

sector with no or low correlation to other sectors. We also observe that the default correlation within sectors is higher than between sectors. This suggests that systematic factors (such as a recession or structural weakness as the general decline of a sector) impact on defaults more than idiosyncratic factors. Hence if General Motors defaults, it is more likely that Ford defaults, rather than Ford benefiting from the default of its rival GM.

Since the intra-sector default correlations are higher than inter-sector default correlations, a lender is advised to have a sector-diversified loan portfolio to reduce default correlation risk.

Defaults are binomial events: either default or no default. Therefore, to model defaults, often a simple binomial model is applied, which we will do in Chapter 5. However, we can also analyse defaults in more detail and look at term structure of defaults. Let's assume a creditor has given loans to two debtors. One debtor is A-rated and one is CC-rated. A historical default term structure of these bonds is displayed in Table 1.4.

To clarify, the number 0.15% in the column corresponding to the fifth year and second row means that an A-rated bond has a 0.15% probability to default in year 5.[15] For most investment-grade bonds, the term structure of default probabilities increases in time, as we see from Table 1.4 for the A-rated bond. This is because the longer the time horizon, the higher the probability of adverse internal events as mismanagement, or external events as increased competition or a recession. For bonds in distress, however, the default term structure is typically inverse, as seen for the CC-rated bond in Table 1.4. This is because for a distressed company, the immediate future is critical. If the company survives the coming problematic years, the probability of default decreases.

For a creditor, the default correlation of his debtors is critical. As mentioned, a creditor will benefit from a low default correlation of their debtors, which spreads the default correlation risk. We can correlate the default term structures in Table 1.4 with the famous (now infamous) copula model, which will be discussed in Chapter 7. This will allow us to answer questions as "What is the joint probability of Debtor 1 defaulting in Year 3 and Debtor 2 defaulting in Year 5?"

"Correlations always increase in stressed markets"
John Hull

CORRELATION RISK AND SYSTEMIC RISK

So far, we have analysed correlation risk with respect to market risk and credit risk and have concluded that correlations are a critical input when quantifying market risk and credit risk. Correlations are also closely related to systemic risk, which we define as the risk that a financial market or an entire financial system collapses.

An example of systemic risk is the collapse of the entire credit market in 2008. At the height of the crisis in September 2008, when Lehman Brothers filed for bankruptcy, the credit markets were virtually frozen with essentially no lending activities. Even as the Federal Reserve guaranteed interbank loans, lending resumed only very gradually and slowly.

The stock market crash starting in October 2007, with the Dow (Dow Jones Industrial Average) at 14,093 points and then falling by 53.54% to 6,547 points by March 2009, is also a systemic market collapse. All but one of the Dow 30 stocks had declined. Walmart was the lone stock, which was up during the crisis. Of the S&P 500 stocks, 489 declined during this timeframe. The 11 stocks that were up were:

❏ Apollo Group (APOL), educational sector; provides educational programmes for working adults and is a subsidiary of the University of Phoenix;
❏ Autozone (AZ0), auto industry; provides auto replacement parts;
❏ CF Industries (CF), agricultural industry; provides fertiliser;
❏ DeVry Inc. (DV), educational sector; holding company of several universities;
❏ Edward Lifesciences (EW), pharmaceutical-industry; provides products to treat cardiovascular diseases;
❏ Family Dollar (FDO), consumer staples;
❏ Gilead Pharmaceuticals (GILD), pharmaceutical industry; provides HIV, hepatitis medication;
❏ Netflix (NFLX), entertainment industry; provides Internet subscription service;
❏ Ross Stores (ROST), consumer staples;

❑ Southwestern Energy (SWN), energy sector; and
❑ Walmart (WMT), consumer staples.

From this list we can see that the consumer staples sector (which provides basic necessities as food and basic household items) fared well during the crisis. The educational sector also typically thrives in a crisis, since many unemployed seek to further their education.

Importantly, systemic financial failures such as the one from 2007 to 2009 typically spread to the economy with a decreasing GDP, increasing unemployment and, therefore, a decrease in the standard of living.

Systemic risk and correlation risk are highly dependent. Since a systemic decline in stocks involves almost the entire stock market, correlations between the stocks increase sharply. Figure 1.8 shows the relationship between the percentage change of the Dow and the correlation between the stocks in the Dow before the crisis from May 2004 to October 2007 and during the crisis from October 2007 to March 2009.

In Figure 1.8 we downloaded daily closing prices of all 30 stocks in the Dow and put them into monthly bins. We then derived monthly 30 × 30 correlation matrices using the Pearson correlation measure and averaged the matrices. We then smoothed the graph by taking the one-year moving average.

From Figure 1.8 we can observe a somewhat stable correlation from 2004 to 2006, when the Dow increased moderately. In the time period from January 2007 to February 2008 we observe that the correlation in the Dow increases when the Dow increases more strongly. Importantly, in the time of the severe decline of the Dow from August 2008 to March 2009 we observe a sharp increase in the correlation from non-crisis levels of an average 27% to over 50%. In Chapter 2, we will observe empirical correlations in detail and we will find that, at the height of the crisis in February 2009, the correlation of the stocks in the Dow reached a high of 96.97%. Hence, portfolios that were considered well diversified in benign times experienced a sharp increase in correlation and hence unexpected losses due to the combined, highly correlated decline of many stocks during the crisis. We will quantify this correlation risk and its associated potential losses in detail in Chapters 10 and 11.

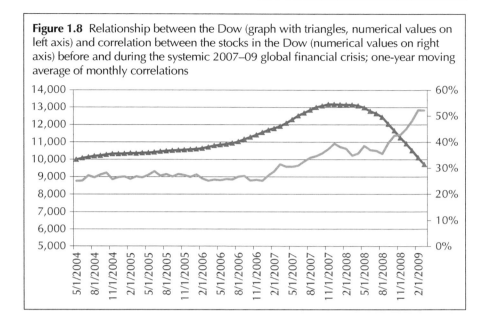

Figure 1.8 Relationship between the Dow (graph with triangles, numerical values on left axis) and correlation between the stocks in the Dow (numerical values on right axis) before and during the systemic 2007–09 global financial crisis; one-year moving average of monthly correlations

CORRELATION RISK AND CONCENTRATION RISK

Concentration risk is a fairly new risk category and therefore not yet uniquely defined. A sensible definition is the risk of financial loss due to a concentrated exposure to a specific group of counterparties.

Concentration risk can be quantified with the concentration ratio. For example, if a creditor has 10 loans of equal size, the concentration ratio would be $1/10 = 0.1$. If a creditor has only one loan to one counterparty, the concentration ratio would be 1. Naturally, the lower the concentration ratio, the more diversified is the default risk of the creditor, assuming the default correlation between the counterparties is smaller than 1.

We can also categorise counterparties into groups – for example, sectors. We can then analyse sector concentration risk. The higher the number of different sectors a creditor has lent to, the higher is their sector diversification. High sector diversification reduces default risk, since intra-sector defaults are higher correlated than counterparties in different sectors, as seen in Table 1.3.

Naturally, concentration and correlation risk are closely related. Let's verify this in an example.

Example 1.3: Case (a) The commercial bank C has lent US$10,000,000 to a single company W. So C's concentration ratio is 1. Company W has a default probability P_W of 10%. Hence the expected loss (EL) for bank C is US$10,000,000 × 0.1 = US$1,000,000. Graphically, we have Figure 1.9.

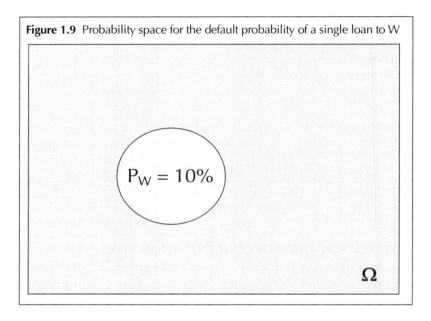

Figure 1.9 Probability space for the default probability of a single loan to W

Case (b) The commercial bank C has lent US$5,000,000 to company X and US$5,000,000 to company Y. Both X and Y have a 10% default probability. So C's concentration ratio is reduced to 1/2.

If the default correlation between X and Y is bigger than 0 and smaller than 1, we derive that the worst-case scenario, ie, the default of X and Y, $P(X \cap Y)$, with a loss of US$1,000,000 is reduced, as seen in Figure 1.10.

The exact joint default probability depends on the correlation model and correlation parameter values, which will be discussed in Chapters 4 to 8. For any model, though, if default correlation between X and Y is 1, then there is no benefit from the lower concentration ratio. The probability space would be as in Figure 1.9.

Case (c) If we further decrease the concentration ratio, the

Figure 1.10 Probability space for loans to companies X and Y

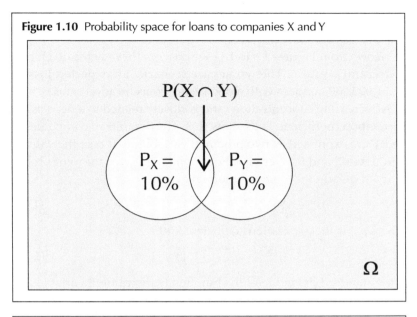

Figure 1.11 Probability space for loans to companies X, Y and Z

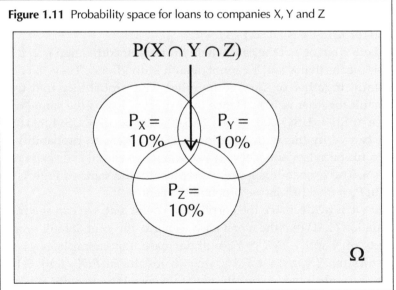

worst-case scenario, ie, the expected loss of 10% decreases further. Let's assume the lender C gives loans to three companies X, Y and Z, of US$3.33 million each. The default probability of X, Y and Z is

10% each. Therefore, the concentration ratio decreases to a third. The probabilities are displayed in Figure 1.11.

Hence, from Figures 1.9 to 1.11 we observe the benefits of a lower concentration ratio. The worst-case scenario, an expected loss of US$1,000,000, reduces with a decreasing concentration ratio.

A decreasing concentration ratio is closely related to a decreasing correlation coefficient. Let's show this. The defaults of companies X and Y are expressed as two binomial variables that take the value 1 if in default, and 0 otherwise. Equation (1.11) gives the joint probability of default for the two binomial events:

$$P(X \cap Y) = \rho_{XY}\sqrt{P_X(1-P_X)P_Y(1-P_Y)} + P_X P_Y \quad (1.11)$$

where ρ_{XY} is the correlation coefficient and

$$\sqrt{P_X(1-P_X)} \quad (1.12)$$

is the standard deviation of the binomially distributed variable X.

Let's assume again that the lender C has given loans to X and Y of US$5,000,000 each. Both X and Y have a default probability of 10%. Following equation (1.12), this means that the standard deviation for X and Y is $\sqrt{0.1 \times (1-0.1)} = 0.3$.

Let's first look at the case where the default correlation is $\rho_{XY} = 1$. This means that X and Y cannot default individually. They can only default together or survive together. The probability that they default together is 10%. Hence the expected loss is the same as in case a) EL = (US$5,000,000 + US$5,000,000) × 0.1 = US$1,000,000. We can verify this with equation (1.11) for the joint probability of two binomial events, $P(X \cap Y) = 1 \times \sqrt{0.1(1-0.1) \times 0.1(1-0.1)} + 0.1 \times 0.1$ = 10%. The probability space is graphically the same as Figure 1.9 with $P_X = P_Y = 10\%$ as the probability event.

If we now decrease the correlation coefficient, we can see from equation (1.11) that the worst-case scenario, the joint default probability of X and Y, $P(X \cap Y)$, will decrease. For example, $\rho_{XY} = 0.5$ results in $P(X \cap Y) = 5.5\%$, $\rho_{XY} = 0$ results in $P(X \cap Y) = 1\%$. Interestingly, even a slightly negative correlation coefficient can result in a positive joint default probability if the standard deviation of the binomial events is fairly low and the default probabilities are high. In our example, the standard deviation of both entities is 30% and a default probability of both entities is 10%. Together with a negative correlation coefficient of −0.1, following equation (1.11) leads to a joint default probability of 0.1%. We will discuss the binomial correlation model in more detail in chapter 5.

In conclusion, we have shown the beneficial aspect of a lower concentration ratio that is closely related to a lower correlation coefficient. In particular, both a lower concentration ratio and a lower correlation coefficient reduce the worst-case scenario for a creditor, the joint probability of default of his debtors.

In Chapter 14 we will verify this result and find that a higher (copula) correlation between assets results in a higher credit value-at-risk (CVaR). CVaR measures the maximum loss of a portfolio of correlated debt with a certain probability for a certain timeframe. Hence CVaR measures correlated default risk and is analogous to the VaR concept for correlated market risk, which we discussed earlier.

A WORD ON TERMINOLOGY

As mentioned in the section "Trading and correlation" above, we find the terms "correlation desks" and "correlation trading" in trading practice. Correlation trading means that traders trade assets or execute trading strategies, whose value is at least in part determined by the co-movement of two or more assets in time. We already mentioned the strategy "pairs trading", the exchange option and the quanto option as examples of correlation trading. In trading practice, the term "correlation" is typically applied quite broadly, referring to any co-movement of asset prices in time.

However, in financial theory, especially in recent publications, the term "correlation" is often defined more narrowly, referring only to the linear Pearson correlation model, as in Cherubini *et al* (2004), Nelsen (2006) and Gregory (2010). These authors refer to other than Pearson correlation coefficients as dependence measures or measures of association. However, in financial theory the term "correlation" is also often applied to generally describe dependencies, as in the terms "credit correlation", "default correlation" and "volatility–asset return correlation", which are quantified by non-Pearson models as in Heston (1993), Lucas (1995) and Li (2000).

In this book, we will refer to the Pearson coefficient, discussed in Chapter 3, as correlation coefficient and the coefficients derived by non-Pearson models as dependency coefficients. In accordance with most literature, we will refer to all methodologies that measure some form of dependency as correlation models or dependency models.

SUMMARY

There are two types of financial correlations: (1) static correlations, which measure how two or more financial assets are associated within a certain time period, for example a year; (2) dynamic financial correlations, which measure how two or more financial assets move together in time.

Correlation risk can be defined as the risk of financial loss due to adverse movements in correlation between two or more variables. These variables can be financial variables such as correlated defaults between two debtors or nonfinancial such as the correlation between political tensions and an exchange rate. Correlation risk can be non-monotonic, meaning that the dependent variable, for example the CDS spread, can increase or decrease when the correlation parameter value increases.

Correlations and correlation risk are critical in many areas in finance such as investments, trading and especially risk management, where different correlations result in very different degrees of risk. Correlations also play a key role in a systemic crisis, where correlations typically increase and can lead to high unexpected losses. As a result, the Basel III accord has introduced several correlation concepts and measures to reduce correlation risk (see Chapters 14 to 16 for details).

Correlation risk can be categorised as its own type of risk. However, correlation parameters and correlation matrices are critical inputs and hence a part of market risk and credit risk. Market risk and credit risk are highly sensitive to changing correlations. Correlation risk is also closely related to concentration risk, as well as systemic risk, since correlations typically increase in a systemic crisis.

The term "correlation" is not uniquely defined. In trading practice "correlation" is applied quite broadly and refers to the co-movements of assets in time, which may be measured by different correlation concepts. In financial theory, the term "correlation" is often defined more narrowly, referring only to the linear Pearson correlation coefficient. Non-Pearson correlation measures are termed "dependence measures" or "measures of association".

APPENDIX A1
Dependence and correlation
Dependence
In statistics, two events are considered dependent if the occurrence of one affects the probability of another. Conversely, two events are considered independent if the occurrence of one does not affect the probability of another. Formally, two events A and B are independent if and only if the joint probability equals the product of the individual probabilities:

$$P(A \cap B) = P(A)P(B) \tag{A1}$$

Solving equation (A1) for $P(A)$, we get

$$P(A) = \frac{P(A \cap B)}{P(B)}$$

Following the Kolmogorov definition

$$\frac{P(A \cap B)}{P(B)} \equiv P(A|B)$$

we derive

$$P(A) = \frac{P(A \cap B)}{P(B)} = P(A|B) \tag{A2}$$

where $P(A|B)$ is the conditional probability of A with respect to B. $P(A|B)$ reads "probability of A given B". In equation (A2) the probability of A, $P(A)$, is not affected by B, since $P(A) = P(A|B)$, hence the event A is independent from B.

From equation (A2), we also derive

$$P(B) = \frac{P(A \cap B)}{P(A)} = P(B|A) \tag{A3}$$

Hence from equation (A1) it follows that A is independent from B and B is independent from A.

Example A1: Statistical independence:
The historical default probability of company A, $P(A) = 3\%$, the historical default probability of company B, $P(B) = 4\%$, and the historical joint probability of default is $3\% \times 4\% = 0.12\%$. In this case $P(A)$ and $P(B)$ are independent. This is because, from equation (A2), we have

$$P(A) = \frac{P(A \cap B)}{P(B)} = P(A \mid B) = 3\% = \frac{3\% \times 4\%}{4\%} = 3\%$$

Since $P(A) = P(A \mid B)$, the event A is independent from the event B. Using equation (A3), we can do the same exercise for event B, which is independent from event A.

Correlation

As mentioned in the section on terminology above, the term "correlation" is not uniquely defined. In trading practice, the term "correlation" is used quite broadly, referring to any co-movement of asset prices in time. In statistics, correlation is typically defined more narrowly and typically referred to as the linear dependency derived in the Pearson correlation model. Let's look at the Pearson covariance and relate it to the dependence discussed above.

A covariance measures how strong the linear relationship between two variables is. These variables can be deterministic (which means their outcome is known), as the historical default probabilities in example A1 above. For random variables (variables with an unknown outcome such as flipping a coin), the Pearson covariance is derived with expectation values:

$$COV(X,Y) = E\big[(X - E(X))(Y - E(Y))\big] = E(XY) - E(X)E(Y) \quad \text{(A4)}$$

where $E(X)$ and $E(Y)$ are the expected values of X and Y respectively, also known as the mean. $E(XY)$ is the expected value of the product of the random variables X and Y. The covariance in equation (A4) is not easy to interpret. Therefore, often a normalised covariance, the correlation coefficient is used. The Pearson correlation coefficient $\rho(XY)$ is defined as

$$\rho(X,Y) = \frac{COV(X,Y)}{\sigma(X)\sigma(Y)} \quad \text{(A5)}$$

where $\sigma(X)$ and $\sigma(Y)$ are the standard deviations of X and Y respectively. While the covariance takes value between $-\infty$ and $+\infty$, the correlation coefficient conveniently takes values between -1 and $+1$.

Independence and uncorrelatedness

From equation (A1) above we find that the condition for independence for two random variables is $E(XY) = E(X) E(Y)$. From equation (A4) we see that $E(XY) = E(X) E(Y)$ is equal to a covariance of zero. Therefore, if two variables are independent, their covariance is zero.

Is the reverse also true? Does a zero covariance mean independence? The answer is no. Two variables can have a zero covariance even when they are dependent! Let's show this with an example. For the parabola $Y = X^2$, Y is clearly dependent on X, since Y changes when X changes. However, the correlation of the function $Y = X^2$ derived by equations (A4) or (A5) is zero! This can be shown numerically and algebraically. For a numerical derivation, see the simple spreadsheet www.dersoft.com/dependenceandcorrelation.xlsm, sheet 1. Algebraically, we have from equation (A4):

$$COV(X,Y) = E(XY) - E(X)E(Y)$$

Inputting $Y = X^2$, we derive

$$= E(X\,X^2) - E(X)\,E(X^2)$$

$$= E(X^3) - E(X)\,E(X^2)$$

Let X be a uniform variable bounded in $[-1, +1]$. Then the mean $E(X)$ and $E(X^3)$ are zero and we have

$$= 0 - 0\,E(X^2)$$

$$= 0$$

For a numerical example, see www.dersoft.com/dependenceandcorrelation.xlsm, sheet 2.

In conclusion, the Pearson covariance or correlation coefficient can give values of zero, ie, tells us the variables are uncorrelated, even if the variables are dependent! This is because the Pearson correlation concept measures only linear dependence. It fails to capture nonlinear relationships. This shows the limitation of the Pearson correlation concept for finance, since most financial relationships are nonlinear. See Chapter 3 for a more detailed discussion on the Pearson correlation model.

APPENDIX A2
On percentage and logarithmic changes

In finance, growth rates are expressed as relative changes, $(S_t - S_{t-1})/S_{t-1}$, where S_t and S_{t-1} are the prices of an asset at time t and $t-1$, respectively. For example, if $S_t = 110$, and $S_{t-1} = 100$, the relative change is $(110 - 100)/100 = 0.1 = 10\%$.

We often approximate relative changes with the help of the natural logarithm:

$$(S_t - S_{t-1})/S_{t-1} \approx \ln(S_t/S_{t-1}) \tag{A6}$$

This is a good approximation for small differences between S_t and S_{t-1}. $\mathrm{Ln}(S_t/S_{t-1})$ is called a log-return. The advantage of using log-returns is that they can be added over time. Relative changes are not additive over time. Let's show this in two examples.

Example 1
A stock price at t_0 is US\$100. From t_0 to t_1, the stock increases by 10%. Hence the stock increases to US\$110. From t_1 to t_2, the stock increases again by 10%. So the stock price increases to US\$110 × 0.1 = US\$121. This increase of 21% higher than adding the percentage increases of 10% + 10% = 20%. Hence percentage changes are not additive over time.

Let's look at the log-returns. The log-return from t_0 to t_1 is $\ln(110/100) = 9.531\%$. From t_1 to t_2 the log-return is $\ln(121/110) = 9.531\%$. When adding these returns, we get $9.531\% + 9.531\% = 19.062\%$. This is the same as the log-return from t_0 to t_2, ie, $\ln(121/100) = 19.062\%$. Hence log-returns are additive in time.[16]

Let's now look at another, more extreme example.

Example 2
A stock price in t_0 is US\$100. It moves to US\$200 in t_1 and back to US\$100 in t_2. The percentage change from t_0 to t_1 is (US\$200 − US\$100)/US\$100 = 100%. The percentage change from t_1 to t_2 is (US\$100 − US\$200)/(US\$200) = −50%. Adding the percentage changes, we derive +100% − 50% = +50%, although the stock has not increased from t_0 to t_2! Naturally this type of performance measure is incorrect and not allowed in accounting.

Log-returns give the correct answer: the log-return from t_0 to t_1 is $\ln(200/100) = 69.31\%$. The log-return from t_1 to t_2 is $\ln(100/200) =$

–69.31%. Adding these log-returns in time, we get the correct return of the stock price from t_0 to t_2 of 69.31% – 69.31% = 0%.

These examples are displayed in a simple spreadsheet at www.dersoft.com/logreturns.xlsx.

Questions for Chapter 1

Answers to these questions can be found at the end of this book.

1. What two types of financial correlations exist?
2. What is "wrong-way correlation risk" or for short "wrong-way risk"?
3. Correlations can be non-monotonous. What does this mean?
4. Correlations are critical in many areas in finance. Name five.
5. High diversification is related with low correlation. Why is this considered one of the few "free lunches" in finance?
6. Create a numerical example and show why a lower correlation results in a higher return/risk ratio.
7. What is "correlation trading"?
8. What is "pairs trading"?
9. Name three correlation options, in which a lower correlation results in a higher option price.
10. Name one correlation option where a lower correlation results in a lower option price.
11. Create a numerical example of a two-asset portfolio and show that lower correlation coefficient leads to a lower VaR number.
12. Why do correlations typically increase in a systemic market crash?
13. In 2005, a correlation crisis with respect to CDOs occurred that led to the default of several hedge funds. What happened?
14. In the global financial crisis 2007–09, many investors in the presumably safe super-senior tranches got hurt. What exactly happened?

15. What is the main objective of the Basel III accord?
16. The Basel accords have no legal authority. So why do most developed countries implement them?
17. How is correlation risk related to market risk and credit risk?
18. How is correlation risk related to systemic risk and concentration risk?
19. How can we measure the joint probability of occurrence of a binomial event as default or no-default?
20. Can it be that two binomial events are negatively correlated but they have a positive probability of joint default?
21. What is value-at-risk (VaR) and credit value-at-risk (CVaR)? How are they related?
22. Correlation risk is quite broadly defined in trading practice, referring to any co-movement of assets in time. How is the term "correlation" defined in statistics?
23. What do the terms "measure of association" and "measure of dependence" refer to in statistics?

---

1 The CDS spread s is the premium or fee that the CDS buyer pays for getting protection. It is called a spread since it is approximately the spread between the yield of the risky bond (the bond of Spain in Figure 1.1) in the CDS minus the yield of a riskless bond. See Meissner 2005, Chapter 2 for details.

2 To hedge means to protect. More precisely, hedging means to enter into a second trade to protect against the risk of an original trade.

3 Log-returns $\ln(S_1/S_0)$ are an approximation of percentage returns $(S_1 - S_0)/S_0$. We typically use log-returns in finance since they are additive in time, whereas percentage returns are not. For details see Appendix A2.

4 Implied volatility is volatility derived (implied) by option prices. The higher the implied volatility, the higher the option price.

5 Simply put, a CDS is an insurance against default of an underlying (eg, a bond). However, if the underlying is not owned, a long CDS is a speculative instrument on the default of the underlying (just like a naked put on a stock is a speculative position on the stock going down). See Meissner (2005) for more.

6 We will use a "variance-covariance VaR" approach in this book to derive VaR. Another way to derive VaR is the "non-parametric VaR". This approach derives VaR from simulated historical data. See Markovich (2007) for details.

7 More mathematically, the vector β_h is the transpose of the vector β_v and vice versa: $\beta_h^T = \beta_v$ and $\beta_v^T = \beta_h$. Hence we can also write Equation (1.9) as $\sigma_P = \sqrt{\beta_h C \beta_v^T}$. See www.dersoft.com/matrixprimer.xlsx sheet "Matrix Transpose" for more.

8 The attentive reader realises that we calculated the covariance differently in Equation (1.3). In Equation (1.3) we derived the covariance "from scratch", inputting the return values and means. In Equation (1.10) we are assuming that we already know the correlation coefficient ρ and the standard deviation σ.

9   This calculation, including Excel matrix multiplication, can be found at www.dersoft.com/2assetVaR.xlsx.
10 Investing in the equity tranche means "assuming credit risk" since a credit deterioration hurts the investor. This is similar to a bond, where the investor assumes the credit risk. Investors in the equity tranche receive the high equity tranche contract spread.
11 To hedge means to protect or to reduce risk. See Chapter 12, subsection titled, "What is hedging?", for details.
12 Going short the mezzanine tranche means being "short credit", ie, benefiting from a credit deterioration. Going short the mezzanine tranche means paying the (fairly low) mezzanine tranche contract spread.
13 Repo stands for repurchase transaction. It can be viewed as a short-term collateralised loan.
14 See also the original ES paper by Artzner (1997), an educational paper by Yamai and Yoshia (2002), as well as Acerbi and Tasche (2001), and McNeil *et al* (2005).
15 For the difference between default probabilities and default intensities, see Chapter 5.
16 We could have also solved for the absolute value 121, which matches a logarithmic growth rate of 9.531%: $\ln(x/110) = 9.531\%$, or, $\ln(x) - \ln(110) = 9.531\%$, or, $\ln(x) = \ln(110) + 9.531\%$. Taking the power of e we get, $e^{(\ln(x))} = X = e^{(\ln(110)+0.09531)} = 121$.

2

Empirical Properties of Correlation: How do Correlations Behave in the real World?

"Anything that relies on correlation, is charlatanism"
– Nassim Taleb

In this chapter we show that, contrary to common beliefs, financial correlations display statistically significant and expected properties.

HOW DO EQUITY CORRELATIONS BEHAVE IN A RECESSION, NORMAL ECONOMIC PERIOD OR STRONG EXPANSION?

In our study, we observed daily closing prices of the 30 stocks in the Dow Jones Industrial Average (Dow) from January 1972 to July 2017. This resulted in 11,214 daily observations of the Dow stocks and hence 11,214 × 30 = 336,420 closing prices. We built monthly bins and derived 900 correlation values (30 × 30) for each month, applying the Pearson correlation approach (see Chapter 3 for details). Since we had 534 months in the study, altogether we derived 534 × 900 = 480,600 correlation values.

The composition of the Dow is changing in time, with successful stocks being input into the Dow and unsuccessful stocks being removed. Our study comprises the Dow stocks that represent the Dow at each particular point in time.

Figure 2.1 shows the 534 monthly averaged correlation levels: we created monthly 30 by 30 bins of the Dow stock returns from 1972 to 2017, derived the Pearson correlation between each Dow stock returns, eliminated the unit correlation on the diagonal and averaged the remaining correlation values. We then differentiated the three states: an expansionary period with GDP (gross domestic product) growth rates of 3.5% or higher, a normal economic period

CORRELATION RISK MODELLING AND MANAGEMENT

Figure 2.1 Average correlation of monthly 30 × 30 Dow stock return bins. The light grey background displays an expansionary economic period, the medium gray background a normal economic period and the white background represents a recession. The horizontal line shows the polynomial trendline of order 4.

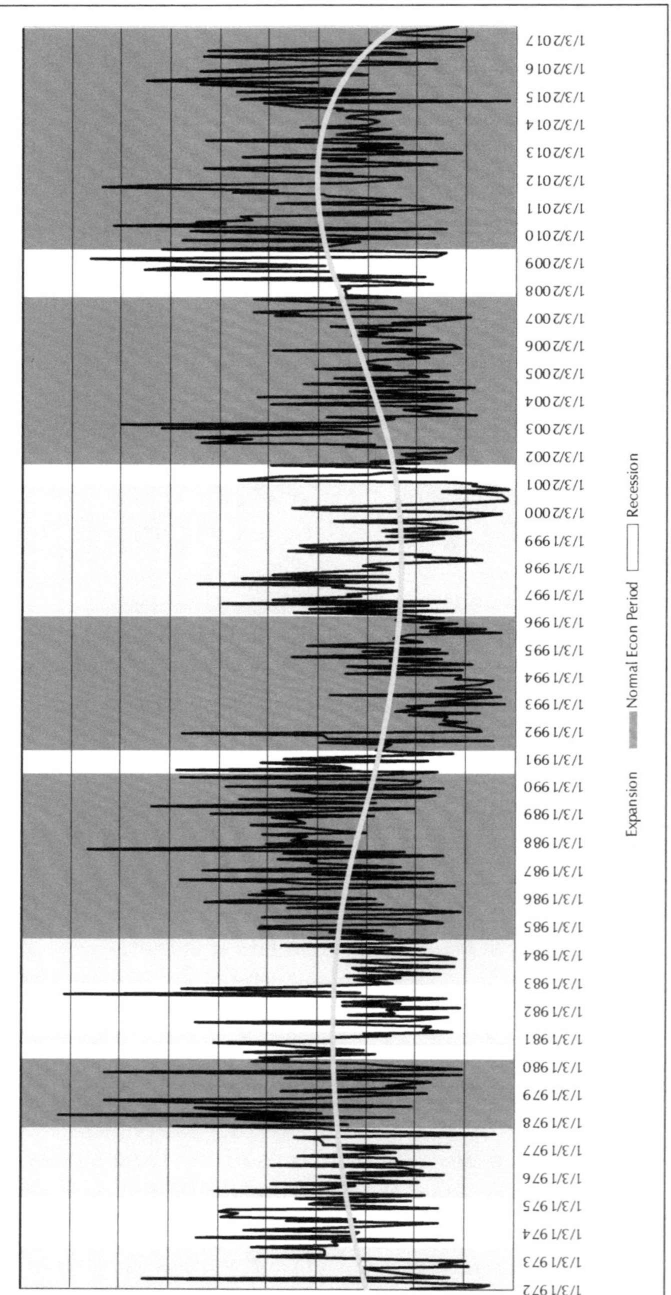

EMPIRICAL PROPERTIES OF CORRELATION: HOW DO CORRELATIONS BEHAVE IN THE REAL WORLD?

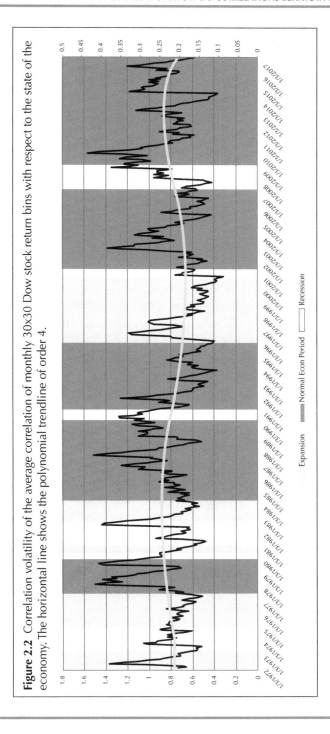

Figure 2.2 Correlation volatility of the average correlation of monthly 30x30 Dow stock return bins with respect to the state of the economy. The horizontal line shows the polynomial trendline of order 4.

with growth rates between 0% and 3.49% and a recession with two consecutive quarters of negative growth rates.

Figure 2.2 shows the volatility of the averaged monthly correlations. For the calculation of volatility, see Chapter 1.

From Figures 2.1 and 2.2, we observe the somewhat erratic behaviour of Dow correlation levels and volatility. However, Table 2.1 reveals some expected results:

Table 2.1 Correlation level and correlation volatility with respect to the state of the economy

	Correlation level	Correlation volatility
Expansionary period	27.46%	71.17%
Normal economic period	33.06%	83.06%
Recession	36.96%	80.48%

From Table 2.1, we observe that correlation levels are lowest in strong economic growth times. The reason may be that in strong growth periods equity prices react primarily to idiosyncratic, not to macroeconomic, factors. In recessions, correlation levels are typically high as shown in Table 2.1. In addition, we had already displayed in Chapter 1, Figure 1.8, that correlation levels increased sharply in the great recession from 2007 to 2009. In a recession, macroeconomic factors seem to dominate idiosyncratic factors, leading to a downturn across multiple stocks.

A further expected result in Table 2.1 is that correlation volatility is lowest in an economic expansion and higher in worse economic states. We did expect a higher correlation volatility in a recession compared with a normal economic state. However, it seems that high correlation levels in a recession remain high without much additional volatility. We will analyse whether the correlation volatility is an indicator for future recessions below. Altogether, Table 2.1 displays the higher correlation risk in bad economic times, which traders and risk managers should consider in their trading and risk management.

From Table 2.1, we observe a generally positive relationship between correlation level and correlation volatility. This is verified in more detail in Figure 2.3.

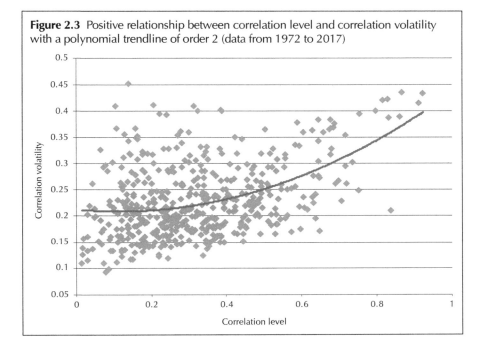

Figure 2.3 Positive relationship between correlation level and correlation volatility with a polynomial trendline of order 2 (data from 1972 to 2017)

DO EQUITY CORRELATIONS EXHIBIT MEAN REVERSION?

Mean reversion is the tendency of a variable to be pulled back to its long-term mean. In finance, many variables, such as bonds, interest rates, volatilities, credit spreads and more, are assumed to exhibit mean reversion. Fixed coupon bonds, which do not default, exhibit strong mean reversion: a bond is typically issued at par – for example, at US$100. If the bond does not default, at maturity it will revert to exactly that price of US$100, which is typically close to its long term mean.

Interest rates are also assumed to be mean-reverting: in an economic expansion, typically, demand for capital is high and interest rates rise. These high interest rates will eventually lead to cooling off of the economy, possibly leading to a recession. In this process capital demand decreases and interest rates decline from their high levels towards their long-term mean, eventually falling below it. Being in a recession, economic activity eventually increases again, often supported by monetary and fiscal policy. In this reviving economy, demand for capital increases, in turn increasing interest rates to their long term mean.

How can we quantify mean reversion?

Mean reversion is present if there is a negative relationship between the change of a variable, $S_t - S_{t-1}$, and the variable at $t-1$, S_{t-1}. Formally, mean reversion exists if

$$\frac{\partial(S_t - S_{t-1})}{\partial S_{t-1}} < 0 \qquad (2.1)$$

where

S_t: Price at time t
S_{t-1}: Price at the previous point in time $t-1$
∂: Partial derivative coefficient

Equation (2.1) tells us: If S_{t-1} increases by a very small amount, $S_t - S_{t-1}$ will decrease by a certain amount and vice versa. In particular, if S_{t-1} has decreased (in the denominator), then at the next point in time t, mean reversion will "pull up" S_{t-1} to S_t, and therefore increasing $S_t - S_{t-1}$. Conversely, if S_{t-1} has increased (in the denominator) and is high in $t-1$, then at the next point in time t, mean reversion will "pull down" S_{t-1} to S_t and therefore decreasing $S_t - S_{t-1}$. The degree of the "pull" is the degree of the mean reversion, also called mean reversion rate, mean reversion speed, or gravity.

Let's quantify the degree of mean reversion. Let's start with the discrete Vasicek 1987 process, which goes back to Ornstein–Uhlenbeck 1930:

$$S_t - S_{t-1} = a(\mu_S - S_{t-1})\Delta t + \sigma_S \sqrt{\Delta t} \qquad (2.2)$$

where

S_t: Price at time t
S_{t-1}: Price at the previous point in time $t-1$
a: Degree of mean reversion, also called mean reversion rate or gravity, $0 \le a \le 1$
μ_S: Long term mean of S
σ_S: Volatility of S
ε: Random drawing from a standardised normal distribution at time t, $\varepsilon(t) = n \sim (0,1)$. We can compute ε as =normsinv(rand()) in Excel/VBA and norminv(rand) in MATLAB. See www.dersoft.com/epsilon.xlsx for details.

We are currently interested only in mean reversion, so for now we will ignore the stochastic part in equation (2.2), $\sigma_S \varepsilon \sqrt{\Delta t}$.

For ease of explanation, let's assume $\Delta t = 1$. Then, from equation (2.2), we see that a mean reversion parameter of $a = 1$ will pull S_{t-1} to the long-term mean μ_S completely at every time step, assuming S_{t-1} was below the mean. For example if S_{t-1} is 80 and μ_S is 100, then $= 1 \times (100 - 80) = 20$ so the S_{t-1} of 80 is "mean-reverted up" to its long-term mean of 100 in one time step. Naturally, a mean-reversion parameter "a" of 0.5 will lead to a mean reversion of 50% at each time step, and a mean-reversion parameter "a" of 0, will result in no mean reversion.

Let's now quantify mean reversion. Setting $\Delta t = 1$, equation (2.2) without stochasticity reduces to

$$S_t - S_{t-1} = a(\mu_S - S_{t-1}) \qquad (2.3)$$

or

$$S_t - S_{t-1} = a\mu_S - aS_{t-1} \qquad (2.4)$$

To find the mean reversion rate "a", we can run a standard regression analysis of the form

$$Y = \alpha + \beta X.$$

Following equation (2.4) we are regressing $S_t - S_{t-1}$ with respect to S_{t-1}:

$$\underbrace{S_t - S_{t-1}}_{Y} = \underbrace{a\mu_S}_{\alpha} - \underbrace{aS_{t-1}}_{\beta X} \qquad (2.5)$$

Importantly, from equation (2.5), we observe that the regression coefficient β is equal to the negative mean-reversion parameter "a".

We now run a regression of equation (2.5) to find the empirical mean reversion of our correlation data. Hence S represents the 30 × 30 Dow stock monthly average correlations from 1972 to 2017. The regression analysis is displayed in Figure 2.4.

The regression function in Figure 2.4 displays a strong mean reversion of 79.03%. This means that, on average in every month, a deviation from the long-term correlation mean (32.38% in our study) is pulled back to that long-term mean by 79.03%. We can observe this strong mean reversion also by looking at Figure 2.1. An upward spike in correlation is typically followed by a sharp decline in the next time period, and vice versa.

CORRELATION RISK MODELLING AND MANAGEMENT

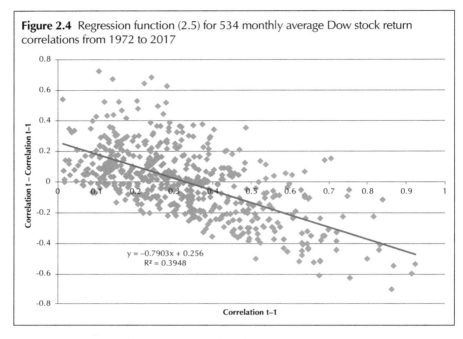

Figure 2.4 Regression function (2.5) for 534 monthly average Dow stock return correlations from 1972 to 2017

Let's look at an example of modelling correlation with mean reversion.

Example 2.1: The long-term mean of the correlation data is 32.38%. In February 2017, the averaged correlation of the 30 × 30 Dow correlation matrices was 26.15%. From the regression function from 1972 to 2017, we find that the average mean reversion is 79.03%. What is the expected correlation for March 2017 following equation (2.3) or (2.4)?

Solving equation (2.3) for S_t, we have $S_t = a(\mu_S - S_{t-1}) + S_{t-1}$. Hence the expected correlation in March is

$$S_t = 0.7903 \times (0.3238 - 0.2615) + 0.2615 = 0.3107$$

As a result, when applying equation (2.3) with the mean reversion rate of 79.03%, we expect the correlation in March 2017 to be 31.07%.[1]

DO EQUITY CORRELATIONS EXHIBIT AUTOCORRELATION?

Autocorrelation is the degree to which a variable is correlated to its past values. Autocorrelation can be quantified with the Nobel

Prize-rewarded ARCH (Autoregressive Conditional Heteroscedasticity) model of Robert Engle (1982) or its extension GARCH (Generalized Autoregressive Conditional Heteroscedasticity) by Tim Bollerslev (1988); see Chapter 9 for more details. However, we can also regress the time series of a variable to its past time series values to derive autocorrelation. This is the approach we will take here.

In finance, positive autocorrelation is also termed "persistence". In mutual-fund or hedge-fund performance analysis, an investor typically wants to know if an above-market performance of a fund has persisted for some time, ie, is positively correlated to its past strong performance.

Autocorrelation is the "reverse property" to mean reversion: the stronger the mean reversion, ie, the stronger a variable is pulled back to its long-term mean, the lower is the autocorrelation, ie, the lower is its correlation to its past values, and vice versa.

For our empirical correlation analysis, we derive the autocorrelation AC for a time lag of one period with the equation

$$AC(\rho_t, \rho_{t-1}) = \frac{COV(\rho_t, \rho_{t-1})}{\sigma(\rho_t)\sigma(\rho_{t-1})} \qquad (2.6)$$

where

AC: Autocorrelation
ρ_t: Correlation values for time period t (in our study, the monthly average of the 30 × 30 Dow stock return correlation matrices from 1972 to 2017, after eliminating the unity correlation on the diagonal)
ρ_{t-1}: Correlation values for time period $t - 1$ (ie, the monthly correlation values starting and ending one month prior than period t
COV: Covariance, see equation (1.3) for details

Equation (2.6) is algebraically identical with the Pearson correlation coefficient equation (1.4). The autocorrelation just uses the correlation values of time period t and time period t – 1 as inputs.

Following equation (2.6), we find the one-period lag autocorrelation of the correlation values from 1972 to 2017 to be 20.97%. As mentioned above, autocorrelation is the "opposite property" of mean reversion. Therefore, not surprisingly, the autocorrelation of 20.97% and the mean reversion is our study of 79.03% (see the

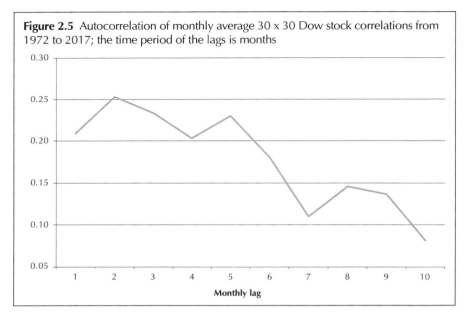

Figure 2.5 Autocorrelation of monthly average 30 × 30 Dow stock correlations from 1972 to 2017; the time period of the lags is months

above section "Do equity correlations exhibit mean reversion?") add up to 1.

Figure 2.5 shows the autocorrelation with respect to different time lags.

From Figure 2.5, we observe that 2-month lag autocorrelation, so autocorrelation with respect to two months prior, produces the highest autocorrelation. Altogether we observe the expected decay in autocorrelation with respect to time lags of earlier periods.

HOW ARE EQUITY CORRELATIONS DISTRIBUTED?

The input data of our distribution tests are daily correlation values between all 30 Dow stocks from 1972 to 2017. This resulted in 464,580 correlation values. The distribution is shown in Figure 2.6.

From Figure 2.6, we observe that most correlations between the stocks in the Dow are positive. In fact, 77.23% of all 464,580 correlation values were positive.

We tested 61 distributions for fitting the histogram in Figure 2.6, applying three standard fitting tests: (a) Kolmogorov–Smirnov, (b) Anderson–Darling and (c) Chi-Squared. Not surprisingly, the versatile Johnson SB distribution with four parameters – γ and δ for the shape, μ for location and σ for scale – provided the best fit.

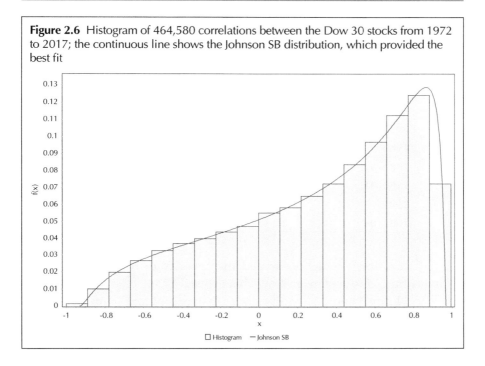

Figure 2.6 Histogram of 464,580 correlations between the Dow 30 stocks from 1972 to 2017; the continuous line shows the Johnson SB distribution, which provided the best fit

Standard distributions such as normal distribution, lognormal distribution or beta distribution provided a poor fit.

We also tested the correlation distribution between the Dow stocks for different states of the economy. The results were slightly but not significantly different; see www.dersoft.com/correlationfitting.docx.

IS EQUITY CORRELATION VOLATILITY AN INDICATOR FOR FUTURE RECESSIONS?

In our study from 1972 to 2017, six recessions occurred: (1) a severe recession in 1973–74 following the first oil price shock, (2) a short recession in 1980, (3) a severe recession in 1981–82 following the second oil price shock, (4) a mild recession in 1990–91, (5) a mild recession in 2001 after the Internet bubble burst and (6) the "great recession" 2007–09, following the global financial crisis. Table 2.2 displays the relationship of a change in the correlation volatility preceding the start of a recession.

From Table 2.2, we observe the severity of the 2007–09 "great

Table 2.2 Decrease in correlation volatility, preceding a recession. The decrease in correlation volatility is measured as a 6-month change of 6-month moving average correlation volatility. The severity of the recession is measured as the total GDP decline during the recession.

	% change in correlation volatility before recession	Severity of recession (% change of GDP)
1973–74	−7.22%	−11.93%
1980	−10.12%	−6.53%
1981–82	−4.65%	−12.00%
1990–91	0.06%	−4.05%
2001	−5.55%	−1.80%
2007–09	−2.64%	−14.75%

recession", which exceeded the severity of the oil price shock induced recessions in 1973–74 and 1981–82.

From Table 2.2, we also notice that, except for the mild recession in 1990–91, before every recession a downturn in correlation volatility occurred. This coincides with the fact that correlation volatility is low in an expansionary period (see Table 2.1), which often precedes a recession. However, the relationship between a decline in volatility and the severity of the recession is statistically non-significant. The regression function is almost horizontal and the R^2 is close to zero. Studies with more data, going back to 1920, are currently being conducted.

PROPERTIES OF BOND CORRELATIONS AND DEFAULT PROBABILITY CORRELATIONS

Our preliminary studies of 7,645 bond correlations and 4,655 default probability correlations display similar properties as equity correlations. Correlation levels were higher for bonds (41.67%) and slightly lower for default probabilities (30.43%) compared with equity correlation levels (34.83%). Correlation volatility was lower for bonds (63.74%) and slightly higher for default probabilities (87.74%) compared with equity correlation volatility (79.73%).

Mean reversion was present in bond correlations (25.79%) and in default probability correlations (29.97%). These levels were lower than the very high equity correlation mean reversion of 77.51%.

The default probability correlation distribution is similar to equity correlation distribution (see Figure 2.4) and can be replicated best by the Johnson SB distribution. However, the bond correlation distribution shows a more normal shape and can be best fitted with the generalised extreme value distribution and quite well with the normal distribution. Some fitting results are at www.dersoft.com/correlationfitting.docx. The bond correlation and default probability results are currently being verified with a larger sample data base.

SUMMARY

The following are the main findings of our empirical analysis:

(a) Our study confirmed that the worse the state of the economy, the higher are equity correlations. Equity correlations were extremely high during the great recession of 2007–09 and reached 96.97% in February 2009.

(b) Equity correlation volatility is lowest in an expansionary period and higher in normal and recessionary economic periods. Traders and risk managers should take these higher correlation levels and higher correlation volatility that markets exhibit during economic distress into consideration.

(c) Equity correlation levels and equity correlation volatility are positively related.

(d) Equity correlations show very strong mean reversion. The Dow correlations from 1972 to 2017 showed a monthly mean reversion of 79.03%. Hence, when modelling correlation, mean reversion should be included in the model.

(e) Since equity correlations display strong mean reversion, they display low autocorrelation. The degree of autocorrelations shows the typical decrease with respect to time (ie, the autocorrelation is higher for more recent time lags).

(f) The equity correlation distribution showed a distribution, which can be replicated well with the Johnson SB distribution. Other distributions such as normal, lognormal and beta distribution do not provide a good fit.

(g) First results show that bond correlations display similar properties as equity correlations. Bond correlation levels and bond correlation volatilities are generally higher in economic bad times. In addition, bond correlations exhibit mean reversion, although lower mean reversion than equity correlations exhibit.

(h) First results show that default correlations also exhibit properties seen in equity correlations. Default probability correlation levels are slightly lower than equity correlation levels, and default probability correlation volatilities are slightly higher than equity correlations. Studies with more data are currently being conducted.

Questions for Chapter 2
Answers to these questions can be found at the end of this book.

1. In which state of the economy are equity correlations the highest?
2. In which state of the economy is equity correlation volatility high?
3. What follows from Questions 1 and 2 for risk management?
4. What is mean reversion?
5. How can we quantify mean reversion?
6. What is autocorrelation? Name two approaches for how to quantify autocorrelation.
7. For equity correlations, we see the typical decrease of autocorrelation with respect to time lags. What does that mean?
8. How are mean reversion and autocorrelation related?
9. What is the distribution of equity correlations?
10. When modelling stocks, bonds, commodities, exchange rates, volatilities and other financial variables, we typically assume a normal or lognormal distribution. Can we do this for equity correlations?

---

1 Note that we have omitted any stochasticity, which is typically included when modelling financial variables, as shown in equation (2.2).

3

The Pearson Correlation Model – Work of the Devil?

"Not one subject in the universe is unworthy of study"
– Karl Pearson 1857–1936

While by far the most applied correlation model in finance, the Pearson correlation model is – due to its simplicity and linearity – also the most heavily criticised: "Anything that relies on correlation is charlatanism" (Nassim Taleb) and "Instruments whose pricing requires the input of correlation ... are accidents waiting to happen" (Paul Wilmott). In this chapter we address this contradiction and evaluate whether the Pearson correlation approach is rigorous and suitable for modelling associations in finance.

INTRODUCTION

The Pearson correlation model is by far the most prominent in finance. It is applied in risk measures such as VaR (value-at-risk), see Chapters 1, 10 and 12; ES (expected shortfall), see Chapter 16; ERM (enterprise risk management); and EVT (extreme value theory). The higher the Pearson correlation between the assets in the portfolio, the higher the risk measures, since high correlation implies a high probability of many assets declining jointly.

Pearson correlations also play a central role in investment analysis. In MPT (modern portfolio theory) a Pearson correlation coefficient matrix serves as an input to derive the portfolio variance, which is interpreted as portfolio risk. In the seminal CAPM (capital asset pricing model), the Pearson covariance is the numerator of the famous β, the measure for the sensitivity of an asset to non-diversifiable systematic risk.

The Pearson correlation measure also serves as an input for more advanced correlation models such as the Heston 1993 model (see

Chapter 5), where the Pearson correlation coefficient correlates the Brownian motions of the two variables of interest. Numerous extensions of the Heston model exist, such as the popular SABR (stochastic alpha beta rho) model of Hagan, Kumar, Lesniewski and Woodward (2002), where stochastic interest rates and stochastic volatility are Pearson-correlated to derive realistic volatility smiles and skews. A further extension of the Heston 1993 model is the Buraschi, Porchia and Trojani 2010 model – see Chapter 9. Here, the critical equations are the stochastic process of the underlying asset vector and the stochastic process of the mean-reverting covariance matrix of the assets. These two equations are correlated with the Pearson correlation model. Pearson correlation matrices are also part of copula correlation modelling, correlating the mapped marginal distributions to derive a single multivariate function – see Chapter 6.

In addition, Pearson correlations are applied in numerous correlation trading strategies. Pearson autocorrelations of indices or stocks can be calculated to find the degree of trending, which has decreased in recent years. Standard multi-asset options derive their value based on the Pearson correlation coefficient between the underlying assets. In addition, dispersion trading applies the Pearson correlation parameter as an input to evaluate the relationship between index volatility derived by the index components and actual index volatility. For details on correlation trading strategies, see Chapter 13.

In summary, the Pearson correlation model is ubiquitous in finance and at the same time heavily criticised. We will evaluate this contradiction and analyse if the Pearson model is a rigorous and proper model for finance.

THE PEARSON CORRELATION MODEL

The Pearson correlation model is a fundamental correlation model and can be found in virtually every descriptive statistics book. We already applied some elements of the Pearson model in Chapter 1, the section called "Investments and correlation". We will discuss it more in detail here.

In the Pearson model, a single number, the correlation coefficient ρ, expresses the strength of a linear association between two variables, here denoted by X and Y:

$$\rho(X,Y) = \frac{COV(X,Y)}{\sigma(X)\sigma(Y)} \qquad (3.1)$$

where X and Y are sets with the elements $\{x_1, ..., x_n\} \in R$ and $\{y_1, ..., y_n\} \in R$, and $\sigma(X)$ and $\sigma(Y)$ are the standard deviation of X and Y respectively. COV is the covariance, which for deterministic variables (eg, the past returns of two assets) is defined as

$$COV(X,Y) = \frac{1}{n-1}\sum_{i=1}^{n}(x_i - \mu_X)(y_i - \mu_Y) \qquad (3.2)$$

where μ_X and μ_Y are the mean of X and Y respectively. See Chapter 1, the section called "Investments and correlation", for a numerical example of the correlation coefficient and the covariance. See also the Excel spreadsheet at www.dersoft.com/matrixprimer.xlsx, sheet "Covariance Matrix".

From equations (3.1) and (3.2) we recognise why ρ is also called the Pearson product-moment correlation coefficient (PPMC). In the numerator of equation (3.1), the variable-adjusted first moments, the means are multiplied; in the denominator the square roots of the second moments are multiplied. Importantly, we recognise that only the first two moments are incorporated in the Pearson correlation coefficient. This property will be critical when analysing the robustness with respect to data distribution later in this chapter.

Conveniently, from equation (3.1) follows that $-1 \leq \rho(X, Y) \leq 1$, so ρ is easy to interpret: the closer ρ is to +1, the higher is the linear strength of the relationship; the closer ρ is to −1, the higher the negative linear relationship between the variables X and Y. A correlation coefficient of 0 means that the variables X and Y are uncorrelated. We will see later that a zero correlation does not necessarily imply independence of X and Y.

A second critical parameter in the Pearson correlation model is the regression coefficient. Given is the unknown true function of a population

$$y_i = \alpha + \beta x_i + \varepsilon_i \qquad (3.3)$$

for $i = 1, ..., n$ observations, and ε_i are the residuals, assumed iid and $n(0, 1)$. The objective is to find the best estimate for β. The Pearson model applies the OLS (ordinary least squares) method to find the best estimate via the regression function

$$\hat{y}_i = \hat{\alpha} + \hat{\beta} x_i \qquad (3.4)$$

The derivation for $\hat{\beta}$ applying the OLS can be found in Appendix 3.2.

From equation (3.4) we easily observe that $\hat{\beta}$ measures the average change of $\hat{Y}$ for a one-unit change of X. The correlation coefficient ρ and the regression coefficient $\hat{\beta}$ are algebraically related by

$$\hat{\beta}(X,Y) = \rho(X,Y) \frac{\sigma(Y)}{\sigma(X)} = \frac{COV(X,Y)}{\sigma^2(X)} \qquad (3.5)$$

Therefore, whereas the correlation coefficient ρ measures the strength and direction of a relationship, the regression coefficient $\hat{\beta}$ measures the sensitivity (slope) and direction of the relationship.

> "Make everything as simple as possible, but not simpler"
> Albert Einstein

BENEFITS OF THE PEARSON CORRELATION MODEL

Original models, which rigorously address a problem for the first time – such as Markowitz and Sharp's CAPM model, the Black–Scholes–Merton option-pricing model (see Chapter 6), the Merton default probability model (see Chapter 6) and Vasicek's one-factor Gaussian copula (see Chapter 7) – deserve recognition and praise. However, while these models find an innovative solution to an original problem, they are first-time models, often based on simple assumptions and analytics. The Pearson correlation model is no exception. It finds a unique and groundbreaking solution to the problem of association between variables. However, the model is somewhat simplistic in its assumptions and scope. This simplicity, while being a limitation, is the main benefit of the model.

The simplicity is highlighted by the fact that the degree of association between two variables is expressed in a single number: the correlation coefficient ρ. The correlation coefficient can be easily derived since virtually every software has a built-in function for it. For example, in Excel/VBA it is "correl"; in MATLAB it is "corrcoef"; in R it is "cor"; in C++ the GNU scientific library has prewritten code. Users can also easily derive the correlation coefficient themselves by calculating the covariance and the individual volatilities and applying equation (3.1).

Since the correlation coefficient conveniently takes values between −1 and +1, it is easily understood, often even by upper management! Hence if the correlation coefficient of the asset returns in a portfolio is close to +1, a supervising manager can order or suggest an allocation of assets that has a lower correlation. Moreover, the regression coefficient can give additional information. For example, a simple partial regression can be run to show the sensitivity of the portfolio value to a change in the price of single assets.

In conclusion, the main benefit of the groundbreaking Pearson correlation model is its simplicity and intuition. While the Pearson correlation parameters are easily derived and understood, Pearson outcomes can also easily be misunderstood and misinterpreted since they are derived on restricting assumptions and analytics, which will be discussed in the following section.

LIMITATIONS OF THE PEARSON CORRELATION MODEL

In this main section, we will discuss the numerous limitations of the Pearson correlation model. The limitations, arguably in order of significance, are:

- linearity;
- non-robustness with respect to data distribution;
- non-robustness with respect to outliers;
- timeframe sensitivity;
- the correlation – causality fallacy (spurious relationships);
- spurious correlations;
- heteroscedasticity;
- multicollinearity;
- transformation invariance; and
- finite variance.

We'll look at each in turn.

Linearity

One of the most critical limitations of the Pearson correlation model is the fact that it assesses the linear strength of an association. However, the vast majority of relationships in finance are nonlinear: the efficient frontier in CAPM, equity prices in time, the bond-yield function, an option function, the equity tranche in a CDO, to name but a few. Nonlinear relationships cannot be evaluated by the Pearson correlation model since it includes only the first two moments, as observed in equations (3.1) and (3.2). A popular example for the failure of the correlation coefficient to evaluate nonlinear relationships is the parabola $Y = X^2$. Here we have a perfect dependency of Y on X, however, the Pearson correlation coefficient of $Y = X^2$ is zero (see Appendix 1A). In fact, for most nonlinear relationships the Pearson correlation model will underestimate the true dependency. We will discuss the dependency–correlation relationship in more depths later in this chapter.

How to deal with nonlinearity?
When addressing the issue of nonlinearity, the first thing to do is to determine whether it is present. Heuristically, we can simply visually evaluate the scatterplot. This gives us a good assessment whether the data is linear or nonlinear. Statistically, several methods exist to test for linearity. We can test if the proportion Y/X converges to a constant $a \in R$ in X. For example, if $Y = X + \varepsilon$, where X and Y are sets $X = \{x_1, ..., x_n\}$ and $Y = \{y_1, ..., y_n\}$ with ε iid and $n(0, 1)$, Y/X will converge to $a = 1$ with increasing i. Hence the function $Y = X + \varepsilon$ is linear in X. Conversely, for nonlinear functions such as $Y = e^X$, Y/X will not converge to a constant $a \in R$ in X.

Another linearity test is to evaluate whether the conditional mean $\mu_Y | X = \mu_Y + \rho(X - \mu_X)\frac{\sigma Y}{\sigma X}$ is a linear function in X and if the conditional mean $\mu_X | Y = \mu_X + \rho(Y - \mu_Y)\frac{\sigma X}{\sigma Y}$ is linear in Y. If so, Y and X will be linear in X and Y.

If the dataset of interest is nonlinear, we can also try to linearise it and then apply the Pearson correlation model. Several methods such as logarithmic transformation, exponential transformation, square-root transformation, inverse transformation, and square transformation exist. For different data plots, different transformations are preferable. For example if the data is exponential, a logarithmic transformation can be applied. If the dataset is parabolic as the before mentioned $Y = X^2$, a square-root transformation will result in $Y = X$ and reveal the perfect dependency when the Pearson model is applied.

In conclusion, a critical limitation of the Pearson model is that it assesses only the linear strength of a relationship. Applying the Pearson model to nonlinear datasets, which occur often in finance, will typically underestimate the true dependency. Hence, before applying the Pearson model, visual or statistical tests on linearity have to be performed. For certain datasets a transformation to linearise the data can be performed. If successful, the Pearson model may be applied, bearing the following limitations.

Non-robustness with respect to data distribution
In the previous section we addressed the limitation that the Pearson correlation model evaluates only the strength and direction of a *linear* relationship between two variables. We will now expand this discussion and analyse which joint data distribution is consistent with the linearity of the Pearson correlation model.

From equations (3.1) and (3.2) we realise that the Pearson model incorporates only the first and second moment, mean and variance. Hence the Pearson model is consistent with joint distributions that are fully characterised by the first two moments. This is the family of elliptical distributions, which comprises the Normal, student-t, Laplace, Cauchy and the logistic distribution.[1] If the joint distribution of variables is elliptical, the linear Pearson correlation model is a suitable correlation measure with respect to data distribution.

However, in only one case, when the joint distribution is normal, does uncorrelatedness (ie, a Pearson covariance of 0) imply independence. Even if the marginal distributions are zero and the joint distribution is not, uncorrelatedness does not imply independence. Furthermore, uncorrelatedness does not imply independence for other elliptical distributions or non-elliptical distributions.

More general, independence implies uncorrelatedness; however, uncorrelatedness does not imply independence. This can be shown in a simple way. In equations (3.1) and (3.2), we derived the Pearson correlation coefficient and covariance with deterministic variables. For random variables, the covariance is expressed with expectation values:

$$COV(X,Y) = E\big[(X - E(X))(Y - E(Y))\big] = E(XY) - E(X)E(Y) \quad (3.6)$$

From basic probability theory we recall that X and Y are statistically independent iff the expectation of the product of the variables $E(XY)$ is equal to the expectation of the individual variables $E(X)$ and $E(Y)$,

$$E(XY) = E(X)E(Y) \qquad (3.7)$$

The independence condition (3.7) implies a covariance of zero; see equation (3.6). Hence it follows that, if X and Y are independent, they are uncorrelated.

To prove that the opposite is not true, ie, that uncorrelatedness does not imply independence, we have to show only one example of uncorrelatedness and dependence. We can do this with our previously mentioned example $Y = X^2$. Here we have perfect dependence of Y on X: if X is known, a unique, deterministic Y results. However, Y and X are uncorrelated, ie, the covariance is zero:

From equation (3.7) we have

$$COV(X,Y) = E(XY) - E(X)E(Y)$$

Inputting $Y = X^2$, we derive

$$= E(XX^2) - E(X)E(X^2)$$
$$= E(X^3) - E(X)E(X^2)$$

Let X be a uniform variable bounded in [-1, +1]. Then the means $E(X) = E(X^3) = 0$ and we have,

$$= 0 - 0E(X^2) = 0$$

Hence, for the perfect dependency $Y = X^2$, the Pearson covariance results in zero, which is naturally quite misleading. As mentioned, only for joint normal distributions is independence identical with uncorrelatedness. Stated in terms of logic, we find that independence is a necessary condition for uncorrelatedness for all non-normal joint distributions. Only for joint normal distributions is independence a necessary and sufficient condition for uncorrelatedness.

Anscombe (1973) showed that almost identical correlation parameters can result from very different data distributions as seen in Figure 3.1.

The fact that different datasets can result in very similar Pearson coefficients is *per se* not necessarily a limitation of the Pearson model. However, the critical point in Figure 3.1 is that the Pearson coefficients may misrepresent the data distribution: in graph II the nonlinearity is not captured and in graphs III and IV a single outlier distorts the relationship. The latter will be discussed in more detail in the next section.

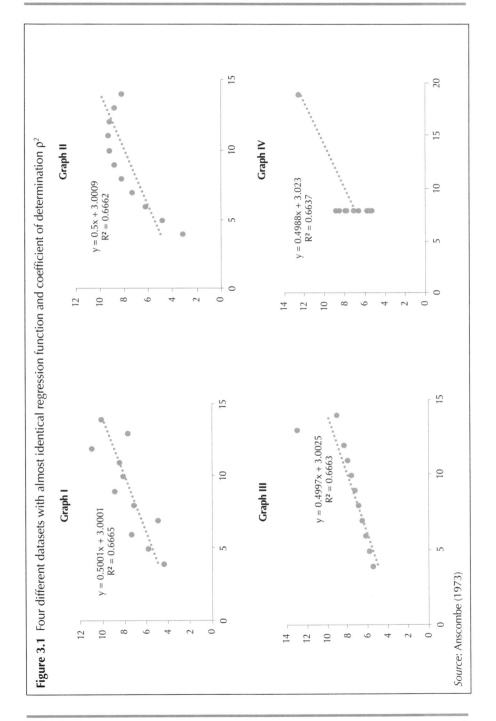

Figure 3.1 Four different datasets with almost identical regression function and coefficient of determination ρ^2

Source: Anscombe (1973)

In conclusion, the Pearson correlation model is highly sensitive and non-robust with respect to the data distribution. The Pearson coefficients can be meaningfully interpreted only if the data distribution is approximately elliptical. Even in this case, Pearson uncorrelatedness does not necessarily imply statistical independence. Pearson uncorrelatedness implies independence only if the joint distribution of the variables is normal. Very different data distributions can result in very similar Pearson coefficients. This may be due to the fact that nonlinearity is present or that outliers distort the results. The latter will be discussed in the following section.

Non-robustness with respect to outliers
In this section we will extend the discussion of the data distribution to outliers. We already observed in Figure 3.1, Graphs III and IV, that the Pearson regression function can be highly sensitive to outliers.

There are several reasons why the Pearson correlation model is prone to outliers. The first is that the Pearson model applies the mean as a measure for the central tendency of the sets X and Y. The mean or arithmetic average is not robust to outliers. Statistically, the breakdown point of the mean is 0 (the lowest possible value), since a single outlier can ruin the mean. For example, an infinitely large outlier results in the mean also approaching infinity. In contrast, the median is outlier-robust: changing a single value above the median to an arbitrarily large value will not change the median.

The second reason why the Pearson model is non-robust to outliers is that it applies the distorted variance as a dispersion measure. In the variance

$$Var(Y) = \frac{1}{n-1} \sum_{i=1}^{n} (y_i - \bar{y})^2$$

outliers are overweighed since differences between the observations and the mean are squared, $(y_i - \bar{y})^2$. In addition, values with a distance to the mean smaller than 1 are underweighed since they are squared.

Lastly, outliers are amplified when deriving the regression function $Y(X)$. In the OLS (ordinary least squares) approach, the sum of

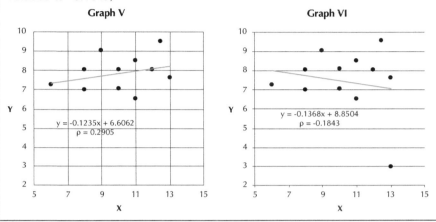

Figure 3.2 The datasets of Graph V and VI are identical, except for the outlier point {13, 3} in Graph VI. The outlier changes the regression function from positive to negative, as seen in the regression coefficient (which changes from +0.1235 to −0.1368) and the correlation coefficient (which changes from +0.2905 to −0.1843)

the vertical error terms is squared and then minimised. The squaring again overweighs vertical outliers, ie, high or low y values. An example of a single vertical outlier distorting the regression function is displayed in Figure 3.1, Graph III. An example of a vertical and horizontal outlier distorting the regression function is displayed in Figure 3.1, Graph IV.

In extreme cases, a single outlier can change the sign of the regression function and the correlation coefficient as seen in Figure 3.2.

How to deal with outliers?

The treatment of outliers in statistics is somewhat controversial. However, there is consensus that outliers cannot be arbitrarily excluded from a given dataset. This would constitute data manipulation and fraudulent statistics. Principally, outliers can be discarded only if there is a high probability that they are erroneous.

However, valuable information can be gained if the regression is run without significant or possibly erroneous outliers; see Figure 3.1, Graphs III and IV, where the regression without outliers would give significantly different results.[2] If the regression is run without certain outliers, this has to be clearly stated in the study. Regressions with and without outliers can be analysed to observe whether a significant difference exists.

In conclusion, the Pearson correlation model is highly sensitive to outliers. The reasons are the use of the mean, variance and OLS (ordinary least squares) in the Pearson model, which are all non-robust to outliers. Naturally, the smaller the dataset and the more prominent the outlier, the more sensitive the Pearson model is to outliers. Hence a simple solution is to work with large datasets, which reduces the impact of individual outliers.

Timeframe sensitivity

In this section we will discuss the sensitivity of the Pearson coefficients with respect to the timeframe chosen.

Let's first clarify: we differentiate two types of correlations, static and dynamic. In static correlations, the dataset is collected at a certain point in time. For example, we can derive correlations between certain bond prices and their respective yields at the end of a day. However, in finance we typically analyse dynamic correlations, ie, we evaluate how financial variables such as prices or values evolve together in time. It turns out that correlations are typically highly sensitive to the timeframe that is observed. We will show this in two theoretical examples and one practical example. Figure 3.3 displays two variables with positive correlation short term but negative correlation longer-term.[3]

From Figure 3.3, we derive the Pearson correlation coefficient ρ for different timeframes, displayed in Figure 3.4.

From Figure 3.4 we observe that the correlation coefficient for $n = 2$ points in time is $+1$, since both variables increase from time 1 to time 2.[4] However, the longer the timeframe, the more the variables in Figure 4 diverge, hence the correlation coefficient approaches -1.

Another example showing the time-frame sensitivity of a correlation coefficient is displayed in Figure 3.5, where the two variables are negatively correlated short term, but positively correlated long-term.

The correlation coefficient resulting from Figure 3.5 is displayed in Figure 3.6.

From Figure 3.6, we observe that the correlation coefficient for

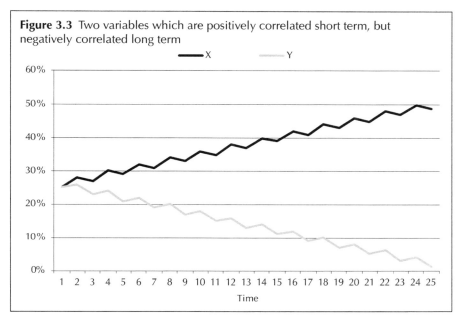

Figure 3.3 Two variables which are positively correlated short term, but negatively correlated long term

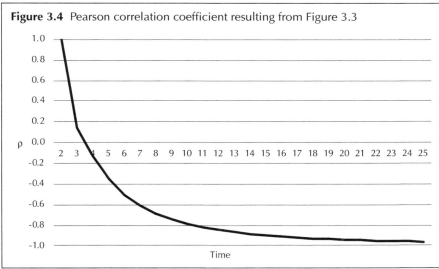

Figure 3.4 Pearson correlation coefficient resulting from Figure 3.3

$n = 2$ points in time is -1, since one variable increases and the other decreases from time t to time $t + 1$. However, the longer the timeframe, the more the functions in Figure 3.6 are positively associated, hence the correlation coefficient approaches $+1$. A spreadsheet of

CORRELATION RISK MODELLING AND MANAGEMENT

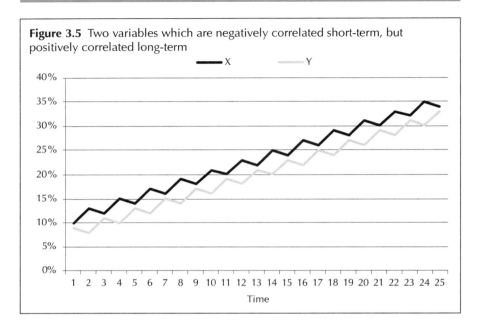

Figure 3.5 Two variables which are negatively correlated short-term, but positively correlated long-term

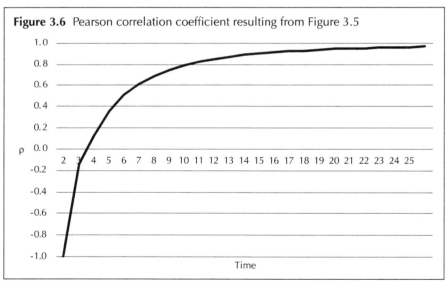

Figure 3.6 Pearson correlation coefficient resulting from Figure 3.5

Figures 3.3 to 3.6 can be found at www.dersoft.com/Pearsontime sensitivity.xlsx.

A real-world example of changing correlations with respect to time is displayed in Figure 3.7.

In Figure 3.7, the correlation coefficient for the entire time period from January 1, 1988, to February 15, 2015, is strongly negative at −0.770, since on average the S&P increased from 1988 to 2015 and the 10-year Treasury yield decreased. However, for sub-periods, the correlation coefficient is quite different: the correlation is negative (−0.429) from January 1, 1988, to August 31, 1998, positive from September 1, 1998, to April 31, 2009 (+0.600), and negative again from May 1, 2009, to February 15, 2015 (−0.397). The example of Figure 3.7 confirms that correlations can vary strongly with respect to the selected time period.

The correlations in Figure 3.7 also confirm that correlations typically increase in economic recessions. The US suffered a recession from 2000 to 2002 after the dotcom bubble burst (the correlation coefficient is +0.838) and the "Great Recession" from September 2007 to March 2009 (the correlation coefficient is +0.826). This confirms our study, which finds that correlation levels and correlation volatility increase in bad economic times, as we discussed in Chapter 2.

In conclusion, correlations can be highly sensitive to the timeframe of observation. In particular, when short timeframes with few data are analysed, the correlation parameters may be misleading. Researches should carefully scrutinise different correlation regimes before drawing any general conclusions. Principally, the more data analysed and the longer the timeframe, the more meaningful the correlation results.

The correlation–causality fallacy

In this section we will discuss the relationship between correlation and causality. The theory of causality has been extensively addressed in philosophy and goes at least as far back as Aristotle (Falcon 2012). Causality is also being discussed in natural sciences, especially physics and chemistry, as well as in logic, medicine and statistics.

Correlation and dependence
Before we address the critical question whether correlation implies causality, let's derive if correlation implies dependence. Does it? The answer is yes. There are several ways to show this. The easiest is to take our derivation of the section "Non-robustness with

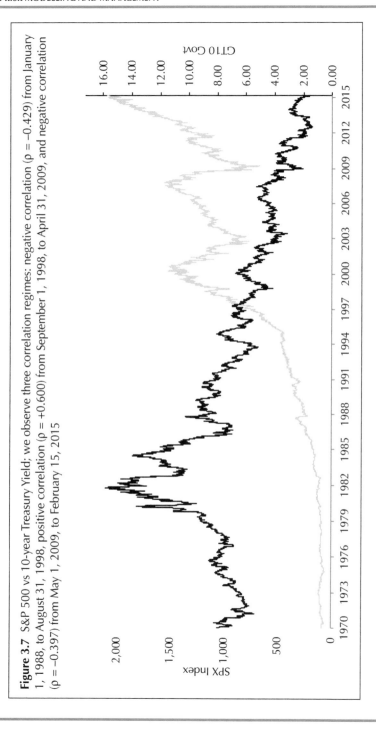

Figure 3.7 S&P 500 vs 10-year Treasury Yield; we observe three correlation regimes: negative correlation ($\rho = -0.429$) from January 1, 1988, to August 31, 1998, positive correlation ($\rho = +0.600$) from September 1, 1998, to April 31, 2009, and negative correlation ($\rho = -0.397$) from May 1, 2009, to February 15, 2015

respect to data distribution", that independence implies uncorrelatedness: let's denote independence with I and uncorrelatedness with U. Hence, formally, we have $I \to U$. Applying the logical equivalence: $I \to U \equiv \neg U \to \neg I$, denoting $\neg U$ with correlatedness and $\neg I$ with dependence, we find that correlatedness implies dependence. Hence if two variables are correlated, they are also dependent. A more elaborate proof of correlatedness implying dependence is in the Appendix 3.1.

The concept of causality

The concept of causality deals with the interaction between a primary event, the cause, and a secondary event, the effect. David Hume (1748) in his "An Enquiry Concerning Human Understanding" stated eight criteria that constitute cause and effect. For a financial-regression analysis the critical properties of cause and effect are as follows.

1. There exist two events, the first, the cause, and a second, the effect.
2. There exists a temporal order, ie, the cause happens before or coincides with the effect. An example of a cause occurring before the effect is Newton's second law of motion, $F = m\,a$, where "F" is the force, "m" is mass and "a" is acceleration. First, a force (the cause) is applied to an object, then the object accelerates (the effect) proportionally with the mass, m.
3. Effects can be probabilistic or deterministic: smoking causing the effect cancer is probabilistic; a sun running out of hydrogen, causing the effect of the sun to explode, is deterministic (in this case not only the effect but also the cause is deterministic).

Direction of causality

Regarding the direction of causality, for two variables X and Y, we have three cases.

1. X causes Y, the reverse not being true. Formally $(X \to Y)$, $\neg(Y \to X)$.
2. Y causes X, the reverse not being true. Formally $(Y \to X)$, $\neg(X \to Y)$.

3. X causes Y and Y causes X, termed bidirectional causation. Formally $(X \rightarrow Y) \cap (Y \rightarrow X)$. An example would be a stock market crash causing investor panic. It is also true that investor panic causes a stock market to crash. Another example would be decreasing housing prices causing mortgagors to default (some mortgagors walk away from their property when it has negative equity). Also, mortgagors' defaults cause housing prices to decline. We remember the bidirectional mortgage default – housing causation from the 2007–09 mortgage crisis. Both examples constitute a vicious cycle.

Correlation does not imply causality
Importantly, the presence of correlation does not imply that the variables in the correlation analysis are directly causally related, indirectly causally related or causally related at all.

Let neither X cause Y, nor Y cause X. Formally, $\neg(Y \rightarrow X)$, $\neg(X \rightarrow Y)$. However, even in this case of no causal relationship between X and Y, there can be a strong Pearson correlation between X and Y. The reason for the strong Pearson correlation may be the existence of a third variable W, termed a confounding, hidden or lurking variable, which causes X and Y to be related, since W causes X, and W causes Y. Formally: $\neg(X \rightarrow Y)$, $\neg(Y \rightarrow X)$, however, $(W \rightarrow X) \cap (W \rightarrow Y)$, creating a non-zero Pearson correlation between X and Y. If a third variable causes the variables of interest to be correlated without direct causation between the variables, this is termed a "spurious relationship". We differentiate two types, as follows.

❏ Spurious relationship, the third variable being time: the third variable W, which causes an effect on the variables of interest X and Y, can simply be time. As an example, in the last years we observed an increase in organic food consumption as well as an increase in autism. Autism and organic food consumption are naturally not causally related but their correlation will be strongly positive. This constitutes the case of nonsense-correlation.

❏ Spurious relationship, the third variable not being time: an example is the default probability of Microsoft P(M) and the default probability of BMW, P(BMW), which are not directly causally related since they are in different countries and different industries. However, a third variable, a worldwide recession, may increase both default probabilities, resulting in a positive correlation. This concept is applied in the CID (conditionally independent) correlation approach, applied in the OFGC, the one-factor Gaussian copula model (Vasicek 1987). The core equation is:

$$x_i = \sqrt{\rho}M + \sqrt{1-\rho}Z_i \qquad (3.8)$$

where

x_i: default indicator variable for $i = 1 \ldots n$ entities;
ρ: Pearson default correlation parameter for pairwise correlation between the $i = 1 \ldots n$ entities;
M: a common factor, which impacts all entities; an example of M would be the general economic environment;
Z_i: idiosyncratic factor of entity i; M and Z_i are random drawings from a standard normal distribution, also termed ε, and can be computed as =normsinv(rand()) in Excel or norminv(rand) in MATLAB (see www.dersoft.com/epsilon.xlsx for a spreadsheet that derives M and Z_i).

The key property of equation (3.8) is that we do not model the default correlation between the entities i directly, but instead we condition defaults on M: if $\rho = 1$, every entity i has a perfect correlation with M, hence all entities are perfectly correlated. If ρ is zero, all assets i depend only on their idiosyncratic factor Z_i, hence the assets are independent. For a ρ of 0.7071 (and therefore $\sqrt{\rho} = 0.5$) all x_i are determined equally by M and Z_i.

Equation (3.8) is simplistic since it implies that all entities have the same pairwise Pearson default correlation and default probability. Numerous extensions of the OFGC exist as applying a default curve with respect to time (not just a default probability scalar) and allowing correlation matrices, ie, different pairwise correlations. We will discuss the OFGC in detail in Chapter 7. The simple copula equation (3.8) with correlation ρ being a function of the default probability, is the basis for deriving CVaR (credit value-at-risk) in the Basel II accord, which presently (2018) is also applied in Basel III (BCBS 2005 and BCBS 2011); see Chapter 14. A spreadsheet of equation (3.8) can be found at www.dersoft.com/xigraphicallydisplayed.xlsx.

Pearson correlation and causation

Importantly, the Pearson correlation model does not include any methodology to determine the existence or the nature of a causal relationship between the variables in the correlation model. Therefore, we have to exogenously determine:

1. the existence of a direct or indirect causal relationship between X and Y; and
2. the direction of the causal relationship (X causing Y, Y causing X, or bidirectional).

Since finance is mainly a non-experimental science, we have to rely on theoretical analysis and empirical observations to assess the criteria 1 and 2. Only after the causality analysis has been completed and accepted can the correlation analysis be conducted, bearing the previously mentioned and forthcoming limitations.

In conclusion, the Pearson correlation model does not include an assessment on the existence or nature of a causal relationship between the variables in the analysis. Therefore, a causal analysis has to be performed exogenously before the correlation analysis is conducted. Spurious relationships are indirect relationships, where a third variable impacts on the primary two (or more) variables. A simple version of the spurious-relationship approach, the OFGC (one-factor Gaussian model), is applied in Basel II and is also expected to be part of the Basel III framework.

Spurious correlations

Spurious correlations should not be confused with spurious relationships, although they often are (see, for example, http://www.thefreedictionary.com/spurious+correlation, http://www.tylervigen.com/ or https://www.youtube.com/watch?v=nt1h8iR0Sac). We discussed spurious relationships earlier (see "The correlation–causality fallacy") and found that it refers to a third variable impacting on the variables of interest.

"Spurious correlation" is a term coined by Karl Pearson (1897). Spurious correlations occur when only the ratios between variables display a non-zero Pearson correlation, but the absolute values of the variables are not correlated. Let X and Y be the variables of interest. Spurious correlation exists if X and Y are not correlated, but the ratios X/Z and Y/Z, $Z \in R$, display a non-zero Pearson correlation. For example, let X and Y be normally distributed random variables with a mean of 10 and variance of 1, ie, $X, Y \sim n(10,1)$. Correlating X and Y will result in a zero Pearson correlation. Let Z be a normally distributed random variable with a mean of 10 and variance of 25, ie, $Z \sim n(10,25)$. Correlating X/Z with Y/Z will result in a 0.99 sample Pearson correlation. Hence, correlating absolute values can give very different correlations than correlating ratios.

Karl Pearson derived approximate equations for spurious correlations. For a single divisor Z and uncorrelated random variables X, Y and Z, the spurious correlation SC between X and Y with common divisor Z, $SC(X, Y; Z)$ ie, the Pearson correlation between X/Z and Y/Z is

$$SC(X,Y;Z) = \rho\left(\frac{X}{Z}, \frac{Y}{Z}\right) = \frac{\frac{\sigma_Z}{\mu_Z}}{\sqrt{\left(\frac{\sigma_X}{\mu_X}\right)^2 + \left(\frac{\sigma_Z}{\mu_Z}\right)^2}\sqrt{\left(\frac{\sigma_Y}{\mu_Y}\right)^2 + \left(\frac{\sigma_Z}{\mu_Z}\right)^2}} \quad (3.9)$$

For our example of $X, Y \sim n(10,1)$ and $Z \sim n(10,25)$, we derive $SC(X, Y; Z) = \rho\left(\frac{X}{Z}, \frac{Y}{Z}\right) = 0.96$ as an approximation of the above-derived sample correlation 0.99. Equations for non-common divisors can be found in Pearson (1897) and Pawlowsky-Glahn and Buccianti (eds) (2011).

In conclusion, in the Pearson framework absolute correlations can differ strongly from correlations on ratios. A researcher working with ratios, as is often done in biosciences, should also derive absolute correlations to test for statistical rigor.

Heteroscedasticity

Heteroscedasticity is a well-defined property in statistics and can be found in virtually every econometrics text book. We will focus here on the properties and potential harm of heteroscedasticity with respect to financial regressions.

While difficult to pronounce and spell, heteroscedasticity (sometimes heteroskedasticity), is a simple concept. It comes from the Greek "hetero" meaning different and "scedasis", meaning dispersion. Heteroscedasticity exists if the error terms ε_i in the regression $Y(X)$ are not constant but have a different dispersion in X. Let's quantify dispersion with the variance Var. Then heteroscedasticity exists if

$$VaR(\varepsilon_i \mid X) = f(X) \qquad (3.10)$$

Since the error terms ε_i express the vertical difference between the data points y_i and the regressed points $\hat{y}_i$, we can also write $VaR(\varepsilon_i \mid X) = VaR(Y \mid X) = f(X)$.

Conversely, homoscedasticity exists if the variance of the error terms is constant in X:

$$VaR(\varepsilon_i \mid X) = \sigma^2 \qquad (3.11)$$

where σ^2 is a constant, representing the constant variance of the error terms.

Homoscedastiticy is one of the three Gauss–Markov assumptions, the other two being that the error terms have zero expectation: $E(\varepsilon_i \mid X) = 0$ and are uncorrelated: $Cov(\varepsilon_i, \varepsilon_j) = 0 \; \forall i, j, \; i \neq j$. Gauss and Markov show that the three assumptions result in the best linear unbiased estimator (BLUE) for the coefficients of the OLS $\hat{\alpha}$ and $\hat{\beta}$. For the derivation of $\hat{\beta}$ with the OLS method, see Appendix 3.2.

Figure 3.8 displays a form heteroscedasticity in which the error terms increase in X^2.

Consequences of heteroscedasticity

Given is the unknown true population function $y_i = \alpha + \beta x_i + \varepsilon_i$. When deriving the optimal values of the regression parameters and of the regression function $y_i = \hat{\alpha} + \hat{\beta} x_i$, we differentiate the squared error terms ε_i^2 with respect to $\hat{\alpha}$ and $\hat{\beta}$. In this process it is irrelevant if the error terms vary in X, ie, if the error terms are heteroscedastic (proof is in the Appendix 3.2). Hence the regression parameters $\hat{\alpha}$ and $\hat{\beta}$ are robust with respect to heteroscedasticity.

However, the conventional standard error term of the regression coefficient $\hat{\beta}$, $se(\hat{\beta})$,

$$se(\hat{\beta}) = \sqrt{\frac{\sigma_\varepsilon^2}{\sum_{i=1}^{n}(x_i - \bar{x})^2}} \qquad (3.12)$$

is a function of the variance of the error term σ_ε^2, hence the standard error $se(\hat{\beta})$ is not heteroscedasticity robust. The standard error is an input for inference tests as the t-test, z-test or F-test. For example,

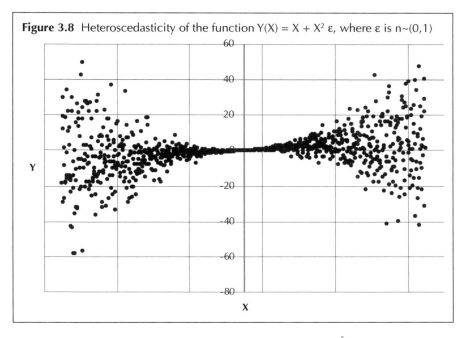

Figure 3.8 Heteroscedasticity of the function $Y(X) = X + X^2 \varepsilon$, where ε is n~(0,1)

the t-statistic for the regression parameter $\hat{\beta}$ is $t_{\hat{\beta}} = \frac{\hat{\beta}-\beta}{se(\hat{\beta})}$. Hence inference tests that include the standard error are non-heteroscedasticity-robust and can give false results as falsely rejecting the null hypothesis (type 1 error) or falsely accepting the null hypothesis (type 2 error).

How to deal with heteroscedasticity?
Similar to the limitation of linearity, the first thing to do when dealing with heteroscedasticity is to find out if it is present. We can investigate the scatterplot visually to get a good idea whether the scatterplot is heteroscedastic. Numerous statistical tests for heteroscedasticity exist: for example, Breusch–Pagan test, which tests the null-hypothesis that error variances are equal. The White test, a special case of Breusch-Pagan, which can be handle non-normal errors, and other tests such as Park test or Glesjer test can be applied.

If heteroscedasticity does exist, we can apply heteroscedasticity-robust standard errors, which are typically credited to Halbert White (1980). However, some groundwork was laid by Eicker (1967) and Huber (1967). The White heteroscedasticity robust standard error statistic $se(\hat{\beta})_W$, also called Eicker–Huber–White standard error, does not apply the variance of the error term σ_ε^2, but the error terms ε_i themselves in the test statistic. Hence equation (3.12) changes to

$$se(\hat{\beta})_W = \sqrt{\frac{\sum_{i=1}^{n}\varepsilon_i^2(x_i-\bar{x})^2}{\left(\sum_{i=1}^{n}(x_i-\bar{x})^2\right)^2}} \qquad (3.13)$$

If the covariance between ε_i^2 and $(x_i - \bar{x})^2$ is negative, ie, if low values of ε_i^2 are associated with high values of $(x_i - \bar{x})^2$, then the conventional standard error of equation (3.12) is biased upwards and vice versa. The proof is in Appendix 3.3.

One question remains: if heteroscedasticity-robust standard errors exist (equation (3.13)), why bother with non-heteroscedasticity-robust standard errors (equation (3.12))? The answer is that if homoscedasticity holds and the errors are normal, then the t-statistics applying equation (3.12) will be exactly student-t-distributed. However, heteroscedasticity-robust standard errors may not be exactly student-t-distributed, especially for small sample sizes. This may lead to biased inference statistics. Therefore some studies derive and report both heteroscedasticity-robust and non-robust standard errors.

Heteroscedasticity and finance

The most prominent application of heteroscedasticity in finance is naturally the Nobel Prize-rewarded ARCH (autoregressive conditional heteroscedasticity) model of Robert Engle (1982). Numerous specifications and extensions of ARCH exist, for nice overview papers see Bollerslev et al (1992), Engle (1995), or Teräsvirta (2006). The original ARCH(q) model is

$$\sigma_t^2 = a_0 + a_1\sigma_{t-1}^2\varepsilon_{t-1}^2 + \ldots + a_q\sigma_{t-q}^2\varepsilon_{t-q}^2 \qquad (3.14)$$

where

σ_t^2 is the variance of the variable of interest and $a_0 > 0$, $a_1 \geq 0$, so that σ^2 is positive, and $q \in N$.

ε is typically derived by a linear autoregressive process of the variable of interest,

$$S_t = f(X_{t-1}, b) + \varepsilon_t \qquad (3.15)$$

where S may be the relative change of a stock price, X_{t-1} is the information set until $t-1$, and b is the parameter vector. In many applications the general equation (3.15) is modelled with a simple univariate autoregressive process $S_t = a_0 + a_1 S_{t-1} + \varepsilon_t$ (see Goodhart (1990) or Meissner and Kawano (2001)).

From equation (3.15) we realise that the higher the fluctuation of S in time, the higher is the error term ε and vice versa. In turn, from equation (3.14) we see that evolution of ε drives the variance σ_t^2: high periods of ε result in high periods of σ^2, and low periods of ε result in low periods of σ^2. Hence, equations (3.14) and (3.15) model volatility clustering, which is found in reality.

In general, in most financial regressions there will be a certain degree of heteroscedasticity. For example, the income distribution will vary for different education levels. Lower education will result in a less disperse income distribution since most lower-educated individuals earn little. Individuals with a higher education will sometimes earn a lot or sometimes, as professors, a little (!). Hence we have heteroscedasticity, a higher income dispersion for higher-educated individuals.

Another example would be the dividend/profit ratio of companies with different profits. Companies with low profits typically have a similar dividend/profit ratio. However, companies with higher profits typically have a higher dispersion in their dividend/profit ratio. Some choose to have a higher dividend/profit ratio; some choose to have a lower one, constituting heteroscedasticity.

Hence in finance the question is not whether heteroscedasticity is present, but (a) how high is the degree of heteroscedasticity and (b) does the degree of heteroscedasticity distort regression results?

The degree of heteroscedasticity can be quantified with the methods we mentioned above, such as the Breusch–Pagan test, Park test and Glesjer test. Regarding the harmfulness, it turns out that the degree of heteroscedasticity in most financial regressions does not distort inference statistics as seen in studies of Box and Pierce (1970), Bey and Pinches (1980), Engle (1982), Schwert and Segui (1990), Hoang V., (2002), or Stevenson (2004).

In conclusion, heteroscedasticity is a somewhat overrated limitation of the Pearson correlation model. The regression parameters $\hat{a}$

and $\hat{\beta}$ are heteroscedasticity-robust. However, standard errors and consequently inference statistics are not heteroscedasticity-robust. Nonetheless, generally, heteroscedasticity has to be quite severe to cause a serious bias in inferences as empirical studies show. In addition, heteroscedasticity-robust standard errors exist, which can be applied. However, they are not exactly t-distributed, which in extreme cases may cause biased inference results. In the presence of severe heteroscedasticity, both heteroscedasticity-robust and non-robust standard errors and their inference statistics may be derived and evaluated to assure statistical rigor.

Multicollinearity
As heteroscedasticity, multicollinearity is a well-defined property of a regression analysis and can be found in virtually every econometrics textbook. Hence, after displaying the key properties, we will concentrate on multicollinearity in financial regression analyses.

As the word implies, multicollinearity refers to two or more variables, in this case regressors (ie, independent or explanatory variables) to be highly linearly related. A special case of multicollinearity is collinearity in which only two regressors are correlated. We differentiate perfect multicollinearity and partial multicollinearity.

Perfect multicollinearity
In the case of perfect multicollinearity, two or more regressors are perfectly linearly correlated, ie, have a correlation coefficient of 1. Perfect multicollinearity is extremely rare and principally occurs only when the researcher has misspecified the model, ie, has made a mistake. For example, the researcher has input the same regressor, just in different dimensions, one in inches and one in centimetres. Or the researcher has fallen into the dummy variable trap: here a redundant variable is input. For example, for the category "gender", a variable male (1) and a variable female (0) is entered. This is redundant since not male implies female, and vice versa. Additionally, if a constant is entered, the sum of the column vectors for gender will have the same value as the constant, resulting in perfect multicollinearity. Remedies to the dummy variable trap are naturally eliminating the redundant variable. In addition, eliminating the constant will also do the trick.

Perfect multicollinearity is easily detected, since the regression model will become unsolvable: let the regression model be

$$Y = \beta_1 + \beta_2 X_2 + \beta_3 X_3 + \varepsilon \tag{3.16}$$

with the two regressors X_2 and X_3 being linearly correlated, ie,

$$X_2 = a_1 + a_2 X_3 \tag{3.17}$$

Inputting equation (3.17) into (3.16), we get

$$Y = \beta_1 + \beta_2 a_1 + X_3 (\beta_2 a_2 + \beta_3) + \varepsilon \tag{3.18}$$

From the third term on the right-hand side, we see that equation (3.18) has infinite solutions for the combination β_2 and β_3.

The same exercise can be done when we use matrix notation: generalising equation (3.16) for $i = 1 \ldots n$ observations, and $1 \ldots k$ regressors, we have

$$y = X\beta + \varepsilon = \begin{pmatrix} y_1 \\ y_2 \\ . \\ . \\ y_n \end{pmatrix} = \begin{pmatrix} x_{11} & x_{12} & \ldots & x_{1k} \\ x_{21} & x_{22} & \ldots & x_{2k} \\ . & . & \ldots & . \\ . & . & \ldots & . \\ x_{n1} & . & \ldots & x_{nk} \end{pmatrix} \begin{pmatrix} \beta_1 \\ \beta_2 \\ . \\ . \\ \beta_k \end{pmatrix} + \begin{pmatrix} \varepsilon_1 \\ \varepsilon_2 \\ . \\ . \\ \varepsilon_n \end{pmatrix} \tag{3.19}$$

During the process of deriving the optimal vector for β, we have to invert the matrix X (see Appendix 3.2 for details). However, if perfect multicollinearity exists, at least one row is a multiple of the other, and the matrix X has a determinant of zero. Consequently, the matrix is singular and cannot be inverted. Put differently, the rank of the matrix X (the number of linearly independent rows) is lower than the number of regressors k, making the matrix non-invertible.

Partial multicollinearity
Partial collinearity exists if two or more regressors are not perfectly but highly correlated. In this case equation (3.17) changes to

$$X_2 = a_1 + a_2 X_3 + u \tag{3.20}$$

Where $u \in R$. Inputting equation (3.20) into (3.16), we get

$$Y = \beta_1 + \beta_2 a_1 + \beta_2 u + X_3 (\beta_2 a_2 + \beta_3) + \varepsilon \tag{3.21}$$

OLS optimisation of equation (3.21) typically leads to a unique solution for β_2 and β_3 since changes in β_2 lead to changes in the error term u via the term $\beta_2 u$. In matrix notation, in the absence of perfect multicollinearity none of the rows in the matrix X in equation (3.19) are a linear combination of another. Hence the matrix has a determinant-unequal zero and is invertible. Put differently, the rank of the matrix X is equal to number of regressors k, hence the matrix is invertible.

Consequences of multicollinearity
Importantly, partial multicollinearity does not violate any assumptions of the Pearson regression model. As a consequence, the analytical results of a regression analysis as a whole are unbiased.

However, since the individual regressors are highly correlated it is difficult to determine their individual impact. Therefore, the analytical power of the individual regressors can be distorted. In this case the betas of the individual regressors are highly sensitive to changes in the dataset. Generally, a high partial multicollinearity leads to high standard errors se_{β_j} of the individual regressor as we can observe from equation (3.22). ρ_j^2 is the coefficient of determination of the jth regressor, which is regressed (input as a dependent variable) against the other regressors; n is the total number of observations and k is the number of regressors

$$se_{\beta_j} = \sqrt{\frac{\sum_{i=1}^{n}(y_i - \hat{y}_i)^2}{\sum_{i=1}^{n}(x_i - \hat{x}_i)^2 (1 - \rho_j^2)(n-k)}} \quad (3.22)$$

(including β_0). As we see from equation (3.22), if the correlation between j and the other regressors is high, the standard error se_{β_j} will be high. These distorted high standard errors may lead to falsely accepting the null-hypothesis beta $j = 0$, a type II error. Put simply, due to multicollinearity, the model fails to recognise the true, strong explanatory power of the regressor. We also observe from equation (3.22) that for total multicollinearity, ie, $\rho_j^2 = 1$, the regression falls apart, ie, the standard errors cannot be evaluated.[5]

How to deal with multicollinearity
Similar to heteroscedasticity, we have first to find out if multicollinearity is present. As we discussed in the section above, multicollinearity typically leads to increased error terms of the individual regressor, hence the statistical significance of individual regressor is low. Therefore, a first indication of multicollinearity is if the overall regression is significant, but the individual regressors are not. To test the individual impact of a single regressor, the regression may be run with that regressor alone. This impact may be compared to the impact of the regressor in the multivariate regression. Large differences in the impacts suggest multicollinearity.

A straightforward way to quantify multicollinearity is to simply correlate the regressors with each other. This will show the degree of correlation between them. However, complex relationships between the regressors, such as a regressor being dependent on several other regressors, will not be revealed. A more rigorous approach is to correlate one regressor, j, with all the others. The coefficient of determination ρ_j^2 can be derived, which we already applied in the error term in equation (3.22). A rule of thumb is that levels of ρ_j^2 above 0.8 or 0.9 may distort the analytical or predictive power of individual regressors due to multicollinearity.

In case a researcher detects severe multicollinearity and is particularly interested in the causal effect of individual regressors, several methods to deal with multicollinearity exist. A preferred method is to increase the data pool. This may lead to more representative and informative data and may prevent incidental multicollinearity. Additionally, from equation (3.22) we observe that an increase in observations n decreases the upwardly biased standard errors.

Researchers may also reduce the degree of multicollinearity in the regression by eliminating regressors with a high degree of correlation to other regressors. Alternatively, regressors with a high degree of correlation may be combined into a single regressor.

Multicollinearity and finance
As mentioned above, the presence of perfect multicollinearity in financial practice is extremely rare. Conversely, the total absence of multicollinearity in financial practice is also extremely rare. The

regressors in a financial regression will typically have some degree of positive or negative correlation, which may include spurious relationships (see the section "The correlation–causality fallacy"). For example, when regressing the relative change of a company's stock price with the company's relative change in revenue, earning per share, dividend yield and country's GDP, in most cases these regressors will be somewhat positively correlated. Or when correlating the relative change of short-term interest rates with the relative change in inflation, country's GDP, currency value and monetary policy, these regressors will typically also be correlated.

Hence, similar to heteroscedasticity, the question with respect to multicollinearity in finance is not if it is present, but (a) how high is the degree of multicollinearity and (b) does the degree of multicollinearity distort regression results?

The degree of multicollinearity can be quantified to a satisfactory degree by applying the methods mentioned above. Regarding the degree of harmfulness of multicollinearity, importantly, the overall regression parameters are not distorted. However, individual regressor coefficients may be misleading since they covary together. This is a bigger problem when the model has a causal nature, rather than a predictive nature. However, even in the presence of multicollinearity, the coefficients typically give satisfactory results as studies by Fabrycy (1975), Harvey (1977), Beery and Feldman (1979), Mansfield and Helms (1982), Greenberg and Parks (1997), and Voss (2004), Obrien (2007) and Seiler (2012) show.

In conclusion, multicollinearity is a somewhat overrated limitation of the Pearson correlation model. The overall regression coefficients are not affected by severe multicollinearity and are still BLUE (the best linear unbiased estimators). However, individual regressor coefficients may be distorted. In particular, standard errors of individual regressors may be higher than the "true" errors, which may lead to type II errors, ie, falsely accepting the null hypothesis. Nonetheless, tests to quantify multicollinearity and, if necessary, remedies exist. Altogether, statistical analysis, as well as empirical studies, show that in most cases multicollinearity, despite its ubiquity, poses little harm to a properly interpreted regression analysis.

TRANSFORMATION INVARIANCE

The Pearson correlation model is robust with respect to linear transformations of one or more variables. However, the Pearson model is not robust, ie, displays transformation invariance for nonlinear transformations. Let X and Y follow discrete geometric Brownian motions, ie,

$$X_{t+\Delta t} = X_t \left(1 + \mu_1 \Delta t + \sigma_1 \varepsilon_t \sqrt{\Delta t}\right) \tag{3.23}$$

$$Y_{t+\Delta t} = Y_t \left(1 + \mu_2 \Delta t + \sigma_2 \varepsilon_t \sqrt{\Delta t}\right) \tag{3.24}$$

The correlation between X and Y is critically determined by the drift rates μ_1 and μ_2. The higher or lower both μ_1 and μ_2, the higher is the correlation, since in this case X and Y will share a similar drift rate. In addition, the lower the volatilities μ_1 and μ_2, the higher the correlation, since low volatility reduces the noise term, the last term on the right-hand side of equations (3.23) and (3.24).

Let's investigate a possible transformation of X and Y to X^T and Y^T, where T is just an index (not an exponent):

$$X_t^T = a_1 + b_1 (X_t + c_1)^{d_1} \tag{3.25}$$

$$Y_t^T = a_2 + b_2 (X_t + c_2)^{d_2} \tag{3.26}$$

Positive increases of the parameters a_1, b_1 and c_1 will move the function X_t linearly higher, or the X, Y scatterplot horizontally to the right (X being on the abscise), vice versa. Importantly, the correlation between X and Y and the transformed X^T and Y will be identical. The same logic applies to transforming Y. Positive increases of the parameters a_2, b_2 and c_2, will move the function Y_t linearly higher, or the X, Y scatterplot higher (Y being on the ordinate), vice versa. Again, the correlations between X and Y and X and the transformed Y^T are the same.

However, changes in the parameters d_1 and d_2 in equations (3.25) and (3.26) will alter the correlation, since changes in d_1 and d_2 result in a nonlinear transformations of X and Y. That is, the correlations between X and Y, and X^T and Y will not be identical, nor will be the correlation between X and Y, and X and Y^T. We already observed an example of nonlinear transformation in the section "Spurious Correlations" above when correlating absolute random variables and ratios of the random variables, this nonlinear transformation led to strongly different correlations.

Is the invariance of the Pearson correlation model to nonlinear transformations a problem? Well, in finance we often like to perform nonlinear transformations, such as taking the logarithm of a function – for example, a stock price – to conveniently display it. Doing so will lead to different correlations since $\rho(X, Y) \neq \rho(\ln(X), \ln(Y))$. However, altogether, the invariance of the Pearson correlation model to nonlinear transformations is only a moderate annoyance. Knowing about the nonlinear transformation invariance, we can circumvent it by simply omitting nonlinear transformations.

FINITE VARIANCE

As a last limitation of the Pearson model, let's discuss finite variances. From equation (3.1) $\rho(X, Y) = \frac{COV(X,Y)}{\sigma(X)\sigma(Y)}$ we observe that the correlation coefficient ρ can be derived only if the standard deviations σ and hence the variances σ^2 exist and are finite. There are several distributions that have an undefined variance, an infinite variance or an infinite variance for certain parameter values. Among the most popular ones are the Cauchy and Levy distribution with an undefined variance, the generalised Pareto distribution (GPD) with a variance defined only for the tail parameter $\zeta < 0.5$, and the Student-t distribution with a variance defined only for $v = m - 2 > 2$ degrees of freedom, where m is the number of observations.

For the Cauchy and Levy distribution with their undefined variances, the Pearson model cannot be applied. For the generalised Pareto distribution, the tail parameter ζ for financial data is mostly between 0.1 and 0.4, hence in this case the Pearson model is functional. For the Student-t distribution, even for extreme events, we often have more than $m = 5$ observations, so the Student-t distributions can typically underlie the Pearson model. Altogether, most distributions applied in finance have finite variances. Therefore, the finite variance limitation is of minor practical concern.

SUMMARY

The answer to the question whether the Pearson correlation model is the work of the devil is clearly no. It is the work of Karl Pearson, who created a groundbreaking, rigorous and seminal model to derive the association between two or more variables. The benefits of the Pearson model lie in its intuition and simplicity. However, simplicity comes at a cost. Numerous assumption and limitations, which are not compatible with finance exist.

❏ The assumption of linearity limits the model to very few financial associations, since most variables and their associations in finance are nonlinear.
❏ More precisely, the Pearson model is consistent only when the joint distribution is fully characterised by the first two moments. This is the family of elliptical distributions, which comprise the normal, Student-t, Laplace, Cauchy and the logistic distribution. If the joint distribution of the variables is non-elliptical, the linear Pearson correlation model is not a suitable correlation measure.
❏ The Pearson model is highly sensitive to outliers. Single outliers, especially for small datasets, can result in very different correlation outcomes.
❏ Financial correlations often display correlation regimes. Hence different timeframes can lead to very different correlation results.
❏ Unlike the cointegration framework, which we will discuss in the next chapter, the Pearson model does not include a methodology to determine the causality between the variables.
❏ Heteroscedasticity and multicollinearity are often cited by practitioners as problems in regression analyses. However, when interpreted properly, they pose little harm.
❏ Transformation invariance and the finite variance condition are typically minor practical annoyances.

In conclusion, given the numerous limitations, extreme care has to be taken when the Pearson correlation model is applied. All the limitations mentioned above have to be taken into consideration before a Pearson regression is performed. Only if the dataset is linear; sufficient data with few outliers is present; different correlation regimes have been scrutinised; and the causality has been exogenously analysed and accepted, can the Pearson model give sensible results.

It has to be noted that if the Pearson correlations are distorted due to limitations mentioned earlier, so will the portfolio measures and risk measures that apply the distorted Pearson correlation measure as an input.

A prominent example of misinterpreting Pearson correlations is the global financial crises of 2007 to 2009. Risk managers fed their VaR (value-at-risk) and ES (expected shortfall) models correlation data from the benign time period 2002 to 2006. It cannot be expected that correlation data from non-crisis periods give sensible results in a crisis. "Garbage in, garbage out" in computer terminology. Naturally, risk managers should have input correlation data from crises as the Great Depression, or at least the 2001 dotcom crash or the recessions in 1973–74 or 1981–82. This would have given much higher and more realistic risk numbers. It is prudent that the stress testing of banks' portfolios required by the Fed and Basel III includes the stress testing of correlations, despite of the limitations of correlation mentioned in this chapter. More advanced correlation models, which we will analyse in the following chapters, although more complex, may find their way into the stress testing methodologies in the future.

Altogether, in light of the severe limitations of the Pearson correlation model, it seems to be a far better choice to model financial associations with more advanced correlation models such as Heston correlations, cointegration, copulas and the very promising, currently emerging stochastic correlation models, which we will discuss in the following chapters.

APPENDIX 3.1: PROOF THAT CORRELATEDNESS (IE, NON-ZERO CORRELATION) IMPLIES DEPENDENCE

Given are the continuous random variables $X \in R$ and $Y \in R$.

Correlatedness between X and Y, ie, non-zero correlation between X and Y, is given when the correlation coefficient ρ is non-zero, or from equation (3.1) $\rho(X, Y) = \frac{COV(X,Y)}{\sigma(X)\sigma(Y)}$, if the covariance COV is non-zero:

$$Corr(X,Y) \neq 0 \Rightarrow COV(X,Y) \neq 0 \qquad (A1.1)$$

Statistical dependence is given iff the expected value of the joint distribution is unequal to the product of the individual distributions, $E(XY) \neq E(X) E(Y)$, or

$$E(XY) - E(X)E(Y) \neq 0 \qquad (A1.2)$$

We will show that uncorrelatedness (equation (A1.1)) implies dependence (equation (A1.2)), ie,

$$\text{If } Corr(X,Y) \neq 0 \Rightarrow E(XY) - E(X)E(Y) \neq 0 \quad (A1.3)$$

Applying

$$E(X) = \int x f_X(x) dx$$

and

$$E(XY) = \int xy f_{X,Y}(x,y) dx dy \quad (A1.4)$$

where $f_X(x)$ is the density of X at x, equation (A1.2) becomes

$$\iint xy f_{X,Y}(x,y) dx dy - \int x f_X(x) dx \int y f_Y(y) dy \neq 0$$

multiplying the second term on the left side, we get

$$\iint xy f_{X,Y}(x,y) dx dy - \iint xy f_X(x) f_Y(y)) dx dy \neq 0$$

factoring out the term xy, becomes

$$\iint xy \left[f_{X,Y}(x,y) - f_X(x) f_Y(y) \right] dx dy \neq 0 \quad (A1.5)$$

Applying equations (A1.4) to equation (9) $COV(X, Y) = E(XY) - E(X) E(Y)$, we have

$$COV(X,Y) = \left[f_{XY}(x,y) - f_X(x) f_Y(y) \right] \quad (A1.6)$$

Equation (A1.5) can be true only if (A1.6) is $\neq 0$, hence correlatedness implies dependence.

APPENDIX 3.2: PROOF THAT THE REGRESSION COEFFICIENT $\hat{\beta}$ IS HETEROSCEDASTICITY ROBUST

There are several ways to show that the regression coefficient $\hat{\beta}$ in the bivariate regression function $\hat{y}_i = \hat{\alpha} + \hat{\beta} x_i$ is robust with respect to different variances in the error terms. The easiest way is to show that when deriving the optimal value for $\hat{\beta}$, the variance of the error term is not part of the derivation. We will take this approach first for the bivariate case, and then generalise it to the multivariate case.

Given is the true unknown population function

$$y_i = \alpha + \beta x_i + \varepsilon_i \quad (3.3)$$

and the to be regressed function

$$\hat{y}_i = \hat{\alpha} + \hat{\beta} x_i \quad (3.4)$$

Since $E(\hat{\alpha}) = \alpha$ and $E(\hat{\beta}) = \beta$, we have $\varepsilon_i = y_i - \hat{y}_i = y_i - \hat{\alpha} - \hat{\beta}x_i$ or

$$\sum \varepsilon_i^2 = \sum (y_i - \hat{y}_i)^2 = \sum (y_i - \hat{\alpha} - \hat{\beta}x_i)^2 \tag{A2.1}$$

Differentiating equation (A2.1) partially with respect to $\hat{\beta}$, we derive

$$\frac{\partial \sum \varepsilon_i^2}{\partial \hat{\beta}} = 2\sum (y_i - \hat{\alpha} - \hat{\beta}x_i)(-x_i) \tag{A2.2}$$

Setting to equation (A2.2) to zero and rearranging, we derive

$$-2\sum (y_i - \hat{\alpha} - \hat{\beta}x_i)(x_i) = 0$$

Dividing by -2, multiplying, and factoring $\hat{\alpha}$ and $\hat{\beta}$ out, we get

$$\hat{\beta}\sum x_i^2 = \sum x_i y_i - \hat{\alpha}\sum x_i$$

Inputting the relationship

$$\hat{\alpha} = \sum \frac{y_i}{n} - \hat{\beta}\sum \frac{x_i}{n}$$

we get

$$\hat{\beta}\sum x_i^2 = \sum y_1 x_1 - \left(\sum \frac{y_i}{n} - \hat{\beta}\sum \frac{x_i}{n} \right)\sum x_i$$

or

$$\hat{\beta}\sum x_i^2 = \sum y_1 x_1 - \frac{\sum y_i \sum x_i}{n} + \left(\hat{\beta}\sum \frac{(x_i)^2}{n} \right)$$

Rearranging and factoring out, we derive

$$\hat{\beta}\left(\sum x_i^2 - \sum \frac{(x_i)^2}{n} \right) = \sum y_i x_i - \frac{\sum y_i \sum x_i}{n}$$

or

$$\hat{\beta} = \frac{\sum y_i x_i - \dfrac{\sum y_i \sum x_i}{n}}{\sum x_i^2 - \sum \dfrac{(x_i)^2}{n}} \tag{A2.3}$$

Equation (A2.3) is identical with equation (1)

$$\beta(X,Y) = \frac{COV(X,Y)}{VaR(X)}$$

Importantly, when deriving $\hat{\beta}$, the homogeneity assumption $VaR(\varepsilon_i|X) = \sigma^2$ is not part of the derivation. Hence $\hat{\beta}$ is heterogeneous robust.

The bivariate analysis above can be easily extended to the multivariate case of the form

$$y_i = \beta_1 + \beta_2 x_{2i} + \beta_3 x_{3i} + \ldots + \beta_k x_{nk} + \varepsilon_i \tag{A2.4}$$

where $i = 1 \ldots n$ are the observations, and $1 \ldots k$ are the regressors.

Writing equation (A2.4) in matrix notation, we have

$$y = X\beta + \varepsilon = \begin{pmatrix} y_1 \\ y_2 \\ . \\ . \\ y_n \end{pmatrix} = \begin{pmatrix} x_{11} & x_{12} & \ldots & x_{1k} \\ x_{21} & x_{22} & \ldots & x_{2k} \\ . & . & \ldots & . \\ . & . & \ldots & . \\ x_{n1} & . & \ldots & x_{nk} \end{pmatrix} \begin{pmatrix} \beta_1 \\ \beta_2 \\ . \\ . \\ \beta_k \end{pmatrix} + \begin{pmatrix} \varepsilon_1 \\ \varepsilon_2 \\ . \\ . \\ \varepsilon_n \end{pmatrix} \tag{A2.5}$$

In equation (A2.5) the vertical y-vector and the matrix X are given from the dataset. The vertical β-vector is unknown and has to be optimised by minimising the unknown squares of vertical ε-vector.

Let the vertical vector b denote the "candidate" for the optimal β-vector, and the vertical vector e denote the 'residual candidate'. The vectors b and e are derived from the regression of the form

$$y = Xb + e$$

or

$$e = y - Xb \tag{A2.6}$$

Hence the sum of the squared errors is

$$\sum_{i=1}^{n} e_i^2 = e^T e = (y - Xb)^T (y - Xb)$$
$$= y^T y - y^T Xb - X^T b^T y + X^T b^T Xb \tag{A2.7}$$

Differentiating equation (A2.7) with respect to b^T and setting to zero, we derive

$$-2X^T y + 2X^T Xb = 0 \tag{A2.8}$$

or

$$b = (X^T X)^{-1} X^T y \tag{A2.9}$$

As expected, during the process of deriving the optimal vertical vector b, the homogeneity assumption is not applied. Hence the optimal b vector is heteroscedasticity robust.

APPENDIX 3.3: PROOF THAT THE CONVENTIONAL STANDARD ERROR IS BIASED UNDER HETEROSCEDASTICITY

The conventional standard error

$$se(\hat{\beta}) = \sqrt{\frac{\sigma_\varepsilon^2}{\sum_{i=1}^{n}(x_i - \bar{x})^2}} \qquad (3.22a)$$

applies the homogeneity assumption of a constant variance of error terms σ_ε^2. White's (1980) heterogeneous robust standard error equation avoids the homogeneity assumption and applies the error term itself:

$$se(\hat{\beta})_W = \sqrt{\frac{\sum_{i=1}^{n}\varepsilon_i^2(x_i - \bar{x})^2}{\left(\sum_{i=1}^{n}(x_i - \bar{x})^2\right)^2}} \qquad (3.23a)$$

If $\varepsilon_i^2(x_i - \bar{x})^2$ has zero mean, we get for the numerator of equation (3.23a)

$$\sqrt{\sum_{i=1}^{n}\varepsilon_i^2(x_i - \bar{x})^2} = E\left(\varepsilon_i^2(x_i - \bar{x})^2\right) \qquad (A3.1)$$

Applying equation $COV(X, Y) = E(XY) - E(X)E(Y)$ to equation (A3.1), we get

$$E\left(\varepsilon_i^2(x_i - \bar{x})^2\right) = E(\varepsilon_i^2)E\left[(x_i - \bar{x})^2\right] + Cov\left[\varepsilon_i^2, (x_i - \bar{x})^2\right] \qquad (A3.2)$$

Rearranging and applying $E(\varepsilon_i^2) = \sigma_\varepsilon^2$ and

$$E\left[(x_i - \bar{x})^2\right] \equiv \sum_{i=1}^{n}(x_i - \bar{x})^2$$

we get

$$E\left(\varepsilon_i^2(x_i - \bar{x})^2\right) - \sigma_\varepsilon^2 \sum_{i=1}^{n}(x_i - \bar{x})^2 = Cov\left[\varepsilon_i^2, (x_i - \bar{x})^2\right] \qquad (A3.3)$$

From equation (3.22a) and (A3.1) we have

$$E\left(\varepsilon_i^2(x_i - \bar{x})^2\right) = \left[se(\hat{\beta})_W\right]^2 \left(\sum_{i=1}^{n}(x_i - \bar{x})^2\right)^2$$

and from equation (3.23a)

$$\sigma_\varepsilon^2 = \left[se\left(\hat{\beta}\right)\right]^2 \sum_{i=1}^{n}(x_i - \bar{x})^2$$

Inputting into (A3.3), we derive

$$\left[se\left(\hat{\beta}\right)_W\right]^2 - \left[se\left(\hat{\beta}\right)\right]^2 = Cov\left[\varepsilon_i^2, (x_i - \bar{x})^2\right] \qquad \text{(A3.4)}$$

Hence the higher the covariance between the error terms ε_i^2 and $(x_i - \bar{x})^2$ (ie, vertical hour-glass shape – see Figure 3.8), the more is the standard error $[se(\hat{\beta})]^2$ downward biased. Vice versa, the lower the covariance between the error terms ε_i^2 and $(x_i - \bar{x})^2$, (rhombus shape) the more is the standard error upward biased.

Questions for Chapter 3

Answers to these questions can be found at the back of this book.

1. What does the Pearson correlation coefficient measure?
2. What does the Pearson regression coefficient measure?
3. The Pearson correlation model incorporates only the first two movements of distribution of the variables. What severe limitation follows from this property?
4. What is the Pearson correlation of $Y = X^2$? Why is it distorted?
5. Why does the Variance overweight outliers?
6. What is nonsense correlation?
7. Correlation is highly time-sensitive. What follows from this property?
8. Does heteroscedasticity distort the Pearson model?
9. Does multicollinearity distort the Pearson model?
10. Do you agree that "Everything that relies on Correlation is Charlatanism" (Nassim Taleb)?

---

1 For more on elliptical distributions, see Embrechts et al (2002).
2 See Cook, R. Dennis (February 1977), "Detection of Influential Observations in Linear Regression", Technometrics, American Statistical Association, 19 (1): 15–18, to quantify the effect of outliers.

3 The idea for Figures 3.3 and 3.6 goes back to Wilmott 2013.
4 The correlation coefficient for two functions observed only at n=2 points in time will either be +1 in case both functions increase or decrease, or –1 in case one function increases and the other decreases.
5 For a nice paper discussing further properties of multicollinearity, see Stephen Voss, "Multicollinearity", *Encyclopedia of Social Measurement*, 2004.

4

Cointegration – A Superior Concept to Correlation?

"If you can't explain it in simple terms, you haven't understood it very well"

– Albert Einstein

In the previous chapter we looked at the numerous limitations of the Pearson correlation model. In this chapter we discuss the concept of cointegration and evaluate if it is a better suited concept to analyse financial time series and their dependence.

SOME BASICS

Cointegration is a 2003 Nobel Prize-rewarded concept and goes back to Robert Engle and Clive Granger (1987). Before we analyse it, we have to understand some statistical properties, which are part of Cointegration.

What is a stationary process?
Definition: A stationary process is a process where mean and variance are constant in time (weak stationary) or all moments (strict stationary) are constant in time.

An example of a stationary process is a random drawing from a standard normal distribution ε_t, which we already encountered in chapter 3. ε can be computed as =normsinv(rand()) in Excel or norminv(rand) in MATLAB. See www.dersoft.com/epsilon.xlsx for a spreadsheet deriving ε. Drawing 10,000 ε_t, we derive Figure 4.1.

However, stocks that grow are not stationary, since their mean increases in time. In addition, the volatility of stocks, ie, the standard deviation of their returns typically varies with time. Sometimes

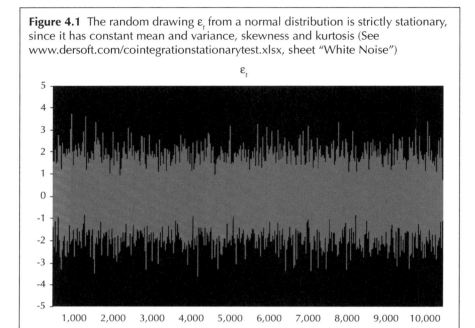

Figure 4.1 The random drawing ε_t from a normal distribution is strictly stationary, since it has constant mean and variance, skewness and kurtosis (See www.dersoft.com/cointegrationstationarytest.xlsx, sheet "White Noise")

constant autocorrelation, also called covariance-stationarity, is added as a criterion of a stationary process. In Figure 4.2, the upper function Y_t has constant autocorrelation, but the lower function X_t does not.

Why is constant autocorrelation sometimes added as a criterion for a stationary process? The answer is that it is difficult to work with processes that have varying autocorrelation. In the example of Figure 4.2 there will be a positive correlation between Y and X in the beginning when both have positive autocorrelation, but we will find negative correlation between Y and X when X displays negative autocorrelation. In particular, applying the cointegration to pairs trading, which we will discuss in detail in Chapter 13, requires a high degree of constant autocorrelation.[1]

Mathematically, we can formulise a stationary process by the following: let X be a portfolio, X_t a stochastic process of that portfolio, and F_X the joint cumulative distribution function. Then X_t is stationary, if for all k, τ, and $t_1 \ldots t_k$

$$F_X(X_{t_1+\tau},\ldots,X_{t_k+\tau}) = F_X(X_{t_1},\ldots,X_{t_k}) \tag{4.1}$$

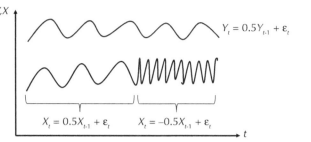

Figure 4.2 The upper function Y_t has fairly constant autocorrelation; the lower function X_t first has positive, then negative autocorrelation

In equation (4.1), the joint distribution F_X is not a function of time τ, ie, the moments of F_X do not change in time, in particular do not follow any trends.

What does integrated to the order d mean?

A second concept that we have to understand before we can discuss cointegration is for a time series to be integrated to a certain order d. Most readers, when they hear the term "integration", probably think of deriving an area under a function. However, we are dealing with time series here, so the domain of integration is one-dimensional. This means that we are simply summing up incremental units over a real line, a function.[2] Let's look at a definition of integration to the order d:

Definition: A time series is integrated to the order d, $I(d)$, if taking repeated differences d times results in a stationary process.

In particular, let Y_t be a time series, L a lag operator (eg, one day), and $1 - L$ the first difference. Then Y_t is integrated to the order d, if

$$(1-L)^d Y_t \qquad (4.2)$$

is stationary. Here is an example:

Example 4.1: Let the lag operator L be a one-unit timeframe (for example, one day). In this case equation (4.2) is $(Y_t - Y_{t-1})^d$. If a time series Y_t is integrated to the order 1, $I(1)$, we have from equation (4.2) $(1 - L)^1 Y_t = (Y_t - Y_{t-1})^1 = \Delta Y$.

Let's look at the first difference ΔY of the function $Y = X^2$. What order of integration does ΔY have? Table 4.1 shows the result.

Table 4.1 The function $Y = X^2$ and its first and second difference

X	$Y = X^2$	$\Delta Y = Y_t - Y_{t-1}$	$\Delta^2 Y = Y_t - Y_{t-1}$ of $(Y_t - Y_{t-1})$
1	1		
2	4	3	
3	9	5	2
4	16	7	2
5	25	9	2
6	36	11	2
7	49	13	2
8	64	15	2
9	81	17	2
10	100	19	2

In Table 4.1, ΔY is displayed in column 3. Taking differences of ΔY results in column 4, which is strictly stationary, since the mean, variance, skewness and kurtosis are constant. Therefore ΔY is integrated to order 1, $I(1)$.

What about the function $Y = X^2$, which is displayed in column 2 of Table 4.1? We observe that taking differences of $Y = X^2$ twice, results in column 4, which as mentioned is stationary. Therefore, the function $Y = X^2$ is integrated to the order 2, $I(2)$. For a simple spreadsheet deriving the results of Table 4.1, see www.dersoft.com/cointegration.xlsx.

Naturally the fourth column in Table 4.1, $\Delta^2 Y$, is integrated to the order 0, $I(0)$. An interesting question is how integrated to the order 0, $I(0)$ and stationarity are related. It turns out that a process integrated to the order of zero $I(0)$ is a necessary (but not sufficient) condition for a stationary process. So all stationary processes are $I(0)$, but not all $I(0)$ processes are stationary. For necessary and sufficient conditions, see Appendix 4.2.

With the tools of stationarity and integration to a certain order d, we are now ready to discuss important properties of the cointegration concept.

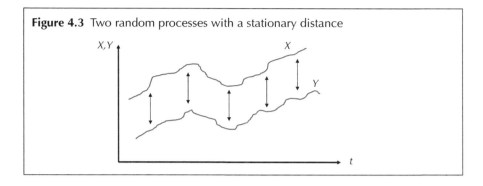

Figure 4.3 Two random processes with a stationary distance

KEY ELEMENTS OF COINTEGRATION

In the following we will study the cointegration concept and its usefulness for finance. Let's start with a definition.

Definition: If two or more time series (eg, two stock prices in time) are individually integrated, but some linear combination (a portfolio) of them has a *lower order of integration*, then the two series are said to be cointegrated.

Michael Murray (1994) in a nice paper explains the concept of cointegration intuitively: a drunk has a puppy. The drunk and her puppy are both individually random processes. However, they belong to each other, so each occasionally assess how far away they are from each other and then partially close the gap. The distance between them is still random, but the distance is stationary. This can be illustrated with Figure 4.3.

APPLICATION OF COINTEGRATION IN FINANCE

How is all this useful in finance? If we find a combination of stocks or other assets that are cointegrated, we can do three things: (1) track an index; (2) do cost-effective hedging; and (3) do pairs trading. Let's discuss these three applications briefly.

Tracking an index

Portfolio managers often try to track an index, such as the S&P 500. Buying all 500 stocks is naturally quite cumbersome and transaction-intensive. However, if we can find a smaller portfolio of maybe 10–20 stocks, whose returns are cointegrated with the returns of the S&P 500, we can track the S&P 500 with this smaller portfolio.

Ideally, the returns of the S&P 500 and portfolio A will be integrated to the order 1, I(1). Then the linear combination of the returns will be stationary and the tracking error small.

Cost-effective hedging

If a trader wants to partially or fully hedge an index such as the S&P 500, a similar concept such as tracking an index can be applied. Assuming that we are long S&P 500, we can simply short the tracking portfolio. Let's assume the trader wants to hedge 50% of their US$1,000,000 S&P 500 position. If they find a small portfolio, which is cointegrated with the S&P 500, they can cost-effectively sell US$500,000 of this small tracking portfolio. Assuming a high degree of cointegration persists into the future, this is a good hedge, since the difference of the mean and variance between the S&P 500 and the tracking portfolio will be small.

Pairs trading

Pairs trading is an assumed market neutral trading strategy that tries to exploit a decrease in correlation or cointegration between the returns of two assets. Let's assume the correlation between the returns of two assets has been fairly constant in the past. Now however the returns have diverged. The asset whose return has increased is shorted and the asset whose return has decreased is bought, assuming that the return gap will narrow again. Cointegration is considered a useful tool of identify stocks for pairs trading, which we will analyse in depth in Chapter 13.

A PRACTICAL APPROACH TO FINDING COINTEGRATED STOCKS

Robert Engle and Clive Granger (1987) suggest a two-step procedure to find cointegrated stocks.

Step 1: If two stocks X and Y are cointegrated, a linear combination is stationary. Formally,

$$Y_t - \beta X_t = u_t \tag{4.3}$$

where u_t is stationary. We first have to find the nature of the possible cointegration, ie, we have to find the value of β in equation (4.3). This is typically done with an OLS (ordinary least square) estimate. Let's assume X and Y are associated as in Figure 4.4. Then $\beta = 0.5$.

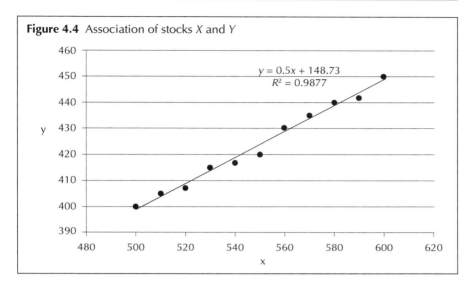

Figure 4.4 Association of stocks X and Y

Step 2: We now have to test if our portfolio of stocks X and Y is really stationary. Several test for stationarity exist such as the Dickey–Fuller test, Phillips–Perron test, Johnson test, or Phillips–Ouliaris test. We will discuss the Dickey–Fuller test here. It involves testing if an autoregressive process is integrated to the order 1, $I(1)$, also called a "unit-root" test. A simple autoregressive function for our portfolio P is

$$P_t = aP_{t-1} + \varepsilon_t \qquad (4.4)$$

The idea is that if the process P_t has high positive auto-regression, eg, high values of P_{t-1} are followed by high values of P_t and vice versa, the process will not revert to its mean, ie, will not have a time-constant mean and variance. So whether our portfolio P is stationary depends on the parameter 'a' in equation (4.4). If $a = 1$, equation (4.4) has a unit root and is not stationary, as seen in Figure 4.5.

From Figure 4.5 we clearly observe that the variance increases in time. Therefore the processes are not stationary. If the parameter $a = -1$, the autoregressive processes $P_t = a\,P_{t-1} + \varepsilon_t$ are also not stationary, but oscillates with again increasing variance, as seen in Figure 4.6.

It turns out that for $|a| < 1$, the process $P_t = a\,P_{t-1} + \varepsilon_t$ is stationary. The Dickey–Fuller test is a special test for stationarity,

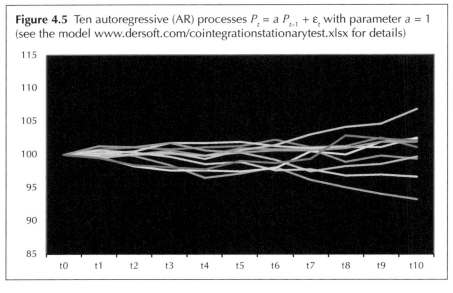

Figure 4.5 Ten autoregressive (AR) processes $P_t = a P_{t-1} + \varepsilon_t$ with parameter $a = 1$ (see the model www.dersoft.com/cointegrationstationarytest.xlsx for details)

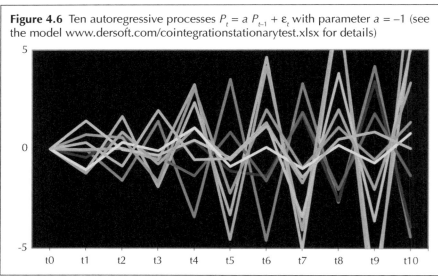

Figure 4.6 Ten autoregressive processes $P_t = a P_{t-1} + \varepsilon_t$ with parameter $a = -1$ (see the model www.dersoft.com/cointegrationstationarytest.xlsx for details)

which tests whether an autoregressive process has a unit root, ie, $a = 1$. So our null hypothesis H_0 is that the process $P_t = a P_{t-1} + \varepsilon_t$ has a unit root, ie, that $a = 1$ (in which case the process is not stationary). Our research or alternative hypothesis H_1 is "The process P is stationary, so $|a| < 1$". We can formulise the Dickey–Fuller test with equation (4.5):

$$P_t = aP_{t-1} + \varepsilon_t \qquad (4.5)$$

and

$$H_0 : a = 1; H_1 : a < |1|$$

Subtracting P_{t-1} from both sides we get $P_t - P_{t-1} = (a - 1)P_{t-1} + \varepsilon_t$, and with $\delta = a - 1$ we get

$$\Delta P_t = \delta P_{t-1} + \varepsilon_t$$

We can now run a standard t-test on δ. Since P_{t-1} under H_0 is nonstationary and therefore the central limit theorem does not apply, we have to compare our t-statistic with some critical value of the Dickey–Fuller (DF) distribution, which takes into consideration the unit root property. If we find that our t-value is smaller than some critical value of the DF distribution, ie, $t < DF_{critical'}$ then we reject the null hypothesis and conclude that our portfolio is stationary. For a model on the DF test, see www.dersoft.com/cointegrationstationarytest.xlsx. In the following we will discuss another key element of cointegration, the Granger causality.

GRANGER CAUSALITY

The search for causation is omnipresent! We want to know what caused the Big Bang, what causes the universe's current expansion, what the final state of the universe will be, what caused life on Earth, earthquakes, hurricanes, cancer, stock-market crashes, economic recessions and much more. Cause and effect are popular topics in philosophy (see, eg, Aristotle and David Hume).[3]

As we discussed in Chapter 3, the Pearson correlation model does not include any methodology to determine the existence or the nature of a causal relationship between the variables in the correlation model. Therefore in the Pearson model, we have to exogenously determine (1) the existence of a direct or indirect causal relationship between X and Y and (2) the direction of the causal relationship (X causing Y, Y causing X, or bidirectional).

Since there is a lack of causality in the Pearson model, "nonsense correlation" or "spurious relationships" are possible, ie, a high correlation between variables, which are not causality-related.

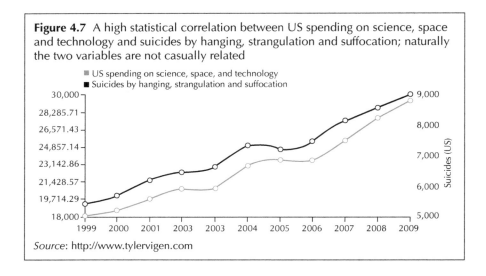

Figure 4.7 A high statistical correlation between US spending on science, space and technology and suicides by hanging, strangulation and suffocation; naturally the two variables are not casually related

Source: http://www.tylervigen.com

Many examples of nonsense correlation exist (see, for example, Figure 4.7).

Clive Granger addresses the lack of causality and the possibility of nonsense correlation in the Pearson model and derives a concept that attempts to find the causality between two variables. The assumptions that Granger makes are that (1) the cause happens before the effect and (2) the cause has unique information about the future values of its effect. Based on these assumptions, we have

$$P[Y_{t+1} \in A \mid I(t)] \neq P[Y_{t+1} \in A \mid I_{-X}(t)] \tag{4.6}$$

where P : Probability, A : non-empty set, I : Information in the universe, I_{-X} : Information in the universe without X.

Equation (4.6) reads: Given an information set $I(t)$, the probability of a variable Y at time $t + 1$ being in set A is different from the probability of the variable Y at time $t + 1$ being in set A when the information set I does not include information on X. Therefore X has a time-lagged impact on Y. This is graphically expressed in Figure 4.8.

Equation (4.6) can be tested with a multiple regression function which includes autoregression terms of the variable Y and time-lagged regressive terms of X. Hence we have

$$Y_t = \underbrace{a_1 Y_{t-1} + a_2 Y_{t-2} + \ldots + a_p Y_{t-p}}_{Y \text{ autoregression term}} + \underbrace{b_1 X_{t-1} + b_2 X_{t-2} + \ldots + b_q X_{t-q}}_{\text{Time-lagged regression term}} + \varepsilon_t \tag{4.7}$$

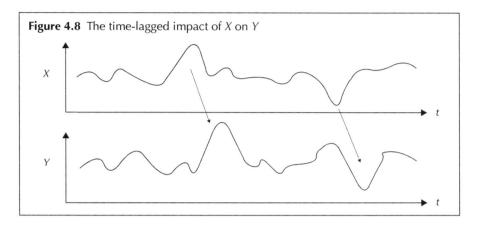

Figure 4.8 The time-lagged impact of X on Y

t-tests on the parameters and F-tests on the time-lagged explanatory variables (on the right side of equation (4.7)) to find their impact can be performed.

Granger causality can be implemented using a Vector Autoregressive Model (VAR). Let's assume we have three variables, Y_1, Y_2 and Y_3. To test a one-time period-lagged impact of these variables on each other, we can write:

$$\begin{pmatrix} y_{t,1} \\ y_{t,2} \\ y_{t,3} \end{pmatrix} = \begin{pmatrix} c_1 \\ c_2 \\ c_3 \end{pmatrix} + \begin{pmatrix} a_{11} & a_{12} & a_{13} \\ a_{21} & a_{22} & a_{23} \\ a_{31} & a_{32} & a_{33} \end{pmatrix} \begin{pmatrix} y_{t-1,1} \\ y_{t-1,2} \\ y_{t-1,3} \end{pmatrix} + \begin{pmatrix} e_{t,1} \\ e_{t,2} \\ e_{t,3} \end{pmatrix} \quad (4.8)$$

where c_i are constants, a_{ij} are partial regression coefficients, and e_i are error terms.

Meissner *et al* (2018) use this three-variable VAR model to test a one-day time-lagged impact of the Asian market (Y_1), the European market (Y_2) and the US market (Y_3) on each other. The parameter values come out to be as in Table 4.2.

The critical parameters a_{11} to a_{33} are partial regression coefficients (not correlation coefficients). For example, the coefficient a_{11} is the autoregressive regression coefficient of the Asian market, meaning if Asia was up one day by 1, on average Asia will be down the next day by 0.086, and vice versa. From the coefficients a_{22} and a_{33}, we observe the same one-day negative autocorrelation for the European market and the US market. In addition:

Table 4.2 Coefficients of testing the one-day lagged impact of the Asian market (Y_1), the European market (Y_2) and the US market (Y_3) on each other, >|5%| values in bold.

	Estimate	Std. error	t value	Pr(>|t|)
c_1	-0.0005206	0.0001947	-2.674	0.00752*
a_{11}	**-0.0867521**	0.0149763	-5.793	7.41e-09*
a_{12}	**0.1054833**	0.0198237	5.321	1.08e-07*
a_{13}	**0.2071458**	0.0198803	10.420	< 2e-16*
c_2	-0.0001035	0.0001600	-0.647	0.518
a_{21}	**-0.0521913**	0.0123077	-4.241	2.27e-05*
a_{22}	-0.1416464	0.0162913	-8.695	< 2e16*
a_{23}	**0.2897228**	0.0163378	17.733	< 2e-16*
c_3	0.000277	0.000162	1.710	0.087388
a_{31}	-0.021642	0.012464	1.736	0.082575
a_{32}	0.014414	0.016499	0.874	0.382361
a_{33}	**-0.063185**	0.016546	-3.819	0.000136*

1. The coefficients a_{12} and a_{13} are significant, which means that the European market (Y_2) and the Dow (Y_3) Granger cause the Nikkei (Y_1). For example, the coefficient a_{12} = 0.1055 means that, if the European market was up by 1, on average the Asian market was up by 0.1055 the next day.
2. The coefficients a_{21} and a_{23} are significant, which means that the Asian market (negatively) and the US market Granger causes the European market (Y_2).
3. The coefficients a_{31} and a_{32} are not significant, which means that the Asian market and Europe do not Granger-cause the Dow.

CONCLUSION: COINTEGRATION MODEL

The cointegration model addresses two main drawbacks of the Pearson model: (1) the fact that the Pearson model evaluates only the linear association between variables and (2) that nonsense correlation is possible.

The cointegration model assesses time series (eg, of stocks), which may be integrated to a high order (ie, are nonlinear). It then tries to find a linear combination of the stocks (a portfolio), which has a lower order of integration, for example is stationary. If this can be achieved, three critical things are possible: (1) tracking an index, (2) cost-effective hedging and (3) pairs trading.

Another key element of cointegration is Granger causality, which attempts to find the causality between variables. On the positive side, Granger causality applies autoregressive and lagged regressive terms to derive the impact on the dependent variable. Hence, it combines standard multiple Pearson regression techniques in one model. This can be rigorously formulated with a VAR. On the negative side, Granger causality, being an extension of the Pearson approach, is still a linear model. So can the Granger causality concept find "true causality"? Besides this being a highly philosophical question, "nonsense correlation" is still possible in the Granger model: "A rooster crows before the sun rises. Therefore, the rooster causes the sun to rise."

Altogether, cointegration is a valuable model for finance, which addresses and enhances critical drawbacks of the Pearson correlation model.

APPENDIX 4.1: TIME SERIES INTEGRATION

The mathematical theory of integration was founded independently by Isaac Newton and Gottfried Leibnitz in the 17th century and later rigorously formulated mainly by Bernhard Riemann and Henri Lebesgue.

When the reader hears the term "integration" they probably think mainly of deriving the area under a function. In this case the domain of integration is two-dimensional. However, when dealing with time series, we are simply summing up incremental units over a real line, a function. Therefore the domain of integration is one-dimensional. Here is an example:

Example 1: What is the expected value of a stock price S at a future time T, $E(S_T)$, when modelled with the geometric Brownian motion

$$\frac{dS}{S} = \mu_S dt + \sigma_S \varepsilon_t \sqrt{dt} \qquad (4A.1)$$

where S is the stock price, μ_S is the expected rate of growth, σ_S is the expected volatility and ε_t is a random drawing from a standard normal distribution. Graphically, we can display equation (4A.1) in Figure A1:

Figure A1 Graphical display of $\frac{dS}{S} = \mu_s dt + \sigma_s \varepsilon_t \sqrt{dt}$

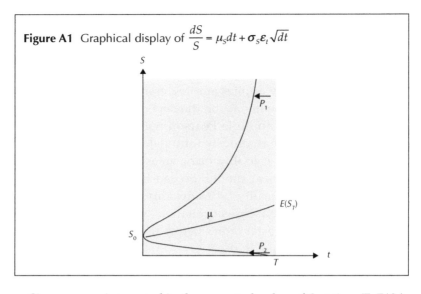

Since we are interested in the expected value of S at time T, $E(S_T)$, and the expected value $E(\varepsilon) = 0$, the second term on the right side of equation (4A.1) drops out and we have

$$\frac{dS}{S} = \mu_s dt \tag{4A.2}$$

To find $E(S_T)$, we now integrate equation (4A.2) from time 0 to time T, ie, we integrate over a real line, so the domain of integration is one-dimensional. Inputting an expectation operator E, we get

$$\int_0^T E\left(\frac{dS}{S}\right) = \int_0^T \mu_s \, dt \tag{4A.3}$$

Applying

$$\int \frac{dS}{S} = \ln S,$$

we get

$$\ln\bigl(E(S_T)\bigr) = \mu_s T + \ln(S_0) \tag{4A.4}$$

where $\ln(S_0)$ is the integration constant. Using $e^{\ln(x)} = x$ and simple algebra, we get

$$E(S_T) = S_0 e^{\mu_s T} \tag{4A.5}$$

Hence the expected value of the stock price at time T, when integration over the real line

$$\frac{dS}{S} = \mu_s dt$$

is simply the starting value of S, S_0, multiplied with $e^{\mu_s T}$.

APPENDIX 4.2: ON NECESSARY AND SUFFICIENT CONDITIONS

In the following we will explain the concept of necessary and sufficient conditions. A necessary condition is a condition that implies another condition. A sufficient condition is the minimum condition to guarantee another condition. Let's look at an example.

Let A be a set and B a subset of A. In particular, A is the set of odd numbers and B is the set of prime numbers:

$$A = \{3, 5, 7, 9, 11, 13, 15, 17, 19\ldots\}$$

$$B = \{3, 5, 7, 11, 13, 17, 19\ldots\}$$

It follows that:

1. A is a necessary condition for B; it follows that B implies A, B $\rightarrow$ A (being prime implies being odd (all primes are odd));
2. A is not a sufficient condition for B, or A does not guarantee B (being odd does not guarantee to be prime (not all odds are prime));
3. B is not a necessary condition for A; it follows that A does not imply B, A not $\rightarrow$ B; (being odd does not imply being prime (not all odds are prime)); and
4. B is a sufficient condition for A, or, B guarantees A (being prime guarantees that the number is odd (all primes are odd)).

In conclusion, the superset A is necessary but not sufficient for the subset B. The subset B is sufficient but not necessary for superset A.

Questions for Chapter 4
Answers to these questions can be found at the end of this book.

1. Which two major drawbacks of the Pearson correlation model mainly sparked the creation of the Cointegration model?
2. What is a stationary process?
3. Is a random drawing from a standard normal distribution ε_t, =normsinv(rand()) in Excel and norminv(rand) in MATLAB a stationary process?
4. Why is constant autocorrelation, also called covariance-stationarity, sometimes added as a criterion of a stationary process?
5. A stationary process can be formulised as

$$F_X\left(x_{t_{1+\tau}},\ldots,x_{t_{k+\tau}}\right)=F_X\left(x_{t_1},\ldots x_{t_k}\right)$$

   Interpret this equation.
6. What does integrated to the order d mean?
7. What is cointegration?
8. What applications does the cointegration concept have in finance?
9. Explain the Granger–Engle two-step process to find cointegrated stocks.
10. What does the Dickey–Fuller test try to achieve?
11. What does Granger causality try to achieve?
12. Which two key elements of the Pearson correlation model does Granger causality combine?
13. Do you think Granger causality is "true causality"?
14. What is the limitation of the Granger causality concept?

---

1 For a graph showing the autocorrelation of the Dow Jones Industrial Average from 1920 to 2017, see Chapter 13.
2 For an example of one-dimensional integration, see Appendix 4.1 of this chapter.
3 *Aristotle on Causality* (2006). *Stanford Encyclopedia of Philosophy*, Dauer, F. Watanabe (2008). *Hume on the Relation of Cause and Effect*, John Wiley

5

Financial Correlation Modelling – Bottom-up Approaches

> "Fortune sides with him who dares"
> – Virgil

In this chapter we address correlation models, which were specifically designed to measure the association between financial variables. We will concentrate on bottom-up correlation models that collect information, quantify it and then aggregate the information to derive an overall correlation result.

CORRELATING BROWNIAN MOTIONS (HESTON 1993)

One of the most widely applied correlation approaches used in finance was generated by Steven Heston in 1993. Heston applied the approach to negatively correlate stochastic stock returns $dS(t)/S(t)$ and stochastic volatility $\sigma(t)$. The core equations of the original Heston model are the two stochastic differential equations (SDEs)

$$\frac{dS(t)}{S(t)} = \mu dt + \sigma(t) dz_1(t) \tag{5.1}$$

and

$$d\sigma^2(t) = a\left[m_\sigma^2 - \sigma^2(t)\right]dt + \xi\sigma(t)dz_2(t) \tag{5.2}$$

where

S: variable of interest, eg, a stock price
μ: expected growth rate of S
σ: expected volatility of S
dz: standard Brownian motion, ie, $dz(t) = \varepsilon(t)\sqrt{dt}$, $\varepsilon(t)$ is i.i.d. (independently and identically distributed). In particular $\varepsilon(t)$ is a random

drawing from a standardised normal distribution at time t, $\varepsilon(t) = n \sim (0, 1)$, which we already encountered in chapters 3 and 4. We can compute ε as =normsinv(rand()) in Excel/VBA and norminv(rand) in MATLAB. See the spreadsheet www.dersoft.com/epsilon.xlsx for a derivation of ε.

a: mean reversion rate (gravity), ie, degree with which σ at time t, σ_t, is pulled back to its long term mean σ_ρ. "a" can take the values $0 \le a \le 1$ (see Chapter 2 for details);
m_σ: long-term mean of the σ;
ξ: volatility of the volatility σ.

In equation (5.1), the underlying variable S follows the standard geometric Brownian motion (GBM), which is also applied in the Black–Scholes–Merton option-pricing model, which, however, assumes a constant volatility σ. For a model, that generates the GBM in equation (5.1), and equation (5.1) with random jumps, see www.dersoft.com/gbmwithconditionaljumps.xlsm. Equation (5.2) models the stochastic volatility with the mean-reverting Cox, Ingersoll, Ross (CIR) process (Cox, Ingersoll and Ross 1985).

Importantly, the correlation between the stochastic processes (5.1) and (5.2) is introduced by correlating the two Brownian motions dz_1 and dz_2. The instantaneous correlation between the Brownian motions is

$$Corr[dz_1(t), dz_2(t)] = \rho dt \qquad (5.3)$$

The definition (5.3) can be conveniently modelled with the identity

$$dz_1(t) = \sqrt{\rho} dz_2(t) + \sqrt{1-\rho} dz_3(t) \qquad (5.4)$$

where $dz_2(t)$ and $dz_3(t)$ are independent, and $dz(t)$ and $dz(t')$ are independent, $t \ne t'$.

Equation (5.4) allows only a positive correlation between dz_1 and dz_2 (since the correlation parameter ρ is input as a square root). We can rewrite equation (5.4) to allow negative correlation by applying $\sqrt{\rho} = \alpha$. Equation (5.4) then changes to

$$dz_1(t) = \alpha dz_2(t) + \sqrt{1-\alpha^2} dz_3(t) \qquad (5.5)$$

From equation (5.5) we observe that, for a dependence coefficient of $\alpha = 1$, the critical Brownian motions $dz_1(t)$ and $dz_2(t)$ are equal at every time t. For $\alpha = 0$, the Brownian motions $dz_1(t)$ and $dz_2(t)$ are not correlated, since $dz_1(t) = dz_3(t)$. For $\alpha = -1$, $dz_1(t)$ and $dz_2(t)$ have an inverse correlation.

Equations (5.4) and (5.5) are mathematically and

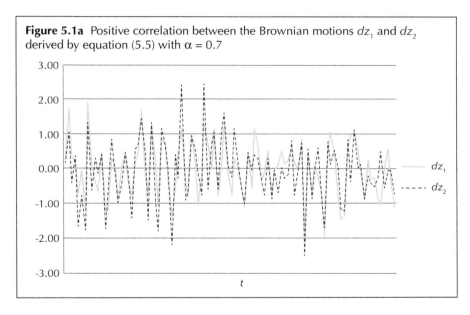

Figure 5.1a Positive correlation between the Brownian motions dz_1 and dz_2 derived by equation (5.5) with $\alpha = 0.7$

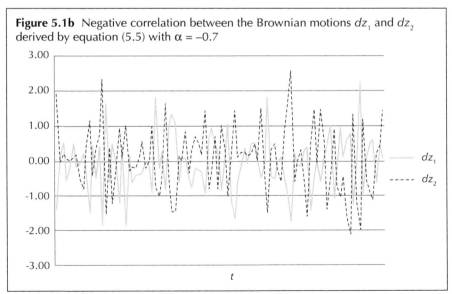

Figure 5.1b Negative correlation between the Brownian motions dz_1 and dz_2 derived by equation (5.5) with $\alpha = -0.7$

computationally convenient. If dz_2 and dz_3 are standard normal, it follows by construction that dz_1 will also be standard normal for any value of $-1 \leq \sqrt{\rho} = \alpha \leq 1$.

Figures 5.1a and 5.1b show the correlation between dz_1 and dz_2 for different dependence parameters α.

In conclusion, the Heston correlation approach is a dynamic, versatile, and mathematically rigorous correlation model. It allows us to positively or negatively correlate stochastic processes and permits dynamic correlation modelling since $dz(t)$ is a function of t. Hence it is not surprising that the approach is an integral part of correlation modelling in finance.

Applications of the Heston model

One prominent application of the Heston model is in the stochastic alpha beta rho (SABR) model of Hagan *et al* (2002), where stochastic interest rates and stochastic volatility are correlated to derive realistic volatility smiles and skews. For extensions of the SABR model see West (2005), Henry-Labordere (2007), Kahl and Jaeckel (2009), and Benhamou *et al* (2009) as well as Chapter 9. Huang and Yildirim (2008) use the Heston approach to correlate the volatility of the inflation process and the volatility of the nominal discount bond process to value TIPS (Treasury inflation-protected security) futures. Langnau (2009) combines the Heston approach with the local volatility model of Dupire (1994). The result is a dynamic "local correlation model" (LCM), which matches the implied volatility skew of equity index options well.

In credit risk modelling, Zhou (2001) derives analytical equations for joint default probabilities in a Black–Cox first-time passage framework applying Heston correlations. Zhou's equations help to explain empirical default properties as being (1) default correlations and asset-price correlations that are positively related and (2) default correlations that are small over short time horizons. They typically first increase in time, then plateau out and then gradually decline, as found by Lucas (1995). Brigo and Pallavicini (2008) apply two Heston correlations. The first correlates two factors that drive the interest-rate process, while the second correlates the interest-rate process with the default intensity process. Meissner *et al* (2013) apply the Heston approach in a reduced-form framework. They correlate the Brownian motion of an LMM (Libor Market

Model) modelled reference asset and an LMM modelled counterparty, and investigate the impact on the CDS spread. They find that just correlating the LMM processes results in a rather low impact on the CDS spread, ie, it leads to higher CDS spreads than correlating the default processes directly. See Chapter 11 for details.

A variation of the Heston approach will be discussed in Chapter 9.

THE BINOMIAL CORRELATION MEASURE

A further popular correlation measure, mainly applied to default correlation, is the binomial correlation approach of Douglas Lucas (1995). Let's assume we have two entities (individuals, companies or sovereigns) X and Y. We define the binomial events

$$1_X = 1_{\{\tau_X \leq T\}} \tag{5.6}$$

and

$$1_Y = 1_{\{\tau_Y \leq T\}} \tag{5.7}$$

where τ_X is the default time of entity X and τ_Y is the default time of entity Y. 1_X is the indicator variable of entity X. We read the equation (5.6) as: if entity X defaults before time T, ie, $\tau_X \leq T$, then 1_X takes the value 1 and 0 otherwise. The same applies to entity Y.

Furthermore, let $P(X)$ and $P(Y)$ be the default probability of X and Y respectively, and $P(XY)$ is the joint probability of default. The standard deviation of a one-trial binomial event is

$$\sqrt{P(X) - (P(X))^2},$$

where P is the probability of outcome X. Hence, modifying the Pearson correlation equation (1.4), we derive the joint default dependence coefficient of the binomial events $1_{\{\tau_X \leq T\}}$ and $1_{\{\tau_Y \leq T\}}$ as

$$\rho\left(1_{\{\tau_X \leq T\}}, 1_{\{\tau_Y \leq T\}}\right) = \frac{P(XY) - P(X)P(Y)}{\sqrt{P(X) - (P(X))^2}\sqrt{P(Y) - (P(Y))^2}} \tag{5.8}$$

By construction, equation (5.8) can only model binomial events, for example default and no default. With respect to equation (1.4), we observe that in equation (1.4) X and Y are sets of $i = 1, \ldots, n$ variates, with $i \in \Re$. $P(X)$ and $P(Y)$ in equation (5.8) however are scalars, eg, the default probabilities of entities X and Y for a certain time period

T respectively, $0 \leq P(X) \leq 1$, and $0 \leq P(Y) \leq 1$. Hence the binomial correlation approach of equation (5.8) is a limiting case of the Pearson correlation approach of equation (1.4). As a consequence, the significant shortcomings of the Pearson correlation approach for financial modelling apply also to the binomial correlation model.

Application of the binomial correlation measure

The binomial-correlation approach (5.8) had been applied by rating agencies to value CDOs; for a discussion see Bank for International Settlements (2004) and Schönbucher (2006). However, the rating agencies have replaced the binomial correlation approach by a structural Merton-based model in combination with Monte Carlo (see Meissner *et al* 2008c). Hull and White (2001) apply the binomial correlation measure to price CDSs with counterparty risk. They find that the impact of the counterparty risk on the CDS is small if the binomial correlation between the reference asset and the counterparty is small. The impact increases if the binomial correlation increases and the creditworthiness of the counterparty declines.

Numerous studies have applied the binomial correlation measure to analyse historical default correlations. Most of the studies show little statistical evidence of default correlation. Erturk (2000) finds no statistically significant evidence of default correlation for less than one-year intervals for 1,500 investment-grade entities in the US. Similarly, Nagpal and Bahar (2001) find low binomial correlation coefficients within 11 sectors in the US from 1981 and 1999. Li and Meissner (2006) study intra-sector and inter-sector default correlations of 10,348 US companies from 1981 to 2003. Inter-sector default correlations show 80.76% positive default dependencies. However, only 8.97% of these were statistically significant at a 5% level. Inter-sector default correlations increased to 100% positive in recessionary periods. Of these, again 8.97% were statistically significant at the 5% level.

COPULA CORRELATIONS

A fairly recent and famous as well as infamous correlation approach applied in finance is the copula approach. Copulas go back to Abe Sklar (1959). Extensions are provided by Schweizer and Wolff (1981) and Schweizer and Sklar (1983). One-factor copulas were introduced to finance by Oldrich Vasicek in 1987. More versatile, multivariate copulas were applied to finance by David Li in 2000.

When flexible copula functions were introduced to finance in 2000, they were enthusiastically embraced but then fell into disgrace when the global financial crisis hit in 2007. Copulas became popular because they could presumably solve a complex problem in an easy way: it was assumed that copulas could correlate multiple assets; for example, the 125 assets in a CDO, with a single, although multidimensional, function. We will devote the entire Chapter 6 to discuss the benefits and limitations of the Gaussian copula for valuing CDOs. Let's first look at the maths of the copula correlation concept.

Copula functions are designed to simplify statistical problems. They allow the joining of multiple univariate distributions to a single multivariate distribution. Formally, a copula function C transforms an n-dimensional function on the interval [0,1] into a unit-dimensional one:

$$C:[0,1]^n \to [0,1] \qquad (5.9)$$

More explicitly, let $G_i(u_i)$ be a univariate, uniform distribution with $u_i = u_1, \ldots, u_n$, and $i \in N$. Then there exists a copula function C such that

$$C[G_1(u_1),\ldots,G_n(u_n)] = F_n\left[F_1^{-1}(G_1(u_1)),\ldots,F_n^{-1}(G_n(u_n)); \rho_F\right] \qquad (5.10)$$

where $G_i(u_i)$ are called marginal distributions and F_n is the joint cumulative distribution function. F_i^{-1} is the inverse of F_i. ρ_F is the correlation structure of F_n.

Equation (5.10) reads: given are the marginal distributions $G_1(u_1)$ to $G_n(u_n)$. There exists a copula function that allows the mapping of the marginal distributions $G_1(u_1)$ to $G_n(u_n)$ via F^{-1} and the joining of the (abscise values) $F^{-1}(G_i(u_i))$ to a single, n-variate function $F_n[F^{-1}(G_1(u_1)), \ldots, F_n^{-1}(G_n(u_n))]$ with correlation structure of ρ_F.

If the mapped values $F_i^{-1}(G_i(u_i))$ are continuous, it follows that C is unique. For detailed properties and proofs of equation (5.10), see Sklar (1959) and Nelsen (2006). A short proof is given in Appendix A2.

Numerous types of copula functions exist. They can be broadly categorised in one-parameter copulas as the Gaussian copula;[1] and the Archimedean copula family, the most popular being Gumbel,

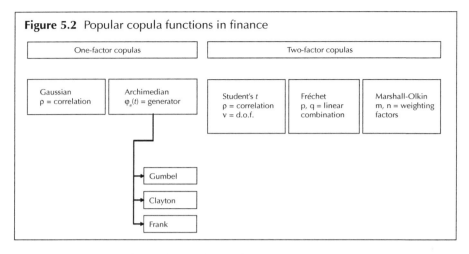

Figure 5.2 Popular copula functions in finance

Clayton and Frank copulas. Often cited two-parameter copulas are student-t, Frechet, and Marshall–Olkin. Figure 5.2 shows an overview of popular copula functions.

The Gaussian copula

Due to its convenient properties, the Gaussian copula C_G is among the most applied copulas in finance. In the n-variate case, it is defined

$$C_G\left[G_1(u_1),\ldots,G_n(u_n)\right] = M_n\left[N^{-1}(G_1(u_1)),\ldots,N^{-1}(G_n(u_n));\rho_M\right] \quad (5.11)$$

where M_n is the joint, n-variate cumulative standard normal distribution with ρ_M, the $n \times n$ symmetric, positive-definite correlation matrix of the n-variate normal distribution M_n. N^{-1} is the inverse of a univariate standard normal distribution.

If the $G_x(u_x)$ are uniform, then the $N^{-1}(G_x(u_x))$ are standard normal and M_n is standard multivariate normal. For a proof, see Cherubini et al 2005.

It was David Li (2000), who transferred the copula approach of equation (5.11) to finance. He defined the cumulative default probabilities Q for entity i at a fixed time t, $Q_i(t)$ as marginal distributions. Hence we derive the Gaussian default time copula $C_{GD'}$

$$C_{GD}\left[Q_i(t),\ldots,Q_n(t)\right] = M_n\left[N^{-1}(Q_1(t)),\ldots N^{-1}(Q_n(t));\rho_M\right] \quad (5.12)$$

Equation (5.12) reads: given are the marginal distributions, ie, the cumulative default probabilities Q of entities $i = 1$ to n at times t,

$Q_i(t)$. There exists a Gaussian copula function C_{GD}, which allows the mapping of the marginal distributions $Q_i(t)$ via N^{-1} to standard normal and the joining of the (abscise values) $N^{-1}Q_i(t)$ to a single n-variate standard normal distribution M_n with the correlation structure ρ_M.

More precisely, in equation (5.12) the term N^{-1} maps the cumulative default probabilities Q of asset i for time t, $Q_i(t)$, percentile to percentile to a univariate standard normal distribution. So the 5th percentile of $Q_i(t)$ is mapped to the 5th percentile of the standard normal distribution; the 10th percentile of $Q_i(t)$ is mapped to the 10th percentile of the standard normal distribution, etc. As a result, the $N^{-1}(Q_i(t))$ in equation (5.12) are abscise (x-axis) values of the standard normal distribution. For a numerical example see example 5.1 and Figure 5.3 below. The $N_i^{-1}(Q_i(t))$ are then joined to a single n-variate distribution M_n by applying the correlation structure of the multivariate normal distribution with correlation matrix ρ_M. The probability of n correlated defaults at time t is given by M_n.

We will now look at the Gaussian copula in an example.

Example 5.1: Let's assume we have two companies, B and Caa, with their estimated default probabilities for years 1 to 10 as displayed in Table 5.1.

Table 5.1 Default probability and cumulative default probability of companies B and Caa

Default time t	Company B Default Probability	Company B Cumulative Default Probability $Q_B(t)$	Company Caa Default Probability	Company Caa Cumulative Default Probability $Q_{Caa}(t)$
1	6.51%	6.51%	23.83%	23.83%
2	7.65%	14.16%	13.29%	37.12%
3	6.87%	21.03%	10.31%	47.43%
4	6.01%	27.04%	7.62%	55.05%
5	5.27%	32.31%	5.04%	60.09%
6	4.42%	36.73%	5.13%	65.22%
7	4.24%	40.97%	4.04%	69.26%
8	3.36%	44.33%	4.62%	73.88%
9	2.84%	47.17%	2.62%	76.50%
10	2.84%	50.01%	2.04%	78.54%

Default probabilities for investment-grade companies typically increase in time, since uncertainty increases with time. However, in Table 5.1 both companies are in distress. For these companies the next years are the most difficult. If they survive these next years, their default probability decreases.

Let's now find the joint default probabilities of the companies B

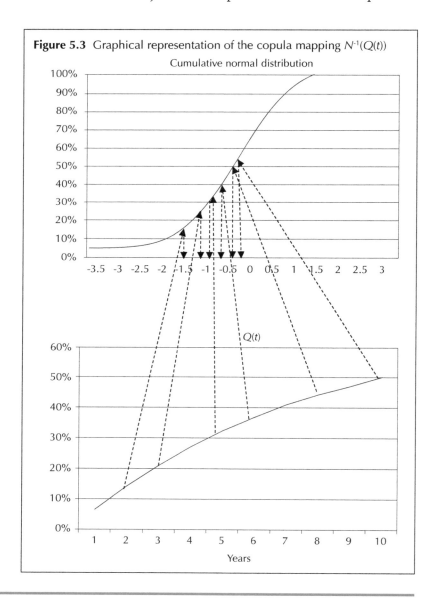

Figure 5.3 Graphical representation of the copula mapping $N^{-1}(Q(t))$

and Caa for any time t with the Gaussian copula function (5.12). First, we map the cumulative default probabilities $Q(t)$, which are in columns 3 and 5 in Table 5.1, to the standard normal distribution via $N^{-1}(Q(T))$. Computationally, this can be done with =normsinv(Q(t)) in Excel or norminv($Q(t)$) in MATLAB. Graphically the mapping can be represented in two steps, which are displayed in Figure 5.3. In the lower graph of Figure 5.3, the cumulative default probability of asset B, $Q_B(t)$, is displayed. We first map these cumulative probabilities percentile to percentile to a cumulative standard normal distribution in the upper graphs of Figure 5.2 (up arrows). In a second step the abscise (x-axis) values of the cumulative normal distribution are found (down arrows).

The same mapping procedure is done for company Caa, ie, the cumulative default probabilities of company Caa, which are displayed in Table 5.1 in column 5 are mapped percentile to percentile to a cumulative standard normal distribution via $N^{-1}(Q_{Caa}(t))$.

We have now derived the percentile to percentile mapped cumulative default probability values of our companies to a cumulative standard normal distribution. These values are displayed in Table 5.2, columns 3 and 5.

We can now use the derived and apply them to equation (5.12).

Table 5.2 Cumulative default probabilities mapped percentile to percentile to standard normal. For example, using Excel, the value –1.5133 is derived using =normsinv(0.0651)= –1.5133

Default time t	Company B Cumulative Default Probability $Q_B(t)$	Company B Cumulative Standard normal Percentiles $N^{-1}(Q_B(t))$	Company Caa Cumulative Default Probability $Q_{Caa}(t)$	Company Caa Cumulative Standard normal Percentiles $N^{-1}(Q_{Caa}(t))$
1	6.51%	–1.5133	23.83%	–0.7118
2	14.16%	–1.0732	37.12%	–0.3287
3	21.03%	–0.8054	47.43%	–0.0645
4	27.04%	–0.6116	55.05%	0.1269
5	32.31%	–0.4590	60.09%	0.2557
6	36.73%	–0.3390	65.22%	0.3913
7	40.97%	–0.2283	69.26%	0.5032
8	44.33%	–0.1426	73.88%	0.6397
9	47.17%	–0.0710	76.50%	0.7225
10	50.01%	0.0003	78.54%	0.7906

Since we have only $n = 2$ companies B and Caa in our example, equation (5.12) reduces to

$$M_2\left[N^{-1}(Q_B(t)), N^{-1}(Q_{Caa}(t)); \rho\right] \quad (5.13)$$

From equation (5.13) we see that since we have only two assets in our example, we have only one correlation coefficient ρ, not a correlation matrix ρ_M.

Importantly, the copula model now assumes that we can apply the correlation structure ρ_M or ρ of the multivariate distribution (in our case the Gaussian multivariate distribution M), to the transformed marginal distributions $N^{-1}(Q_B(t))$ and $N^{-1}(Q_{Caa}(t))$. This is done for mathematical and computational convenience.

The bivariate normal distribution M_2 is displayed in Figure 5.4.

The code for the bivariate cumulative normal distribution M can be found on the Internet. It is also displayed at www.dersoft.com/2assetdefaulttimecopula.xlsm in Module 1.

We now have all necessary ingredients to find the joint default probabilities of our companies B and Caa. For example, we can answer the question: what is the joint default probability Q of companies B and Caa in the next year assuming a one-year Gaussian default correlation of 0.4? The solution is

$$Q(t_b \leq 1 \cap t_{Caa} \leq 1) \equiv M(x_B \leq -1.5133 \cap x_{Caa} \leq -0.7118, \rho = 0.4) = 3.44\% \quad (5.14)$$

where t_B is the default time of company B and t_{Caa} is the default time of company Caa. x_B and x_{Caa} are the mapped abscise values of the bivariate normal distribution, which are derived from Table 5.2.

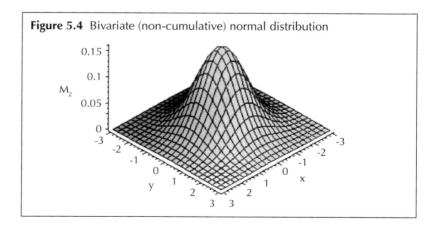

Figure 5.4 Bivariate (non-cumulative) normal distribution

In another example, we can answer the question: what is the joint probability of company B defaulting in year 3 and company Caa defaulting in year 5? It is

$$Q(t_B \leq 3 \cap t_{Caa} \leq 5) \equiv M(x_B \leq -0.8054 \cap x_{Caa} \leq 0.2557, \rho = 0.4) = 16.93\% \quad (5.15)$$

Equations (5.14) and (5.15) show why this type of copula is also called "default-time copula". We are correlating the default times of two or more assets t_i. A spreadsheet that correlates the default times of two assets can be found at www.dersoft.com/2assetdefaulttimecopula.xlsm. The numerical value of 3.44% of equation (5.14) is in cell Q17.

Simulating the correlated default time for multiple assets

The preceding example considers only two assets. We will now find the default time for an asset that is correlated to the default times of all other assets in a portfolio using the Gaussian copula. To derive the default time τ of asset i, τ_i, which is correlated to the default times of all other assets $i = 1, \ldots, n$, we first derive a sample $M_n(\cdot)$ from a multivariate copula (r.h.s. of equation (5.13) in the Gaussian case), $M_n(\cdot) \in [0, 1]$. This is done via Cholesky decomposition, which is explained in Appendix A1 of this chapter. The sample includes the default correlation via the default correlation matrix ρ_M of the n-variate standard normal distribution M_n. An example of a default correlation matrix was displayed in Chapter 1 in Table 1.3. We equate the sample $(\cdot)$ from M_n, $M_n(\cdot)$ with the cumulative individual default probability Q of asset i at time τ, $Q_i(\tau_i)$. Therefore,

$$M_n(\cdot) = Q_i(\tau_i) \text{ or} \quad (5.16)$$

$$\tau_i = Q_i^{-1}(M_n(\cdot)) \quad (5.17)$$

There is no closed-form solution for equation (5.16) or (5.17). To find the solution, we first take the sample $M_n(\cdot)$ and use equation (5.16) to equate it to $Q_i(\tau_i)$. This can be done with a search procedure such as Newton–Raphson. We can also use a simple lookup function in Excel.

Let's assume the random drawing from $M_n(\cdot)$ was 35%. We now equate 35% with the market-given function $Q_i(\tau_i)$ and find the expected default time of asset i, τ_i. This is displayed in Figure 5.5, where $\tau_i = 5.5$ years. We repeat this procedure numerous times, for

Figure 5.5 Finding the default time τ of 5.5 years from equation (5.16) for a random sample of the n-variate normal distribution $M_n(\cdot)$ of 35%

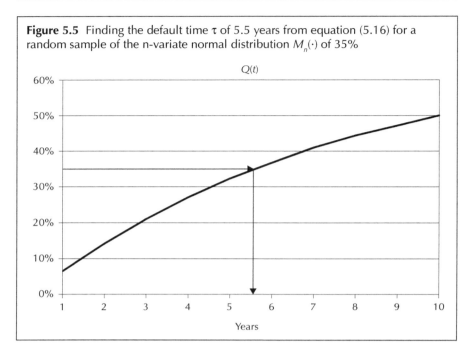

example 100,000 times and average each τ_i of every simulation to find our estimate for τ_i. Importantly, the estimated default time of asset i, τ_i, includes the default correlation with the other assets in the portfolio, since the correlation matrix is an input of the n-variate standard normal distribution M_n.

Finding the correlated default time in a continuous time framework using survival probabilities

In the idealised intensity model framework, we admit a continuous exponential default intensity function $\lambda_i(t)$. The default intensity for entity i is the default probability of entity i for a future time period, assuming the default of the entity i has not occurred until the beginning of the future period. For example, the default intensity from the end of year 6 to the end of year 7 (the 7th year), is the default probability for that time period, conditional on no default until the end of year 6. The default intensity from the end of year 6 to the end of year 7 is higher than the forward default probability for that time period, since when standing at the end of year 6, defaulting in year 7 is higher. Let's look at a numerical example.

Example 5.2: The 6-year default probability Q_6 of entity i is 36.73% and the 7-year default probability Q_7 of entity i is 40.97%. What is forward default probability in year 7 and what is the default intensity in year 7? The forward default probability, which is viewed today at time 0, is

$$q(0)_{6,7} = Q(7) - Q(6) = 40.97\% - 36.73\% = 4.24\%.$$

The forward default intensity, viewed at the end of time 6, is

$$\lambda(6)_{6,7} = (Q_7 - Q_6) / (1 - Q_6) = 40.97\% - 36.73\% / (1 - 36.73\%) = 6.70\%.$$

$(1-Q_6)$ represents the survival probability until the end of year 6.

We can find the probability of survival of entity i until t, $\Pr[\tau_i > t]$ as the area under the given default intensity function for which the default time τ_i is bigger than t. This is displayed in Figure 5.6.

The default intensity function in Figure 5.6 is similar to the default probability curve of our bond B in Table 5.1 in column 2. However, default intensity functions can have different shapes. For investment-grade bonds, they typically increase in time, since uncertainty and therefore default probabilities increase in time. Formally, we can express the survival probability $\Pr[\tau_i > t]$ in Figure 5.6 as

$$\Pr[\tau_i > t] = \exp\left\{-\int_0^{\tau_i} \lambda_i(t)dt\right\} \tag{5.18}$$

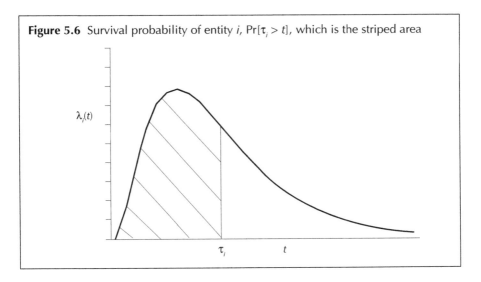

Figure 5.6 Survival probability of entity i, $\Pr[\tau_i > t]$, which is the striped area

where τ_i is the default time of asset i, which we are looking for. In equation (5.18) we are "discounting" with the default intensity λ_i to find the survival probability. This methodology was derived by Lando (1998), and Duffie and Singleton (1999). They found that the present value of a risky claim (as a risky bond) can be derived by discounting with the default-adjusted rate. For example, if a Treasury bond is discounted with the risk-free rate r, a risky bond can be discounted with $r + s$, where s is the credit spread (see Lando (1998) and Duffie and Singleton (1990) for details).

To find τ_i, we first draw a random sample $(\cdot)$ from the n-variate standard normal distribution (M_n), $(M_n(\cdot))$. We then equate the survival probability with the barrier $M_n(\cdot)$, ie,

$$\exp\left\{-\int_0^{\tau_i} \lambda_i(t)dt\right\} = M_n(\cdot) \qquad (5.19)$$

or

$$\int_0^{\tau_i} \lambda_i(t)dt = -\ln\left[M_n(\cdot)\right] \qquad (5.20)$$

and solve numerically for τ_i. In the case of a constant default intensity λ_i, equation (5.20) simplifies and we find the correlated default time closed form as

$$\tau_i = \frac{-\ln\left[M_n(\cdot)\right]}{\lambda_i} \qquad (5.21)$$

Importantly, the derived default time of entity i, τ_i, is correlated to the default times of the other assets in the portfolio, since the barrier $M_n(\cdot)$ includes the default correlation via the default correlation matrix of $M_{n,}\rho_M$ (see equation (5.11)).

Copula applications

There are numerous applications of copula functions in finance.

1. One prominent copula application is the valuing of structured products such as CDOs. We will devote the whole next chapter on the topic of valuing CDOs with copulas.
2. A further prominent application of the multivariate Gaussian copula is the modelling of credit-rating changes by CreditMetrics. First, a copula dependence coefficient is derived for all asset pairs. This is often derived from equity correlation. A correlated sample from the bivariate copula

equation (5.13) is then derived. The sample is then compared to the historical rating percentile to determine whether a rating change occurs. Monte Carlo simulation is conducted to derive the entire rating distribution. This approach has to be applied to all company pairs in question. Hence it is computationally quite intensive. For details see Finger (2009).
3. Copulas are also popular tools to model CDSs with counterparty risk. Typically the bivariate Gaussian copula is applied to model the default correlation between the CDS seller and the reference asset; see Kim and Kim (2003), Hamp *et al* (2007) and Brigo and Chourdakis (2008).
4. Recently, copula functions have also been applied outside the credit-risk framework. Copulas have been applied to constant maturity spread options, foreign-exchange cross options and basket options; see Au (2005). Outside of finance, copulas are applied in civil engineering, meteorology and medicine.

Limitations of the Gaussian copula

As with any model, the Gaussian Copula has limitations with respect to its application to financial reality. The main limitations are tail dependence, calibration and risk management. Let us deal with each in turn.

Tail dependence
In a crisis, correlations typically increase, as studies by Das *et al* (2007) and Duffie *et al* (2009) show, and as we derived in Figure 1.3 in Chapter 1 and in the empirical Chapter 2. Hence, it would be desirable to apply a correlation model with high co-movements in the lower tail of the joint distribution. Following the tail-dependence definition of Joe (1999), a bivariate copula has lower tail dependence if

$$\lim_{y_1 \downarrow 0, y_2 \downarrow 0} P\left[\left(\tau_1 < N_1^{-1}(y_1)\right) | \left(\tau_2 < N_2^{-1}(y_2)\right)\right] > 0 \qquad (5.22)$$

where τ_i is the default time of asset i, y_i is the marginal distribution of asset i, and N^{-1} is the inverse of the standard normal distribution. Equation (5.22) reads: if the functions y_1 and y_2 both approach 0 from above, tail dependence exists if the following holds: the

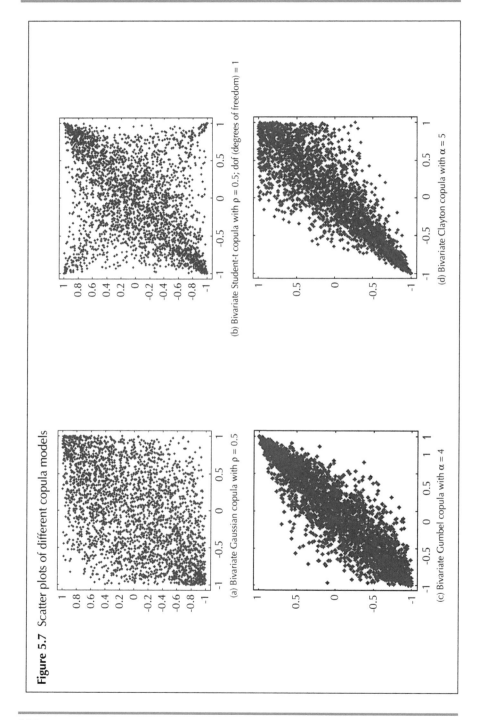

Figure 5.7 Scatter plots of different copula models

probability of τ_1 being smaller than $N_1^{-1}(y_1)$, given that τ_2 is smaller than $N_2^{-1}(y_2)$, is bigger than 0. However, it can be easily shown that the Gaussian copula has no tail dependence for any correlation parameter ρ: $\lim_{y_1 \downarrow 0, y_2 \downarrow 0} P\left[\left(\tau_1 < N_1^{-1}(y_1)\right) | \left(\tau_2 < N_2^{-1}(y_2)\right)\right] = 0, \rho \in \{-1, 1\}$. In contrast, the student-t copula, equation (5.10) with F_n being the n-variate student-t distribution and F^{-1} being the inverse of F, satisfies equation (5.22) for any $\rho \in \{-1, 1\}$. Hence it may be more desirable to apply the student-t copula in financial-crisis modelling. Figure 5.7 (a) to (d) shows several copula scatterplots.

As seen in Figure (c), the Gumbel copula exhibits high tail dependence especially for negative co-movements. Since correlations typically increase when asset prices decrease, as we verified in Chapter 2, the Gumbel copula might also be a good correlation approach for financial modelling.

Calibration

A further criticism of the Gaussian copula is the difficulty to calibrate it to market prices. In practice, typically a single correlation parameter (not a correlation matrix) is used to model the default correlation between any two entities in a CDO; see Chapter 6 for details. Conceptually, this correlation parameter should be the same for the entire CDO portfolio. However, traders randomly alter the correlation parameter for different tranches in order to derive desired tranche spreads. Traders increase the correlation for "extreme" tranches such as the equity tranche or senior tranches, referred to as the correlation smile. This is similar to the often-cited implied-volatility smile in the Black–Scholes–Merton model. Here traders increase the implied volatility especially for out-of-the money puts, but also for out-of-the money calls to increase the option price. We will discuss this limitation further in Chapter 6.

Another criticism of the Gaussian copula is that for certain parameter constellations it may not be possible to imply a market CDO tranche spread for a correlation parameter between 0 and 1. Kherraz (2006) tests the LHP (large homogeneous portfolio) version of the Gaussian copula (see Chapters 6 and 7) and finds that the lowest 40% and highest 20% of losses of the equity tranche cannot be explained by the model. However, Kherraz uses a fairly high default probability of 40% in his study and does not mention the frequency or timing of the occurrence. Finger (2009) tests the calibration of the LHP model with base correlation, a correlation with zero attachment point, which is bootstrapped from the implied correlation; see JP Morgan 2004 for details on base correlation. Finger finds calibration failures for just 20 days for the iTraxx and 21 days for the CDX indices before July 2007. He finds no calibration failures after July 2007.

Several other studies, such as Hull and White (2004), Andersen and Sidenius (2004) and Burtschell *et al* (2008) test the one-factor Gaussian copula as well as other copulas such as Marshall–Olkin, Clayton or double-t. None of the studies finds any calibration failures for these copulas.

Risk management
A further criticism of the Copula approach is that the copula model is static and consequently allows only limited risk management (see Finger (2009) and Donnelly and Embrechts (2010)). The original copula models of Vasicek (1987) and Li (2000) and several extensions of the model such as Hull and White (2004) and Gregory and Laurent (2004) do have a one-period time horizon, ie, are static. In particular, there is no stochastic process for the critical underlying variables' default intensity and default correlation. However, even in these early copula formulations, back testing and stress testing the variables for different time horizons can give valuable sensitivities; see Whetten and Adelson (2004) and Meissner *et al* (2008b).

In addition, the copula variables can be made a function of time as in Hull *et al* (2006). However, this still does not create a fully dynamic stochastic process with drift and noise, which allows flexible hedging and risk management.

In the following we will discuss a further bottom-up financial correlation model, the contagion-correlation approach.

CONTAGION-CORRELATION MODELS

The basic idea in contagion-correlation modelling is that the default intensity of an entity is a function of the default of another entity. Hence contagion default modelling incorporates counterparty risk, ie, the direct impact of a defaulting entity on the default intensity of another entity.

Contagion default modelling was pioneered by Davis and Lo

(1999 and 2001) and Jarrow and Yu (2001). Davis and Lo model the latent variable Z of entity i, Z_i with equation

$$Z_i = X_i + (1-X_i)\left(1-\prod_{\substack{i=1\\i\ne j}}^{n}(1-X_j K_{ij})\right) \qquad (5.23)$$

where

Z_i: binomial default indicator variable of entity i
X_i and X_j: Bernoulli random variable[2] of entity i and j, respectively
K_{ij}: contagion variable, ie, the degree of with the default of j impacts on the default intensity of entity i.

Let's understand equation (5.23). Z_i is a binomial default indicator variable of entity i. This means if $Z_i = 1$, entity i defaults, and $Z_i = 0$, entity i survives. Entity i can default "directly", when it is not being affected by entity j. In this case the Bernoulli random variable $X_i = 1$. Entity i can also default indirectly, ie, when it is affected by the default of entity j. In this case, the Bernoulli random variable $X_j = 1$. The degree of infection is modelled with the Bernoulli random "contagion variable" K_{ij}. Formally

$$\Pr(X_i = 1) = p$$
$$\Pr(X_j = 1) = q \qquad (5.24)$$
$$\Pr(K_{ij} = 1) = r$$

where p, q and r and input parameters which are $\in [0, 1]$. In a dynamic setting, the persistence of the contagion variable K_{ij} may be modelled as an exponentially decreasing function of time t. A parameter $g(t)$ (gravity) determines the degree of decreasing contagion in t, ie, $K_{ij}(t) = e^{-g(t)t}$ where $g(t) > 0$ and $\partial g / \partial t < 0$.

Jarrow and Yu (2001) introduce default intensity contagion with a set of linear equations

$$\lambda_A(t) = a_1 + a_2 \mathbf{1}_{\{\tau_B \le 1\}} \qquad (5.25)$$

$$\lambda_B(t) = b_1 + b_2 \mathbf{1}_{\{\tau_A \le 1\}} \qquad (5.26)$$

where λ_X is the default probability of X and a_1, a_2, b_1 and b_2 are parameters, which are bigger than zero and have to be calibrated. τ_X is the default time of entity X. In equation (5.25) **1** is an indicator variable. 1 takes the value 1 if the default time of entity B, τ_B, is smaller than a certain time t. We can simulate τ_B randomly, for example with a copula model, which we have done in equations (5.14) or (5.17). Multiple sampling will result in many outcomes of the experiment $\tau_B \leq t$. For example, if 10% of the outcomes are that $\tau_B \leq t$, then the probability of $\tau_B \leq t$, ie, the probability of the entity B defaulting before t, is 10%. From equation (5.25) we see that the higher the probability of $1_{\{\tau_B \leq t\}}$, the higher the default probability of A, λ_A. The same logic applies to equation (5.26).

Introducing symmetric contagion among all entities creates the problem of circularity, which Jarrow and Yu (2001) call "looping defaults". In this case, the construction of a joint distribution is rather complex. Jarrow and Yu solve the problem by introducing the concept of "asymmetric dependence", ie, the default of primary entities impacts on the default intensity of secondary entities, but not vice versa. In this case, the joint default distribution conveniently becomes the product of the individual primary default times.

Contagion-correlation modelling can be combined with CID (conditionally independent default) correlation modelling. These combinations are discussed in Chapter 7.

SUMMARY

In this chapter, we evaluated correlation approaches, which were especially designed to model financial correlations. We concentrated on "bottom-up" approaches, which collect information, quantify it and then aggregate the information to derive an overall correlation result.

One of the most widely applied correlation concepts is correlating Brownian motions, introduced by Steven Heston (1993). In the Heston model the Brownian motions of two variables are correlated with a simple equation. The model was originally designed to replicate the negative correlation between stock returns and volatility. However, the model has been applied to other financial relationships such as stochastic interest rates and stochastic volatility, as in the popular SABR (stochastic alpha beta rho) model, to stochastic interest rates and stochastic default intensities and many more. Altogether the Heston approach is mathematically rigorous, dynamic, and flexible. Therefore it is one of the most valuable and applied correlation models in finance.

The binomial correlation model of Douglas Lucas (1995) models by design binomial events, for example default or no default. The binomial model is a special limiting case of the Pearson correlation model. Whereas in the Pearson model the inputs are sets of variables, in the binomial model the inputs are scalars. Since the binomial correlation model is a special case of the Pearson correlation model, the significant shortcomings of the Pearson correlation approach for financial modelling also apply to the binomial correlation model.

Copula correlations were first enthusiastically embraced, but then fell into disgrace when the global financial crisis hit in 2007. Copulas go back to Abe Sklar in 1959 and were introduced to finance by Oldrich Vasicek (1987) and David Li (2000). Copula functions simplify statistical problems. They allow the joining of multiple univariate distributions to a single multivariate distribution. In this way copulas can evaluate n correlation functions with a single, although n-dimensional function. Many different types of copulas and extensions exist. The Gaussian copula is the most popular one due to its simplicity and convenient programming.

The bottom line is that copulas are rigorous statistical approaches that can have value in finance. However, severe limitations of copulas for finance exist: (1) most copulas, especially the Gaussian copula, have low tail dependence; (2) calibration to market prices is problematic, especially for one-factor copulas; (3) copulas are principally static. However, they can be extended to be dynamic such as in Hull and White (2006) and Albanese *et al* (2010).

Contagion-correlation modelling, pioneered by Davis and Lo (1999 and 2001) and Jarrow and Yu (2001), is based on the idea that the default of one entity impacts the default intensity of another. The degree of the impact can be modelled with an exponentially decreasing function of time. However, introducing symmetric contagion among all entities creates the problem of circularity. In this case, the construction of a joint distribution is rather complex. One solution is to model "asymmetric dependence", ie, the default of primary entities impacts on the default intensity of secondary entities, but not vice versa.

Questions for Chapter 5

Answers to these questions can be found at the end of this book.

1. The original Heston (1993) model correlates the Brownian motion of which two financial variables? What is the most significant result of the original Heston model?
2. To create negative correlation between asset 1 and asset 2 in the Heston (1993) model, what value does the correlation coefficient α take in equation $dz_1(t) = \alpha dz_2(t) + \sqrt{1-\alpha^2} dz_3(t)$?
3. The Heston model is one of the most widely applied correlation models in finance. Why?
4. What is the difference between the Pearson correlation model and the binomial correlation model of Lucas (1995)?
5. What are the limitations of the binomial correlation model of Lucas (1995)?
6. What is the basic principle of the copula correlation model?
7. Why is the Gaussian copula model the most popular copula model in finance?
8. What does "In the copula mapping process, the marginal distribution are preserved" mean?
9. Given are the marginal default probabilities 5% for asset 1 and 7% for asset 2. If the Gaussian correlation coefficient is 0.3, what is the joint probability of default in year 1, assuming asset 1 and asset 2 are jointly bivariately distributed?
10. Given are the five-year default probability of entity i of 40% and the six-year default probability of entity i of 45%. What is forward default probability in year 6 and what is the default intensity in year 6?
11. What are the limitations of the Gaussian copula for financial applications?
12. Since the Gaussian copula has low tail dependence, which other copulas seem more suitable to model financial correlations?

13. Can the Copula model be blamed for the great recession 2007 to 2009?
14. What is the basic idea in contagion-correlation models?
15. Name the limitations of contagion models!
16. Derive correlated samples x_1, x_2 and x_3 from a multivariate standard normal distribution, which are correlated by the matrix

$$\Sigma = \begin{bmatrix} 1 & 0.2 & 0.3 \\ 0.2 & 1 & 0.4 \\ 0.3 & 0.4 & 1 \end{bmatrix}$$

applying Cholesky decomposition (see Appendix A2 for details).

APPENDIX 5.1: CHOLESKY DECOMPOSITION

The Gaussian copula model creates a multidimensional normal distribution from standard normal marginal distributions. Monte Carlo simulations derive samples from the distribution, which are compared with the default threshold. The standard procedure to derive correlated samples from a multivariate normal distribution is Cholesky decomposition. We will outline the method here.

Given is the n-dimensional correlation matrix Σ.[3]

$$\Sigma = \begin{bmatrix} c_{11} & c_{11} & \cdots & c_{1n} \\ c_{21} & c_{22} & \cdots & c_{2n} \\ \cdot & \cdot & & \cdot \\ c_{n1} & c_{n2} & \cdots & c_{nn} \end{bmatrix}$$

We decompose Σ into $\Sigma = M\,M^T$, where M is a special symmetric, positive definite, lower triangular matrix, and M^T is the transpose of M:[4]

$$\begin{bmatrix} c_{11} & c_{12} & \cdots & c_{1n} \\ c_{21} & c_{22} & \cdots & c_{2n} \\ \cdot & \cdot & & \cdot \\ c_{n1} & c_{n2} & \cdots & c_{nn} \end{bmatrix} = \begin{bmatrix} m_{11} & 0 & \cdots & 0 \\ m_{21} & m_{22} & \cdots & 0 \\ \cdot & \cdot & & \cdot \\ m_{n1} & m_{n2} & \cdots & m_{nn} \end{bmatrix} \times \begin{bmatrix} m_{11} & m_{12} & \cdots & m_{nn} \\ 0 & m_{22} & \cdots & m_{2n} \\ \cdot & \cdot & & \cdot \\ 0 & 0 & \cdots & m_{nn} \end{bmatrix}$$

From the decomposed matrix, we can find equations for m_{ij} (see Example A1 below). We then generate uncorrelated random samples from a standard normal distribution ε, (ε = normsinv(rand()) in Excel and norminv(rand) in MATLAB) and find correlated random values x_i from $x_i = M\varepsilon_i$.

Let's look at an example of Cholesky decomposition for three assets:

Example A1: Given is the correlation matrix Σ, which we decompose into $\Sigma = M\, M^T$,

$$\begin{bmatrix} c_{11} & c_{12} & c_{13} \\ c_{21} & c_{22} & c_{23} \\ c_{31} & c_{32} & c_{33} \end{bmatrix} = \begin{bmatrix} m_{11} & 0 & 0 \\ m_{21} & m_{22} & 0 \\ m_{31} & m_{32} & m_{33} \end{bmatrix} \times \begin{bmatrix} m_{11} & m_{21} & m_{31} \\ 0 & m_{22} & m_{32} \\ 0 & 0 & m_{33} \end{bmatrix}$$

We can find the equations for m_{ij} from matrix multiplication:

$c_{11} = m_{11} \times m_{11} \rightarrow m_{11} = \sqrt{c_{11}}$

$c_{21} = m_{21} \times m_{11} \rightarrow m_{21} = c_{21} / m_{11}$

$c_{22} = m_{21} \times m_{21} + m_{22} \times m_{22} \rightarrow m_{22} = \sqrt{c_{22} - (m_{21})^2}$

$c_{31} = m_{31} \times m_{11} \rightarrow m_{31} = c_{31} / m_{11}$

$c_{32} = m_{31} \times m_{21} + m_{32} \times m_{22} \rightarrow m_{32} = (c_{32} - m_{31} \times m_{21}) / m_{22}$

$c_{33} = m_{31} \times m_{31} + m_{32} \times m_{32} + m_{33} \times m_{33} = \rightarrow m_{33} = \sqrt{c_{33} - (m_{31})^2 - (m_{32})^2}$

We now generate uncorrelated random samples from a standard normal distribution ε, (ε = normsinv(rand()) in Excel) and find correlated random values x_i from $x_i = M\varepsilon_i$

$$\begin{bmatrix} x_1 \\ x_2 \\ x_3 \end{bmatrix} = \begin{bmatrix} m_{11} & 0 & 0 \\ m_{21} & m_{22} & 0 \\ m_{31} & m_{32} & m_{33} \end{bmatrix} \times \begin{bmatrix} \varepsilon_1 \\ \varepsilon_2 \\ \varepsilon_3 \end{bmatrix}$$

Hence, the values for the three correlated random samples x_i are

$x_1 = m_{11} \times \varepsilon_1$
$x_2 = m_{21} \times \varepsilon_1 + m_{22} \times \varepsilon_2$
$x_3 = m_{31} \times \varepsilon_1 + m_{32} \times \varepsilon_2 + m_{33} \times \varepsilon_3$

We can now apply Monte Carlo simulation, ie, simulate the equations for x_i multiple times to derive robust values for the x_i.

A numerical example of Cholesky decomposition can be found at www.dersoft.com/matrixprimer.xlsx sheet "Cholesky Decomposition".

Try to solve the numerical Cholesky decomposition problem 16 above.

APPENDIX 5.2: A SHORT PROOF OF THE GAUSSIAN DEFAULT TIME COPULA

Given are the cumulative default probabilities Q of entities $i = A, B, \ldots, n$ at various times t, $Q_i(t_i)$. There exists a copula function C

$$C\left[Q_A(t_A), Q_B(t_B), \ldots, Q_n(t_n)\right] = M_n(t_A, t_B, \ldots, t_n) \qquad (5A.1)$$

where M_n is an n-dimensional Gaussian distribution function.
Proof:
Let R_i, $i = A, B, \ldots, n$ be a uniform random variable. We define

$$\Pr\left[R_A \leq Q_A(t_A), R_B \leq Q_B(t_B), \ldots, R_n \leq Q_n(t_n)\right] \qquad (5A.2)$$

Applying $R_i \leq Q_i(t_i) = Q_i^{-1}(R_i) \leq t_i$ to equation (5.A2), we derive

$$\Pr\left[Q_A^{-1}(R_A) \leq t_A, Q_B^{-1}(R_B) \leq t_B, \ldots, Q_n^{-1}(R_n) \leq t_n\right] \qquad (5A.3)$$

Let T_i be the abscise value of the default distribution $Q_i^{-1}(R_i)$. Hence

$$\Pr\left[T_A \leq t_A, T_A \leq t_B, \ldots, T_n \leq t_n\right] \qquad (5A.4)$$

For the n-dimensional Gaussian distribution M_n, equation (5A.4) is

$$M_n(t_A, t_B, \ldots, t_n)$$

---

1 Strictly speaking, only the bivariate Gaussian copula is a one-parameter copula, the parameter being the copula correlation coefficient. A multivariate Gaussian copula may incorporate a correlation *matrix*, containing various correlation coefficients.
2 A Bernoulli random variable can take values of 0 and 1 with certain probabilities for each value. See http://mathworld.wolfram.com/BernoulliDistribution.html for details.
3 The reader may study some basic matrix algebra at www.dersoft.com/matrixprimer.xlsx.
4 The matrix transpose A^T is the matrix obtained by exchanging A's rows and columns. Hence if we have a matrix

$$A = \begin{bmatrix} a_{11} & a_{12} \\ a_{21} & a_{22} \end{bmatrix}$$

it follows that

$$A^T = \begin{bmatrix} a_{11} & a_{21} \\ a_{12} & a_{22} \end{bmatrix}$$

See also, www.dersoft.com/matrixprimer.xlsx sheet, "Matrix Transpose".

6

Valuing CDOs with the Gaussian Copula – What Went Wrong?

"Take risks: if you win, you will be happy; if you lose, you will be wise"

– author unknown

When the global financial crisis hit from 2007 to 2009, the Gaussian copula was widely blamed for the crisis, especially when applied to valuing collateralised debt obligations (CDOs).[1] In this chapter we analyse the pricing methodology of CDOs and evaluate whether the Gaussian copula is to blame. Let's first look at some CDO basics.

CDO BASICS – WHAT IS A CDO? WHY CDOS? TYPES OF CDOS
What is a CDO?
A CDO (collateralised debt obligation) is a financial structure in which the credit risk from a pool of securities is transferred from one counterparty, the originating bank, to another, the investor. The investor can invest money in different CDO tranches. Each tranche has a different degree of credit risk. The credit risk is distributed with a waterfall principle: if losses accumulate and the detachment level of a tranche is breached, additional credit losses flow into the adjacent higher tranche. A CDO is typically arranged by an SPV (special-purpose vehicle), which is AAA-rated to minimise counterparty credit risk.

Why CDOs?
There are three main parties in a CDO:

1. the originator (or protection buyer), who transfers the credit risk;

2. the investor, who assumes the credit risk; and
3. the SPV who manages to CDO (see Figures 6.2 and 6.3).

The motivation for the originator is naturally to transfer the credit risk, which improves their credit rating, frees credit lines, reduces regulatory capital and lowers funding cost. The motivation for the investor is to receive high yields. The motivation for the SPV is fee income.

CDOs include several sound financial properties: diversification, subordination and overcollateralisation.

Diversification: since typically 125 assets are in a CDO, a skilled originator will choose assets with a low correlation to achieve high diversification benefits (see Chapter 1, "Investments and correlation").

Subordination: this means that mezzanine and higher tranches are protected by lower tranches, since lower tranches absorb default losses from the underlying basket of credits first.

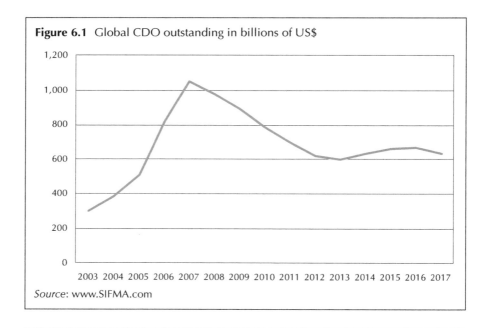

Figure 6.1 Global CDO outstanding in billions of US$

Source: www.SIFMA.com

Overcollateralisation: typically, the assets in a CDO have a higher value than the liabilities that the SPV owes to the investors. This overcollateralisation adds an additional element of protection for investors.

The drawback of CDOs lies in their relative pricing complexity. We have to find the default probability function with respect to time of 125 assets for the duration of the CDO which can be up to 10 years. This alone is difficult to estimate. Furthermore, we have to correlate the default functions of the 125 assets! This is where the copula function comes in.

First, let's have a look at where the CDO market is today.

From Figure 6.1 we observe that the CDO market peaked in 2007 and basically plateaued from 2012 to 2017.

Types of CDOs

There are three main types of CDOs, which are displayed in Figure 6.2.

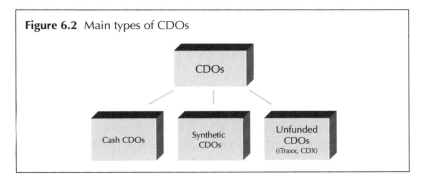

Figure 6.2 Main types of CDOs

In a cash CDO, the originating bank sells assets to the SPV, which then creates tranches. Each tranche is exposed to a certain degree of default risk. The first losses from asset defaults flow into the equity tranche. Further losses flow into the next higher mezzanine tranche and so on. Figure 6.3 shows the cashflows of a typical Cash CDO.

In a synthetic CDO, displayed in Figure 6.4, assets are not sold from the originating bank to the SPV, but the SPV assumes the credit risk via selling CDSs (credit default swaps). The SPV receives the CDS spreads from the originating bank and the cash from the investor, and invests these cashflows into risk-free assets, as seen in Figure 6.4.

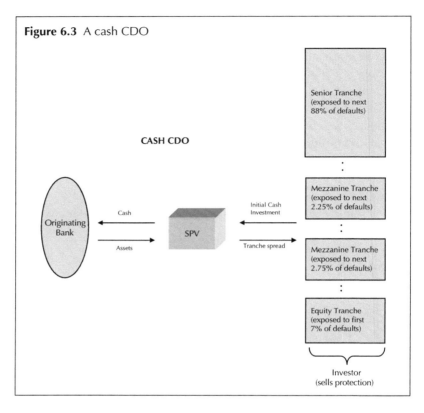

Figure 6.3 A cash CDO

A third type of CDO consists of unfunded CDOs such as the family of CDX indices or the iTraxx indices, also called credit-default-swap indices. The most popular CDX index is the CDX.NA.IG, which references 125 investment-grade CDSs in North America. The most popular iTraxx index is the iTraxx Europe, which references 125 investment-grade CDSs on that continent. Importantly, the CDX and iTraxx are unfunded, therefore no initial principal amount is exchanged between the buyer (investor) and the seller. Hence the trading of the CDX and iTraxx is similar to buying and selling futures contracts. The cashflows of an unfunded, tranched CDO is displayed in Figure 6.5.

VALUING CDOS

There are three main input factors when valuing a CDO:

1. the default probability of each of the 125 assets;

VALUING CDOS WITH THE GAUSSIAN COPULA – WHAT WENT WRONG?

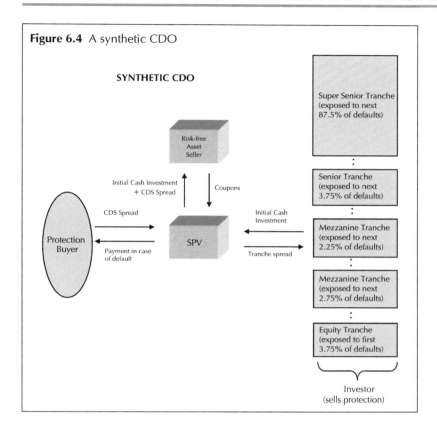

Figure 6.4 A synthetic CDO

2. the default correlation between the 125 assets in the portfolio; and
3. the recovery rate in case of default.

Let's discuss briefly how to derive the default probability function before we concentrate on the most significant element, the default correlation.

Deriving the default probability for each asset in a CDO

Most investment banks, hedge funds and SPVs use an extension of the seminal Merton 1974 model to derive the default probability for each asset in a CDO. Let's calculate this default probability.

In 1973, Fischer Black and Myron Scholes, and separately Robert Merton, created their famous Black–Scholes–Merton (BSM) option pricing model. The well-known equation for a call is

CORRELATION RISK MODELLING AND MANAGEMENT

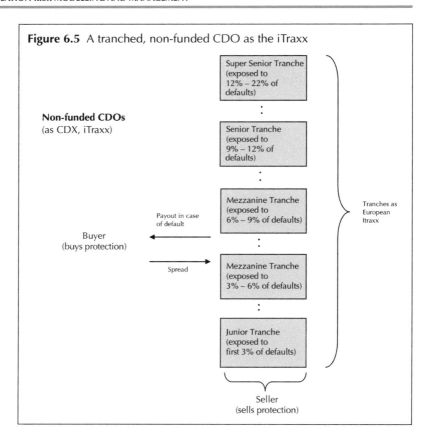

Figure 6.5 A tranched, non-funded CDO as the iTraxx

$$C = S_0 N(d_1) - Ke^{-rT} N(d_2) \qquad (6.1)$$

where

$$d_1 = \frac{\ln\left(\dfrac{S_0}{Ke^{-rT}}\right) + \left(r + \dfrac{\sigma^2}{2}\right)T}{\sigma\sqrt{T}}$$

and

$$d_2 = d_1 - \sigma\sqrt{T}$$

C: Call price
S_0: Current stock price
N: Cumulative standard normal distribution
K: Strike price
r: Continuously compounded risk-free interest rate,

T: Option maturity, measured in years
σ: Implied volatility of S

One year later, in 1974, Robert Merton transferred the option framework of equation (6.1) to corporate finance. He applied the equation Equity = Assets − Liabilities and argued that the equity value of a company has similar properties to a call: if the asset value of a company increases, equity increases with unlimited upside potential. In addition, the value of equity is asymmetric, since it can only go to zero. This is the case when the asset value drops below the debt value, which is the case of default. With this rational, Merton derived

$$E = V_0 N(d_1) - De^{-rT} N(d_2) \qquad (6.2)$$

with

$$d_1 = \frac{\ln\left(\dfrac{S_0}{De^{-rT}}\right) + \dfrac{\sigma^2}{2}T}{\sigma\sqrt{T}}$$

and

$$d_2 = d_1 - \sigma\sqrt{T}$$

where

V_0 : Current asset value of the company
D : Debt of the company
σ : Implied volatility of V
T : Time to maturity of debt D
Other variables defined as in equation (6.1)

Note that equations (6.1) and (6.2) are mathematically identical. Just the variables are redefined.

The asymmetric payoff of equity implies, as is the case with a call, that there is time value of equity, as seen in Figure 6.6., which outlines the relationship between a company's equity value and its asset value at a certain point in time before debt maturity. If we assume that the asset value grows with a certain rate r, we derive the probability of default as the probability of the asset value being smaller than the value of debt at debt maturity T, as seen in Figure 6.7.

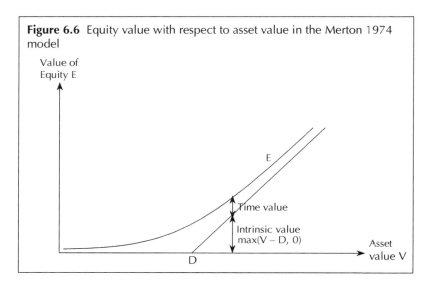

Figure 6.6 Equity value with respect to asset value in the Merton 1974 model

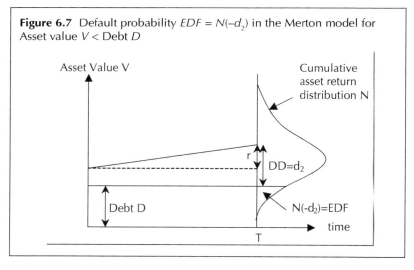

Figure 6.7 Default probability $EDF = N(-d_2)$ in the Merton model for Asset value $V <$ Debt D

In Figure 6.7, using Moody's–KMV's terminology, EDF is the expected default frequency, ie, the default probability, and DD is the distance to default, which is a representation of the risk-neutral d_2 of equation (6.2). DD is the difference between the expected asset value and debt value at debt maturity T. There is an inverse relationship between EDF and DD.

Importantly, in equation (6.1) the probability of exercising a call option at option maturity T is $\text{Prob}(S_T > K) = N(d_2)$. The probability of not exercising the call option is $1 - N(d_2) = N(-d_2)$. In analogy, the probability of the asset value V being smaller than the debt value D at time T, which means default at T, follows from the Merton 1974 model of equation (6.2) as $N(-d_2)$. Hence, the default probability in the Merton model is derived conveniently with a closed form solution as $N(-d_2)$.[2]

The ingenious Merton 1974 model outlines the principles of a company's default using structural properties such as asset and debt. The main limitations of the model are that only one form of debt D is modelled and that default can occur only at debt maturity T. Naturally, numerous extensions of the model have been created to bring the model in line with the complexities of reality. In particular, the following.

1. The first passage time models of Black and Cox 1976, Kim, Ramaswamy and Sundaresan (1993), Longstaff and Schwartz (1995) and Briys and de Varenne (1997) evaluate the default probability before debt maturity T by introducing an exogenous, continuous default barrier. Once the asset value falls below the barrier, default occurs. Hence the first time passage models effectively turn the European-style model of equation (6.2) into an American-style model.
2. The asset return does not grow with the risk-free rate r and is not assumed normally distributed at debt maturity T (see Figure 6.7). Instead a real-world historical asset growth rate and asset distribution is applied. For example, Moody's–KMV database contains 30 years of information on over 6,000 public and 150,000 private company default events.
3. The debt value is not considered constant as in Figure 6.7. Instead, empirical data is used to project a realistic increase or decrease in debt.
4. Other default criteria besides asset and debt values are taken into consideration, such as liquidity risk and systemic risk, as well as company-specific data such as product line, competition, quality of management, etc.

The Merton model, which we just discussed, is called a structural approach, since it uses the capital structure of the entity as inputs to derive the default probability. A different way to determine the default probability of an entity is the reduced-form approach. Here market prices such as bond prices or credit-default-swap prices are the inputs to derive the default probabilities; see Jarrow and Turnbull (1995), Jarrow, Lando and Turnbull (1997) and Duffie and Singleton (1999). The approach is called reduced form, since it does not apply the capital structure of an entity as inputs.

Let's now discuss the critical aspect of the Gaussian copula with respect to valuing CDOs.

Deriving the default correlation of the assets in a CDO

In the previous section, we derived the individual default probability λ of each asset i, λ_i, in the CDO. The probability of default of an asset λ_i is now mapped via

$$N^{-1}(\lambda_i) \qquad (6.3)$$

where N^{-1} is the inverse of a standard normal distribution (=normsinv(λ_i) in Excel, norminv(λ_i) in MATLAB). Equation (6.3) maps the default probabilities to a standard normal distribution. For example, if $\lambda_i = 5\%$, then $N^{-1}(0.05) = -1.645$, which is the x-axis value of the 5th percentile of a standard normal distribution.[3] This procedure allows a comparison of the default probabilities with samples from an n-variate normal asset distribution M_n.

We will now determine the default threshold. This is the value that, when breached, will constitute default of the entity or asset in question. To derive the threshold, typically the popular Gaussian copula model is applied. We slightly modify equation (5.12) and derive the default threshold as

$$M_n\left[N^{-1}(u_1),\dots,N^{-1}(u_n);\rho_M\right] \qquad (6.4)$$

M_n is the n-variate Gaussian distribution, N^{-1} is again the inverse of a standard normal distribution, and u_x is a uniform random vector $u_x \in [0,1]$, =rand() in Excel/VBA or randn() in MATLAB. ρ_M is the asset-correlation matrix. An example of a correlation matrix is shown in Table 6.1.

We now look at a certain timeframe t and derive the mapped default probability of asset i at time t, $N^{-1}(\lambda_{i,t})$, following equation

(6.3). We also derive M_n in equation (6.4) for a certain time t, $M_{n,t}$, and then derive a sample $M_{n,t}(.)$ using Cholesky decomposition, which was explained in the first appendix of Chapter 5. If the mapped individual default probability $N^{-1}(\lambda_{i,t})$ is bigger than the threshold sample $M_{n,t}(.)$, default of asset i occurs and vice versa. Formally:

$$\tau_{i,t} = 1_{\{N^{-1}(\lambda_{i,t}) > M_{n,t}(.)\}} \tag{6.5}$$

In equation (6.5), 1 is an indicator variable. That is 1 assumes the value 1 if $N^{-1}(\lambda_{i,t}) > M_{n,t}(.)$ and zero otherwise. We now perform Monte Carlo simulations, ie, we derive multiple results, for example 100,000, of equation (6.5) and average those results. This gives us a certain probability of default of asset i at time t. For example, if the average result of equation (6.5) for a certain asset i in the CDO is 0.1, then the default probability of this asset is 10% at time t. We apply equation (6.5) for all n assets in the CDO. This gives us the correlated default distribution of all assets in the CDO. The defaults in the distribution are correlated, since the threshold $M_{n,t}(.)$ includes the correlation of the defaults via the correlation matrix ρ_M. Figure 6.8 shows a possible default distribution generated by the Gaussian copula model.

In Figure 6.8, the defaults are put into 10% bins. We observe that there is approximately a 19% probability that 10% of the assets default, and approximately a 26% probability that 20% of the asset

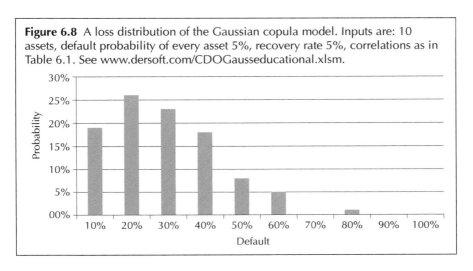

Figure 6.8 A loss distribution of the Gaussian copula model. Inputs are: 10 assets, default probability of every asset 5%, recovery rate 5%, correlations as in Table 6.1. See www.dersoft.com/CDOGausseducational.xlsm.

Table 6.1 (Fictitious) asset-correlation matrix underlying Figure 6.8

Asset-Correlation Matrix									
1	0.15	0.15	0.15	0.15	0.15	0.05	0.05	0.05	0.05
0.15	1	0.15	0.15	0.15	0.05	0.05	0.05	0.05	0.05
0.15	0.15	1	0.15	0.15	0.15	0.15	0.05	0.05	0.05
0.15	0.15	0.15	1	0.15	0.15	0.05	0.05	0.05	0.05
0.15	0.15	0.15	0.15	1	0.15	0.15	0.05	0.05	0.05
0.15	0.05	0.15	0.15	0.15	1	0.15	0.05	0.05	0.05
0.05	0.05	0.15	0.05	0.15	0.15	1	0.15	0.05	0.05
0.05	0.05	0.05	0.05	0.05	0.05	0.15	1	0.15	0.05
0.05	0.05	0.05	0.05	0.05	0.05	0.05	0.15	1	0.05
0.05	0.05	0.05	0.05	0.05	0.05	0.05	0.05	0.05	1

default, etc. We see that the loss distribution is somewhat lognormal, however, other simulations display other shapes.

We now map the default distribution to the tranches of the CDO. Assuming a continuous default distribution, the mapping is shown in Figure 6.9.

Figure 6.9 gives us the correlated default probability of each tranche. The tranche spread s, which is effectively a "coupon" that

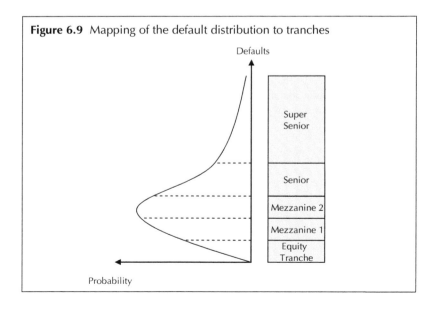

Figure 6.9 Mapping of the default distribution to tranches

the tranche investor receives (see Figures 6.3 to 6.5) is directly related to the default probability λ via equation

$$s \approx \lambda(1-R) \qquad (6.6)$$

where R is the recovery rate. Equation (6.6) is also called the "credit triangle", since three parameters are involved and two parameters are necessary to derive the remaining third. If the recovery rate is already included in the loss distribution, we have $s \approx \lambda$. This relationship is intuitive since the default probability λ is the risk that the investor takes, and he should be compensated for this risk by receiving a similar amount, the spread s. The relationship $s \approx \lambda (1 - R)$ was formally derived by Lando (1998) with $R = 0$ and by Duffie and Singleton (1990) with $R \neq 0$.

Once we have derived the correlated default probability distribution λ, we can derive the loss distribution L via

$$L = EAD\ \lambda(1-R) \qquad (6.7)$$

where EAD is the exposure at default, which for a CDO is the invested amount in the tranche. Equation (6.7) assumes that the default probability distribution of λ does not include the recovery rate R.

A model that derives the default distribution and loss distribution in a Gaussian copula framework can be found at www.dersoft.com/CDOGausseducational.xlsm.

Recovery rate

The default probability of the assets in the CDO and the default correlation of the assets are the critical inputs when valuing a CDO. A third input is the recovery rate in case the asset defaults. However, the recovery rate is not as critical an input as the default probability and default correlation.

Generally, recovery rates depend on the type of security, seniority, country and state of the economy. The United States enjoys one of the highest recovery rates due to its lenient Chapter 11 bankruptcy law, while recovery rates in Japan are among the lowest. Several studies find that recovery rates are higher in an economic expansion than in a recession (Altman 2002; Doshi 2011).

Recovery rates are often approximated using historical recovery rates of defaulted companies. Interestingly, the rating agency Fitch

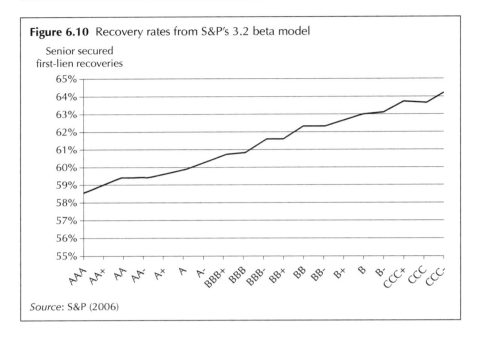

Figure 6.10 Recovery rates from S&P's 3.2 beta model

Source: S&P (2006)

assigns a lower recovery rate to higher-rated entities. The logic is that higher-rated entities will default only in a recession, in which recovery rates are lower. Lower-rated entities are assigned a higher recovery rate, since they can also default in an economic expansion. Fitch refers to this concept as "tiered recovery rates". This is in line with S&P's model to forecast recovery rates with respect to ratings, as seen in Figure 6.10.

In addition, the thinner the tranche, the higher is the loss severity, since thinner tranches can be wiped out more quickly. Equity and junior mezzanine tranches are typically thinner than senior tranches. Hence some rating agencies typically assign lower ratings and in some cases lower recovery rates to equity and junior tranches.

In the standardised iTraxx and CDX indices, the assumed recovery rates range from 20% to 35%, depending on the credit quality of the index (see http://www.markit.com/en/products/data/indices/credit-and-loan-indices/itraxx/news.page for details).

CONCLUSION: THE GAUSSIAN COPULA AND CDOS – WHAT WENT WRONG?

As mentioned in the beginning of this chapter, the Gaussian copula is occasionally blamed for the global financial crisis of 2007 to 2009. Let's get the facts straight.

Complexity of CDOs

As mentioned earlier, CDOs are useful financial products since they include sound financial principles such as diversification, subordination and overcollateralisation. However, from a valuation perspective CDOs are complex instruments. Generating the default probabilities of 125 assets for the maturity of a CDO, typically 5–10 years, is not an easy task. This is because many variables such as future economic environment, sector-specific developments, products, changing competition and changing company management, are difficult to predict. In addition, typically the assets in the CDO have never defaulted before, so empirical data of analogous companies has to be analysed.

Even more difficult is finding the default correlation between all the 125 assets in a CDO, which principally requires us to generate a 125-by-125 default correlation matrix. In addition, these correlations are typically quite unstable, as we have seen in Chapter 2.

The Gaussian copula model to value CDOs

The Gaussian copula model is a mathematically rigorous and adequate model to value a CDO. The Copula model allows the joining of n default probability functions to a single n-variate distribution. The correlation structure of the newly created n-variate distribution is then applied.

Naturally, the Gaussian copula has its limitations. We discussed some of those limitations in Chapter 5. They include low tail dependence, difficulties in calibration, and traders violating correlation assumptions by using their own tranche-specific correlation inputs. In addition, the original copula function is static, ie, has a one-period time horizon. However, default probability functions and correlation matrices can be derived to different time horizons. This does not create a truly stochastic process with drift and noise, but it gives valuable information for different times t. One-factor copulas can be made dynamic, such as in Hull *et at* (2005). However, the one-factor copulas, which assume a single correlation value for all assets in a CDO, are simplistic and should not be applied when valuing complex CDOs.

The main problem in 2007 and 2008 when valuing CDOs with the Gaussian copula was inadequate calibration. Benign default probability functions were applied and low default correlations between the assets in the CDO were input in correlation matrices. When data from non-crisis periods are input into a model, it cannot be expected that the model will produce correct outputs in a crisis! In programming terminology, "garbage in, garbage out". In the future, crisis scenarios have to be tested, ie, default probabilities and default correlations from crisis periods have to be applied. Basel III and the Federal Reserve have adopted this approach by requiring financial institutions to stress-test their models. In conclusion, "Don't blame the models, blame the people that misuse them."

SUMMARY

In this chapter we discussed the Gaussian copula correlation model and its application for valuing CDOs (collateralised debt obligations). Several non-quantitative articles have blamed the copula model for the global financial crisis of 2007 and 2009.

There are three main types of CDOs: (a) cash CDOs, (b) synthetic CDOs and (c) unfunded CDOs such as the iTraxx and CDX. However, many variations of these three basic types exist. The three main players in a CDO are (1) the originator (or protection buyer), who transfers the credit risk, (2) the investor, who assumes the credit risk, and (3) an SPV (special-purpose vehicle), who manages the CDO. CDOs have been misleadingly called "toxic", especially by those who do not want to take responsibility for their own incompetence and trading losses. CDOs include sound financial principles such as (a) diversification, (b) subordination, and (c) overcollateralisation.

The drawback of CDOs lies in their relative pricing complexity, especially with respect to correlation. If the CDO has 125 assets, we have to evaluate a 125 × 125 asset-correlation matrix! Here is where the copula function comes in. It allows the joining of n (for example $n = 125$) univariate distributions to one, however – n-dimensional distribution. Cholesky decomposition lets us easily sample from this distribution (see the first Appendix in Chapter 5). This sample serves as a default threshold: if the individual default probability of an asset is equal or exceeds the threshold, default of the asset occurs. Monte Carlo simulations are then conducted and the average of the outcomes constitute the default probability of the asset. Conveniently, the default correlation of the assets is included in the default probabilities, since they are incorporated in the threshold.

Naturally, as with every model, the Gaussian copula has its limitations such as low tail dependence, problems in calibration and its principally static nature. However, the main problem in the 2007–2009 crisis was the overinvestment in CDOs, the lack of hedging and, importantly, the data feed. Benign default probabilities and default correlation data from non-crisis periods were input into the model. Of course, it cannot be expected that this data can realistically value the behaviour of a financial structure like a CDO in a severe crisis. This is why the central banks and the Basel III committee have required all financial institutions to perform stress tests to evaluate the risks under extreme crises scenarios.

Questions for Chapter 6
The answers to these questions can be found at the end of this book.

1. What is the basic idea of a CDO?
2. Name the three main types of CDOs.
3. Which are the three main players in a CDO? Why is the SPV typically AAA-rated?
4. Name the motives of these three players to enter into a CDO.
5. Name the three financial principles that are incorporated in a CDO and explain them briefly.
6. What is the default probability of an entity based on the Merton 1974 model, if the current asset value V_0 = US\$4,000,000, the debt value D = US\$3,000,000, the maturity T of the debt is in 1 year, the risk-free interest rate r is 2% and the volatility of the assets σ is 20%? (A simple model, which derives the answer is available upon request.)

7. In the Merton 1974 model, there is a closed-form solution for the default probability. What is it?
8. The elegant Merton 1974 model principally serves as a basis for more realistic extensions. What are the limitations of the Merton 1974 model?
9. The Merton 1974 model is the basis for all structural models. Why is the Merton model called structural? Why are reduced-form models called reduced-form?
10. When valuing the default probability in a CDO, why do we map the default probability of asset i, λ_i to standard normal via $N - 1(\lambda_i)$?
11. The multivariate copula function Mn serves as the default threshold. How is the default of asset i derived in the copula model?
12. The credit triangle is $s \approx \lambda (1 - R)$, where s is the credit spread, λ is the default intensity, and R is the recovery rate. When $R = 0$, we have $s \approx \lambda$. Explain the intuition of $s \approx \lambda$.
13. The recovery rate is often modelled as the higher, the lower the credit rating of an asset. This seems counterintuitive. But why is it rational?
14. Can the Gaussian copula be blamed for the global financial crisis of 2007 to 2009?
15. What were the main reasons for the misevaluation of CDOs before and during the crisis?

---

[1] See "Recipe for Disaster: The Formula that killed Wall Street", *Wired* (2009); "Wall Street Wizards Forgot a Few Variables", *New York Times* (2009); "The formula that felled Wall Street", *Financial Times* (2009).
[2] For an analysis of this property, see Meissner 2007.
[3] See Chapter 5 for details of copula mapping.

7

The One-Factor Gaussian Copula Model – Too Simplistic?

> "Make everything as simple as possible, but not simpler"
> – Albert Einstein

In Chapter 6 we discussed the standard copula model. It joins n marginal distribution to a single n-variate distribution. The n marginal distributions are correlated in a correlation matrix. This matrix is $n \times n$ dimensional, so if the CDO has 125 assets, the matrix is 125×125 dimensional. This is mathematically and computationally quite challenging. Often financial institutions take a shortcut, putting the assets into sectors and correlating the different sectors. This reduces the dimension of the correlation matrix.

A further shortcut is to assume that all assets in the portfolio have the same pairwise correlation. This seems simplistic, and it is. However, if the assets in the portfolio are homogeneous – ie, they are very similar, for example they have the same or similar credit rating and/or they belong to the same sector – this assumption may be tolerable.

If we simplify further, we can also assume that the default probability of all assets in the portfolio is the same. This again seems simplistic and it again is. However, if the assets in the portfolio are homogeneous – ie, they have the same or similar credit rating, they belong to the same sector, have a similar maturity and coupon – this simplification may be adequate.

A model in which the correlations and the default probability are assumed the same for all assets, is called "homogeneous" or LHP: "large homogeneous portfolio". In 1987 Oldrich Vasicek developed a methodology to price the credit risk for such an LHP, which is called the one-factor Gaussian copula (OFGC) model. The OFGC is a special type of the conditionally independent correlation (CID) approach, which we will explain in this chapter.

Let's just look at some basics that are necessary to evaluate the credit risk in a portfolio. We need three main inputs.

1. Default intensity. As explained in Chapter 5, Example 5.2, default intensity for period t to t + 1 is the default probability from t to t + 1 conditional on no default until period t. If t = 0, ie, we look at a time period starting today, default intensity and default probability are identical.
2. Default correlation, which measures the likelihood of two or more assets to default together. The standard copula model, discussed in Chapter 5, includes a default correlation matrix of the assets in the portfolio (displayed in Chapter 1, Figure 1.3). The OFGC applies a conditionally independent correlation (CID) approach, which includes a single correlation coefficient, ie, the same pairwise correlation between all assets in the portfolio.
3. Recovery rate. This can be modelled as explained in the previous chapter, or derived by historical data.

Let's look at the evolution of the one-factor Gaussian copula, which is displayed in Table 7.1.

Table 7.1 Large homogeneous portfolio (LHP) evaluated by the one-factor Gaussian copula (OFGC) model and extensions

	Default intensity λ	Correlation coefficient ρ	Recovery rate R
Vasicek's 1987 LHP, valued on OFGC (used in Basel III to calculate Credit Value at Risk CVaR, see chapter 14)	Same for all assets i	Same for all assets i	Same for all assets i
Extension of LHP: OFGC with different λ_i (used to value homogeneous CDOs)	Different λ_i for each asset i, λ_i can be a function of t, $\lambda_i(t)$	Same for all assets i	Same for all assets i
Multivariate Gaussian Copula David Li (2000) (is typically applied to value CDOs, see chapter 6)	λ is a function of i and t, $\lambda_i(t)$	Different for each asset pair since a correlation matrix ρ_M is applied	Different for each asset class

THE ORIGINAL OFGC

We first define a variable i, $i = 1, \ldots, n$. The variable i represents a certain company i, whose asset is part of a portfolio, for example, a CDO. We then derive an "auxiliary default indicator variable" x_i for every company i. x_i can be thought of as the overall "strength" of company i. The x_i are derived by

$$x_i = \sqrt{\rho}\, M + \sqrt{1-\rho}\, Z_i \qquad (7.1)$$

where

ρ: Default correlation parameter between the assets in the portfolio, $0 \le \rho \le 1$. ρ is assumed identical and constant for all asset pairs in the portfolio.

M: Systematic market factor, which impacts all companies. M can be thought of as the general economic environment, for example the return of the S&P 500. M is a random drawing from a standard normal distribution, formally $M = n \sim (0, 1)$. M is the same as ε in Chapter 6. (See the spreadsheet www.dersoft.com/epsilon.xlsx for a derivation of ε.)

Z_i: Idiosyncratic factor of company i. Z_i expresses i-th company's individual strength, possibly measured by company i's stock price return. Just like M, Z_i is a random drawing from a standard normal distribution.

x_i: The value for x_i results from equation (7.1) and is interpreted as a "Default indicator variable" for company i. The lower i, the earlier is the default time T for company i. x_i is by construction standard normally distributed.

The variables M, Z_i and the resulting x_i in equation (7.1) are sometimes referred to as "latent variables" or "frailty variables", because the lower M or Z_i, the lower is x_i and hence the earlier is the default time of company i. Equation (7.1) is the key equation in the OFGC. It can be graphically represented with Figure 7.1.

Although equation (7.1) is rather simple, it includes several important properties, as follows.

(a) The key property of equation (7.1) is that we do not model the default correlation between the assets i in the portfolio directly, but instead we condition defaults on M. We assume that ρ is identical for all asset pairs. Therefore, we have the

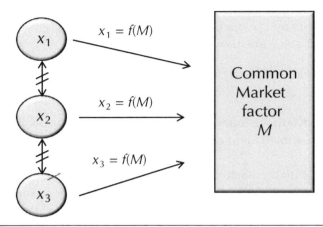

Figure 7.1 Graphical representation of the correlation concept of equation (7.1) for $n = 3$ entities. The x_i are not directly correlated, but indirectly correlated by conditioning on the common factor M.

same relationship between every asset i and M: if ρ is one, every asset i has a perfect correlation with M, hence all assets are perfectly correlated. If ρ is zero, all assets i only depend on their idiosyncratic factor Z_i, hence the assets are independent. For a ρ of 0.7071 (and therefore $\sqrt{\rho} = 0.5$) all x_i are determined equally by M and Z_i. Importantly, once we have determined M (by a random drawing from a standard normal distribution), the assets i are conditionally (on M) independent, meaning the correlation coefficient between the x_i is zero. Therefore, we name this approach "conditionally independent correlation" (CID) modelling. (For a spreadsheet explaining conditional independence, see www.dersoft.com/xigraphicallydisplayed.xlsx.)

(b) Since M and Z_i are random drawings from a standard normal distribution, it conveniently follows that x_i is standard normal.

(c) The higher x_i, the higher the default time t_i, hence the later the default of asset i.

We will now derive how the OFGC can evaluate the spreads of the tranches in a CDO.

Table 7.2 A sample-simulation for deriving the correlated default time of five assets, which is displayed in the last column; default intensity λ for all assets is 5%, copula correlation coefficient $\rho = 0.5$, maturity is four years. Note that the market factor M (second column) is identical for all assets i. (The spreadsheet can be found at www.dersoft.com/ofgceducational.xls.)

	M	Z_i	Correlated x_i	Normsdist(x_i)=P_i	$1-P_i$	Years to default	Default in year
Asset 1	−1.7710	−0.5560	−1.6454	0.0499	0.9501	1.00	1
Asset 2	−1.7710	0.3338	−1.0162	0.1548	0.8452	3.28	4
Asset 3	−1.7710	1.3042	−0.3300	0.3707	0.6293	9.03	No default
Asset 4	−1.7710	0.7198	−0.7433	0.2287	0.7713	5.06	No default
Asset 5	−1.7710	−0.5345	−1.6302	0.0515	0.9485	1.03	2

VALUING TRANCHES OF A CDO WITH THE OFGC

The roadmap for deriving the fair spread of each tranche consists of the following six steps. They are displayed in Table 7.2

The six steps to derive the fair spread of a CDO tranche are:

1. Drawing random samples for M and Z_i and deriving x_i

We start with drawing random samples from a standard normal distribution (=normsinv(rand()) in Excel or norminv(rand) in MATLAB). For every simulation we draw one sample M and one sample for each asset i, Z_i (Table 7.2, columns 2 and 3). Together with a (market-given) ρ, we derive x_i from equation (7.1) for every asset i (Table 7.2, column 4).

2. Converting the x_i into probabilities P_i

Next, we convert the x_i, which are $-\infty \leq x_i \leq \infty$ to cumulative probabilities P_i using the cumulative standard normal distribution N (=normsdist(x_i) in Excel, normcdf(x_i) in MATLAB), hence $N(x_i) = P_i$, $0 \leq P_i \leq 1$, (Table 7.2, column 5). The usage of standard normal distributions for M and Z_i and the resulting cumulative normal distribution via $N(x_i)$ is why the approach is called the Gaussian copula. Our simulated default probabilities P_i are uniform (=rand()

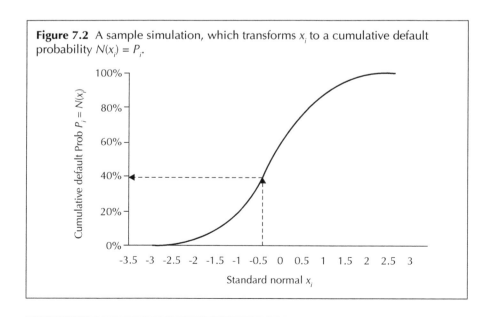

Figure 7.2 A sample simulation, which transforms x_i to a cumulative default probability $N(x_i) = P_i$.

in Excel, rand in MATLAB), since we just reversed =normsinv(rand()) from step 1. Graphically, this is displayed in Figure 7.2.

3. Deriving market survival thresholds 1 − P_i

We calculate the market survival threshold $1 - P_i$ (Table 7.2, column 6), which includes the idiosyncratic factor Z_i, the market factor M, and the correlation between the x_i with Z_i and M. From step 2, we see that the $1 - P_i$ are calculated in the same way for every asset i. However, the numerical values of each $1 - P_i$ differ, since they depend on the random drawing for every asset i, Z_i (the $1 - P_i$ in each simulation will be identical only if the random drawings Z_i are identical by coincidence and/or in the case of $\rho = 1$).

4. Deriving individual survival probabilities of asset i, s_i

(a) Constant (flat) default intensity curve λ in time

In this case, we take the market-given default intensity h for asset i, h_i, at time t and derive the survival probability s for asset i at time t via $(1 - h_i)^t = s_t^i$.[1]

(b) Default intensity is a function of time $\lambda(t)$

If we have a market-given, non-constant default intensity curve for each company i with respect to time, we have to derive the idiosyncratic survival curve for every asset i. We take the annual, market-given default probability curve $p_i(t)$ for every asset i. We derive the default intensity (also called hazard rate) at a specific time T, $h_i(T)$, from

$$h_i(T) = \frac{p_i(T)}{1 - \sum_{t=1}^{T-1} p_i(t)},$$

$t = 1, \ldots, T$. $h_i(T)$ is the default probability from time T to time $T + 1$, assuming no default until time T. We find the annual survival probabilities $s_i(t) = 1 - h_i(t)$. We derive the cumulative survival time

$$S_i(T) = \prod_{t=1}^{T} s_i(t)$$

A curve of $S_i(t)$ is shown in Figure 7.3. It is generated from default probabilities of 5% in year 1 to 14% in year 10, linearly increasing.

5. Deriving the correlated default time (Table 7.2, column 7)

(a) Constant (flat) default intensity curve λ:
We derive the default time t of asset i, by equating asset i's (market-given) survival probability at t, s_i^t with the market survival threshold $1 - P_{i'}$ which were derived in steps 2 and 3.

$$s_i^t = 1 - P_i \qquad (7.2)$$

We solve equation (7.2) for the default time t of asset i, t_i.[2] We then use Monte Carlo simulation to derive many default times t for an asset i. We average the default times t for each i. Note that the default time t includes the default time correlation of all assets in the portfolio, since $1 - P_i$ includes the default correlation.

(b) Default intensity as a function of time $\lambda(t)$
We relate the simulated survival probabilities from step 3, $1 - P_{i'}$ to asset i's idiosyncratic cumulative survival probability curve $S_{i'}$ generated in step 4. We find the default time of asset i with a look-up function (see Figure 7.3). We then use Monte Carlo simulation to derive many default times t for an asset i and average the default times t for each i.

The fact that we find the default time t by equating the

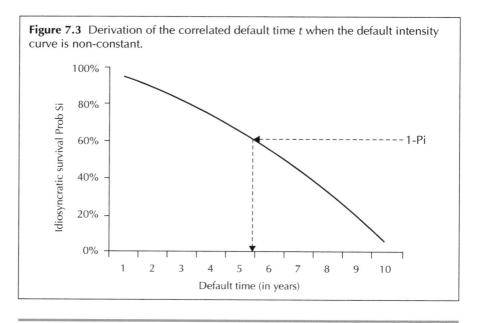

Figure 7.3 Derivation of the correlated default time t when the default intensity curve is non-constant.

idiosyncratic survival probability S_i with the simulated survival threshold $1 - P_i$ relates to standard Gaussian copula, which we discussed in Chapter 6. In the standard Gaussian copula the default of an asset at time τ was determined by equating the inverse of the default intensity with a market threshold (see equation (6.5)).

In Table 7.2, $M = -1.7710$. M can be interpreted as the state of the economic environment. M is a random drawing from a standard normal distribution and takes values $-\infty \leq M \leq \infty$. So in the displayed simulation in Table 7.2, $M = -1.7710$ means that we have a somewhat negative economic environment. This is why several of the names in Table 7.2 default. In particular, assets 1, 2 and 5 default, since their Z_i are also relatively low. Asset 2's Z_i is the lowest, therefore it defaults earliest, ie, in year 1.

6. Deriving the tranche spread

Once we have derived the average default time for each asset i, it is easy to find the fair tranche spread. Each tranche of a CDO consists of a portfolio of credit default swaps (CDSs). The number of CDSs in a certain tranche is determined by the attachment and detachment point. For example, the equity tranche of the iTraxx and CDX contain 0% – 3% of defaults of the 125 assets. Hence 3% × 125 = 3.75 of all defaults fall into the equity tranche (so the fourth default falls to 75% into the equity tranche and to 25% into the next higher tranche).

Since we have derived the expected default time of every asset i (step 5), we also know the losses at any time t. From the losses of every asset i, we can find the outstanding notional ON of the CDO at any time t. With this outstanding notional in hand, we can price the tranche:

Each CDO tranche is evaluated with simple swap valuation techniques. The present value PV of the spread leg of tranche j is

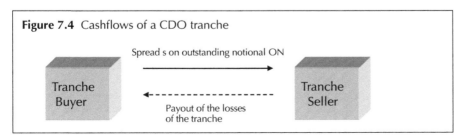

Figure 7.4 Cashflows of a CDO tranche

$$PV\left(\text{Spread tranche}_j\right) = \text{Spread}_j E\left(\sum_{t=1}^{n} e^{-rt} ON_j(t)\right) \qquad (7.3)$$

where E stands for expected value, $ON_j(t)$ is the outstanding notional of tranche j at time t, and r is the continuously compounded risk-free interest rate. The present value of the payout leg of tranche j is

$$PV\left(\text{Payout leg}_j\right) = E\left(\sum_{t=1}^{n} e^{-rt}\left(ON_j(t-1) - ON_j(t)\right)(1-R)\right) \qquad (7.4)$$

where R is the recovery rate.

Equating (7.3) and (7.4), setting to zero and solving for "Spread$_j$" gives the fair market spread of tranche j:

$$\text{Spread}_j = \frac{E\left(\sum_{t=1}^{n} e^{-rt}\left(ON_j(t-1) - ON_j(t)\right)(1-R)\right)}{E\left(\sum_{t=1}^{n} e^{-rt} ON_j(t)\right)} \qquad (7.5)$$

For an educational model showing steps 1 to 6, see www.dersoft.com/ofgceducational.xls.

Let's derive the fair tranche spread in a numerical example.

Example 7.1: Deriving the fair tranche spread of a CDO with the OFGC (one-factor Gaussian copula) model

Let's look at a CDO with a three-year maturity. The starting notional is US$1,000,000,000, with 125 equally weighted companies. Hence each asset has a notional of US$8,000,000.

Next assume that the spread payments and payouts are annually in arrears. The recovery rate for every asset is 40%. Interest rates are constant at 10%. We consider an equity tranche with a detachment point of 3%. Hence the equity tranche has a starting notional of US$30,000,000.

Let's also assume that from our analysis of steps 1 to 5 we derived the fact that one asset defaults after 1.5 years and one asset defaults in 2.5 years. Hence the starting notional of US$30,000,000 reduces to US$22,000,000 for t_2 (end of year 2) and to US$14,000,000 for t_3 (end of year 3).

From equation (7.4), the numerator is

$$e^{-0.1\times 1} \times 0 \times 0.6 + e^{-0.1\times 2} \times (\$30,000,000 - \$22,000,000) \times 0.6 +$$
$$e^{-0.1\times 3} \times (\$22,000,000 - \$14,000,000) \times 0.6 = \$8,782,153$$

From equation (7.4), the denominator is

$$e^{-0.1\times 1} \times \$30,000,000 + e^{-0.1\times 2} \times \$22,000,000 + e^{-0.1\times 3} \times \$14,000,000 = \$55,528,654$$

Hence the fair equity tranche spread, paid annually in arrears is

US$8,782,153 / US$55,528,654 = 15.82%.

Note that we abstracted from any accrued interest of the asset. Furthermore, we have abstracted from any accrued interest on the spread premium.

Randomness in the OFGC model

The reader might be surprised by all the randomness in generating the default time t. Since both M and Z_i are random drawings from a normal distribution, does it matter what value ρ has in equation (7.1)? A similar question is: since all P_i are random, uniform probabilities (=rand() in Excel), why don't we just start the process at step 2) and derive uniform drawings, hence P_i = rand()?

The answer is that ρ in equation (7.1) represents the default correlation between the assets in the CDO. We generate one M for every asset i and a unique Z for every asset i in each Monte Carlo simulation. Hence ρ serves as a weighting factor between M and Z_i. The higher ρ, the more the x_i depend on the common factor M, hence the higher the default correlation of the assets in the CDO, vice versa. This will be discussed in detail in the following section.

THE CORRELATION CONCEPT IN THE OFGC MODEL

As mentioned above, a key property of the OFGC model is that the default correlation between the assets in the CDO is not modelled directly, but instead indirectly by conditioning the defaults on a common market factor M.

The higher ρ in equation (7.1), the higher is the dependence of each asset i on the common factor M, hence the higher is the correlation between the assets. This is expressed in the standard deviation of the simulated survival probabilities $1 - P_i$. The higher ρ, the lower is the standard deviation of the $1 - P_i$'s in a simulation, hence the higher is the probability that the assets default together.

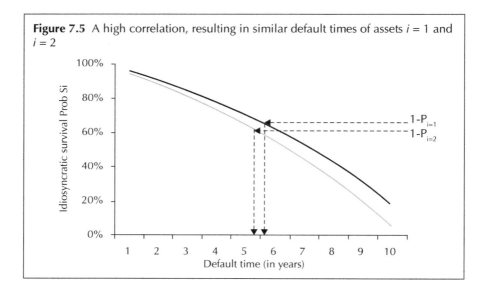

Figure 7.5 A high correlation, resulting in similar default times of assets $i = 1$ and $i = 2$

Figure 7.5 shows the idiosyncratic survival curves of two assets, $i = 1$ and $i = 2$. If ρ is high (close to 1), the $1 - P_i$'s of each asset i will have a low standard deviation in each simulation (ie, will have similar values). Since the simulated $1 - P_i$'s are quite similar, the probability of the assets defaulting together is high, as seen in Figure 7.5.

In the extreme case of $\rho = 1$, each simulation will generate the same $1 - P_i$ for every asset i (since the x_i and the resulting $1 - P_i$ only depend on the common factor M). If additionally the hazard rates of every asset i are identical, the OFGC will generate the same default time for every asset i.

For a low correlation, eg, $\rho = 0.05$, from equation (7.1), the x_i, P_i and $1 - P_i$ are mainly determined by the idiosyncratic Z_i. In this case the survival times $1 - P_i$ in each simulation have a high standard deviation, ie, they are quite different (unless by coincidence the random drawings Z_i are similar). Therefore, the OFGC model typically generates quite different default times, as seen in Figure 7.6.

The loss distribution of the OFGC model

As we have seen, there are two main input factors that determine the price of a CDO. One is the default probability of the assets in

THE ONE-FACTOR GAUSSIAN COPULA MODEL – TOO SIMPLISTIC?

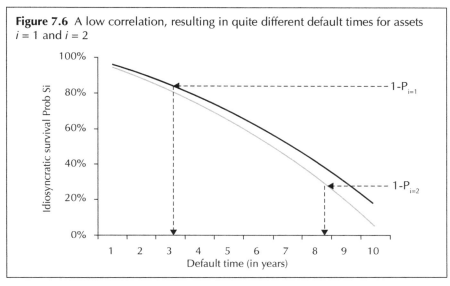

Figure 7.6 A low correlation, resulting in quite different default times for assets $i = 1$ and $i = 2$

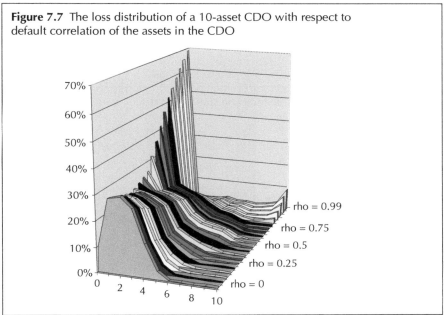

Figure 7.7 The loss distribution of a 10-asset CDO with respect to default correlation of the assets in the CDO

the CDO. Naturally, the higher the default probability, the higher the spread of the tranches in the CDO. The second crucial input factor is the default correlation of the assets in the CDO. Figure 7.7

shows the loss distribution with respect to correlation of a 10 asset CDO with a two-year maturity and a 10% hazard rate.

As seen in Figure 7.7, for zero correlation, the OFGC model displays a somewhat lognormal distribution of losses. For medium correlation, the losses are more evenly distributed and descending. For very high correlation, the probability of extreme events increases. Hence, there is a high probability of zero losses and an increased probability that all assets default. For a model deriving the loss distribution of the OFGC, see www.dersoft.com/basecorrelationgeneration.xls.

The tranche spread – correlation relationship

From Figure 7.8 we can deduct the tranche spread – correlation relationship in the OFGC model. Interestingly, the equity tranche spread is negatively related to default correlation, while the senior tranche is positively related.

The negative relationship between the equity tranche spread and default correlation is intuitive: the higher the default correlation of the companies in the CDO, the higher the probability of extreme

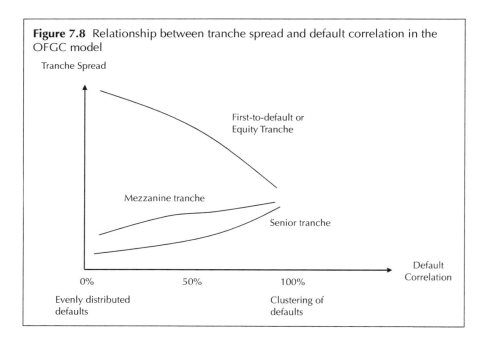

Figure 7.8 Relationship between tranche spread and default correlation in the OFGC model

events, ie, the probability of many or no defaults at all is high. The high probability of no defaults reduces the riskiness and hence reduces the equity tranche spread. The high probability of many defaults increases the riskiness of the equity tranche, which increases the equity tranche spread. However, this effect does not impact on the equity tranche significantly, since the losses are capped at the detachment level.

The opposite logic applies to the senior tranche: if default correlation is high, many defaults may occur at the same time. Therefore, the senior tranche may be impacted; hence the riskiness and the spread are high.

It should be mentioned that the relationship between tranche spread and correlation in Figure 7.8 is a specific result of the OFGC model. Other models with different distribution assumptions and correlation approaches derive a different spread–correlation relationship, eg, a positive relationship between equity spread and correlation.[3]

THE RELATIONSHIP BETWEEN THE OFGC AND THE STANDARD COPULA

The core equation of the OFGC was displayed earlier in equation 7.1:

$$x_i = \sqrt{\rho}\, M + \sqrt{1-\rho}\, Z_i \qquad (7.1)$$

By construction, x_i in equation (7.1) is standard normal. Therefore, we can easily create the cumulative standard normal distribution of the x_i

$$N(x_i) \qquad (7.1a)$$

where N is the one-dimensional cumulative standard normal distribution. Importantly, $N(x_i)$ includes the default correlation between the $i = 1, \ldots, n$ assets via the correlated x_i, derived in equation (7.1).

In comparison, the n-dimensional cumulative standard normal distribution M_n was derived earlier in the standard Gaussian copula framework with equation (5.12):

$$M_n\left[N^{-1}(Q_1(t)), \ldots, N^{-1}(Q_n(t)); \rho_M\right] \qquad (5.12)$$

where $Q_i(t)$ is the cumulative default distribution of asset i with respect to t and ρ_M is the correlation matrix of the assets in the portfolio.

Let's look at the differences in the OFGC of equations (7.1) and (7.1a), and standard copula of equation (5.12).

(a) The correlations between the assets i in equation (7.1) are modelled indirectly by conditioning the auxiliary variable of asset i, x_i, on a common factor M. In contrast, equation (5.12) applies the typical correlation matrix ρ_M (for an example see Chapter 1, Table 1.3).
(b) As a consequence, in the OFGC all asset pairs in the portfolio have the same correlation. The standard Gaussian copula is richer as it can model asset-pair correlation individually in the correlation matrix.
(c) The cumulative normal distribution in equation (7.1a), which includes the correlation between the assets i via x_i, is conveniently one-dimensional. The cumulative normal distribution in equation (5.12) is n-dimensional.
(d) The bivariate case of the standard Gaussian copula is equivalent with the OFGC: sampling from equation (5.12) is achieved by Cholesky decomposition (as explained in the Appendix A1 of Chapter 5). In the bivariate case, Cholesky sampling of two correlated variables x_1 and x_2 from equation (5.12) reduces to

$$x_i = \varepsilon_1$$
$$x_2 = \sqrt{\rho}\,\varepsilon_1 + \sqrt{1-\rho}\,\varepsilon_2$$

where ε_1 and ε_2 are independent samples from $n \sim (0, 1)$. This is equivalent to samples $i = 1, 2$ from equation (7.1).

EXTENSIONS OF THE OFGC

The OFGC is principally static, ie, has a one-period time horizon. However, the static property of the OFGC can be relaxed, as in Hull et al (2005), who apply a dynamic OFGC model. Hence they modify equation (7.1) and model

$$dz_i(t) = \sqrt{\rho(t)}\,dM(t) + \sqrt{1-\rho(t)}\,dZ_i(t) \qquad (7.6)$$

where

$dM(t)$ and $dZ_i(t)$ are $n \sim (0, 1)$ and independent. It follows from equation (7.6) that $dz_i(t)$ is also $n \sim (0, 1)$. The dependence on $M(t)$

again determines indirectly the correlation between assets i. For example, if $\rho(t) = 1$, $dz_i(t)$ depends only on $dM(t)$, hence all assets i have the same Brownian motion at time t. If $\rho(t) = 0$, $dz_i(t) = dZ_i(t)$, hence the Brownian motions of assets i are uncorrelated at time t.

Furthermore, additional common factors M can be modelled. In this case equation (7.1) generalises to

$$x_i = \sum_{k=1}^{m} \sqrt{p_{i,k}} M_k + Z_i \sum_{k=1}^{m} \sqrt{p_{i,k}}$$

and the correlation between x_i and x_j is

$$\sum_{k=1}^{m} \sqrt{p_{i,k} p_{j,k}}$$

Numerous further extensions of the OFGC approach exist. One of the most popular is the one-factor student-t copula.

$$\bar{x}_i = \sqrt{\rho} M + \sqrt{1-\rho} Z_i \qquad (7.7)$$

where M and Z_i are independent and $n \sim (0, 1)$. $x_i = \bar{x}_i \sqrt{W}$ where W follows an inverse gamma distribution. It follows that the latent variable x_i is student-t distributed.

Another popular extension of the OFGC in equation (7.1) is the double-t copula. It is defined as

$$x_i = \sqrt{\rho} M_s + \sqrt{1-\rho} Z_{s,i} \qquad (7.8)$$

where M_s and $Z_{s,i}$ are independent and follow a student-t distribution. Since the student-t distribution is not stable under convolution, the latent variable x_i in equation (7.8) is not student-t distributed.

Another extension of the OFGC is integrating a binomial representation of stochastic correlation. Burtschell et al (2007) model the latent variable x_i as

$$x_i = B_i \left(\sqrt{\rho_1} M + \sqrt{1-\rho_1} Z_i \right) + \left(1 - B_i \right) \left(\sqrt{\rho_2} M + \sqrt{1-\rho_2} Z_i \right)$$

where B_i is a Bernoulli random variable. We define a Bernoulli cutoff $B^* \in [0, 1]$ and model

$$B_i = \begin{cases} 0 \text{ if } r < B^* \\ 1 \text{ if } r \geq B^* \end{cases}$$

where r is a random drawing from a uniform distribution $n \in [0, 1]$. If we set $p_1 > p_2$, the cutoff level B^* can be set low to model high correlation in distressed times.

A further extension of the OFGC is creating a local correlation model (LCM) (see Turc et al (2005)), where the correlation is state-dependent. In particular, Turc et al assume that the correlation ρ is dependent on the state of the economy M. Hence, the OFGC changes to

$$x_i = -\sqrt{\rho(M)}\,M + \sqrt{1-\rho(M)}\,Z_i$$

The approach is similar in nature to the local volatility model of Dupire (1994), where volatility at time t, σ_t, is a function of the state of the underlying S at time t and t, $\sigma_t(S_t,t)$. Whereas Dupire is able to model the implied volatility skew and smile in the equity option market well, the local correlation model is able to reproduce the implied correlation smile of CDO tranches spreads quite accurately. As a result, the marked-to-market and hedge ratios of the local correlation model outperform those of the original OFGC.

A further extension of the OFGC is by Schönbucher and Schubert (2001), who integrate stochastic dynamics into the Gaussian copula model. Andersen and Sidenius (2004/2005) introduce randomness to the factor M with their RFL (random factor loading) model, allowing default correlation to be higher in a recession. Andersen (2006) adds jumps in both factors and residuals to the RFL model. Willeman (2005) applies lognormal jumps, and Baxter (2006) uses Brownian variance-gamma jumps to model the credit process.

Further extensions of the OFGC model: hybrid CID – contagion modelling

As derived in the early section "The original one-factor Gaussian copula model", the OFGC applies a conditionally independent correlation (CID) approach. CID models offer realistic correlation features such as default clustering. For example, if the correlation coefficient ρ is high and the market environment M is negative (see equation (7.1)), many entities will default together.

As mentioned in Chapter 5, contagion correlation approaches can model counterparty default contagion. Hence, it is not surprising that several models incorporate the CID common factor feature as well as contagion properties. In these models, typically a contagion term is simply added to the CID process. Schönbucher and Schubert (2001), Frey and Backhaus (2003), Giesecke and Weber (2004) and Yu (2007) propose

$$\lambda_i = \alpha_i M + Z_i + \sum_{j \neq i} \beta_{i,j} N_j \quad (7.9)$$

where M and Z_i are defined as in equation (7.1). $\beta_{i,j}$ is a function that models the contagion of firm i to a default of firm j and N_j is a default counting process

$$N_j = \sum_{j \geq 1} 1_{\{T_j \leq t\}}$$

where T_j is the stopping time (ie, default time) of firm j. A special case of equation (7.9) is derived by Giesecke and Weber (2006) with $Z_i = 0$ and $\alpha_i M = c_t$. Hence the deterministic function c_t, which models the "base intensity" may not incorporate a systematic factor M.

Alternatively, Schönbucher (2005), Giesecke, Goldberg and Ding (2009), and Duffie, Eckner, Horel and Saita (2009) suggest

$$\lambda_i = \alpha_i M + Z_i + \beta_i \hat{U}$$

where β_i is a deterministic function and $\bar{U}$ is a common factor, which is unobservable. However, the factor $\bar{U}$ is transformed into an observable process $U = E(\bar{U}_t | \mathcal{F}_t)$, where $\mathcal{F}_t$ is the filtration, which contains all events. The filtered process U is updated with observable information, in particular information about default events, which constitutes the contagion of firm i on defaults of other firms j.

CONCLUSION: IS THE OFGC TOO SIMPLISTIC TO EVALUATE CREDIT RISK IN PORTFOLIOS?

Let's answer this question by first looking at the benefits and limitations of the OFGC model.

Benefits of the OFGC model

The OFGC model is simple. Similar to the Black–Scholes–Merton model, the OFGC model has high intuition and is easy to implement. More complex approaches, as non-factor copulas, have to use multivariate methods such as Gaussian quadrature or recursion techniques (Andersen *et al* 2003, Hull and White 2004), Inverse Fast Fourier Transforms (Laurent and Gregory 2003) or saddle-point approximations (Martin *et al* 2001) to generate the cumulative loss distribution. However, the OFGC model uses a simple univariate function $N(x_i)$ to generate the simulated loss distribution, since the x_i already includes the correlation. The default time of an asset can be derived easily by equating the market survival threshold with individual survival probability, see equation (7.2).

Limitations of the OFGC model

The OFGC model is simple. It is essentially static, with no underlying stochastic process.[4] Hence dynamic delta and gamma hedging are difficult to implement.

The most significant drawback is that traders do not seem to agree with the model. Just as option traders increase the implied volatility to derive higher prices for out-of-the-money puts and calls in the Black–Scholes–Merton model, CDO traders alter the crucial input factor correlation in the OFGC. The often-cited correlation smile looks as in Figure 7.9.

However, there is a crucial difference between the volatility smile of options and the correlation smile of CDOs. While an increase in the implied correlation increases the senior tranche

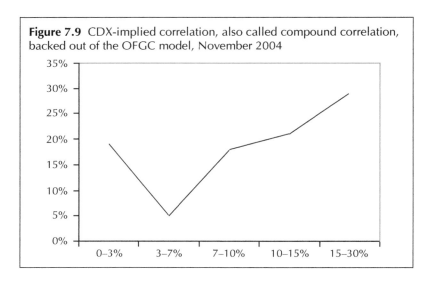

Figure 7.9 CDX-implied correlation, also called compound correlation, backed out of the OFGC model, November 2004

spread, an increase in the implied correlation decreases the equity tranche spread. This is because the equity tranche spread has a negative dependence on implied correlation (see Figure 7.8). Hence CDO traders arbitrarily decrease the equity tranche spread and arbitrarily increase the senior tranche spread.

In practice traders do not like to work with implied correlation. It does not allow easy interpolation, eg, the pricing of an off the run tranche as, for example, the 2%–8% tranche. Hence traders typically derive a base correlation curve, which has an attachment point of zero and the detachment points of the standard tranches, hence 0%–3%, 0%–7%, 0%–10%, 0%–15% and 0%–30% in case of the CDX. The derived base correlation curve is typically upward sloping and allows easier interpolation of off the run tranches, as seen in Figure 7.10.

The transformation of "forward" implied correlation to "spot" base correlation reminds us of the calculation of spot rates from Eurodollar future rates in the interest rate market. For a model, which bootstraps the base correlation curve from CDO tranche spreads, see www.dersoft.com/basecorrelationgeneration.xls.

In conclusion, the OFGC is an elegant, simple and intuitive model that traders like. It bears similar benefits and limitations as the Black–Scholes–Merton model. Similar to the Black–Scholes–Merton model, the benefits are simplicity and intuition. One

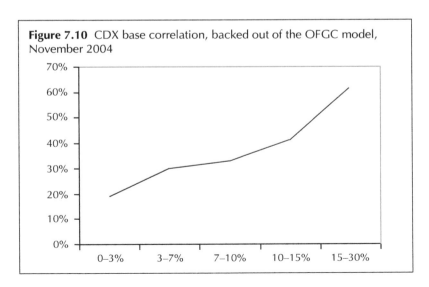

Figure 7.10 CDX base correlation, backed out of the OFGC model, November 2004

limitation of the OFGC with respect to application is that traders violate the assumptions of the model. They randomly alter the crucial input factor correlation to derive desired tranche spreads.

While traders like simplicity, simplicity comes at a cost. The critical question is whether the assumptions of the OFGC – ie, same default probability of all assets in the portfolio and same correlation between all asset pairs in the portfolio – are too simplistic to derive the credit risk of that portfolio. The answer is: only in rare cases – if the assets in the portfolio are very homogeneous, ie, have similar default probabilities and similar default correlation – is the OFGC an adequate model. Most portfolios of investment banks, however, are highly diversified with assets from different sectors, different geographical regions and hence have different default probabilities and default correlations. In this case the OFGC is an inappropriately simplistic model! It is a bit surprising that the Basel III accord applies the OFGC to evaluate credit risk for the portfolios of financial institutions. For more details, see the Basel III CVaR approach discussed in Chapter 14.

SUMMARY

In this chapter we discussed a shortcut of the Gaussian copula function: the one-factor Gaussian copula (OFGC). We evaluated whether it is too simplistic, especially with respect to valuing CDOs.

The OFGC was created by Oldrich Vasicek in 1987. The OFGC makes the following strong simplistic assumptions: (1) all assets in a portfolio have the same default probability; (2) all assets in a portfolio have the same pairwise default correlation; and, less critically, (3) all assets in the portfolio have the same recovery rate. These assumptions constitute a large homogeneous portfolio. In fact, the simplistic assumptions of the OFGC are justifiable only if the portfolio in question is very homogeneous, for example contains assets of the same sector with the same or similar credit ratings, maturities, and coupons.

The OFGC applies the conditionally independent correlation (CID) approach. In this approach, the assets are not correlated directly, but indirectly by conditioning on a common factor, which is shared by all assets. For example, all assets depend on the current state of the economy. The higher the dependence of the assets on the state of the economy, the higher is also the correlation between the assets. For example in the extreme case, if all assets' dependence on the common factor is 1, all assets are perfectly correlated. If the dependence on the common factor is 0, the assets are uncorrelated. For dependence values on the common factor between 0 and 1, naturally there is a partial correlation between the assets.

The correlated default time of an asset is derived in a similar fashion as in the standard Gaussian copula: a threshold is created, which contains the default correlations of the assets in the portfolio. This threshold is equated with the survival probability of the asset, and, in the case of a constant default probability function, this equation can be solved for the default time t. In case of a non-constant default probability function, a search procedure finds the default time. Monte Carlo simulations are applied to derive numerous default times and the result is averaged to determine the final default time. The default times of the different tranches are then mapped to the tranches of the CDO to find the tranche spread.

Since the OFGC is simplistic, many extensions exist, which attempt to bring the OFGC closer to reality. A dynamic OFGC model can be created, multiple common factors can be introduced, or different distributions for the latent variables can be applied.

In conclusion, the OFGC is a simple, intuitive model that traders like. However, simplicity comes at a cost. The assumptions of identical default probability of all assets and identical default correlation between all assets in the portfolio are justifiable only for a portfolio with highly homogeneous assets, possibly in the same sector and with similar credit ratings. For the heterogeneous portfolios of most investment banks, the OFGC seems too simplistic. In addition, as with the Black–Scholes–Merton option pricing model, traders seem to disagree with the OFGC: they randomly alter the tranche correlations to derive desired tranche spreads, which violates the basic principle of the OFGC, which assumes a constant CDO-wide, tranche-non-specific default correlation.

Questions for Chapter 7

Answers to these questions can be found at the back of this book.

1. Name the three strongly simplistic assumptions of the one-factor Gaussian copula (OFGC) model.
2. For which portfolios are those assumptions justifiable?
3. The correlation concept of the OFGC is incorporated in the simple equation (7.1) $x_i = \sqrt{\rho}\, M + \sqrt{1-\rho}\, Z_i$. Explain the correlation concept with this equation.
4. Equation (7.1) applies the conditionally independent correlation (CID) approach. Explain the term "conditionally independent"!
5. Why are the variables M, Z_i, and the resulting x_i in equation (7.1) called "latent" and "frailty" variables?
6. In equation (7.1), the x_i are standard normally distributed. How are the x_i transformed into probabilities?
7. In equation (7.2) $s_i^t = 1 - P_{i'}$ is the survival probability of asset i at time t, and $1 - P_i$ is the default threshold, which includes the correlation. Solve equation (7.2) for the default time t of asset i. What is the default time of asset i if $s_i^t = 80\%$ and $P_i = 50\%$?
8. Calculate the fair equity tranche spread of a CDO for the following CDO with a three-year maturity: the starting notional is US$2,000,000,000, with 125 equally weighted companies. Hence each asset has a notional of US$16,000,000. Let's assume spread payments and payouts are annually in arrears. The recovery rate for every asset is 30%. Interest rates are constant at 5%. We consider an equity tranche with a detachment point of 3%. Hence the equity tranche has a starting notional of US$60,000,000. Let's assume that we have derived that one asset defaults after 1.5 years and one asset defaults at 2.5 years. Hence the starting notional of US$60,000,000 reduces to US$44,000,000 for t_2 (end year 2) and to US$28,000,000 for t_3 (end of year 3). What is the equity tranche spread derived by the OFGC?

9. The tranche spread of the equity tranche and the senior tranche behave very differently with respect to changes in the correlation of the assets in the CDO. Draw a graph showing the tranche-spread–correlation dependence for the equity tranche and a senior tranche.
10. Explain the graph that you created in problem 9.
11. Name the main differences between the standard Gaussian copula and the OFGC.
12. The OFGC is a first, simplistic approach to derive the tranche spread in a CDO and the credit risk in portfolios. Name three extensions of the OFGC.
13. Should we apply the OFGC to value CDOs? Should we apply the OFGC to value credit risk in portfolios?
14. Why do "traders seem to disagree" with the OFGC?
15. Explain the "correlation smile" that traders apply to derive tranche spreads. How is the correlation smile related to the "volatility smile" when pricing options?

---

1 We do this because it is easy to work with survival probabilities. For example, if the survival probability for year 1 is 90% and the survival probability for the second year is also 90%, the survival probability from time 0 to the end of year 2 is 90% × 90% = 81%, assuming the survival probabilities are independent.
2 We solve equation (7.2) for t by taking the natural logarithm of both sides: $\ln s_i^t = \ln (1 - P_i)$ or $t \ln(s_i) = \ln(1 - P_i)$ or $t = \ln(1 - P_i) / \ln(s_i)$.
3 See Jarrow and van Deventer (2008).
4 See Schoenbucher and Schubert (2001) for integrating stochastic dynamics into the Gaussian copula model.

8

Financial Correlation Models – Top-Down Approaches

> Imagination is more important than knowledge
> – Albert Einstein

Financial credit models, which derive correlated default risk, can be characterised by the way the portfolio default intensity distribution is derived. In the bottom-up models of Chapters 3 to 7, the distribution of the portfolio intensity is an aggregate of the individual entities' default intensity. In a top-down model the evolution of the portfolio intensity distribution is derived directly, ie, abstracted from the individual entities' default intensities.

Top-down models are typically applied in practice if (1) the default intensities of the individual entities are unavailable or unreliable; (2) the default intensities of the individual entities are unnecessary (this may be the case when evaluating a homogeneous portfolio such as an index of homogeneous entities); or (3) the sheer size of a portfolio makes the modelling of individual default intensities problematic.

Top-down models are typically more parsimonious, computationally efficient and can often be calibrated better to market prices than bottom-up models. Although seemingly important information – such as the individual entities' default intensities – is disregarded, a top-down model can typically capture properties of the portfolio such as volatility or correlation smiles better than bottom-up models. In addition, the individual entities' default information can often be inferred by random thinning techniques.

In this chapter we analyse the correlation modelling of several top-down approaches. In particular we revisit Vasicek's 1987 one-factor Gaussian copula (OFGC) model, discuss the Markov chain models of Hurd and Kuznetsov (2006a, 2006b), and Schönbucher (2006); as well as the top-down contagion model of Giesecke et al (2009). Top-down models are mathematically somewhat more complex than bottom-up models. So, mathematically, readers who are not well equipped may take this chapter with caution. Mathematicians will hopefully like it.

VASICEK'S 1987 OFGC MODEL REVISITED

The OFGC model can be considered a top-down correlation model, since it abstracts from the individual default intensities of each asset i. Rather, one default intensity is assumed for all assets in the portfolio.

We devoted Chapter 7 entirely to the OFGC, where we discussed properties and practical applications such as valuing CDOs. In this more theoretical chapter, we will briefly show that a realistic default distribution can be derived with the OFGC.

Vasicek 1987 assumes (a) a constant and identical default intensity of all entities in a portfolio and (b) the same default correlation between the entities. These two conditions constitute a "large homogeneous portfolio" (LHP), which is evaluated with the OFGC framework.

The OFGC model allows creating a loss distribution to find k=1,...,n defaults of a basket of n entities at time T. We start with the core equation

$$x_i = \sqrt{\rho}\, M + \sqrt{1-\rho}\, Z_i \qquad (7.1)$$

variables defined as in Chapter 7.

We now map the cumulative default probabilities $Q(T)$, which are identical for all entities in the portfolio, to standard normal via $N^{-1}(Q(T))$, where N^{-1} is the inverse of the cumulative standard normal distribution. We equate the $N^{-1}(Q(T))$ with the correlated frailty variable x_i of equation (7.1), hence $x_i = N^{-1}(Q(T))$. This equation satisfies the OFGC property that:

$$\text{Prob}\,(x_i < x) = \text{Prob}\,(T_i < T)$$

ie, the frailty variable x_i (which includes the default correlation) is mapped percentile to percentile to default times T_i.[1]

Inputting $x_i = N^{-1}(Q(T))$ into equation (7.1) and solving for Z_i, we derive

FINANCIAL CORRELATION MODELS – TOP-DOWN APPROACHES

$$Z_i = \frac{N^{-1}(Q(T)) - \sqrt{p}M}{\sqrt{1-p}} \qquad (8.1)$$

The correlation between the $i = 1, \ldots, n$ entities is modelled indirectly by conditioning on M. Once we determine the value of M (by a random drawing from a standard normal distribution), it follows that defaults of the entities are mutually independent. In particular, the cumulative default probability of the idiosyncratic factor Z_i, $N(Z_i)$, can be expressed as the cumulative default probability dependent on M, $Q(T \mid M)$. Hence we have

$$Q(T \mid M) = N\left(\frac{N^{-1}(Q(T)) - \sqrt{p}M}{\sqrt{1-p}}\right) \qquad (8.2)$$

Equation (8.2) gives the cumulative default probability conditional on the market factor M. We now have to find the unconditional default probabilities. We do this by first discretely integrating over M. Since M is standard normal, this is computationally easy, we can use the discrete Gaussian quadrature (Norm (x) – Norm (x – 1)) in MATLAB. We now have to derive all possible $k = 0, \ldots, n$ default combinations. We do this by applying the binomial distribution B, hence $B(k; n, Q(T \mid M))$ and weighing it with the piecewise integrated units of M. The result is a distribution of the number of defaults until T, as shown in Figure 8.1.

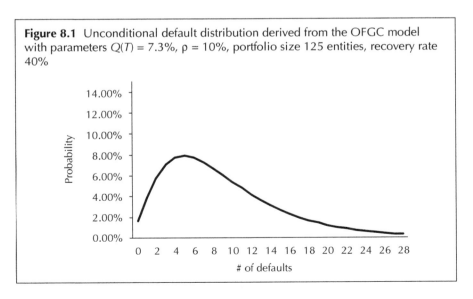

Figure 8.1 Unconditional default distribution derived from the OFGC model with parameters $Q(T) = 7.3\%$, $\rho = 10\%$, portfolio size 125 entities, recovery rate 40%

A spreadsheet that derives the default distribution in the OFGC framework can be found at www.dersoft.com/basecorrelationgeneration.xls.

MARKOV CHAIN MODELS

In the following section, we discuss two models that generate correlation in the Markov chain framework.

Inducing correlation via transition rate volatilities

Philipp Schönbucher (2006) generates different transition and default correlation properties via different transition rate[2] volatilities in a time-inhomogeneous, finite-state Markov chain[3] framework. The model is inspired by the Heath–Jarrow–Morton (HJM) (1992) interest-rate model. Whereas the HJM model generates an interest-rate term structure at future times t, Schönbucher creates a stochastic evolution of transition rates to derive the loss distribution at future times t. In analogy to the HJM model, Schönbucher applies the current (time 0) term structure of transition rates as inputs. Hence the model does not require any calibration.

Specifically, the model consists of a time-inhomogeneous, hypothetical Markov chain of cumulative losses $L(t)$, $t \geq 0$ with discrete states $\{0, 1, 2 \ldots I\}$ of the I entities of the portfolio. The generator matrix[4] $A(t, T)$, $t \leq T$, of transition probabilities satisfies the usual conditions; see Jarrow et al 1997 on deriving the risk-neutral generator matrix for continuous and discrete time. Integrating the Kolmogorov differential equations

$$\frac{dP(t,T)}{dT} \frac{1}{P(t,T)} = A(T),$$

we find the transition probability matrix $\Lambda(t, T)$, which reproduces the loss distribution $\mathbf{p}(t, T) = (p_0(t, T), \ldots, p_I(t, T))$. The components of the loss distribution, the probabilities $p_n(t, T)$, are set so that

$$p_n(t,T) := P[L(T) = n \mid \mathcal{F}_t] \qquad (8.3)$$

ie, $p_n(t, T)$ represents the probability of exactly n losses in the portfolio, viewed at time t for maturity T. $\mathcal{F}_t$ is the filtration, which contains all events.

In order to create a no-arbitrage framework and a unique

correspondence of transition probabilities to the loss distribution, Schönbucher initially allows only one-step transitions (ie, only to the next lower rating class). Therefore, the transition probability matrix at time t for maturity T, $\Lambda(t, T)$, contains only zero entries, except on the diagonal and directly adjacent higher nodes (see Figure 8.2).

Figure 8.2 Original transition matrix in the Schönbucher 2006 model

$$\Lambda(t,T) = \begin{pmatrix} a_{1,1} & a_{1,2} & 0 & ..0 & 0 \\ 0 & a_{2,2} & a_{2,3} & ..0 & 0 \\ : & : & : & ...: & : \\ 0 & 0 & 0 & ..a_{I-1,I-1} & a_{I-1,I} \\ 0 & 0 & 0 & ..0 & 0 \end{pmatrix}$$

In Figure 8.2 $a_{i,i}$, $0 \le i \le I$ is the probability of staying in the same state and $a_{i,j}$, $0 \le j \le I$ is the transition probability of moving from state i to state j. The transition probabilities evolve stochastically in time to reproduce the arbitrage-free term structure of loss distributions $\mathbf{p}(t, T)$ at future times t with maturity T. In particular, the transition probability of entity n, seen at time t for maturity T, $a_n(t, T)$, $0 < n < I$, follows a standard generalised Wiener process, ie,

$$da_n(t,T) = \mu_{a_n}(t,T)dt + \sigma_{a_n}(t,T)dz \qquad (8.4)$$

where μ_{a_n} is the drift rate of a_n, and σ_{a_n} is the volatility of a_n. Equation (8.4) brings us to the correlation properties of the model. Default correlation is induced by the dynamics of the transition volatility. Schönbucher specifies a parameter constellation in which an increase in the factor loading of the transition rates a_n increases the volatility of a_n, and vice versa. Importantly, in this framework, a higher volatility of a_n means a higher transition rate of all entities n to a lower state, hence a higher default correlation; conversely a lower volatility of a_n means a lower transition rate of all entities n to a lower state, hence lower default correlation. The model can also replicate "local correlation" by specifying a higher volatility, hence higher correlation only for a short period of time ie,

$$\frac{\partial \sigma_{a_n}(t,T)}{\partial t} = x$$

for the current time t, and a lower correlation for a future time

$$t + dt \frac{\partial \sigma_{a_n}(t,T)}{\partial t} = y$$

where $x > y$.

Inducing correlation via stochastic time change

To the best of our knowledge it was Peter Clark (1973) who first applied stochastic time processes to financial modelling. Clark proposed a stochastic time process $T(t)$ with independent increments drawn from a lognormal distribution. $T(t)$ is a "directing process", a stochastic clock that determines the speed of the evolution of the stock price process $S(t)$, forming the new process $S(T(t))$. This new process $S(T(t))$ serves as a "subordinator process" for the stock price process $S(t)$. Clark finds that the subordinated distributions can explain futures cotton prices better than alternative standard distributions.

The Variance-gamma model of Dilip Madan et al (1998) applies stochastic time change to option pricing, generalising previous work by Madan and Seneta (1990) and Madan and Milne (1991). The model consists of a standard Brownian motion, whose drift μ, however, is evaluated at random time changes t, which are modelled by a gamma process. The model has the same subordinated structure as Clark (1973):

$$S(t;\mu,\sigma,\upsilon) = \mu \Gamma(t;1,\upsilon) + \sigma \, dz(\Gamma(t;1,\upsilon)) \quad (8.5)$$

with variables as defined in equation (8.4) and $\Gamma(t; 1,\upsilon)$ is a gamma distribution with unit mean and variance υ. By controlling the skew via μ and the kurtosis via υ, the model is able to match volatility smiles in the market well. Further models that apply stochastic time change to option pricing are Geman et al (2001), Carr et al (2003) and Cont and Tankov (2004).

The stochastic time models above help to explain certain phenomena in financial practice. In the following, we discuss Hurd and Kuznetsov (2006a) and (2006b), who were the first to induce correlation via stochastic time change. Their time-homogeneous Markov chain model of K discrete rating classes $Y_t \in \{1, 2 \dots, K\}$

assumes that transition and default intensities are identical for entities in the same rating category. Hence the model does not directly reference individual transition and default intensities and therefore it qualifies primarily as top-down.

At the core of the model is a continuous time, time-homogeneous Markov chain with time-constant generator matrix L_Y

$$L_Y = \begin{pmatrix} 1_{1,1} & 1_{1,2} & 1_{1,3} & \cdots & 1_{1,K} \\ 1_{2,1} & 1_{2,2} & 1_{2,3} & \cdots & 1_{2,K} \\ \vdots & \vdots & \vdots & \vdots & \vdots \\ 1_{K-1,1} & 1_{K-1,2} & 1_{K-1,3} & \cdots & 1_{K-1,K} \\ 0 & 0 & 0 & \cdots & 0 \end{pmatrix}$$

where K is the absorbing bankruptcy state. This means that once an entity has defaulted, it stays in default. This is not necessarily the case in the US, where many companies emerge from bankruptcy. Hence the model could be extended to include a non-absorbing bankruptcy state. The $l_{i,j}$, $i \in \{1, 2 ..., K-1\}$, $j = \in \{1, 2 ..., K\}$, are the instantaneous transition intensities of migrating from rating class i to j under the historical (real-world or reference) measure P.

Hurd and Kuznetsov further introduce a vector-valued process

$$\mathbf{X}_t = \{r_t, u_t, \lambda_t\} \tag{8.6}$$

where r_t is the risk-free interest rate, the recovery rate is $R_t = e^{-u_t t}$ and, importantly, λ_t is the stochastic migration intensity process. The vector $\mathbf{X}_t$ captures macroeconomic data and represents a common factor, which affects all entities. The credit migration process of the rating classes $Y_t \in \{1, 2 ..., K\}$ is conditioned on the vector $\mathbf{X}_t$. Hence the Y_t are conditionally independent, applying the CID (conditionally independent) approach, discussed in Chapter 7. Hence $\mathbf{X}_t$ has a similar interpretation as the scalar M in equation (6.1) $x_i = \sqrt{\rho}M + \sqrt{1-\rho}Z_i$. The main motivation for this approach is again to reduce complexity.

More specifically, the correlation dynamics of the model can be derived by a probability measure change. From the generator matrix L_Y we have

$$E^P(Y_{t+dt} = j | Y_t = i) = 1_{ij} dt \tag{8.7}$$

where, P is the historical probability measure. Hurd and Kuznetsov now introduce a time-changed process, a stochastic clock τ_t, which may have continuous components and jump components. τ_t is a function of λ_t,

$$\tau_t = \int_0^t \lambda_s \, ds \qquad (8.8)$$

Under the Girsanov theorem (see Neftci 1996 for an intuitive discussion) we can define a new stochastic process under the risk-neutral measure Q with the changed drift (and jump) but constant volatility

$$E^Q(Y_{t+dt} = j \mid Y_t = i) = 1_{ij} \lambda_t dt \qquad (8.9)$$

Since λ_t is an element of the conditioning market factor X_t (see equation 8.6), the migration processes Y_t in the new process under Q are now dependent. Importantly, from equations (8.8) and (8.9) we observe that default correlation is induced by the speed of the stochastic clock τ_t. An increase in the speed of the clock increases the speed of migration of all entities and hence increases the probability of simultaneous defaults. If the stochastic clock jumps, the probability of simultaneous defaults is even higher.

We find that the induction of correlation via volatility changes (Schönbucher 2006) and the induction of correlation via stochastic time change have a similar interpretation. An increase in transition volatility as well as an increase in the stochastic clock both increase the migration within the transition matrix, hence increase the probability of simultaneous defaults, and vice versa.

CONTAGION DEFAULT MODELLING IN TOP-DOWN MODELS

In a popular credit risk model applied in financial practice, Giesecke *et al* (2011) derive a random thinning process, which allocates the portfolio intensity to the sum of the individual entities' intensities. Giesecke *et al* show that this process uniquely exists and can be realised analytically. More formally, the thinning process Z^k under the reference measure μ is predictable and has the form

$$Z^k = \frac{\lambda^k}{\lambda} \qquad (8.10)$$

where λ is the portfolio default intensity and λ^k is the default intensity of entity k, $k = 1, \ldots, m$ and $\lambda = \lambda^1 + \ldots + \lambda^m$. The model has the property that the thinning processes add up to one,

FINANCIAL CORRELATION MODELS – TOP-DOWN APPROACHES

$$\sum_{k=1}^{m} Z^k = 1$$

and that immediately after entity k defaults, the thinning process of this entity k drops to zero, $Z^k_{\tau^{k+}} = 0$.

The thinning process and a resulting basic default dependence can be explained with a m=2 entity portfolio with an assumed loss distribution N of

$$P(N_T = n) = \begin{cases} (.) & \text{for } n = 0 \\ 1 - e^{-T} & \text{for } n = 1 \\ 1 - e^{-T} - Te^{-T} & \text{for } n = 2 \end{cases} \quad (8.11)$$

where P is an integrable probability measure, n is the number of entities defaulting with the associated probability in (8.11) and N is a Poisson process with stopping time T^2. The thinning process can be parameterised with a non-negative constant q^{k1}.

$$Z^k_t = \frac{\lambda^k_t}{\lambda_t} = \begin{cases} q^{kl} & \text{for } t \leq T^1 \\ 1_{\tau^{kl} = T^1} & \text{for } T^1 < t \leq T^2 \\ 0 & \text{for } T^2 < t \end{cases} \quad (8.12)$$

From equation (8.12) we observe that the thinning process K^k_t equals q^{k1} before or at time T^1 and equals 1 if the first entity defaults before or at T^1 since $\sum_{k=1}^{m} Z^k = 1$ and $Z^k_{\tau^{k+}} = 0$ as can be seen above. The parameter q^{k1} governs the joint default dependence structure via $P(\tau^1 \leq T \cap \tau^2 \leq T) = 1 - e^{-T} - (1 - q^{kl})Te^{-T}$. From this equation and equation (8.11), we see that the extreme values of $q^{k1} = 1$ and $q^{k1} = 0$ generate the probability of exactly one default or two defaults, respectively. The name of the entity that defaults is revealed at the default time, highlighting the fact that random thinning allocates the portfolio intensity to the individual entities.

To incorporate a more rigorous joint default dependency, Giesecke *et al* suggest that the joint default distribution is governed by the portfolio intensity λ. In particular, they suggest that the process of the portfolio default intensity λ has an exponentially mean-reverting drift with a stochastic jump component, which models default contagion:

$$d\lambda_t = g(\lambda_L - \lambda_t) + \delta dJ_t \quad (8.13)$$

where J is the jump with magnitude $\delta \geq 0$ at default of an entity. The jump elevates the level of the portfolio default intensity λ, ie, the default intensity of all entities. After the jump, the contagion reverts exponentially at rate $g \geq 0$ (gravity) to its long term non-contagious mean λ_L.

In Chapter 5, we discussed contagion default modelling in a bottom-up framework. In this framework the contagion is modelled at an individual entity level, ie, the default of entity i directly impacts on the default intensity of entity j. This had led to problems of 'circularity', which complicates the derivation of a joint default distribution significantly. In the top-down environment, the default contagion is modelled conveniently at a portfolio level, circumventing the problem of circularity.

Calibrating the parameters in equation (8.13) and those of the thinning process to the CDX high-yield index during the crisis in September 2008, Giesecke finds that their model outperforms copula-based hedges. In addition, the mean profit is higher compared with the copula approach.

In an extension to the Giesecke et al (2009)[5] model, Giesecke and Tomecek (2005) incorporate a stochastic time change. However, in contrast to Hurd and Kuznetsov (2006a) and (2006b), where stochastic time change is applied to induce correlation, Giesecke and Tomecek 2009 utilise the stochastic time change to transform a standard Poisson into a counting process N of default arrival times T_n. The counting process is represented by a standard Poisson process of the form

$$N_t = \sum_{k=1}^{\infty} 1_{\{S_n \leq t\}} \qquad (8.14)$$

where

$$S_n = \sum_{i=1}^{n} V_i \qquad (8.15)$$

and the V_i are i.i.d., in particular the V_i are exponential random variables.

The continuous process

$$G(t) = \int_0^t \lambda_s$$

defines the time change. G is adapted to the filtration $G = (G_t)t \geq 0$, where G_t represents all information available at time t. Hence the process $G(t)$ is predictable.

The Poisson process (8.14) is mapped to arrival times T_n by the inverse of the time change process G. Hence

$$T_n = G^{-1}(S_n) \qquad (8.16)$$

For a rigorous proof see Giesecke *et al* (2009). Equation (8.16) implies that the Poisson arrivals S_n serve as a Merton style barrier to derive the arrival times T_n:

$$T_n = G^{-1}(S_n) = \inf\{t : G(t) \geq S_n\} = \inf\left\{t : \int_0^t \lambda_s \, ds \geq S_n\right\} \qquad (8.17)$$

Since $G(t)$ and S_n are generated independently, the model has the form of a doubly stochastic process.

We observe that generating the default time in the copula approach, which we derived in Chapter 6, equation (6.5) $\tau_{i,t} = 1_{\{N^{-1}(\lambda_{i,t}) > M_{n,t}(\cdot)\}}$, is conceptually similar to equation (8.17). However, in equation (6.5), the default time is modelled individually for each entity i with respect to the entity's default intensity function λ_i. In the top-down approach (8.17), the intensity λ is modelled at a portfolio level. A further difference is that in equation (6.5) the default correlation is elegantly incorporated in the barrier $M_{n,R}(\cdot)$. In the approach (8.17) the default correlation is modelled separately in the core equation (8.17). One benefit of the model (8.17) is that by construction the default times T_n are ordered, ie, $T_1 = \min(T_k)$ and $T_m = \max(T_k)$, $k = 1, \ldots, m$. In the copula model the default distribution is built by numerical integration over unordered default times, which we explained earlier.

SUMMARY

A fairly new, mathematically quite intensive class of correlation models are top-down approaches. In this framework the evolution of the portfolio intensity distribution is derived directly, ie, abstracting from the individual entities' default intensities. Top-down models are typically applied if:

1. the default intensities of the individual entities are unavailable or unreliable;
2. the default intensities of the individual entities are

unnecessary; this may be the case when evaluating a homogeneous portfolio such as an index of homogeneous entities; or

3. the sheer size of a portfolio makes the modelling of individual default intensities problematic.

Vasicek's large homogeneous portfolio (LHP) can be considered a top-down model, since it assumes (a) a constant and identical default intensity of all entities in a portfolio and (b) the same default correlation between the entities. The model is a one-factor version of the Gaussian copula. The model is currently (year 2018) the basis for credit-risk management in the Basel II and III accords. The benefits of the model are simplicity and intuition. One of the main shortcomings of the model is that traders randomly alter the correlation parameter for different tranches to achieve desired tranche spreads. Conceptually, however, the correlation parameter should be identical for the entire portfolio.

Within the top-down framework, Philipp Schönbucher (2006) creates a time-inhomogeneous Markov-chain of transition rates. Default correlation is introduced by changes in the volatility of transition rates. For certain parameter constellations, higher volatility means faster transition to lower states such as default, hence implies higher default correlation, and vice versa. Similarly, Hurd and Kuznetsov (2006a) and (2006b) induce correlation by a random change in the speed of time. A faster speed of time means faster transition to a lower state, possibly default, hence increases the default correlation, and vice versa.

In conclusion, top-down models are attractive, elegant and mathematically rigorous correlation models. They can be applied if a portfolio is highly homogeneous with respect to default probabilities and default correlation. The models do depend on reliable transition data as inputs and come at the cost of relatively high mathematical and computational complexity.

Questions for Chapter 8
Answers to these questions can be found at the back of this book.

1. What is the difference between "bottom-up" and "top-down" correlation models?
2. For which types of portfolios are top-down correlation models appropriate?
3. Why can the one-factor Gaussian copula (OFGC) be considered a top-down model?
4. Markov processes are "memoryless". What does this mean? Give an example.
5. What is a transition rate?
6. Why does a higher transition rate volatility mean higher default correlation in the Schönbucher 2006 model?
7. Why does an increase in stochastic time change mean a higher default correlation in the Hurd–Kuznetsov 2006a model?
8. What is the "random thinning" process in top-down models and what does it accomplish?

---

1 For more on the Copula mapping, see Chapter 5 and www.dersoft.com/2assetdefaulttime-copula.xlsm.
2 Transition rates are probabilities to move from one credit state to another.
3 A Markov chain is a stochastic "memoryless" process. This means that only the present information, not the past, is relevant. A discrete Markov process is referred to as Markov chain, although occasionally authors (such as Jarrow *et al* 1997) use continuous time when referring to a Markov chain.
4 A generator matrix is a "starting matrix", which serves as a basis to derive matrices at future times. In our context the matrices are transition matrices.
5 The first version of the Giesecke *et al* (2009) model was published in 2004.

9
Stochastic Correlation Models

"I think correlation modelling is basically at the stage volatility modelling was about 15 years ago"

– Vladimir Piterbarg

In finance, many variables such as equities, bonds, commodities, exchange rates, interest rates and volatility are often modelled with a stochastic process. In addition, from our empirical Chapter 2, we derived that financial correlations behave somewhat erratic and random. Therefore, it seems like a good idea to model financial correlations with a stochastic process.

The modelling of financial correlation with a stochastic process is fairly new, but several promising approaches exist. We will discuss them, but, before we do, let's look at some basics.

WHAT IS A STOCHASTIC PROCESS?

The reader who has made it all the way to this chapter has, hopefully, a good idea of what a stochastic process is. But let us have a closer look. Let's start with a deterministic process. A deterministic process is a process with a known outcome. For example counting numbers by one and the movement of the sun are deterministic processes. The opposite of a deterministic process is a stochastic process, also called "random process". Hence, heuristically (meaning non-mathematically), we can define a stochastic process as a process with an unknown outcome.

Examples of a stochastic process are the flipping of a coin and the rolling of a die. Most stochastic processes display the Markov property, meaning they are "memoryless". For example, even if the last three rolls of a die all resulted in a 6, the probability of rolling a 6 again is still 1/6.

The formal definition of a stochastic process is not overly

enlightening. A stochastic process is simply defined as a collection of ordered random variables X at time t:

$$\{X_t, t \in T\} \qquad (9.1)$$

where

X_t: state of the random variable at time t (for example "heads" or "tails" when flipping a coin)
T: points in time. For a discrete stochastic process $T \in N = \{0, 1, 2, 3 \ldots\}$

For a rigorous paper on stochastic processes, see Nualart (2008) or Lamberton and Lapeyre (1996). The terms "stochastic process" and "stochastic model" are often used synonymously, or a stochastic process can be part of a stochastic model. In finance, one popular stochastic model is the geometric Brownian motion (GBM), which we discussed in Chapter 5, equation (5.1). The stock price in the famous Black–Scholes–Merton 1973 option pricing model follows a GBM. Slightly re-writing equation (5.1), we have

$$\frac{d\rho}{\rho} = \mu\, dt + \sigma\, \varepsilon \sqrt{dt} \qquad (9.2)$$

where

S: variable that follows the GBM, for example a stock price
μ: expected growth rate of S
σ: expected volatility of S
dz: "Wiener process" or "Brownian motion" $dz = \varepsilon\sqrt{dt}$, where ε is a random drawing from of standard normal distribution with a mean of 0 and a standard deviation of 1. Formally, $\varepsilon = n \sim (0, 1)$. For a spreadsheet deriving ε see www.dersoft.com/epsilon.xlsx.

Therefore, stochasticity enters equation (9.2) via ε. For a model that generates the GBM in equation (9.2), and equation (9.2) with random jumps, see www.dersoft.com/gbmpathwithjumps.xlsm.

In the recent past, several stochastic correlation models have been suggested. Let us discuss them.

SAMPLING CORRELATION FROM A DISTRIBUTION (HULL AND WHITE 2010)

A simple way to model correlation as a stochastic variable is to sample it from a statistical distribution. In finance, we often sample from a standard normal distribution. For example, the ε in the dz-term of equation (9.2) is such a sample. However, in some research, samples from other distributions are taken. In the variance-gamma model, introduced by Madan et al (1998), and briefly discussed in Chapter 8, a value from the gamma distribution is sampled at random times t to create a stochastic drift rate of the underlying variable.

Hull and White (2010) extend their dynamic OFGC model, which we discussed in Chapter 7. The core equation is

$$dz_i(t) = \sqrt{\rho(t)}dM(t) + \sqrt{1-\rho(t)}dZ_i(t) \qquad (9.3)$$

where

ρ: Asset correlation parameter for the assets of the companies in the portfolio, $0 \le \rho \le 1$. ρ is assumed identical and constant for all company pairs in the portfolio.

M: Systematic market factor, which impacts all companies in the portfolio. M can be thought of as the general economic environment; for example, the return of the S&P 500. M is a random drawing from a standard normal distribution, formally $M = n \sim (0, 1)$. M is the same as ε in Chapter 5.

Z_i: Idiosyncratic factor of asset i. Z_i expresses i-th company's individual strength, possibly measured by company i's stock price return. Z_i is a random drawing from a standard normal distribution.

z_i: Results from equation (9.3) and is interpreted as a "Default indicator variable" for company i. The higher z_i, the less likely is the default of company i at a certain time T. Hence z_i is also interpreted as the asset value of company i. z_i is by construction standard normal.

Replacing $\sqrt{\rho(t)} = \alpha(t)$ in equation (9.3) to allow for negative correlation between $M(t)$ and $z(t)$, we derive

$$dz_i(t) = \alpha_i(t)dM(t) + \sqrt{1-\alpha^2(t)}dZ_i(t) \qquad (9.4)$$

Hull and White now introduce stochastic correlation by sampling $\alpha(t)$ from a beta distribution. This sample serves to create a dependency between $\alpha(t)$ and $dM(t)$. To match empirical CDX (credit default index) prices, they choose the dependency to be $-\sqrt{0.5}$. This creates a positive relationship between α and default probability: if α increases, the market environment dM decreases. This increases the default probability of company i.

The asset correlation between companies i and j is $\alpha_i \alpha_j$ (see Chapter 14 for details). A higher α_i or α_j means a higher asset correlation between i and j, and, as derived above, means a higher joint default probability. This relationship of higher asset correlation and higher default probability was empirically verified by Servigny and Renault (2002) and Das et al (2006).

Therefore, it is not surprising that the approach with the stochastic correlation sample $\alpha(t)$ in the model of equation (9.4) is able to match empirical CDX prices in most cases significantly better compared to the case without stochastic correlation (see Hull White (2010) for details).

DYNAMIC CONDITIONAL CORRELATIONS (ENGLE 2002)

In Chapter 3, equation (3.3), we had defined the Pearson correlation coefficient for a random variable as

$$\rho(X,Y) = \frac{E(XY) - E(X)E(Y)}{\sqrt{E(X^2) - (E(X))^2}\sqrt{E(Y^2) - (E(Y))^2}} \qquad (3.3)$$

Assuming the variables X and Y have a mean of zero, ie, $E(X) = E(Y) = 0$, equation (3.3) reduces to

$$\rho(X,Y) = \frac{E(XY)}{\sqrt{E(X^2)E(Y^2)}} \qquad (9.5)$$

In 2002, Robert Engle introduced dynamic conditional correlations (DCCs) in a model developed by Tim Bollerslev in 1990. The correlation at time t, ρ_t, is conditioned on the information given in the previous period $t - 1$. Hence, equation (9.5) changes to

$$\rho_t(r_1, r_2) = \frac{E_{t-1}(r_{1,t} r_{2,t})}{\sqrt{E_{t-1}(r_{1,t}^2) E_{t-1}(r_{2,t}^2)}} \qquad (9.6)$$

where r is the variable of interest. $r_{1,t}$ may be the return of asset 1 and $r_{2,t}$ may be the return of asset 2 at time t (see Chapter 1, on returns).

Conditional correlation is a concept within the ARCH (autoregressive conditional heteroscedasticity) framework (Engle 1982), which was extended to GARCH (generalised autoregressive conditional heteroscedasticity) by Bollerslev (1986).

In the ARCH framework, the variable of interest, the return r, is defined as the product of its standard deviation and an error term.

$$r_{i,t} = \sigma_{i,t} \varepsilon_{i,t} \qquad (9.7)$$

where

$r_{i,t}$: return of asset i at time t
$\sigma_{i,t}$: standard deviation of the return of asset i at time t (also called volatility)
$\varepsilon_{i,t}$: random drawing of a standard normal distribution for asset i and time t, $\varepsilon = n \sim (0, 1)$.

The variance σ^2 or the standard deviation σ in equation (9.7) are modelled with an ARCH process (or one of many extensions such as GARCH, NGARCH, EGARCH and TGARCH)[1] of the form

$$\sigma_t^2 = a_0 + a_1 \sigma_{t-1}^2 \varepsilon_{t-1}^2 + \ldots + a_q \sigma_{t-q}^2 \varepsilon_{t-q}^2 \qquad (9.8)$$

where $a_0 > 0$, $a_1 \geq 0$, so that σ^2 is positive and $q \in N$.

From equation (9.8), we can observe that the variance is a function of past error terms ε. The error term ε is typically derived from a linear regression of the underlying variable of interest (in equation (9.7) the return of asset i). The critical idea in equation (9.8) is that, if the past error terms ε_{t-x} are high, so will be the future variance at time t, σ_t^2. Vice versa, if the past error terms ε_{t-x} are low, so will be the future variance at time t, σ_t^2. The model of equation (9.8) and extensions of the model have been successfully tested (see, for example, Enders (1995) and Hacker and Hatemi-J (2005). The main contribution of the ARCH and GARCH approach is that the empirical persistence or clustering of volatility can be modelled. In reality, high volatility often persists for a certain period of time, as does low volatility.

The correlation at time t in equation (9.6)

$$\rho_t(r_1, r_2) = \frac{E_{t-1}(r_{1,t} r_{2,t})}{\sqrt{E_{t-1}(r_{1,t}^2) E_{t-1}(r_{2,t}^2)}} \qquad (9.6)$$

depends on information given at time $t-1$. Given certain assumptions, the correlation can be expressed purely in errors terms ε. Let us show this. We express the variance of returns as a function of the return, given the information in the previous period.

$$\sigma_{i,t}^2 = E_{t-1}(r_{i,t}^2) \qquad (9.9)$$

Assuming the return r is standard normal, we have $E_{t-1}(r_{i,t}^2) = 1$ and from equation (9.9) $\sigma_{i,t}^2 = 1$. Hence from equation (9.7), we derive that the return r is just the error term ε, and together with $E_{t-1}(r_{i,t}^2) = 1$, equation (9.6) reduces to

$$\rho_t(r_1, r_2) = E_{t-1}(\varepsilon_{1,t}, \varepsilon_{2,t}) \qquad (9.10)$$

The conditional correlation expressed in equations (9.6) and (9.10) correlates just two assets, 1 and 2. The model can be generalised to include multiple assets. In this case, we derive the conditional correlation matrix R, which contains the pairwise conditional correlations $\rho_t(r_{ij})$ between the n asset returns. Formally, from equation (9.10), we have

$$E_{t-1}(\varepsilon_{i,t}, \varepsilon_{j,t}) = R_{ij} \qquad (9.11)$$

where

R: conditional correlation matrix, containing the pair-wise conditional correlations of the returns of the assets $i = 1, \ldots, n$.

In equation (9.11), the correlation matrix R_{ij} is constant. The approach can be made dynamic, ie, R_{ij} can be time varying, $R_{ij}(t)$. This constitutes DCCs as suggested by Engle (2002). Parameterisation of the dynamic conditional correlation matrix $R_{ij}(t)$ in a GARCH framework can be achieved by exponential smoothing, with certain parameter constellations allowing mean reversion of the matrix process. See Engle (2002) for details.

STOCHASTIC CORRELATION – STANDARD MODELS

In the following, we will introduce three approaches, which model stochastic correlation. All three models are quite closely related.

The geometric Brownian motion

The geometric Brownian motion (GBM), whose basic idea was derived by the biologist Robert Brown in 1827, has already been

STOCHASTIC CORRELATION MODELS

mentioned several times in this book (see Chapter 5, equation (5.1)) and in this chapter – equation (9.2).[2] In finance, variables such as stocks, bonds, commodities, interest rates and volatility are often modelled with the GBM. When modelling correlation with the GBM, we derive

$$\frac{d\rho}{\rho} = \mu dt + \sigma \varepsilon \sqrt{dt} \qquad (9.2)$$

where

ρ: Correlation between two or more variables
μ: expected growth rate of ρ
σ: expected volatility of ρ
ε: random drawing from of standard normal distribution. Formally, $\varepsilon = n \sim (0, 1)$. We can compute ε as =normsinv(rand()) in Excel/VBA and norminv(rand) in MATLAB

Duellmann, Küll and Kunisch (2008) model correlation with equation (9.2). They study whether stock prices or default rates can better estimate asset correlations. Applying stochastic asset correlation in equation (9.2) rather than constant asset correlation, they find that the stochastic correlation model weakens but does not reject the result that stock prices are superior to estimating asset correlations compared to default rates.

Is the GBM in equation (9.2) a good approach to model correlation? It actually has two limitations.

(a) Equation (9.2) is not bounded, meaning correlation ρ can take values bigger than 1 and smaller than –1. From equation (9.2) we see that a value of $\rho > 1$ is more likely to happen when the growth rate μ is high, if the volatility σ is high and if we have a high value of ε in a simulation. Conversely, values of $\rho < -1$ are more likely to occur for low values of μ, and high values of σ and ε.
(b) Mean reversion, ie, the tendency of correlation to revert to its mean, is not modelled with equation (9.2). In the empirical Chapter 2, we derived that financial correlations exhibit strong mean reversion.

For computational purposes, we discretise equation (9.2). With $d\rho = \rho_{t+1} - \rho_t$, we derive

$$\rho_{t+1} = \rho_t + \rho_t \mu \Delta t + \rho_t \sigma \varepsilon_t \sqrt{\Delta t} \qquad (9.12)$$

Figure 9.1 shows a sample path of the GBM.

In Figure 9.1, at each time step, equation (9.12) is applied. The different values for correlation at each time step occur since the random drawing ε is different at each t.[3] See spreadsheet www.dersoft.com/stochasticcorrelation.xlsx for details.

The Vasicek 1977 model

Another approach to model stochastic correlation is what is known as the Vasicek 1977 model, which, however, should be credited to Uhlenbeck and Ornstein (1930). The model is

$$d\rho = a(m_\rho - \rho_t)dt + \sigma_\rho \varepsilon_t \sqrt{dt} \qquad (9.13)$$

where

a: mean reversion speed (gravity), ie, degree with which the correlation at time t, ρ_t, is pulled back to its long term mean m_ρ. a can take the values $0 \leq a \leq 1$.

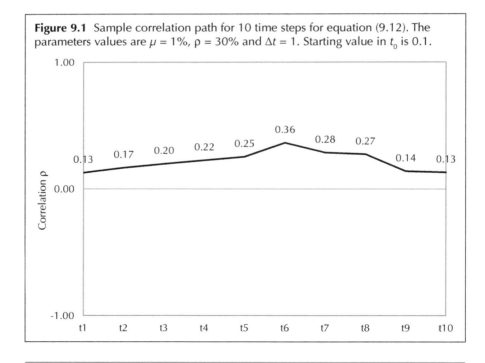

Figure 9.1 Sample correlation path for 10 time steps for equation (9.12). The parameters values are $\mu = 1\%$, $\rho = 30\%$ and $\Delta t = 1$. Starting value in t_0 is 0.1.

m_ρ: long term mean of the correlation ρ
Other variables defined as in equation (9.2)

Equation (9.13) is an improvement to the GBM in equation (9.12) since it includes mean reversion, ie, the tendency of a variable to be pulled back to its long-term mean. We derived in Chapter 2 that financial correlations exhibit strong mean reversion.

The limitation of the Vasicek 1977 model with respect to modelling correlation is that the model is not bounded, ie, correlation values of bigger than 1 and smaller than –1 can occur. These values are more likely to occur when mean reversion "a" is low and volatility σ_ρ is high.

For computational reasons, we again discretise. With $d\rho = \rho_{t+1} - \rho_t$, equation (9.13) then becomes:

$$\rho_{t+1} = \rho_t + a\left(m_\rho - \rho_t\right)\Delta t + \sigma_\rho \varepsilon_t \sqrt{\Delta t} \qquad (9.14)$$

Figure 9.2 shows a sample path of the Vasicek model.

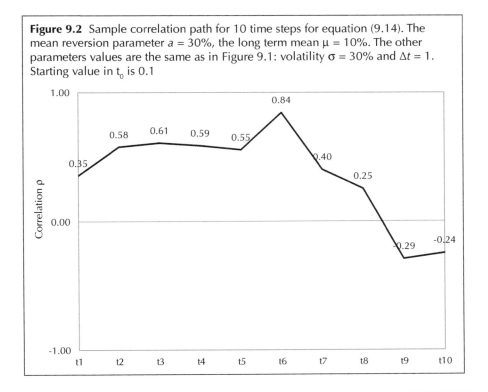

Figure 9.2 Sample correlation path for 10 time steps for equation (9.14). The mean reversion parameter $a = 30\%$, the long term mean $\mu = 10\%$. The other parameters values are the same as in Figure 9.1: volatility $\sigma = 30\%$ and $\Delta t = 1$. Starting value in t_0 is 0.1

Comparing Figures 9.1 and 9.2, we observe the higher volatility in Figure 9.2. This is mainly because the relative change $d\rho/\rho$ is modelled in Figure 9.1, whereas the absolute change $d\rho$ is modelled in Figure 9.2, compare equations (9.12) and (9.14).

The bounded Jacobi process

The two approaches that we have introduced so far, the geometric Brownian motion and the Vasicek model, both have the limitation that correlation values can become bigger than 1 and smaller than −1. This is an undesired property if the correlation is modelled in the Pearson correlation framework, where the correlation coefficient is bounded between −1 and +1.[4]

A model that can comply with correlation bounds is the bounded Jacobi process.[5] Applying the bounded Jacobi process to correlation, we derive

$$d\rho = a(m_\rho - \rho_t)dt + \sigma_\rho \sqrt{(h-\rho_t)(\rho_t - f)}\, \varepsilon_t \sqrt{dt} \qquad (9.15)$$

where h : upper boundary level, f : lower boundary level, ie, $h \geq \rho \geq f$. Other variables are defined as in equations (9.2) and (9.13).

With equation (9.15) the user can choose specific upper and lower boundaries. For correlation modelling in the Pearson framework, these boundaries are $h = +1$ and $f = -1$. In this case equation (9.15) reduces to

$$d\rho = a(m_\rho - \rho_t)dt + \sigma_\rho \sqrt{(1-\rho_t^2)}\, \varepsilon_t \sqrt{dt} \qquad (9.16)$$

Equation (9.15) requires correlation values within a lower-bound f and an upper-bound h (otherwise the term $\sqrt{(h-\rho_t)(\rho_t-f)}$ cannot be evaluated). Equation (9.16) requires correlation values within the bounds −1 to +1 (otherwise the term $\sqrt{(1-\rho_t^2)}$ cannot be evaluated). However, for low mean reversion levels "a" and high volatility σ_ρ, it can happen that the model generates correlation levels smaller than −1 and higher than +1. Therefore, we have to introduce boundary conditions. These boundaries conditions for equation (9.15) are

$$a \geq \frac{\sigma^2(h-f)/2}{(m_\rho - f)} \qquad (9.17)$$

for the lower-bound f and

$$a \geq \frac{\sigma^2(h-f)/2}{(h-m_\rho)} \qquad (9.18)$$

for the higher-bound h.

Applying the boundary levels $f = -1$ and $h = +1$, we derive the boundary levels for equation (9.16) as

$$a \geq \frac{\sigma^2}{(m_\rho + 1)} \qquad (9.19)$$

for the lower-bound f and

$$a \geq \frac{\sigma^2}{(1 - m_\rho)} \qquad (9.20)$$

for the higher-bound h.

From equations (9.17) to (9.20), we observe the intuitive feature that the bounds are more likely to be satisfied for high values of mean reversion 'a' and low values of volatility σ. See Emmerich (2006) and Wilmott (1998) for the derivation of the boundaries.

Ma (2009a) and (2009b) applies the bounded Jacobi process to

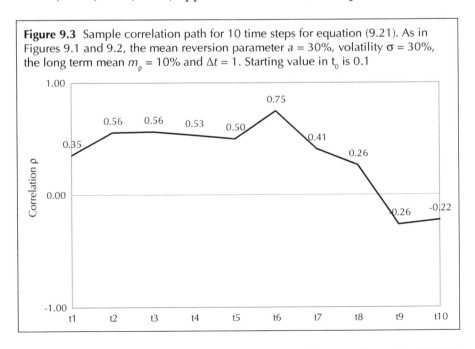

Figure 9.3 Sample correlation path for 10 time steps for equation (9.21). As in Figures 9.1 and 9.2, the mean reversion parameter $a = 30\%$, volatility $\sigma = 30\%$, the long term mean $m_\rho = 10\%$ and $\Delta t = 1$. Starting value in t_0 is 0.1

value correlation dependent Quanto options and Multi-asset options. This inclusion of stochastic correlation in the Black-Scholes-Merton model improves the valuation of these options compared to the standard Black-Scholes-Merton model.

Discretising equation (9.16), again applying $d\rho = \rho_{t+1} - \rho_t$, we derive

$$\rho_{t+1} = \rho_t + a(m_\rho - \rho_t)\Delta t + \sigma_\rho \sqrt{(1-\rho_t^2)} \varepsilon_t \sqrt{\Delta t} \qquad (9.21)$$

Figure 9.3 shows a sample path of the equation (9.21).

Comparing Figures 9.2 and 9.3, we observe somewhat minor differences between the correlation modelling with Vasicek in equation (9.14) and the bounded Jacobi process in equation (9.21). The correlation models introduced so far in this chapter can be found at www.dersoft.com/stochasticcorrelation.xlsx.

EXTENDING THE HESTON MODEL WITH STOCHASTIC CORRELATION (BURASCHI *ET AL* 2010, DA FONSECA 2012)

In Chapter 5, we analysed and praised the Heston 1993 correlation model. It is a mathematically rigorous, dynamic correlation model, which is widely applied in finance. Slightly rewriting the equations in Chapter 5, the Heston model consists of three main equations.

$$\frac{dS}{S} = \mu dt + \sigma_t dz_1 \qquad (9.22)$$

$$d\sigma_t^2 = a(m_\sigma^2 - \sigma_t^2) dt + \xi \sigma_t dz_2 \qquad (9.23)$$

where

S: variable of interest, eg, a stock price
μ: expected growth rate of S
σ: expected volatility of S
dz: Brownian motion or Wiener process $dz(t) = \varepsilon(t)\sqrt{dt}$ with ε: random drawing from of standard normal distribution with a mean of 0 and a standard deviation of 1. Formally, $\varepsilon = n \sim (0, 1)$.
a: mean reversion rate (gravity), ie, degree with which σ at time t, σ_t, is pulled back to its long-term mean σ_ρ. "a" can take the values $0 \le a \le 1$.
m_σ: long term mean of the σ
ξ: volatility of the volatility σ.

The stochastic process of S in equation (9.22) and the stochastic volatility of S, σ in equation (9.23) are correlated with the identity

$$dz_1(t) = \sqrt{\rho_1} dz_2(t) + \sqrt{1-\rho_1} dz_3(t) \qquad (9.24)$$

where $dz_2(t)$ and $dz_3(t)$ are independent, and $dz(t)$ and $dz(t')$ are independent, $t \neq t'$.

Buraschi et al (2010) – first version of the paper appeared in 2006 – and Da Fonesca (2012) extend the Heston 1993 model with a more rigorous correlation structure. The model is based on the Wishart Affine Stochastic Correlation model (WASC), introduced by Bru (1991) and extended by Gourieroux and Valery (2004).

The model is presented as an n-dimensional stochastic process of covariance matrices.[6] For ease of exposition, we will concentrate on $n = 2$ assets. In this case, S in equation (9.22) expands to a price vector of 2 assets, S_1 and S_2, formally $S = (S_1, S_2)^T$, where T stands for "transpose". The stochastic process for S is

$$dS_t = I_s \left[\mu dt + \sqrt{\Sigma_t} dZ_t \right] \qquad (9.25)$$

where

$I_s = \mathrm{Diag}[S_1, S_2]$, ie, a diagonal 2×2 matrix (with entries of equation (9.25) on the diagonal and zero entries otherwise).
μ: expected growth rate of the 2-dimensional vector S
σ: expected volatility of the 2-dimensional vector S
dZ_t: 2-dimensional Brownian motion
Σ_t: Covariance matrix of the returns of asset S_1 and S_2

In our 2-asset case, the covariance matrix Σ_t takes the form

$$\Sigma_t = \begin{bmatrix} \Sigma_t^{11} & \Sigma_t^{12} \\ \Sigma_t^{21} & \Sigma_t^{22} \end{bmatrix} \qquad (9.26)$$

where Σ_t^{11} and Σ_t^{22} are the variance of the returns of asset 1 and asset 2, respectively, and Σ_t^{12} and Σ_t^{21} are the covariances of the returns of assets 1 and 2. Note that the covariance of a single asset is equal to its variance, ie, Covariance(i,i) = Variance(i). Therefore, a covariance matrix has variances on its main diagonal and is therefore also called "variance – covariance" matrix. Also note the covariance of 2 assets is commutative, ie, Covariance(ij) = Covariance(ji), hence in the matrix (9.26) $\Sigma_t^{12} = \Sigma_t^{21}$.

At the core of the model, the covariance matrix (9.26) follows a stochastic process of the form

$$d\Sigma_t = \left(\Omega\Omega^T + M\Sigma_t + \Sigma_t M^T\right)dt + \sqrt{\Sigma_t}\,dW_t Q + Q^T \left(dW_t\right)^T \sqrt{\Sigma_t} \quad (9.27)$$

where

Q: volatility of co-volatility matrix $\sqrt{\Sigma_t}$, corresponding to ξ in equation (9.23).
M: negative semi-definite matrix,[7] which controls the degree of mean reversion of Σ_t, corresponding to "a" in equation (9.23).
Ω: related to the long term mean of the covariance matrix Σ_t, corresponding to m_σ in equation (9.23).
W: two-dimensional Brownian motion.

In the original Heston model, the stochastic process for the underlying asset S and the stochastic process of the volatility σ are correlated by correlating the Brownian motions of these processes (see equation (9.24)). Accordingly, the Brownian motions of equations (9.25) and (9.27) are correlated:

$$dZ(t) = \rho\,dW(t) + \sqrt{1 - \rho^T \rho}\,dB(t) \quad (9.28)$$

where $dW(t)$ and $dB(t)$ are independent, and $dZ(t)$ and $dZ(t')$ are independent, $t \neq t'$.

Equation (9.28) correlates the Brownian motions of equations (9.25) and (9.27). Conveniently, the model admits a closed-form-solution for the correlation between the underlying return assets S and its variance Σ. For asset 1, we have

$$Corr\left(d\ln S_1, d\Sigma^{11}\right) = \frac{\rho_1 Q_{11} + \rho_2 Q_{21}}{\sqrt{Q_{11}^2 + Q_{21}^2}} \quad (9.29)$$

For asset 2,

$$Corr\left(d\ln S_2, d\Sigma^{22}\right) = \frac{\rho_1 Q_{12} + \rho_2 Q_{22}}{\sqrt{Q_{12}^2 + Q_{22}^2}} \quad (9.30)$$

If we assume that there is no correlation between the volatility of volatility of asset 1 and the volatility of volatility of asset 2, then $Q_{12} = Q_{21} = 0$. In this case, the matrix Q is diagonal and equation (9.29) reduces to

$$Corr\left(d\ln S_1, d\Sigma^{11}\right) = \rho_1 \quad (9.31)$$

Equation (9.30) reduces to

$$Corr\left(d\ln S_2, d\Sigma^{22}\right) = \rho_2 \quad (9.32)$$

In reality we observe a negative relationship between returns S and its variance Σ, sometimes called "leverage".[8] This can be modelled for asset 1 with $\rho_1 < 0$ and for asset 2 with $\rho_2 < 0$.

Buraschi et al (2006/2010) assume a rather simple correlation structure, setting $\rho_1 = 1$ and $\rho_2 = 0$. The negative relationship between the returns S and their variance Σ is then generated with negative values of $Q_{12} = Q_{21}$; see equations (9.29) and (9.30) (Q_{11} and Q_{22} are by definition positive). Da Fonesca (2012) applies a more flexible correlation structure, ie, allows $\rho \in (-1,1)$ for all ρ.

Critical appraisal of the Buraschi et al (2010) and Da Fonesca (2012) models

The model presented above has numerous parameters and can therefore replicate financial reality well. Especially the negative relationship between returns and volatility (sometimes called "leverage") and the higher correlation in a recession (sometimes referred to as "asymmetric correlation"), which we also found in the empirical Chapter 2, can be modelled. In addition, volatility skews (ie, higher volatility when returns are negative) and the right balance between correlation persistence correlation mean-reversion can be modelled. Note that the higher the persistence, the lower is the mean reversion and vice versa (for details see Chapter 2). Buraschi et al also find evidence that part of the hedge fund industries' alpha (ie, achieving higher returns than the market) can be attributed to hedge funds exposure to correlation risk.

The drawback of the model lies in its relative mathematical and computational complexity. This may limit its application in reality.

STOCHASTIC CORRELATION, STOCHASTIC VOLATILITY AND ASSET MODELLING

In a recent paper, Lu and Meissner (2017) build a stochastic volatility and stochastic correlation model. Whereas in the Heston 1993 model – extended by Buraschi et al (2010) and Da Fonesca (2012) (see the section "Extending the Heston model with stochastic correlation" above) – stochastic returns and stochastic volatility are correlated, Lu and Meissner correlate stochastic volatility and stochastic correlation.

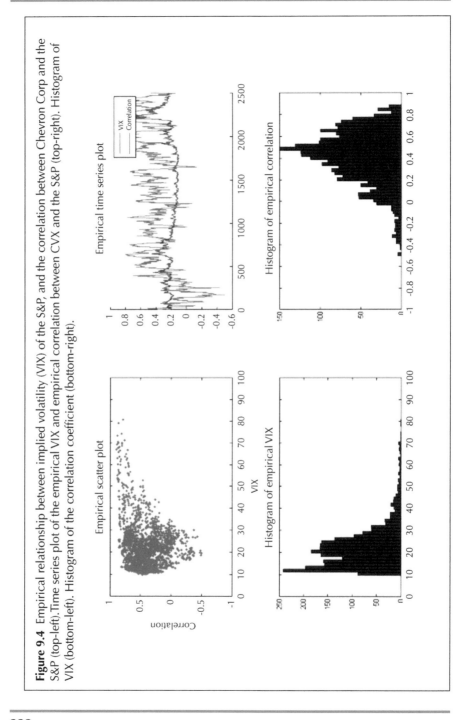

Figure 9.4 Empirical relationship between implied volatility (VIX) of the S&P, and the correlation between Chevron Corp and the S&P (top-left). Time series plot of the empirical VIX and empirical correlation between CVX and the S&P (top-right). Histogram of VIX (bottom-left). Histogram of the correlation coefficient (bottom-right).

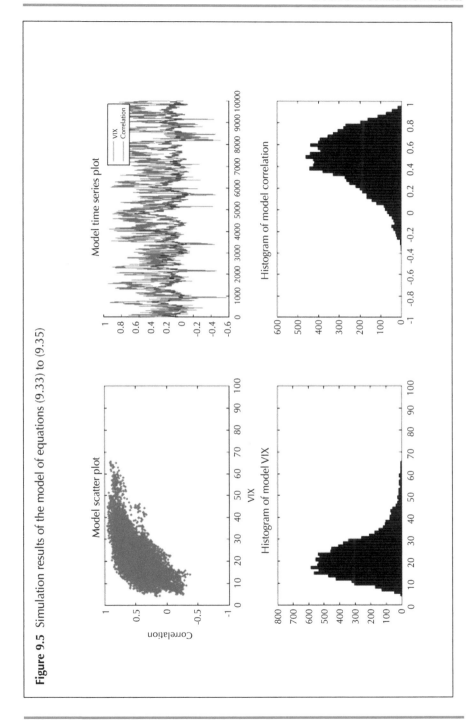

Figure 9.5 Simulation results of the model of equations (9.33) to (9.35)

Therefore the core equations of the model are

$$d\sigma = a_\sigma(m_\sigma - \sigma_t)dt + v_\sigma\sqrt{\sigma}dw_1 \tag{9.33}$$

$$d\rho = a_\rho(m_\rho - \sigma_t)dt + v_\rho\sqrt{1-\rho^2}dw_2 \tag{9.34}$$

$$dw_1 = \rho_w dw_2 + \sqrt{1-\rho_w^2}dw_3 \tag{9.35}$$

where

σ: Volatility of the variable of interest, the S&P 500, modelled by the VIX[9]
m_σ: long term mean of the S&P 500
a_σ: mean reversion of the S&P 500
v_σ: volatility of volatility σ of the S&P 500
ρ: Correlation between an individual stock and the S&P 500
a_ρ, m_ρ, v_ρ: mean reversion, long-term mean and volatility of the correlation ρ, respectively
ρ_w: correlation coefficient, which correlates the Brownian motions dw_1 and dw_2.

Equation (9.33) models stochastic volatility with the Cox–Ingersoll–Ross (1985) model. Equation (9.34) models stochastic correlation with a modified Jacobi process. The term $\sqrt{1-\rho^2}$ bounds correlation between –1 and +1. However, as discussed above, for low mean-reversion levels a_ρ and high-volatility v_ρ, it can happen that the model generates correlation levels smaller than –1 and higher than +1. Therefore, we have to introduce boundary conditions. These boundary conditions are as displayed in equations (9.19) and (9.20).

The model of equations (9.33) to (9.35) intends to replicate real-world volatility – correlation properties. As seen from the model output of Figure 9.5, the real-world volatility – correlation relationships of Figure 9.4 are replicated well by the model.

Of special interest is the relationship between volatility σ (of the S&P 500 in the example above, modelled by the VIX) and the correlation ρ (between a particular stock, Chevron, and the S&P in the example above), displayed in top left graph of Figures 9.4 and 9.5. We observe that the relationship is somewhat "triangular", ie, it is (a) positive, and (b) the correlation volatility v_ρ decreases if the volatility σ (represented by the VIX) increases.

The positive relationship between correlation ρ and σ in Figure 9.4 is replicated if ρ_w is positive. In addition, the decreasing correlation volatility v_ρ as a function of the increase in σ (the VIX) is incorporated in the model: if σ increases, ρ increases (if ρ_w is positive). From the term $v_\rho \sqrt{1-\rho^2}$ it follows that, if ρ increases, the volatility of ρ, v_ρ, decreases. Hence it follows that if σ (represented by the VIX) increases, v_ρ decreases as displayed in Figures 9.4 and 9.5 top left.

Asset modelling

The model of equations (9.33) and (9.35) can be applied to model assets. Asset modelling is often done with geometric Brownian motion (GBM), which we discussed in equations (5.1) and (9.2) and (9.22). Here is the GBM once again

$$\frac{dS_i}{S_i} = \mu_i dt + \sigma_i dz \qquad (9.36)$$

where

S_i: asset price of a particular asset i
μ_i: expected drift of S_i,
σ_i: expected volatility of S_i

Lu and Meissner now expand the GBM and model to

$$\frac{dS_i}{S_i} = \mu_i dt + \sigma_i dz + \beta_i \rho \sigma dw \qquad (9.37)$$

where

β_i: constant with $0 \leq \beta_i \leq 1$
ρ: correlation between an individual stock and the market, represented by the S&P 500. ρ is modelled as a stochastic process by equation (9.34).
σ: volatility of the market, represented by the VIX of the S&P 500, which is modelled by equation (9.33).
The Brownian motions of ρ and σ are correlated via equation (9.35); dw is the Brownian motion of the market component.

Equation (9.37) has a CAPM (capital asset pricing model) interpretation. The first two terms on the right side of equation (9.37) represent the idiosyncratic stock component. The term $\sigma\, dw$

CORRELATION RISK MODELLING AND MANAGEMENT

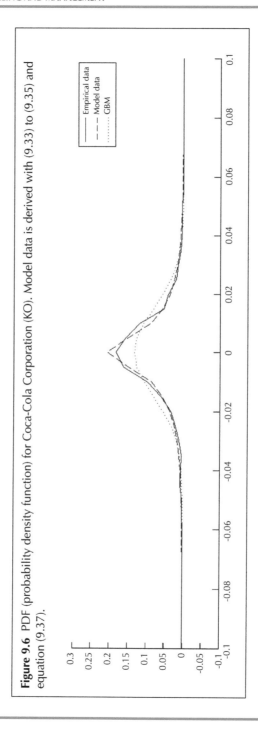

Figure 9.6 PDF (probability density function) for Coca-Cola Corporation (KO). Model data is derived with (9.33) to (9.35) and equation (9.37).

represents the systematic market-risk factor, which is shared by all stocks. The impact magnitude of systematic component on the stock is $\beta_i \rho$.

In Figure 9.6, the performance of the model of equations (9.33) to (9.35) and (9.37) is compared to the standard GBM of equation (9.35).

From Figure 9.6 we observe that the model of equations (9.33) to (9.35) and equation (9.37) outperforms the standard GBM in equation (9.36). This is verified by standard statistics. The chi-square goodness-of-fit test shows a p-value of 0.8164 (chi^2 = 5.986) between the model distribution and the empirical distribution, while the p-value is 0.054 (chi^2 = 19.411) between the GBM-normal distribution and the empirical distribution. The model gives similar results for other stocks that were tested.

Lu and Meissner (2017) extend the model to include correlation between individual stocks in a portfolio approach, applying the conditionally independent (CID) correlation concept, which we discussed in Chapter 7. This improves the performance of the model further.

CONCLUSION: SHOULD WE MODEL FINANCIAL CORRELATIONS WITH A STOCHASTIC PROCESS?

Many assets in finance are modelled with a stochastic process. Assets that are assumed to have little or no mean-reversion, such as stocks, exchange rates or real-estate values, are modelled with a non-mean-reverting stochastic process such as the GBM, displayed in equations (5.1), (9.2) and (9.22), or they can be modelled with no-arbitrage, non-mean-reverting models as Ho Lee (1986).

Assets that display a certain degree of mean reversion such as bonds, interest rates or default probabilities are typically modelled with a stochastic process that includes mean reversion such as the Vasicek (1977) model displayed in equation (9.13) or with mean-reverting no-arbitrage models such as Hull and White (1990) or the Black–Derman–Toy (1990) model. The continuous time, mean-reverting HJM (Heath, Jarrow and Morton) (1990) model and its discrete version, the Libor Market Model (LMM) (1997) model (credited to three groups of authors: Brace, Gatarek and Musiela; Miltersen, Sandmann and Sondermann; and Jamshidian) are generalised models and include the aforementioned models as special cases.

Since many financial assets are successfully modelled with a stochastic process, should we also model financial correlations with a stochastic process? This is mainly an empirical question: do financial correlations in the real world behave in a way that can be captured with a certain stochastic model? The research in this area has just started, but the first results are promising.

We discussed the conditional correlation modelling approach of Bollerslev (1990), generalised by Engle (2002); sampling correlation values from a stochastic distribution (Hull and White 2010); the Vasicek model applied by Duellmann et al (2008); modelling correlation with a modified Jacobi process by Ma (2009a), (2009b), the Wishart Affine Stochastic Correlation (WASC) model applied by Buraschi et al (first version 2006) and an extension by Da Fonseca (2012); as well as the approach by Lu and Meissner (2017). All these approaches show that, when a certain form of stochasticity for financial correlations is applied, correlation properties in reality can be replicated quite well. In addition, the valuation of correlation-dependent structures such as multi-asset options or quanto options (Ma 2009a and 2009b) can be improved if correlation is modelled with as a stochastic process.

In conclusion, while stochastic correlation modelling is still in its infancy, first results are promising. Just as other financial variables as stocks, bonds, interest rates, commodities, volatility and more are modelled with a stochastic process, it can be expected that, in the near future, financial correlations will also be typically modelled with a stochastic process.

SUMMARY

The modelling of financial correlations with a stochastic process is fairly new, but several promising approaches exist. We discussed them in this chapter.

Hull and White (2010) find a simple way to address stochastic correlation. They create a dynamic version of the one-factor Gaussian copula (OFGC) model (see Chapter 7 for details). Hull and White then sample the critical correlation parameter, which indirectly correlates the variables with a beta distribution. The model matches empirical CDX prices in most cases better than a comparable model without stochastic correlation.

In 2002 Robert Engle introduced a dynamic conditional

correlation (DCC) concept within the ARCH and GARCH framework. The correlation depends on expectations given at a previous point in time. In addition, the correlation matrix can be made a function of time, constituting a dynamic stochastic correlation model.

A further way to model financial correlations is to use the standard geometric Brownian motion (GBM), which is often applied to model other financial variables such as stocks, exchange rates, commodities and more. However, the standard GBM suffers from two drawbacks: (a) mean reversion, a critical property of financial correlations, as we derived in Chapter 2, is not incorporated in the GBM; (b) the model is not bounded, meaning correlation values of larger than 1 and smaller than −1 can occur.

An improvement of the GBM for modelling financial correlations is the Vasicek (1977) model, which incorporates mean reversion, or the bounded Jacobi process, which incorporates mean reversion and is also bounded, ie, the correlation values lie between −1 and +1 if boundary conditions are imposed.

A rigorous, mathematically quite intensive approach to modelling financial correlations is based on the Wishart Affine Stochastic Correlation model (WASC). Here a stochastic covariance matrix follows a stochastic process, which is – as in the Heston 1993 model – correlated with the stochastic process of the underlying price matrix. The model has numerous parameters and is able to replicate several real-world correlation properties well.

In the related stochastic correlation model of Lu and Meissner, which correlates stochastic correlation with stochastic volatility, it is shown that asset modelling can be improved compared with the standard GBM.

Questions for Chapter 9
Answers to these questions can be found at the back of this book.

1. What is a deterministic process? Name two examples.
2. What is a stochastic or random process? Name two examples.

3. Why does it seem like a good idea to model financial correlations as a stochastic process? Give two reasons.
4. How is stochasticity modelled in the Dynamic Conditional Correlation (CDD) concept?
5. The geometric Brownian motion (GBM) is applied to model many financial variables such as stock prices, commodities and exchange rates. What are two of the limitations of the GBM model financial correlations?
6. The Vasicek model is an improvement over the GBM to model financial correlations. Why?
7. The bounded Jacobi process seems like a good choice to model financial correlations. What advantage does it have over the GBM and the Vasicek model?
8. In the Buraschi, Porchia and Trojani 2010 stochastic correlation model, which two stochastic processes are correlated?
9. In the Buraschi, Porchia and Trojani 2010 model, which financial properties can be replicated? Name two.
10. Should we model correlation with a deterministic or stochastic process?

---

1 The N in "NGARCH" stands for nonlinear, the E in "EGARCH" stands for exponential, the T in "TGARCH" stands for truncated. See Bollerslev (2008) for a nice overview of all ARCH extensions.
2 It was actually the Dutch biologist Jan Ingenhousz who first published papers in German and French in 1784 and 1785 on the dispersion of charcoal particles on alcohol. Therefore, he should be credited with what is known today as the Brownian motion.
3 Although the correlation values at t_1 and t_{10} are both 0.13, ε in t_1 and t_{10} are different since ρ increases from t_0 to t_1, from 0.1 to 0.13, and decreases from t_9 to t_{10}, from 0.14 to 0.13.
4 For a paper discussing correlation coefficients >1 and <−1, see Burgin and Meissner 2016.
5 For a nice paper on the Jacobi process see Gourieroux and Valery (2004).
6 We will use some matrix algebra in the following. See www.dersoft.com/matrixprimer.xlsx for some basic matrix operations.
7 See www.dersoft.com/matrixprimer.xlsx for details.
8 Unfortunately, the term "leverage" has many meanings in finance. In corporate finance, leverage typically refers to the debt–equity ratio. In derivatives, leverage is the relative change of derivatives gain (or loss) with respect to the relative change of underlying. If the derivative is a call C and the underlying is a stock S, the leverage is $\partial C/C/\partial S/S$.
9 The VIX is the implied volatility of the S&P 500 (ie, the volatility implied by options prices).

10

Quantifying Market Correlation Risk

> "The [financial] industry is more technical than ever, and there is as much need to understand the risks of the system as ever"
> – Robert Merton

In this chapter we will discuss and quantify the correlation risk of financial products whose primary focus is market risk. Let us just clarify what market risk is. Market risk is the risk of financial loss due to an adverse change in the price of a financial security.

We typically differentiate four main types of markets: (a) the equity market; (b) fixed-income market; (c) commodity market; and (d) foreign-exchange-rate market. However, other markets can be categorised as energy market, real-estate market, weather market, economic variables, etc. A financial security is a tradable asset in one of these markets, such as stocks, bonds, commodities, exchange rates, real estate, or futures, options and swaps on these securities.

THE CORRELATION RISK PARAMETERS CORA AND GORA

In Chapters 3 to 5 we discussed models to quantify the correlations among one or more financial variables. We will now discuss how to quantify correlation risk, ie, the risk that the correlations change. We introduce a correlation risk parameter, which we will call Cora.

Definition: Cora measures how much a dependent variable changes if the correlation among two or more independent variables changes by an infinitesimally small amount. Formally,

$$\text{Cora} = \frac{\partial V}{\partial \rho(x_{i=1},\ldots,_n)} \qquad (10.1)$$

where V is the value of a dependent financial variable and $\rho(x_{i=1,\ldots n})$ is the correlation or correlation matrix of the independent variables $x_{i=1,\ldots n}$.

We typically calculate Cora for a portfolio of assets. In this case, V can be the following.

1. The return/risk ratio μ_p/σ_p of the portfolio. We already implicitly derived Cora for the return/risk ratio μ_p/σ_p in Chapter 1 for a two-asset portfolio. This was displayed in Figure 1.3, where Cora is the slope of the μ_p/σ_p function.
2. The risk of a portfolio, measured by the standard deviation of asset returns.
3. The risk of a portfolio measured by the value-at-risk (VaR) concept. We already implicitly derived the Cora in Chapter 1 in the section called "Risk management and correlation" for a two-asset portfolio. Hence in this case V in equation (10.1) is the VaR. The result was displayed in Figure 1.6. In this chapter we will generalise the result for a portfolio of $n > 2$ assets.

V in equation (10.1) can also be a type of correlation option, or a correlation swap. We already discussed the impact of correlation on the risk of these products in Chapter 1 in the section "Trading and correlation". V can also be a standard option, which is valued on a model that includes correlations; see "Option Vanna" below.

V in equation (10.1) can also be the price of a credit product as a credit default swap (CDS) or a structured product such as a collateralised debt obligation (CDO). This is because the market price of a CDS or CDO changes when correlation changes, hence there is market price risk. This shows the close relationship between market risk and credit risk: when the market price of an asset decreases (possibly due to a recession), typically the default risk increases. Vice versa, if the default risk of an asset increases (maybe due to bad management), typically the market price decreases.

We already discussed the dependence of a CDS with respect to the correlation between the reference entity and the counterparty in Chapter 1, displayed in Figure 1.1. Graphically, Cora is the slope of the CDS function. We will discuss correlation risk with respect to credit products in Chapter 11.

In a portfolio context, the x_i in equation (10.1) are the returns of the assets in the portfolio, which are correlated in a correlation matrix $\rho(x_1,...,x_n)$; see example 10.1, below. We can calculate Cora for all asset returns, but we can also analyse how the risk changes for a single pairwise change in the correlation matrix. We will call this GAP-Cora in an analogy with the GAP analysis in interest rate risk management, where a single interest rate is "bumped up" or "bumped down" by a certain amount to see the impact on the present value or on risk.

From Figures 1.2, 1.3, 1.4, 1.6 and 1.7 in Chapter 1, we can see that Cora can be positive or negative. Cora can also be positive and negative within the same function, as in Figure 1.2, where Cora is positive for correlation values of –1 to about –0.3 and negative for correlation values of about –0.3 to 1.

We can also look at the sensitivity of Cora, ie, how much Cora changes. We will call this Gora.

Definition: Gora measures how much Cora changes if the correlation between two or more independent variables changes by an infinitesimally small amount. Formally,

$$\text{Gora} = \frac{\partial \text{Cora}}{\partial \rho(x_{i=1},\ldots,_n)} = \frac{\partial^2 V}{\partial \rho^2(x_{i=1},\ldots,_n)} \qquad (10.2)$$

variables as defined in equation (10.1). Hence, Gora is the first partial derivative of the Cora function or the second partial derivative of the original function V with respect to correlation; ie, Gora measures the curvature of a function with respect to correlation. Since Cora can be negative and positive, it follows that Gora can also be negative and positive.

EXAMPLES OF CORA IN FINANCIAL PRACTICE
Option Vanna
Measuring the impact of changes in correlation is not totally new. It is already formalised in option theory and called "Vanna". It was introduced in the famous "stochastic alpha beta rho model" (SABR) by Hagan *et al* (2002). The core equations of the model are

$$\frac{dF}{F^\beta} = \sigma\, dW \qquad (10.3)$$

$$\frac{d\sigma}{\sigma} = \alpha\, dZ \qquad (10.4)$$

and

$$\text{Corr}(dW,dZ) = \rho dt \tag{10.5}$$

This model is named after its parameters α, which is the volatility of volatility, β, which determines the skew of the volatility, ie, how lopsided or asymmetric the volatility function is, and ρ, which determines the correlation between the Brownian motions dW and dZ of forward rate F and the volatility σ of forward rate F. The model of equations (10.3) to (10.5) reduces to the zero-drift Brownian motion for $\alpha = \beta = 0$. The model is identical to the "Constant Variance of Elasticity" (CEV) model of John Cox (1975) for $\alpha = 0$.

The model includes the correlation between the forward rate or price F and volatility σ via equation (10.5). This correlation influences the call C and put price P, since the call and put price are functions of F and σ. We derive the sensitivity of the option price V^* with respect to correlation. Hence, we have

$$\text{Vanna} = \frac{\partial^2 V^*}{\partial \rho(F,\sigma)} \tag{10.6}$$

From equations (10.1) and (10.6), we see that Vanna is a special case of Cora, with the dependent variable being the option price V^* and the correlated variables being the forward price or rate F and the volatility of F, σ. We can replace the functional relationship $\rho(F, \sigma)$ in equation (10.6) and write

$$\text{Vanna} = \frac{\partial \left(\frac{\partial V^*}{\partial F} \right)}{\partial \sigma} = \frac{\partial^2 V^*}{\partial F \partial \sigma} \tag{10.7}$$

From equation (10.7), we see that Vanna calculates how much the delta $\frac{\partial V^*}{\partial F}$ changes if volatility σ changes. The term $\frac{\partial^2 V^*}{\partial F \partial \sigma}$ of equation (10.7) tells us that Vanna is a second-order mathematical derivative: the option price V^* is partially differentiated with respect to F *and* with respect to σ as seen in the last term of equation (10.7).

Option Cora and Gora

The model of equations (10.6) to (10.7) above shows that, even when pricing plain vanilla options, we can include correlations, which determine the option value. Naturally, especially for correlation options, ie, options whose payoff is at least in part determined by the correlation of two or more variables, correlations are critical.

QUANTIFYING MARKET CORRELATION RISK

In Chapter 1, in the section "Trading and correlation", we already discussed several correlation options. Let's derive Cora for an exchange option.

An exchange option E is the right to exchange asset S_1 for asset S_2 (ie, the right to give away asset S_1 and receive asset S_2 at option maturity). Therefore, an exchange option has the payoff = max (0, $S_2 - S_1$). The pricing formula is

$$E = S_2 e^{-q_2 T} N\left(\frac{\ln\left(\frac{S_2 e^{-q_2 T}}{S_1 e^{-q_1 T}}\right) + \frac{1}{2}(\sigma_1^2 + \sigma_2^2 - 2\rho\sigma_1\sigma_2)T}{\sqrt{\sigma_1^2 + \sigma_2^2 - 2\rho\sigma_1\sigma_2}\sqrt{T}}\right)$$

$$- S_1 e^{-q_1 T} N\left(\frac{\ln\left(\frac{S_2 e^{-q_2 T}}{S_1 e^{-q_1 T}}\right) + \frac{1}{2}(\sigma_1^2 + \sigma_2^2 - 2\rho\sigma_1\sigma_2)T}{\sqrt{\sigma_1^2 + \sigma_2^2 - 2\rho\sigma_1\sigma_2}\sqrt{T}}\right) \quad (10.8)$$

where

q_2 is the return of asset 2
q_1 is the return of asset 1
σ_1 is the volatility of asset S_1
σ_2 is the volatility of asset S_2
ρ is the correlation coefficient for assets S_1 and S_2
$N(x)$ is the cumulative standard normal distribution of x.

Note, that a distinction between a call and put is not sensible with an exchange option. Interestingly, an interest rate is not an input parameter in equation (10.8). This is because in a risk-neutral framework, both asset S_1 and S_2 are expected to grow with the risk-neutral interest rate r and hence r cancels out.

Differentiating equation (10.8) partially with respect to the correlation parameter ρ requires some stamina, but it can be done. The result is the Cora of an exchange option E:

$$\text{Cora}_E = \frac{\partial E}{\partial \rho} = -\frac{e^{-q_2 T}\sqrt{T}S_2\sigma_1\sigma_2 n\left[\frac{\ln\left[\frac{S_2 e^{-q_2 T}}{S_1 e^{-q_1 T}}\right] + \frac{1}{2}T(\sigma_1^2 - 2\rho\sigma_1\sigma_2 + \sigma_2^2)}{\sqrt{T}\sqrt{\sigma_1^2 - 2\rho\sigma_1\sigma_2 + \sigma_2^2}}\right]}{\sqrt{\sigma_1^2 - 2\rho\sigma_1\sigma_2 + \sigma_2^2}} \quad (10.9)$$

where $n(x)$ is the standard normal distribution of x. For the derivation of equation (10.9) see Problem 11 at the end of this chapter.

Equation (10.9) tells us how much the exchange option price E changes if the correlation ρ between the assets S_1 and S_2 changes by a very small amount.

From equation (10.9) we observe that the Cora of an exchange option is negative, since all terms in equation (10.9) are positive and there is a negative sign in front of the right term. The negative Cora makes sense, since the lower the correlation between the assets S_1 and S_2, measured by ρ, the higher is the expected payoff max(0, $S_2 - S_1$) and the higher the exchange option price E. We already observed Cora in Figure 1.4 in Chapter 1 and saw that the slope of E with respect to ρ, ie, the Cora, is negative. For a model that calculates Cora of an exchange option, see www.dersoft.com/exchangeoption.xlsm, cell J19.

Differentiating equation (10.9) again with respect to ρ gives us the Gora, which we defined in equation (10.2). It measures the curvature of the option function. In addition, Gora tells us how sensitive Cora is to changes in ρ. In other words, it tells us how instable the correlation hedge is. The higher the Gora, the more often we have to adjust the correlation hedge.

A normal distribution $n(x)$ is conveniently differentiated by using $\frac{\partial n(x)}{\partial x} = -xn(x)$. Applying the product rule and chain rule to equation (10.9), we derive the Gora as:

$$\text{Gora}_\varepsilon = \frac{\partial \text{Cora}_\varepsilon}{\partial \rho}$$

$$= -\frac{\left(e^{-q_2 T} S_2 \sigma_1^2 \sigma_2^2 \left(-4\ln\left[\frac{S_2 e^{-q_2 T}}{S_1 e^{-q_1 T}}\right]^2 + T(\sigma_1^2 - 2\rho\sigma_1\sigma_2 + \sigma_2^2)(4 + T\sigma_1^2 - 2T\rho\sigma_1\sigma_2 + T\sigma_2^2) \right) \right)}{n\left[\frac{\ln\left[\frac{S_2 e^{-q_2 T}}{S_1 e^{-q_1 T}}\right] + \frac{1}{2}T(\sigma_1^2 - 2\rho\sigma_1\sigma_2 + \sigma_2^2)}{\sqrt{T}\sqrt{\sigma_1^2 - 2\rho\sigma_1\sigma_2 + \sigma_2^2}} \right]}$$

$$/\left(4\sqrt{T}(\sigma_1^2 - 2\rho\sigma_1\sigma_2 + \sigma_2^2)^{5/2}\right) \tag{10.10}$$

The programmed Gora of equation (10.10) is in cell J20 of www.dersoft.com/exchangeoption.xlsm.

CORA AND GORA IN INVESTMENTS

In Chapter 1, we have already briefly discussed the relationship between investments and correlation. We found that a decrease in correlation enhances the effects of diversification, ie, increases the return/risk ratio of a portfolio. We displayed this in Figure 1.3. We will now formalise this finding. We define the Cora of a portfolio Cora_p as

$$\text{Cora}_p = \frac{\partial \left(\frac{\mu_p}{\sigma_p} \right)}{\partial \rho(x_{i=1,\ldots,n})} \quad (10.11)$$

where μ_p is the portfolio return mean and σ_p is the standard deviation of the portfolio returns.

The x_i in equation (10.11) are the pairwise correlations of the returns of the assets in the portfolio. Hence equation (10.11) tells us how much the risk-adjusted return of a portfolio μ_p/σ_p changes, if all pairwise correlations of all n asset returns in the portfolio $\rho(x_{i=1,\ldots,n})$ change by an infinitesimally small amount.

For a two-asset portfolio, the mean of the portfolio value μ_p is derived by equation (1.1) as $\mu_p = w_A \mu_A + w_B \mu_B$. The standard deviation σ_p of the two-asset portfolio return, is derived in equation (1.5) as $\sigma_p = \sqrt{w_A^2 \sigma_A^2 + w_B^2 \sigma_B^2 + 2w_A w_B COV_{AB}}$.

For a two-asset portfolio, we can derive Cora_p from equation (10.11) as

$$\frac{\partial \left(\frac{\mu_p}{\sigma_p} \right)}{\partial \rho} = -(w_A \mu_A + w_B \mu_B) \frac{1}{2} \left(w_A^2 \sigma_A^2 + w_B^2 \sigma_B^2 + 2w_A w_B \sigma_A \sigma_B \rho \right)^{-\frac{1}{2}} (2w_A w_B \sigma_A \sigma_B)$$

However, typically we have more than 2 assets in a portfolio. In this case, we can use equations

$$\mu_p = \sum_{i=1}^{n} w_i \mu_i$$

and equation (1.9)

$$\sigma_p = \sqrt{\beta_h C \beta_v}.$$

If we have more than two assets in a portfolio, we have to simulate an increase in every pairwise correlation of the assets returns and observe the impact on the risk-adjusted return μ_p/σ_p of the portfolio. The magnitude of the simulation can range from a small number as +1% to a much higher number to stress test the correlation impact.

We can also analyse the impact of correlation on just the risk of a portfolio, measured by standard deviation of asset returns, σ_p,

$$\text{Cora}^*_p = \frac{\partial \sigma_p}{\partial \rho(x_{i=1,\dots,n})} \quad (10.11a)$$

To derive the Cora$^*_p$ in equation (10.11a) for a 2-asset portfolio, we can use equation (1.5) $\sigma_p = \sqrt{w_A^2\sigma_A^2 + w_B^2\sigma_B^2 + 2w_Aw_B\sigma_A^2\sigma_B^2\rho}$ and differentiate partially with respect to ρ. We derive

$$\frac{\partial(\sigma_p)}{\partial_\rho} = \frac{1}{2}\left(w_A^2\sigma_A^2 + w_B^2\sigma_B^2 + 2w_Aw_B\sigma_A\sigma_B\rho\right)^{-\frac{1}{2}}(2w_Aw_B\sigma_A\sigma_B).$$

Calculating the portfolio return standard deviation σ_p gives some information of the risk of a portfolio. However, σ_p is part of the VaR concept, which includes a timeframe and a confidence level and is therefore a more informative risk measure. Calculating Cora for the VaR concept is done below in the section "Cora in market risk management".

We can also look at the sensitivity of Cora to changes in the correlation ρ of a portfolio, ie, calculate the Gora of a portfolio.

$$\text{Gora}_p = \frac{\partial(\text{Cora}_p)}{\partial \rho(x_{i=1,\dots,n})} = \frac{\partial^2\left(\frac{\mu_p}{\sigma_p}\right)}{\partial \rho^2(x_{i=1,\dots,n})} \quad (10.12)$$

Equation (10.12) tells us how much the Cora of a portfolio changes if correlation of all assets in the portfolio changes by an infinitesimally small amount. So the Gora of a portfolio tells us how stable the correlation hedge is (see Chapter 12 for correlation hedging). The higher the Gora, the more frequently we have to change the hedge if correlation changes. Graphically, Gora is the curvature of the original μ_p/σ_p function of Figure 1.3.

CORA IN MARKET RISK MANAGEMENT

Arguably the most important application of Cora and Gora is in risk management. In Chapter 1 we have already outlined the basic relationship between correlation and risk. We found that a lower correlation reduces portfolio risk measured by VaR, which was displayed in Figure 1.6. As mentioned in Chapter 1, VaR stands for value-at-risk. It measures the maximum loss of a portfolio with respect to a certain probability for a certain timeframe. VaR is the most widely applied risk management concept in financial practice. It can be calculated with equation

$$VaR_p = \sigma_p \alpha \sqrt{x} \qquad (10.13)$$

where VaR_p is the value-at-risk for portfolio P

α: Abscise value of a standard normal distribution, corresponding to a certain confidence level. It can be derived as =normsinv(confidence level) in Excel or normsinv(confidence level) in MATLAB. α takes the values $-\infty < \alpha < +\infty$.
x: Time horizon for the VaR, typically measured in days
σ_p: Volatility of the portfolio P, which includes the correlation between the assets in the portfolio. We calculate σ_p via

$$\sigma_p = \sqrt{\beta_h C \beta_v} \qquad (10.14)$$

where β_h is the horizontal β vector of invested amounts (price times quantity, "position" in Table 10.1 in example 10.1 below)
β_v is the vertical β vector of invested amounts (also price times quantity, "position" in Table 10.1)[1]
C is the covariance matrix of the returns of the assets (Table 10.4 below)

Naturally VaR has some limitations, especially slim tails and non-additivity. For more on VaR, we recommend Jorion (2006) and Hull (2018).

We will now quantify correlation risk with a real-world example with respect to VaR. We can write

$$\text{Cora}_{VaR} = \frac{\partial(VaR)}{\partial \rho(x_{i=1,\ldots n})} \qquad (10.15)$$

where the x_i are the pairwise correlations between all asset returns in the portfolio. Equation (10.15) measures how much VaR changes for an infinitesimally small change in all pairwise correlations of all asset returns in the portfolio. There is no closed-form solution for equation (10.15), so we have to simulate the change in correlation,

Table 10.1 Stock portfolio of 10 unequally weighted stocks, position in thousands

Portfolio		AT&T	Citi	Ford	GE	GM	HPQ	IBM	JPM	Microsoft	P&G
Spot price		$26.88	$72.50	$10.79	$15.12	$27.05	$58.10	$174.40	$35.58	$24.52	$58.89
Number of shares		79	12	100	90	38	82	20	35	140	70
Position (price × quantity)	$23,513.82	$2,123.52	$870.00	$1,079.00	$1,360.80	$1,027.90	$4,764.20	$3,488.00	$1,245.30	$3,432.80	$4,122.30
Weight (%)		9%	4%	5%	6%	4%	20%	15%	5%	15%	18%

Table 10.2 Correlation matrix ρ between returns of 10 stocks from July 31, 2011 to August 1st, 2012

	AT&T	Citi	Ford	GE	GM	HPQ	IBM	JPM	Microsoft	P&G
AT&T	1.00	0.06	0.49	0.65	0.00	0.50	-0.10	0.52	0.50	-0.02
Citi	0.06	1.00	0.01	-0.04	-0.14	0.04	-0.05	-0.01	0.01	-0.16
Ford	0.49	0.01	1.00	0.68	0.03	0.64	0.02	0.71	0.61	0.11
GE	0.65	-0.04	0.68	1.00	-0.06	0.70	-0.12	0.75	0.65	0.03
GM	0.00	-0.14	0.03	-0.06	1.00	0.02	0.58	-0.01	0.08	0.46
HPQ	0.50	0.04	0.64	0.70	0.02	1.00	-0.05	0.64	0.60	0.05
IBM	-0.10	-0.06	0.02	-0.12	0.58	-0.05	1.00	-0.05	-0.02	0.53
JPM	0.52	-0.01	0.71	0.75	-0.01	0.64	-0.05	1.00	0.57	0.05
Microsoft	0.50	0.01	0.61	0.65	0.08	0.60	-0.02	0.57	1.00	0.02
P&G	-0.02	-0.16	0.11	0.03	0.46	0.05	0.53	0.05	0.02	1.00

possibly with a 1% increase in all pairwise correlations. Let's do this in a real-world example. We first calculate VaR and then Cora$_{VaR}$.

Example 10.1: What is the VaR, Cora$_{VaR}$ and Gora$_{VaR}$ of a 10-asset portfolio of unequally weighted stocks AT&T, Citi, Ford, GE, GM, HPQ, IBM, JPM, MSFT, P&G for a one-year time horizon for a 99% confidence level? This example and the following results are displayed in a spreadsheet at www.dersoft.com/vareducational. xlsm. A model that calculates VaR, Cora$_{VaR}$ and Gora$_{VaR}$ for n assets, can be found at www.dersoft.com/varnassetcoragora.xlsm.

Table 10.1 shows the numerical values of this example.

We first downloaded the stocks' daily closing prices (for example from Yahoofinance.com) from August 1, 2011 to July 31st, 2012. We then calculated the daily returns for stock price S as $R = \ln(S_t/S_{t-1})$.[2] We then correlate the daily returns for all 10 stock pairs to find the correlation coefficient ρ for all stock pairs. Mathematically this is done by equation

$$\frac{\sum_{i=1}^{n}(x_i - \bar{x})(y_i - \bar{y})}{\sqrt{\sum_{i=1}^{n}(x_i - \bar{x})^2 \sum_{i=1}^{n}(y_i - \bar{y})^2}}$$

where x is the return of asset X and y is the return of asset Y, and $\bar{x}$ and $\bar{y}$ are the means of the asset returns of asset X and Y, respectively. Computationally we can use Excel's "Correl" function or MATLAB's "corrcoef" function to find ρ. This gives us $n(n-1)/2 = 10 \times 9/2 = 45$ correlation pairs. Table 10.2 shows the correlation matrix.

From Table 10.2 we observe that the return correlation of the 10 stocks is mostly positive.

We now derive the daily standard deviation σ of the stock returns R via equation (1.2)

$$\sigma_R = \sqrt{\frac{1}{n-1}\sum_{t=1}^{n}(R_t - \mu_R)^2},$$

which are displayed in Table 10.3.

We now build the covariance matrix by using $CoV_{AB} = \sigma_A \sigma_B \rho_{AB}$. Table 10.4 shows the result.

Table 10.3 Standard deviation of daily returns

	Standard Deviation σ
AT&T	1.02%
Citi	3.19%
Ford	2.08%
GE	1.69%
GM	2.73%
HPQ	3.00%
IBM	1.42%
JPM	2.65%
Microsoft	1.43%
P&G	1.00%

Now we are ready to derive the portfolio standard deviation. We use equation (10.14) $\sigma_P = \sqrt{\beta_h C \beta_v}$, which we already used in chapter 1 for a two-asset portfolio.

We first derive $C\beta_v$. Hence, we have

$$\begin{pmatrix} 0.0001031 & 0.0000182 & 0.0001026 & 0.0001113 & 0.0000013 & 0.0001529 & -0.0000148 & 0.0001405 & 0.0000726 & -0.0000018 \\ 0.0000182 & 0.0010178 & 0.0000060 & -0.0000212 & -0.0001209 & 0.0000344 & -0.0000287 & -0.0000123 & 0.0000025 & -0.0000508 \\ 0.0001026 & 0.0000060 & 0.0004332 & 0.0002378 & 0.0000153 & 0.0004002 & 0.0000053 & 0.0003897 & 0.0001822 & 0.0000239 \\ 0.0001113 & -0.0000212 & 0.0002378 & 0.0002847 & -0.0000258 & 0.0003546 & -0.0000294 & 0.0003344 & 0.0001564 & 0.0000048 \\ 0.0000013 & -0.0001209 & 0.0000153 & -0.0000258 & 0.0007477 & 0.0000142 & 0.0002234 & -0.000079 & 0.0000304 & 0.0001260 \\ 0.0001529 & 0.0000344 & 0.0004002 & 0.0003546 & 0.0000142 & 0.0009015 & -0.0000232 & 0.0005058 & 0.0002590 & 0.0000146 \\ -0.00002148 & -0.0000287 & 0.0000053 & -0.0000294 & 0.0002234 & -0.0000232 & 0.0002006 & -0.0000192 & -0.0000043 & 0.0000753 \\ 0.0001405 & -0.0000123 & 0.0003897 & 0.0003344 & -0.0000079 & 0.0005028 & -0.0000192 & 0.0007032 & 0.0002155 & 0.0000133 \\ 0.0000726 & 0.0000025 & 0.0001822 & 0.0001564 & 0.0000304 & 0.0002590 & -0.0000043 & 0.0002155 & 0.0002059 & 0.0000034 \\ -0.0000018 & -0.0000508 & 0.0000239 & 0.0000048 & 0.0001260 & 0.0000146 & 0.0000753 & 0.0000133 & 0.0000034 & 0.0001009 \end{pmatrix} \begin{pmatrix} 2,124 \\ 870 \\ 1,397 \\ 1,360 \\ 1,027 \\ 4,764 \\ 3,488 \\ 1,245 \\ 3,432 \\ 4,122 \end{pmatrix} = \begin{pmatrix} 1.59 \\ 0.63 \\ 4.16 \\ 3.40 \\ 2.11 \\ 7.08 \\ 1.00 \\ 5.17 \\ 2.81 \\ 0.89 \end{pmatrix}$$

We now calculate $\beta_h (C\beta_v)$.

$$(2{,}124 \ \ 870 \ \ 1{,}079 \ \ 1{,}360 \ \ 1{,}027 \ \ 4{,}764 \ \ 3{,}488 \ \ 1{,}245 \ \ 3{,}432 \ \ 4{,}122) \begin{pmatrix} 1.59 \\ 0.63 \\ 4.16 \\ 3.40 \\ 2.11 \\ 7.08 \\ 1.00 \\ 5.17 \\ 2.81 \\ 0.89 \end{pmatrix} = 72{,}141$$

Hence, we have $\sigma_P = \sqrt{72{,}141} = 268.59$. We are considering a 99% confidence level. Hence, $\alpha = \text{normsinv}(0.99) = 2.3263$. We have about 252 trading days in a year. It follows that the portfolio VaR is

Table 10.4 Covariance matrix for the portfolio in Table 10.1 with the correlation matrix of Table 10.2 and standard deviation in Table 10.3

	AT&T	Citi	Ford	GE	GM	HPQ	IBM	JPM	Microsoft	P&G
0.0001031		0.0000182	0.0001026	0.0001113	0.0001529	-0.0000148	0.0001405	0.0000726	-0.0000018	
0.0000182		0.0010178	0.0000060	-0.0000212	-0.0001209	0.0000344	-0.0000287	-0.0000123	0.0000025	-0.0000508
0.0001026		0.0000060	0.0004332	0.0002378	0.0000153	0.0004002	0.0000053	0.0003897	0.0001822	0.0000239
0.0001113		-0.0000212	0.0002378	0.0002847	-0.0000258	0.0003546	-0.0000294	0.0003344	0.0001564	0.0000048
0.0000013		-0.0001209	0.0000153	-0.0000258	0.0007477	0.0000142	0.0002234	-0.0000079	0.0000304	0.0001260
0.0001529		0.0000344	0.0004002	000003546	0.0000142	0.0009015	-0.0000232	0.0005058	0.0002590	0.0000146
-0.0000148		-0.0000287	0.0000053	-0.0000294	0.0002234	-0.0000232	0.0002006	-0.0000192	-0.0000043	0.0000753
0.0001405		-0.0000123	0.0003897	0.0003344	-0.0000079	0.0005058	-0.0000192	0.0007032	0.0002155	0.0000133
0.0000726		0.0000025	0.0001822	0.0001564	0.0000304	0.0002590	-0.0000043	0.0002155	0.0002059	0.0000034
-0.0000018		-0.0000508	0.0000239	0.0000048	0.0001260	0.0000146	0.0000753	0.0000133	0.0000034	0.0001009

$$VaR_p = \sigma_p \alpha \sqrt{x} = 268.59 \times 2.3263 \times \sqrt{252} = 9{,}918.97.$$

Interpretation: We are 99% sure that we will not lose more than US$ 9,918,970 (since numbers are in units of US$1,000) in the next year due to price changes of the stocks in our portfolio. Note that this VaR number includes the correlation between the stocks via σ_p.

Simulation: We now simulate changes in the correlation matrix of Table 10.2 to derive Cora_{VaR}. Cora is defined for an infinitesimally small change in correlation as we can see from equation (10.1). However, even if we increase the correlation by a larger amount, we will derive the exact value in VaR, since we are performing a numerical simulation. This is different to option theory, where we can apply closed form mathematical derivatives. For example the delta of an option V with the underlying S, $\partial V/\partial S$, is the first mathematical derivate of V with respect to S. For larger increases in S, the change in V, ∂V, derived by the closed form solution will be imprecise, since the option function V is non-linear with respect to S.

Figure 10.1 shows the impact of a simulated discrete (not infinitesimally small) change in correlation on VaR, ie, $\text{DiscreteCora}_{\text{VaR}}$.

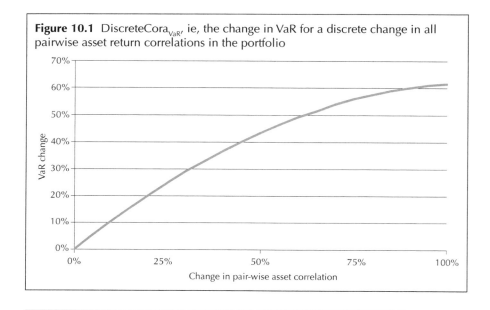

Figure 10.1 $\text{DiscreteCora}_{\text{VaR}}$, ie, the change in VaR for a discrete change in all pairwise asset return correlations in the portfolio

From Figure 10.1 we observe that the higher the increase in the pairwise correlations, the higher is VaR. The impact of a correlation is strong. VaR increases by over 60% for high correlations.

GAP-Cora

In Figure 10.1 we observe a change in correlation of all pairwise correlations in the correlation matrix of Table 10.2. We may also be interested in deriving the correlation exposure of a single asset in our portfolio. In an analogy to interest rate risk management, we will call this GAP analysis, or GAP-Cora. We can derive two types of GAP-Cora.

First, GAP-Cora$_{i,P}$ of a single asset i with respect to all other assets in the portfolio P. Formally,

$$GAP\text{-}Cora_{i,P} = \frac{\partial(VaR)}{\partial \rho(x_{i,j=1,\ldots,n})} \qquad (10.16)$$

Equation (10.16) reads: How much does VaR change, if the correlation between asset i and all other $j = 1, \ldots, n$ assets in the portfolio P changes by an infinitesimally small amount. We can approximate GAP-Cora$_{i,P}$ with a 1%-point increase. For our portfolio, if asset i is AT&T, GAP-Cora$_{i,P}$ = US$12,364. We interpret this number as: if the correlations between AT&T and all other assets in the portfolio increase by 1% point, VaR increases by US$12,364. (The interested reader can confirm this number with the spreadsheet at www.dersoft.com/vareducational.xlsm.)

We can also stress-test GAP-Cora$_{i,P}$. For example, we can increase the correlation by a random number, for example by one standard deviation of the vector of correlations between AT&T and the other assets in the portfolio, which comes out to 35.74%. In this case GAP-Cora$_{AT\&T,P}$ = US$432,752. We interpret this number as: if the correlation between AT&T and all other assets in the portfolio increases by 35.74%, VaR increases by US$432,752.

Second, we can also derive the exposure of the correlation between a single asset with respect to another single asset. Formally,

$$GAP\text{-}Cora_{i,j} = \frac{\partial(VaR)}{\partial \rho(x_{i,j})} \qquad (10.17)$$

Equation (10.17) reads: How much does VaR change, if the correlation between the returns of asset i and j changes by an infinitesimally small amount? We can approximate GAP-Cora$_{i,j}$ with a 1% increase. For our portfolio, if asset i is AT&T, and asset j is Citi, GAP-Cora$_{i,j}$ = US$823. We interpret this number as: if the correlation between AT&T and Citi increases by 1%, VaR increases by US$823. The interested reader can confirm this number with the spreadsheet at www.dersoft.com/vareducational.xlsxm.

We can again also stress-test GAP-Cora$_{i,j}$. For example, we can increase the correlation between AT&T and Citi by a random number. We could, for instance, calculate the historical correlation of AT&T and Citi and derive the standard deviation of this historical correlation. Let's assume this standard deviation is 50%. In this case GAP-Cora$_{AT\&T,Citi}$ = US$41,051. We interpret this number as: if the correlation between AT&T and Citi increases by 50%, VaR increases by US$41,051. The interested reader can again confirm this number with the spreadsheet at www.dersoft.com/vareducational.xlsm.

GORA IN MARKET RISK MANAGEMENT

As defined in equation (10.2), Gora is the second partial derivative of a function, ie, the change in the slope of that function. With respect to VaR we can define

$$\text{Gora}_{VaR} = \frac{\partial \text{Cora}_{VaR}}{\partial \rho(x_{i=1},\dots,_n)} = \frac{\partial^2(VaR)}{\partial \rho^2(x_{i=1},\dots,_n)} \qquad (10.18)$$

Equation (10.18) reads: How much does Cora of VaR change if the correlation of all assets in the portfolio changes; or, what is the curvature of the original VaR function?

From Figure 1.3 in Chapter 1 and Figure 10.1, above, we observe that the curvature of the VaR function is negative (since the slope decreases for increasing correlation). Hence, Gora of VaR is negative. Let's derive Gora of VaR numerically and interpret the result.

There are several ways how we can simulate Gora for market risk.

1. We can calculate the change in VaR for a y% increase between the correlation of all assets in the portfolio and a y% decrease

between the correlation of all assets in the portfolio and then take the average. Formally,

$$\text{Gora}_{VaR} \approx \left(\frac{\left[VaR(+y\% \text{ in } \rho(x_{i=1,\ldots,n})) - VaR \right] + \left[VaR(-y\% \text{ in } \rho(x_{i=1,\ldots,n})) - VaR \right]}{2} \right) \quad (10.19)$$

For our example 10.1, Gora_{VaR} for a $y = 10\%$ simulation comes out to

$$\text{Gora}_{VaR} \approx \left(\frac{1{,}053.60 + (-1{,}179.78)}{2} \right) = -63.09.$$

Since this number is in units of US$1,000, we interpret it as follows. As an approximation, for a 1%-point increase in all correlations in the portfolio, the Cora will reduce by US$6,309, hence we have to reduce our correlation hedge by this amount. The reader can verify this number at www.dersoft.com/vareducational.xlsm (cell P19 on sheet "Portfolio VaR simulation").

2. We can also simulate Gora of VaR by comparing different Coras. For example, we could calculate Cora for an increase in correlation from 10% to 11%, and Cora for an increase in correlation from 0% to 1% and then look at the difference. Formally, $\text{Gora}^*_{VAR} \approx \text{Cora}_{VAR}(\rho = 10\% \to \rho = 11\%) - \text{Cora}_{VAR}(\rho = 0\% \to \rho = 1\%)$, where ρ is the pairwise correlation of all assets in the portfolio. We expect Gora^*_{VaR} to be negative since the slope of Cora for an increase in correlation from 10% to 11% is lower than Cora for an increase in correlation from 0%–1%, as we can see in Figure 10.1. For our example 10.1, we derive $\text{Gora}^*_{VAR} \approx 99.84 - 110.34 = -10.5$. Since this number is again in units of US$1,000, we can interpret this as: if all correlations in the portfolio increase by 10%, we have to reduce our correlation hedge by US$10,500. The reader can verify this number at www.dersoft.com/vareducational.xlsm (cell T17 on sheet "Portfolio VaR simulation").

SUMMARY

In this chapter we discussed how to quantify market correlation risk. Market risk is the risk of an unfavourable change in the market price or rate in four main markets: (a) equity market; (b) fixed-income market; (c) commodity market; and (d) foreign exchange market. However, other markets, such as real estate, energy and weather, can be categorised. Market correlation risk is the risk that the correlations between the prices in one market or between these markets change.

We can quantify market correlation risk with two measures.

1. Cora measures how much a dependent financial variable changes if the correlation between independent variables changes. For example, Cora can measure how much VaR in a portfolio changes if the correlation of the assets in the portfolio changes. However, the dependent financial variable can be any financial variable that is exposed to correlation risk: the return/risk ratio of portfolio, the price of an option, a CDS, a CDO and many more. Graphically, Cora is the slope of the variable's function with respect to correlation. If we hedge correlation risk, Cora tells us the magnitude of the correlation hedge.
2. Gora measures how much Cora changes. Hence it tells how much we have to adjust our correlation hedge. Mathematically, Gora is the second mathematical derivative of the variable's function with respect to correlation.

Arguably, Cora and Gora are most critical in risk management. We find that one of the most widely applied market risk measures of a portfolio, VaR, is highly sensitive to Cora, ie, highly sensitive to changes in correlation of the assets in the portfolio. The sensitive of VaR to Gora is only moderate.

Cora and Gora can be extended in numerous ways: we can calculate Cora not only for a correlation change of *all* assets in the portfolio, but for a change in (a) the correlation between one particular asset with all other assets, or (b) the correlation between two specific assets. This provides the risk manager with the correlation risk of specific assets, possibly critical assets in the portfolio. The same exercise can be done for Gora.

Cora and Gora can also be applied to stress testing. In this case, we can simulate the correlation change between the independent variables by a large amount to observe correlation risk in crises scenarios. See Chapter 16 for correlation stress testing in the Basel III accord.

Questions for Chapter 10

Answers to these questions can be found at the back of this book.

1. When we talk about "market risk", which four markets are typically included?
2. Name several other markets, not included in the four markets mentioned in (1).
3. What is market correlation risk?
4. We can measure market correlation risk with the Cora. What information does Cora give us?
5. What is Cora mathematically?
6. Name three applications of Cora in finance.
7. Measuring correlation risk is not totally new. In option theory, a "Vanna" exists. What information does Vanna give us?
8. What is the relationship between Vanna and Cora?
9. What information does Gora give us?
10. What is Gora mathematically?
11. OK, here is a tough one: differentiate the price function of an exchange option

$$E = S_2 e^{-q_2 T} N\left(\frac{\ln\left(\frac{S_2 e^{-q_2 T}}{S_1 e^{-q_1 T}}\right) + \frac{1}{2}\left(\sigma_1^2 + \sigma_2^2 - 2\rho\sigma_1\sigma_2\right)T}{\sqrt{\sigma_1^2 + \sigma_2^2 - 2\rho\sigma_1\sigma_2}\sqrt{T}}\right)$$

$$-S_1 e^{-q_1 T} N\left(\frac{\ln\left(\frac{S_2 e^{-q_2 T}}{S_1 e^{-q_1 T}}\right) + \frac{1}{2}\left(\sigma_1^2 + \sigma_2^2 - 2\rho\sigma_1\sigma_2\right)T}{\sqrt{\sigma_1^2 + \sigma_2^2 - 2\rho\sigma_1\sigma_2}\sqrt{T}}\right)$$

with respect to the correlation coefficient ρ. Try first yourself. After rearranging, you can just use the chain rule. If you give up, look at www.dersoft.com/exchangeoptioncora.docx for the answer.

12. Arguably, the most important application of correlation risk is in risk management. In practice, the risk of a portfolio is often measured with the VaR concept. Is VaR sensitive to changes in the correlation of the assets in the portfolio, ie, what is the Cora of VaR?
13. What is the Gora of VaR?
14. Cora and Gora can be extended in many ways. Name two.

---

1 More mathematically, the vector β_h is the transpose of the vector β_v, and vice versa: $\beta_h^T = \beta_v$ and $\beta_v^T = \beta_h$. Hence we can also write equation (10.14) as $\sigma_p = \sqrt{\beta_h^T C \beta_h}$. See www.dersoft.com/matrixprimer.xlsx sheet 'Matrix Transpose' for more.
2 See Appendix of chapter 1, why we prefer to use $\ln(S_t/S_{t-1})$ instead of $(S_t - S_{t-1})/S_{t-1}$ to calculate returns.

11

Quantifying Credit Correlation Risk

"A key aspect of any credit risk VaR model is credit correlation"
– John Hull

In this chapter we will discuss and quantify the correlation risk of financial products whose primary focus is credit risk. Let us just clarify what credit risk is: credit risk is the risk of financial loss due to an adverse change in the credit quality of a debtor.

There are principally two types of credit risk: (a) migration risk; and (b) default risk. Figure 11.1 gives an overview of credit risk.

In Figure 11.1, migration risk refers to a migration from one credit state to another: for example, a downward migration from AAA to B. An upward migration from B to AAA can also hurt an investor, if they are short a bond or if the investor is paying fixed in a credit default swap (CDS); see Figure 11.2. Default risk is a special case of migration risk for a migration of the debtor into the default state. Default risk exists only for a long credit position: for example, being long a bond or long a tranche in a collateralised debt obligation (CDO).

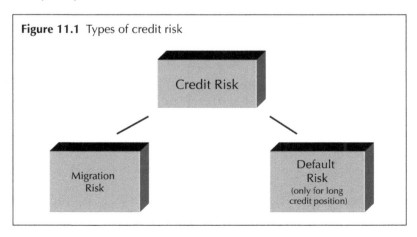

Figure 11.1 Types of credit risk

However, migration risk and default risk have quite different dynamics. For instance, if a bond migrates to a lower state – say from B to CCC – the bond investor just suffers a paper loss and will receive their principal investment back at maturity if the bond does not default. However, if a bond defaults and stays in default, the bond investor will not receive their principal investment back, just the recovery rate of the bond.

What is credit correlation risk? Credit correlation risk is the risk that credit quality correlations between two or more counterparties change unfavourably.

All loan portfolios of financial institutions, as well as all structured products such as CDOs, mortgage-backed securities (MBSs) and so forth, are exposed to credit correlation risk. In addition, all portfolios that apply derivatives as a hedge also include credit correlation risk. Let us explain credit correlation risk with a portfolio of a bond and a CDS, which is used as a hedge.

CREDIT CORRELATION RISK IN A CDS

Let us just clarify what a CDS is: a CDS is a financial product in which the credit risk of an underlying asset is transferred from the CDS buyer to the CDS seller.

We have already briefly discussed some aspects of credit correlation risk of CDSs in Chapter 1. We will expand this discussion now. In a CDS often the CDS buyer owns the underlying asset. We will discuss this case here. If the CDS buyer owns the underlying reference asset, the CDS can be viewed as an insurance against credit risk of the underlying asset: if the reference asset r defaults, the counterparty (CDS seller) c will compensate the investor and default swap buyer i. Figure 11.2 displays this graphically.

Figure 11.2 shows the CDS in case of cash settlement. N is the notional amount, RR_r is the recovery rate of the reference asset, $RR_r a$ is the accrued interest of the reference asset from the time of default to the next coupon date.[1]

Let us outline the credit correlation risk between these entities.

Credit correlation between the counterparty c and the reference asset r

We briefly discussed this critical correlation in Chapter 1. We found that the credit correlation between the counterparty and the

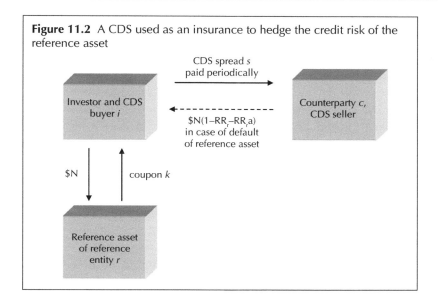

Figure 11.2 A CDS used as an insurance to hedge the credit risk of the reference asset

reference asset significantly influences the CDS price; see Figure 1.2. We will discuss the counterparty–reference asset correlation relationship in detail shortly.

Credit correlation between the investor i and the reference entity r, and the impact for the counterparty c

This case is relevant if the investor pays the CDS spread s periodically, which is typically the case in practice. If the investor would pay the CDS spread upfront, the counterparty would have no credit risk with the investor and hence no correlation exposure with respect to the correlation between the investor and the reference entity. In case the CDS spread is paid periodically, we have four cases.

❏ The credit correlation between the investor i and the reference entity r is negative with the credit quality of the investor decreasing and the credit quality of the reference asset increasing. This is the worst-case scenario for the counterparty: an increase in the credit quality of the reference entity increases the present value of the CDS for the counterparty since the counterparty is now receiving an above market spread (this is beneficial from a profit perspective but negative from a risk perspective since a higher present value means more credit exposure). In addition, the decrease in the credit quality of the investor means higher credit risk for the counterparty with respect to the investor.

- The credit correlation between the investor i and the reference entity r is negative with the credit quality of the investor increasing and the credit quality of the reference asset decreasing. From a risk perspective this is the best-case scenario for the counterparty because an increasing credit quality of the investor means a higher probability that the investor can pay the credit spread s. In addition, a lower credit quality of the reference asset means the present value of the CDS decreases (possibly getting negative). Hence the credit exposure of the counterparty with respect to the investor will decrease.
- The credit correlation between the investor i and the reference entity r is positive with the credit quality of the investor increasing and the credit quality of the reference asset also increasing. In this scenario there is a compensation effect: a higher credit quality of the investor makes future payments of the credit spread s more likely. However, the higher credit quality of the reference asset increases the present value of the CDS for the counterparty, which increases the counterparty's credit exposure to the investor.
- The correlation between the investor i and the reference entity r is positive with the credit quality of the investor decreasing and the credit quality of the reference asset decreasing. In this scenario there is again a compensation effect: a lower credit quality of the investor makes future payments of the credit spread s less likely. However, a lower credit quality of the reference asset decreases the present value of the CDS for the counterparty, which decreases the counterparty's credit exposure to the investor.

In conclusion, the correlation between the investor and the reference asset should be included when deriving a CDS spread, since it impacts the credit exposure of the counterparty. For more details see below, especially Figure 11.11.

The correlation between the investor i and the counterparty c
The default correlation between the investor i and the counterparty c is not a critical correlation to be considered in the default-swap pricing process. If the investor goes into bankruptcy, they do not have to be too concerned if the counterparty also enters bankruptcy. The same logic applies to the counterparty with respect to the investor. We will look shortly at more details on the correlation between the investor i and the counterparty c.

In the following we will discuss how to derive the CDS spreads, including the critical default correlation between the reference entity r and he counterparty c.

Pricing CDSs, including reference entity–counterparty credit correlation

The most critical credit correlation for pricing CDSs is the one between the reference entity r and the counterparty c. See Figure 11.2 for the role the reference entity r and the counterparty c play in a CDS. The correlation between the counterparty and the reference asset has received quite a bit of media attention recently, since financial institutions had sold CDSs on their own home country; see, for example, *Risk* (2011) and European Central Bank (2009). In this case, the counterparty–reference asset credit correlation should be high and consequently the CDS spread s low. In the following we will derive a closed-form solution for the CDS spread s including reference asset–counterparty credit correlation.[2] We use the following notation:

λ_t^r: default intensity of reference entity r, during time t to $t + 1$ (hence λ_t^r is the default probability of r from t to $t + 1$ conditional on survival until t).
Λ_t^r: Cumulative default probability of reference entity r until t.
$\Delta \tau_t$: time between nodes $t - 1$ and t, expressed in years.
s_t: annual default swap spread to be paid at time t.
τ_t: time between time 0 and time t, expressed in years.
Td_t: Time of default, measured between time $t - 1$ and default time, expressed in years.
N: notional amount of the swap.
r_t: risk-free interest rate from time 0 to time $t + 1$.
RR_r: exogenous recovery rate of the reference entity.

$S_f(T_{dt})$: Fair value of the default swap from the time the CDS was issued until the time of reference asset default without the possibility of counterparty default. $S_f(T_{dt})$ includes the notional amount N.

a: Accrued interest on the reference asset from the last coupon date until the default date, hence $a = k\,T_d$, where:

k: coupon of the reference asset

As displayed in Figure 11.2, we assume that the obligation that the counterparty has in case of default of the reference entity r is $N(1 - RR_r - RR_r a)$, where N is the notional amount of the swap, RR_r is the recovery rate of the reference asset issuer of the reference bond, and $RR_r a$ is the accrued interest of the reference bond from the last coupon date until default.

In analogy of the default intensity of the reference asset λ_t^r, we define the default intensity of the counterparty λ_t^c as:

λ_t^c: default intensity of counterparty (ie, default swap seller) c, during time t to $t + 1$ (hence is the default probability of c from t to $t + 1$ conditional on survival until t)

Λ_t^c: Cumulative default probability of counterparty c until t

RR_c: exogenous recovery rate of the counterparty

The model

We now build a quadruple CDS payoff tree and a quadruple CDS premium tree and then use swap evaluation techniques to find the fair CDS spread s. In both trees we have four scenarios.

(a) Both counterparty c and reference entity r default, $\lambda(r \cap c)$.
(b) Both counterparty c and reference entity r do not default, $\lambda(\bar{r} \cap \bar{c})$.
(c) The reference entity r defaults but not the counterparty c, $\lambda(r \cap \bar{c})$.
(d) The reference entity r survives but the counterparty c defaults, $\lambda(c \cap \bar{r})$.

We now build the payoff tree and the CDS spread tree and assign cashflows to each of the scenarios (a), (b), (c) and (d).

The CDS payoff tree
The payoff is the amount of cash that the counterparty c pays to the investor i in case of default of the reference entity r (see Figure 11.2 for the role of these three entities in a CDS).

We assume that if both the reference entity and the counterparty default, $\lambda(r \cap c)$, the standard payoff in case of default of the reference entity will be reduced by the recovery rate of the counterparty. Hence the payoff will be $N(1 - RR_r - RR_r a)RR_c$. There will be no payoff if neither the reference entity nor the counterparty default, $\lambda(\bar{r} \cap \bar{c})$. There will be the standard payoff $N(1 - RR_r - RR_r a)$ if only the reference entity defaults, $\lambda(r \cap \bar{c})$. We assume that if only the counterparty defaults, $\lambda(c \cap \bar{r})$, the counterparty will pay the time t fair value of the default swap, $S_f(t)$, without counterparty default risk, multiplied by the recovery rate of the counterparty, hence $S_f(t) RR_c$. Graphically we derive Figure 11.3

From Figure 11.3 we observe that the payoff tree only continues if both the reference asset and the counterparty survive, $\lambda(r \cap c)$. In all other cases the CDS terminates. Including discount factors e^{-rt}, we derive from Figure 11.3 the present value of the payoff of a two-period default swap as

$$\begin{bmatrix} \lambda_0(r \cap c)N(1-RR_r - RR_r a)RR_c + \lambda_0(\bar{r} \cap \bar{c})N0 \\ +\lambda_0(r \cap \bar{c})N(1-RR_r - RR_r a) + \lambda_0(c \cap \bar{r})S_f(1)RR_c \end{bmatrix} e^{-r_0 \tau_1}$$
$$+\lambda_0(\bar{r} \cap \bar{c}) \begin{bmatrix} \lambda_1(r \cap c)N(1-RR_r - RR_r a)RR_c + \lambda_1(\bar{r} \cap \bar{c})N0 \\ +\lambda_1(r \cap \bar{c})N(1-RR_r - RR_r a) + \lambda_1(c \cap \bar{r})(S_f(2)RR_c) \end{bmatrix} e^{-r_1 \tau_2} \quad (11.1)$$

Generalising equation (11.1) for T periods, we derive

$$\sum_{t=1}^{T} \left\{ \begin{bmatrix} \lambda_{t-1}(r \cap c)N(1-RR_r - RR_r a)RR_c + \lambda_{t-1}(r \cap \bar{c}) \\ N(1-RR_r - RR_r a) + \lambda_{t-1}(c \cap \bar{r})S_f(t)RR_c \end{bmatrix} e^{-r_{t-1}\tau_t} \prod_{u=0}^{t-2} \lambda_u(\bar{r} \cap \bar{c}) \right\} \quad (11.2)$$

Equation (11.2) requires the critical inputs default intensity of the reference asset λ_r, and default intensity of the counterparty, λ_c. These can be derived with a structural Merton 1974-based model (see Chapter 5), which requires the inputs asset value and debt value. Alternatively we can derive λ_r and λ_c with a reduced form model, which abstracts from asset and debt values of the underlying entity and uses market prices as bonds or swaps in a stochastic model to derive the default probabilities λ_r and λ_c. Alternatively, λ_r and λ_c can

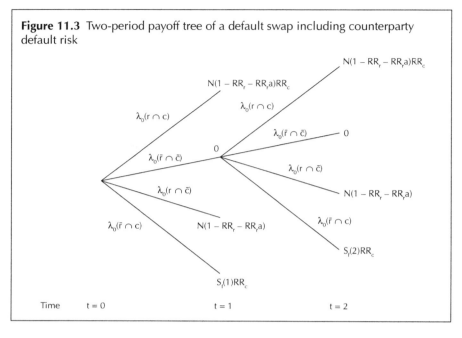

Figure 11.3 Two-period payoff tree of a default swap including counterparty default risk

be derived with a term structure model as the Libor Market Model (LMM),[3] which requires the inputs' forward default intensity and default volatility. In the model presented here λ_r and λ_c are simulated with a LMM model.

The CDS spread tree s

In most credit-default-swap contracts, the CDS spread s is paid in arrears, ie, at the end of each period. In case of default, the default-swap buyer typically has to pay the accrued spread amount from the last spread payment date to the default date. In addition, the solvent party still has to honour its obligations to the defaulting party. Hence, we associate the following spread payments for the four default scenarios.

1. If both the reference asset and the counterparty default, $\lambda(r \cap c)$, the default swap buyer will make a final accrual payment, which is capped at the payoff level in default, ie, $\min[s\,N\,\Delta\tau\,Td, N(1-RR_r-RR_r a)RR_c]$. This scenario nets the obligations in case of $s\,N\,\Delta\tau\,Td \geq N(1-RR_r-RR_r a)RR_c$ and gives a payoff of $N(1-RR_r-RR_r a)RR_c - s\,N\,\Delta\tau\,Td$ in case of $N(1-RR_r-RR_r a)$

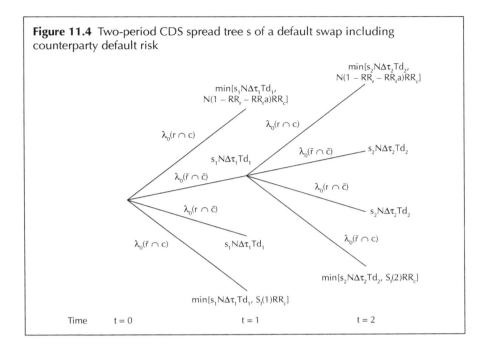

Figure 11.4 Two-period CDS spread tree s of a default swap including counterparty default risk

$RR_c \geq s\, N\, \Delta\tau\, Td$. This guarantees that the investor does not pay more CDS premium s than they receive as a payoff in case of both r and c defaulting.

2. If both the reference asset and the counterparty survive, $\lambda(\bar{r} \cap \bar{c})$, the spread payment will be the standard $s\, N\, \Delta\tau$. Only in this case will the spread payment tree continue.
3. If the reference asset defaults but not the counterparty, $\lambda(r \cap \bar{c})$, the spread payment will be $s\, N\, \Delta\tau\, Td$.
4. If the reference asset survives but the counterparty defaults, $\lambda(c \cap \bar{r})$, the spread payment $s\, N\, \Delta\tau\, Td$ will be capped at the fair value of the swap times the recovery value, ie, $\min[s\, N\, \Delta\tau_t\, Td_t,\, S_f(t)RR_c]$. This again guarantees that the investor does not pay more CDS premium s than they receive as a payoff in case the counterparty c defaults.

Applying these cashflows, we derive the swap spread payment tree as seen in Figure 11.4.

From Figure 11.4, we get for the present value of the CDS spread payments:

$$\begin{aligned}&\begin{cases}\lambda_0(r\cap c)\min\left[sN\Delta\tau_1 Td_1, N(1-RR_r-RR_r a)RR_c\right]+\lambda_0(\bar{r}\cap \bar{c})s_1 N\Delta\tau_1 Td_1\\+\lambda_0(r\cap \bar{c})s_1 N\Delta\tau_1 Td_1+\lambda_0(c\cap \bar{r})\min\left[sN\Delta\tau_1 Td_1, S_f(1)RR_c\right]\end{cases}e^{-r_0\tau_1}\\&+\lambda_0(\bar{r}\cap \bar{c})\begin{cases}\lambda_1(r\cap c)\min\left[s_2 N\Delta\tau_2 Td_2, N(1-RR_r-RR_r a)RR_c\right]+\lambda_1(\bar{r}\cap \bar{c})s_2 N\Delta\tau_2\\Td_2+\lambda_1(r\cap \bar{c})s_2 N\Delta\tau_2 Td_2+\lambda_0(c\cap \bar{r})\min\left[s_2 N\Delta\tau_2 Td_2, S_f(2)RR_c\right]\end{cases}e^{r_1\tau_2}\end{aligned}$$

Assuming a constant swap spread s, ie, $s_1 = s_2 = s_3 \ldots$, generalising for T periods and simplifying the notation by using $\min[s\, N\, \Delta\tau_t\, Td_t, N(1 - RR_r - RR_r a)RR_c] \equiv \min[x_t]$ and $\min[s\, N\, \Delta\tau_t\, Td_t, S_f(t)RR_c] \equiv \min[y_t]$, we derive

$$\sum_{t=1}^{T}\left\{\begin{bmatrix}\lambda_{t-1}(r\cap c)\min[x_t]+\lambda_{t-1}(\bar{r}\cap \bar{c})sN\Delta\tau_t Td_t\\+\lambda_{t-1}(r\cap \bar{c})sN\Delta\tau_t Td_t+\lambda_{t-1}(c\cap \bar{r})\min[y_t]\end{bmatrix}e^{-r_{t-1}\tau_t}\prod_{u=0}^{t-2}\lambda_u(\bar{r}\cap \bar{c})\right\} \quad (11.3)$$

As mentioned above, the default intensity of reference entity r, λ_t^r, and default intensity of counterparty (ie, default swap seller) c, λ_t^c, are inputs, which will be modelled with a LMM process.

Combining the CDS payoff tree and the CDS spread payment tree
We derive the value of the CDS from the viewpoint of the CDS buyer by subtracting equation (11.3) from equation (11.2):

$$\sum_{t=1}^{T}\left\{\begin{bmatrix}\lambda_{t-1}(r\cap c)N(1-RR_t-RR_t a)RR_c+\lambda_{t-1}(r\cap \bar{c})\\N(1-RR_t-RR_t a)+\lambda_{t-1}(c\cap \bar{r})S_f(t)RR_c\end{bmatrix}e^{-r_{t-1}\tau_t}\prod_{u=0}^{t-2}\lambda_u(\bar{r}\cap \bar{c})\right\}$$

$$-\sum_{t=1}^{T}\left\{\begin{bmatrix}\lambda_{t-1}(r\cap c)\min[x_t]+\lambda_{t-1}(\bar{r}\cap \bar{c})sN\Delta\tau_t Td_t\\+\lambda_{t-1}(r\cap \bar{c})sN\Delta\tau_t Td_t+\lambda_{t-1}(c\cap \bar{r})\min[y_t]\end{bmatrix}e^{-r_{t-1}\tau_t}\prod_{u=0}^{t-2}\lambda_u(\bar{r}\cap \bar{c})\right\} \quad (11.4)$$

Setting equation (11.4) to zero and solving for the fair default swap spread s, which gives the credit default swap a value of zero, we derive

$$s=\frac{\sum_{t=1}^{T}\left\{\begin{bmatrix}\lambda_{t-1}(r\cap c)N(1-RR_t-RR_t a)RR_c+\lambda_{t-1}(r\cap \bar{c})\\N(1-RR_t-RR_t a)+\lambda_{t-1}(c\cap \bar{r})S_f(t)RR_c\end{bmatrix}e^{-r_{t-1}\tau_t}\prod_{u=0}^{t-2}\lambda_u(\bar{r}\cap \bar{c})\right\}}{\sum_{t=1}^{T}\left\{\begin{bmatrix}\lambda_{t-1}(r\cap c)\min[y_t]/s+\lambda_{t-1}(\bar{r}\cap \bar{c})N\Delta\tau_t Td_t\\+\lambda_{t-1}(r\cap \bar{c})N\Delta\tau_t Td_t+\lambda_{t-1}(c\cap \bar{r})\min[y_t]/s\end{bmatrix}e^{-r_{t-1}\tau_t}\prod_{u=0}^{t-2}\lambda_u(\bar{r}\cap \bar{c})\right\}} \quad (11.5)$$

Equation (11.5) is a convenient and practical result. It is a closed-form solution for valuing a CDS, including counterparty default risk and the correlation between reference asset and counterparty default. In addition, equation (11.5) is versatile in excluding counterparty default risk, and counterparty–reference asset correlation. This enables the user to isolate counterparty risk, and counterparty–reference asset correlation.

(a) To exclude counterparty default risk, we can apply equation (11.5) and set the default intensity of the counterparty λ^c to zero. In this case all terms except $\lambda_{t-1}(r \cap \bar{c})N(1 - RR_r - RR_r a)$ and $\lambda_{t-1}(r \cap \bar{c})N\Delta\tau_{t-1}$ and drop out, and $\lambda(\bar{r} \cap \bar{c})$ becomes $\lambda(\bar{r})$

(b) To include counterparty default risk, which is, however, not correlated to the reference asset, we apply equation (11.5) and set the dependence parameter of the particular correlation approach ρ to zero.[4]

(c) To use the full version of the model, ie, include counterparty risk, which is correlated to the reference asset, we use equation (11.5) with $\lambda^c \neq 0$ and apply a correlation concept and $\rho \neq 0$.

Testing the impact of different dependence approaches on the CDS price

Besides λ_r and λ_c, which are modelled with an LMM (Libor Market Model) process, equation (11.5) also requires the critical input joint default correlation $\lambda(r \cap c)$. We can use different dependence approaches, which we have already discussed in this book, to derive the joint default probability. We will test the impact of five different dependency approaches and apply them to equation (11.5) to study the impact on the CDS s. The five dependency approaches are:

1. Correlating Brownian motions via the Heston 1993 model. We discussed this model in Chapter 5. In the Heston model the Brownian motions dz_1 and dz_2 are correlated by the identity

$$dz_1 = \sqrt{\rho_1}dz_2 + \sqrt{1-\rho_1}dz_3 \qquad (5.4)$$

where dz_2 and dz_3 are $n \sim (0, 1)$ and independent.

In this model we will correlate the Brownian motions dz_1 and dz_2 of two LMM processes. One LMM process models the default intensity of the reference asset λ_r and one models the default intensity of the counterparty λ_c.

2. The binomial correlation approach of Lucas (1995), which we analysed in Chapter 4. Here a variable takes the value 1 if entity r defaults and 0 otherwise. Equally, a variable takes the value 1 if entity c defaults and 0 otherwise. Applying the binomial approach to entities r and c, hence rewriting equation (4.8), we have

$$\lambda(r \cap c) = \lambda^r \lambda^c + \rho_2 \sqrt{\left[\lambda^r - (\lambda^r)^2\right]\left[\lambda^c - (\lambda^c)^2\right]} \qquad (4.8a)^5$$

3. The one-factor copula approach by Vasicek (1987), which we discussed in Chapter 6. We will test 3 different versions.

   3a. The one-factor Gaussian copula. The core equation is

   $$x_i = \sqrt{\rho}M + \sqrt{1-\rho}Z_i \qquad (6.1)$$

   where M and Z_i are independent and $n \sim (0, 1)$. As a result, the latent variable x_i is $n \sim (0, 1)$.

   3b. The Student-t copula. The core equation is

   $$\bar{x}_i = \sqrt{\rho}M + \sqrt{1-\rho}Z_i \qquad (6.7)$$

   where M and Z_i are independent and $n \sim (0, 1)$. $x_i = \bar{x}_i \sqrt{W}$ where W follows an inverse Gamma distribution. It follows that the latent variable x_i is Student-t distributed.

   3c. the double-t copula. The core equation is

   $$x_i = \sqrt{\rho}M_s + \sqrt{1-\rho}Z_{i,s} \qquad (6.8)$$

   where M_s and $Z_{i,S}$ are independent and follow a Student-t distribution. Since the Student-t distribution is not stable under convolution, the latent variable x_i in equation (6.8) is not Student-t distributed.

   Once we have generated λ_r and λ_c with an LMM process, and by one of the dependency approaches 1 to 3c, we can find the other dependency inputs of equation (11.5) via basic statistics:

   $$\lambda(r \cap \bar{c}) = \lambda^r - \lambda(r \cap c)$$

   $$\lambda(c \cap \bar{r}) = \lambda^c - \lambda(r \cap c)$$

   $$\lambda(\bar{r} \cap \bar{c}) = 1 - \lambda(r \cup c) = 1 - [\lambda^r + \lambda^c - \lambda(r \cap c)]$$

Results

We now present the results when applying different dependence approaches to equation (11.5). We first do a naïve comparison of the dependency approaches, ie, plot the dependence parameter of each approach on the abscise and derive the CDS spread.

Figure 11.5 displays the resulting CDS spread for a relatively low default environment. Figure 11.5 shows the very different CDS prices that result from different dependence parameters of a particular correlation approach. Hence dependence parameters cannot be compared directly, but must be viewed within their correlation context.

From Figure 11.5 we observe that just correlating the noise terms of the LMM processes in a low volatility-environment has no noticeable effect on the CDS spread. The binomial approach displays the strongest correlation, ie, results in the lowest CDS spread relative to its dependence parameter. Of the three-factor copula approaches, the Student-t exhibits the highest correlation. The double-t correlation is lower (ie, produces a higher spread)

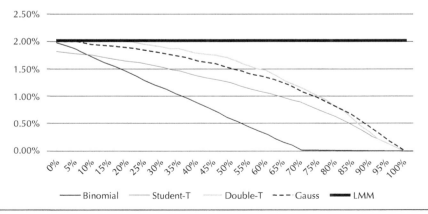

Figure 11.5 Three-year CDS spread derived by equation (11.5) with respect to different correlation approaches. The default probabilities λ_r and λ_c are derived with an LMM model (forward reference entity volatility 2% and 3%, forward counterparty volatility 3% and 4% for year 2 and 3 respectively; reference entity default intensity constant at 2%, counterparty default intensity constant at 4%). There are 110,000 simulations per dependency parameter, which takes about 25 seconds on a Core i5 PC. Upper and lower 95% confidence intervals are below 1.5%.

than the Student-t, since the t-distribution for the idiosyncratic factor Z_i in the double-t generates fatter tails for Z_i. Hence the dependence of x_i on the idiosyncratic factor Z_i increases, reducing correlation between the entities i.

Figure 11.6 displays the CDS spread in a high-volatility environment to show how the models compare in a stressed market environment.

Figure 11.6 shows a slight impact of higher correlation in the LMM approach on the CDS spread. The high volatility also smoothes the binomial correlation function, similar to the effect higher volatility has on the delta function of an option. The non-zero CDS spread for 100% correlation is due to the fact that sampling from the LMM process in case of high volatility produces some simulations in which the reference asset default rates are higher than counterparty default rates. This means that, if the reference asset defaults, the counterparty can survive. Hence the CDS has some value and the CDS spread is non-zero.

For a model that derives the CDS spread including reference asset–counterparty default correlation, see www.dersoft.com/cdswithdefaultcorrelation.xlsm.

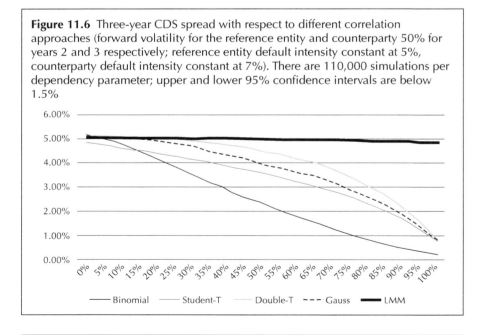

Figure 11.6 Three-year CDS spread with respect to different correlation approaches (forward volatility for the reference entity and counterparty 50% for years 2 and 3 respectively; reference entity default intensity constant at 5%, counterparty default intensity constant at 7%). There are 110,000 simulations per dependency parameter; upper and lower 95% confidence intervals are below 1.5%

Pricing CDSs including the credit correlation of all three entities

From Figure 11.1, we observe the three entities in a CDS:

1. the investor and default swap buyer i;
2. the counterparty or default swap seller c; and
3. the reference entity r, who issued the reference asset.

In section "Credit correlation risk in a CDS", above, we outlined the correlation properties between the three entities in a CDS. We concluded that the credit correlation between the counterparty c and the reference asset r is critical. In addition, the credit correlation between the investor i and the reference asset r is important to the counterparty c. The correlation between the investor i and the counterparty c is less critical, but can be included in the valuation of the fair CDS spread s.

We will now present a model that includes the credit correlation between all three entities in a CDS. The only other study to include the default correlation of all three entities to value a CDS is Brigo and Capponi (2009). They apply a tri-variate copula function in a reduced form continuous time setting to evaluate the CDS spread s. The approach presented here is more practical since it is a discrete time model, in which the user can alter the cashflows if desired.

In the following we will outline this model, which is an extension of the model presented earlier (see "Pricing CDSs including reference entity–counterparty credit correlation").[6]

In an analogy to the definitions of the reference asset r and the counterparty c, above, we define,

λ_t^i: default intensity of investor (ie, default swap buyer) i, (hence λ_t^i is the default probability of i from t to $t + 1$ conditional on survival until t)
Λ_t^i: Cumulative default probability of counterparty i until t
RR_i: exogenous recovery rate of the investor

The model

In the following we will build a CDS payoff tree, a CDS spread tree and use swap evaluation techniques to find the fair CDS spread s. The trees will include the correlation between all three entities in the CDS.

Figure 11.7 Two-period CDS payoff tree with associated cashflows

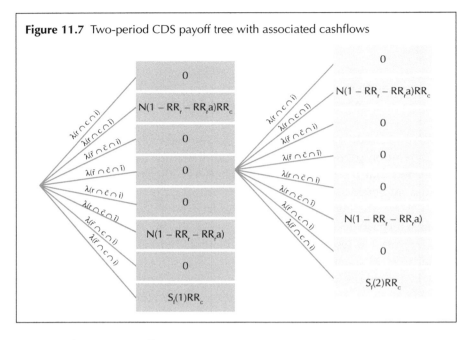

The CDS payoff tree

We assume that if both reference entity and the counterparty default but the investor survives, $\lambda(r \cap x \cap \bar{\imath})$, the standard payoff in case of default of the reference asset $N(1 - RR_r - RR_r a)$ will be reduced by the recovery rate of the counterparty. Hence the payoff will be $N(1 - RR_r - RR_r a)RR_c$. There will be the standard payoff $N(1 - RR_r - RR_r a)$ if only the reference entity defaults and the counterparty and the investor survive, $\lambda(r \cap \bar{c} \cap \bar{\imath})$. We assume that if only the counterparty defaults, $\lambda(c \cap \bar{r} \cap \bar{\imath})$, the counterparty will pay the time t value of the default swap, $S_f(t)$, multiplied by the recovery rate of the counterparty, hence $S_f(t)\,RR_c$. If no entity defaults, $\lambda(\bar{r} \cap \bar{c} \cap \bar{\imath})$ there will be no payoff. Only in this case will the CDS stay alive and enter into the second period octuple tree. This brings us to Figure 11.7.

Displaying Figure 11.7 mathematically for multiple points in time t, we get

$$\sum_{t=1}^{T} \begin{bmatrix} \lambda_t(r \cap c \cap \bar{\imath})(N(1-RR_r-RR_r a)RR_c) \\ +\lambda_t(r \cap \bar{c} \cap \bar{\imath})(N(1-RR_r-RR_r a)) \\ +\lambda_t(\bar{r} \cap c \cap \bar{\imath})(S_f(t)RR_c) \end{bmatrix} e^{-r_{t-1}\tau_t} \prod_{u=0}^{t-2} \lambda_u(\bar{r} \cap \bar{c} \cap \bar{\imath}) \quad (11.6)$$

where T is the maturity date of the CDS and $(t + 1) - t$ is the length of each time step.

Equation (11.7) assumes a zero payoff in many default scenarios. A user can easily adjust payoffs in Figure (11.7) and equation (11.6) if the CDS contract specifies otherwise.

The CDS spread payment tree

We apply in our model that in most CDS contracts the CDS spread is paid in arrears, ie, at the end of each period. In addition, in case of default, the default-swap buyer typically has to pay the accrued spread amount "a" from the last spread payment date to the default date. Also, the US bankruptcy law requires that the solvent party still has to honour its obligations to the defaulting party. Hence we associate the following spread payments for specific default scenarios.

(a) If the investor survives, but both the reference asset and the counterparty default, $\lambda(r \cap c \cap \bar{i})$, the CDS buyer will make a final accrual spread payment, which is capped at the payoff level in default, ie, min $[s\, N\, \Delta\tau\, Td, N(1 - RR_r - RR_r a)RR_c]$. This guarantees that the investor will not pay more CDS spread than the payout they receive. Specifically, this scenario nets the obligations in case of $s\, N\, \Delta\tau\, Td\, N(1 - RR_r - RR_r a)RR_c$ and gives a payoff of $N(1 - RR_r - RR_r a)RR_c - s\, N\, \Delta\tau\, Td$ in case of $N(1 - RR_r - RR_r a)RR_c \geq s\, N\, \Delta\tau\, Td$.

(b) If all three entities survive, $\lambda(\bar{r} \cap \bar{c} \cap \bar{i})$, the spread payment with be the standard $s\, N\, \Delta\tau$. Only in this case will the CDS spread payment tree continue.

(c) If the reference asset defaults but the counterparty and investor survive $\lambda(r \cap \bar{c} \cap \bar{i})$, the spread payment will be $s\, N\, \Delta\tau\, Td$.

(d) If the counterparty defaults, but the reference asset and the investor survive, $\lambda(c \cap \bar{r} \cap \bar{i})$, the spread payment $s\, N\, \Delta\tau\, Td$ will be capped at the fair value of the swap times the recovery value, ie, min$[s\, N\, \Delta\tau_t\, Td_t, S_f(t)RR_c]$. This guarantees, as in scenario (a) that the investor will not pay more CDS spread than the payout she receives.

Applying these cashflows, we derive the swap spread payment tree as seen in Figure 11.8.

Displaying Figure 11.8 mathematically for multiple t, we derive

$$\sum_{t=1}^{T}\begin{bmatrix}\lambda_t(r\cap c\cap \bar{i})\min(sN\Delta t Td_t, N(1-RR_r-RR_ra)RR_c)\\ +\lambda_t(\bar{r}\cap\bar{c}\cap\bar{i})(sN\Delta t)+\lambda_t(r\cap\bar{c}\cap\bar{i})(sN\Delta t Td_t)\\ +\lambda_t(\bar{r}\cap c\cap\bar{i})\min(sN\Delta t Td_t, S_f(t)RR_c)\end{bmatrix}e^{-r_{t-1}\tau_t}\prod_{u=0}^{t-2}\lambda_u(\bar{r}\cap\bar{c}\cap\bar{i}) \quad (11.7)$$

where $t = 1, \ldots, T$ are the CDS spread payment points in time and $(t+1) - t$ is the length of each time period between spread payments s according to the CDS contract.

We have again assumed that in many default scenarios the CDS spread payment is zero. The user can easily alter this in case the CDS contract specifies this otherwise.

Combining the CDS payoff tree and the CDS spread payment tree
We derive the value of the CDS from the viewpoint of the CDS buyer by subtracting equation (11.7) from equation (11.6)

$$\sum_{t=1}^{T}\begin{bmatrix}\lambda_t(r\cap c\cap \bar{i})(N(1-RR_r-RR_ra)RR_c)\\ +\lambda_t(r\cap\bar{c}\cap\bar{i})(N(1-RR_r-RR_ra))\\ +\lambda_t(\bar{r}\cap c\cap\bar{i})(S_f(t)RR_c)\end{bmatrix}e^{-r_{t-1}\tau_t}\prod_{u=0}^{t-2}\lambda_u(\bar{r}\cap\bar{c}\cap\bar{i})$$

$$-\sum_{t=1}^{T}\begin{bmatrix}\lambda_t(r\cap c\cap \bar{i})\min(sN\Delta t Td_t, N(1-RR_r-RR_ra)RR_c)\\ +\lambda_t(\bar{r}\cap\bar{c}\cap\bar{i})(sN\Delta t)+\lambda_t(r\cap\bar{c}\cap\bar{i})(sN\Delta t Td_t)\\ +\lambda_t(\bar{r}\cap c\cap\bar{i})\min(sN\Delta t Td_t, S_f(t)RR_c)\end{bmatrix}e^{-r_{t-1}\tau_t}\prod_{u=0}^{t-2}\lambda_u(\bar{r}\cap\bar{c}\cap\bar{i}) \quad (11.8)$$

Setting equation (11.8) to zero and solving for the CDS spread s, which gives the CDS a value of zero, we derive

$$s = \frac{\sum_{t=1}^{T}\begin{bmatrix}\lambda_t(r\cap c\cap \bar{i})(N(1-RR_r-RR_ra)RR_c)\\ +\lambda_t(r\cap\bar{c}\cap\bar{i})(N(1-RR_r-RR_ra))\\ +\lambda_t(\bar{r}\cap c\cap\bar{i})(S_f(t)RR_c)\end{bmatrix}e^{-r_{t-1}\tau_t}\prod_{u=0}^{t-2}\lambda_u(\bar{r}\cap\bar{c}\cap\bar{i})}{\sum_{t=1}^{T}\begin{bmatrix}\lambda_t(r\cap c\cap \bar{i})\min(sN\Delta t Td_t, N(1-RR_r-RR_ra)RR_c)/s\\ +\lambda_t(\bar{r}\cap\bar{c}\cap\bar{i})(N\Delta t)+\lambda_t(r\cap\bar{c}\cap\bar{i})(N\Delta t Td_t)\\ +\lambda_t(\bar{r}\cap c\cap\bar{i})\min(sN\Delta t Td_t, S_f(t)RR_c)/s\end{bmatrix}e^{-r_{t-1}\tau_t}\prod_{u=0}^{t-2}\lambda_u(\bar{r}\cap\bar{c}\cap\bar{i})}$$

(11.9)

Equation (11.9) is a closed-form solution for valuing a CDS, including default correlation of all involved parties, ie, the investor i (CDS buyer), counterparty c (CDS seller) and reference asset r.

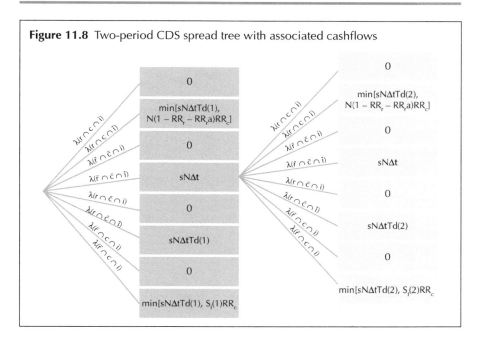

Figure 11.8 Two-period CDS spread tree with associated cashflows

Underlying equation (11.9) is the set of basic probability equations:

$$\lambda(r \cap c \cap \bar{i}) = \lambda(r \cap c) - \lambda(r \cap c \cap i)$$
$$\lambda(r \cap \bar{c} \cap i) = \lambda(r \cap i) - \lambda(r \cap c \cap i)$$
$$\lambda(\bar{r} \cap c \cap i) = \lambda(c \cap i) - \lambda(r \cap c \cap i)$$
$$\lambda(r \cap \bar{c} \cap \bar{i}) = \lambda(r) - \lambda(r \cap c) - \lambda(r \cap i) + \lambda(r \cap c \cap i)$$
$$\lambda(\bar{r} \cap c \cap \bar{i}) = \lambda(c) - \lambda(r \cap c) - \lambda(c \cap i) + \lambda(r \cap c \cap i)$$
$$\lambda(\bar{r} \cap \bar{c} \cap i) = \lambda(i) - \lambda(r \cap i) - \lambda(c \cap i) + \lambda(r \cap c \cap i)$$
$$\lambda(\bar{r} \cap \bar{c} \cap \bar{i}) = 1 - \lambda(r \cup c \cup i)$$
$$= 1 - [\lambda(r) + \lambda(c) + \lambda(i) - \lambda(r \cap c) - \lambda(r \cap i) - \lambda(c \cap i) + \lambda(r \cap c \cap i)] \quad (11.10)$$

Equation set (11.10) can be graphically displayed as shown in Figure 11.9.

The equation set (11.10) is quite versatile. We can eliminate the default risk of an entity by simply setting the default intensity of that entity $\lambda(\cdot)$ to zero. We can include the default intensity of the entities but without default correlation between two of the entities

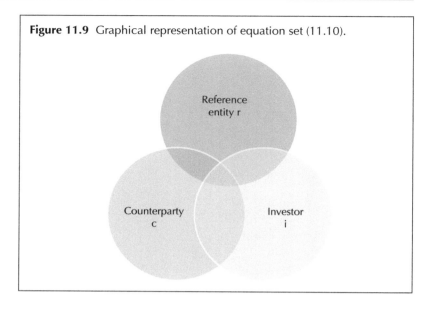

Figure 11.9 Graphical representation of equation set (11.10).

by setting the joint correlation coefficient ρ of the specific correlation approach to zero. The same logic applies to any of the three entities: we can include their default intensities $\lambda(\cdot)$ in the CDS valuation without correlating them by setting the entries in the correlation matrix ρ_M to zero.

Input parameters of the model

The critical input variables that the model requires, $\lambda(r)$, $\lambda(c)$, $\lambda(i)$, $\lambda(r \cap c)$, $\lambda(r \cap i)$, $\lambda(c \cap i)$ and $\lambda(r \cap c \cap i)$, can be derived from historical data and input into the model. However, we can also model $\lambda(r)$, $\lambda(c)$ and $\lambda(i)$ with a term structure approach as with Cox–Ingersoll–Ross (CIR), Heath–Jarrow–Morton (HJM) or the Libor Market Model (LMM). For details see Meissner (1998).

In addition, different approaches to model the joint probabilities can be applied. The bivariate default probabilities $\lambda(r \cap c)$, $\lambda(r \cap i)$, $\lambda(c \cap i)$ can be modelled by the binomial correlation model (Lucas 1995) or the Heston model (1993) approach, which correlates Brownian motions. We can also apply a bivariate copula to model $\lambda(r \cap c)$, $\lambda(r \cap i)$, $\lambda(c \cap i)$ and a trivariate copula to model $\lambda(r \cap c \cap i)$, as done in Brigo and Pallavicini (2008).

Results

We will display four main results with respect to the CDS spread s.

1. We first investigate the impact of the default intensity of the investor $\lambda(i)$ on the CDS spread, which is displayed in Figure 11.10.

    Figure 11.10 shows an expected result. The lower the rating class of the investor, the higher the CDS spread that the investor has to pay. This is because the counterparty will incur a loss if the investor defaults and the present value of the CDS is positive for the counterparty. The model also displays little difference between the CDS spreads when the input parameters are input directly (non-LMM) or when the input parameters are being modelled by an LMM process.
2. The most critical correlation in a CDS is the default intensity correlation between reference asset r and the counterparty c, $\lambda(r \cap c)$. We have discussed this relationship already in

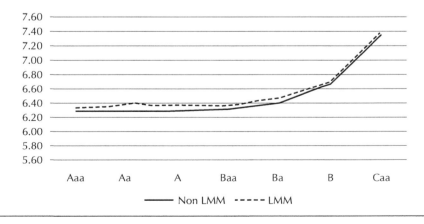

Figure 11.10 CDS spread for different investor rating classes derived by equation (11.9) CDS maturity five years, rating-class reference asset: B, which in 2011 represented $\lambda(r) = 5.27\%$; rating class counterparty: Aa, which in 2011 represented $\lambda(c) = 0.1\%$; rating-class investor: Abscise of Figure 11.10; default correlation between entities 3%; recovery rate of reference asset, counterparty and investor 20%; coupon of reference asset 9%; coupon frequency: semiannual; interest rates constant at 3%; for the LMM process: forward volatility of default intensity of all entities, constant at 15%; forward volatility of interest rates: constant at 9%.

Chapter 1, Figure 1.1. We concluded that the CDS spread is highly sensitive to the default intensity correlation $\lambda(r \cap c)$. This correlation risk also constitutes wrong-way risk (WWR). WWR means that if the exposure (to the reference entity r) increases, it is more unlikely that the insurance provider (the counterparty) can honour its obligation; see Chapter 15 on wrong-way risk.

3. Another important correlation of the CDS is the correlation between the investor i and the reference asset r, $\lambda(i \cap r)$. Regarding this correlation, we have discussed the four possible scenarios. We concluded that a negative credit correlation with credit quality of the reference entity r increasing and the credit quality of the investor i deteriorating, is the worst-case scenario for the counterparty c. A negative credit correlation, however, can also mean best-case scenario if credit quality of the reference entity r decreases and the credit quality of the investor i increases. For a positive credit correlation between the reference entity r investor i, there are offsetting effects.

The model of equation (11.10) derives the sensitivity of the CDS spread with respect to investor–reference asset counterparty default intensity correlation, ie, $\lambda(r \cap i)$ as shown in Figure 11.10.

From Figure 11.11 we observe a slightly negative dependence of the CDS spread with respect to the investor–reference asset-default intensity correlation. This is due to the fact that the worst-case scenario 2a (see above) for the counterparty can occur for high negative correlation and the counterparty wants to be compensated for this risk with a higher CDS spread.

4. The model shows that the CDS spread has close to zero sensitivity with respect to investor i and counterparty c default intensity correlation, $\lambda(c \cap i)$. This is because the possible effects net:

   (a) For negative correlation, $\lambda(i)$ may increase, while $\lambda(c)$ can decrease. Both effects tend to increase s. A decrease in $\lambda(i)$ and an increase in $\lambda(c)$ both tend to decrease s. (b) For positive correlation, both $\lambda(i)$ and $\lambda(c)$ may increase. An increase in $\lambda(i)$ tends to increase s, while an increase in $\lambda(c)$

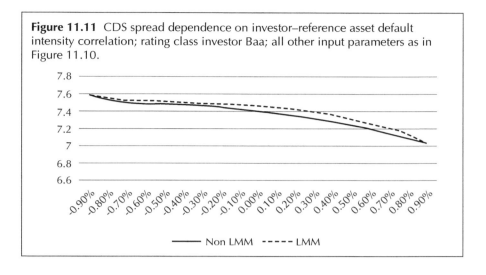

Figure 11.11 CDS spread dependence on investor–reference asset default intensity correlation; rating class investor Baa; all other input parameters as in Figure 11.10.

tends to decrease s. For positive correlation both $\lambda(i)$ and $\lambda(c)$ may also decrease. While a decrease in $\lambda(i)$ tends to decrease s, a decrease in $\lambda(c)$ tends to increase s. Since both the investor and the counterparty have credit risk with respect to each other, these effects net.

It is generally questionable whether an entity should consider its own default intensity and subsequently its own default correlation with other entities. This "bilateral counterparty risk" or debt-value adjustment (DVA) is appealing from a mathematical perspective since it creates congruence and symmetry in pricing. However, if company "a" takes into account its own default intensity, the debt value of company "a" decreases in the case of its own default, and company "a" pays only the recovery rate on its debt. This arguably artificially increases the debt/equity ratio and can possibly increase the credit rating of "a". We will discuss the aspect of DVA in detail in Chapters 15 and 16.

A code, which prices a CDS with the default intensity correlation between all three entities, can be found at www.dersoft.com/ LMMpricingcode.docx.

Cora for CDSs

As seen in equation (10.1), a Cora measures how much a dependent variable changes, if the correlation between one or more independent variables changes. For a CDS, we have four Coras. The most critical Cora is the change in the CDS value for a change in the reference asset–counterparty default correlation:

$$\text{CDSCora}_1 = \frac{\partial \text{CDS}}{\partial \lambda(r \cap c)} \qquad (11.11)$$

Equation (11.11) reads: How much does the value of a CDS change, if the default intensity correlation between the reference asset r and the counterparty c, $\lambda(r \cap c)$, changes by a very small amount? For the role r and c play in a CDS, see again Figure 11.2. We already analysed this correlation in Chapter 1, Figure 1.2. We concluded that the impact of the default correlation between the reference entity r and the counterparty c on the CDS is significant. For the extreme case of the default correlation $\lambda(r \cap c) = 1$, the CDS is worthless, since, if the reference entity defaults, so will the insurance seller c.[7]

We can derive a second Cora for a CDS as displayed in equation (11.12):

$$\text{CDSCora}_2 = \frac{\partial \text{CDS}}{\partial \lambda(r \cap i)} \qquad (11.12)$$

Equation (11.12) reads: How much does the value of CDS change, if the default correlation between the reference asset r and the investor i, $\lambda(r \cap i)$, changes by a very small amount? The CDSCora$_2$ function is displayed in Figure 11.11. We observe that CDSCora$_2$ values are in a relatively narrow range from 7 to 7.6% of the notional amount. Therefore, the counterparty does not have to change their correlation hedge much if the correlation between the reference entity r and the investor i, $\lambda(r \cap i)$, changes.

We can derive a third function of the Cora in a CDS.

$$\text{CDSCora}_3 = \frac{\partial \text{CDS}}{\partial \lambda(i \cap c)} \qquad (11.13)$$

However, we earlier concluded that CDSCora$_3$ is close to 0, since the effects of a change in the correlation between the investor i and the counterparty c net.

Lastly, we can derive the sensitivity of the CDS value with a change in the joint default correlation of all entities in a CDS. This is expressed in equation (11.14).

$$\text{CDSCora}_4 = \frac{\partial \text{CDS}}{\partial \lambda(r \cap c \cap i)} \qquad (11.14)$$

Equation (11.14) reads: How much does the value of CDS change, if the default correlation between the reference asset r, the counterparty c and the investor i, $\lambda(r \cap c \cap i)$ changes by a very small amount? The default intensity correlation $\lambda(r \cap c \cap i)$ can be simulated by a trivariate copula as in Brigo and Pallavicini (2008) or can be simulated by Monte Carlo as discussed earlier. The numerical values for CDSCora_4 are complex and depend on the default-intensity input parameter values $\lambda(r)$, $\lambda(c)$, $\lambda(i)$, the volatilities of $\lambda(r)$, $\lambda(c)$, $\lambda(i)$ and the correlation $\lambda(r \cap c \cap i)$. Different sensitivities of the CDS spread result for different combinations of the input parameters.

Gora for CDSs

In equation (10.2), we defined Gora as the changes of Cora for a small change in the correlation of two more variables. Since we have four different Coras for a CDS, we have four different Goras. The most critical Cora for a CDS is CDSCora_1 in equation (11.11). Therefore the most critical Gora is the Gora with respect to CDSGora_1. Hence, we derive

$$\text{CDSGora}_1 = \frac{\partial \text{CDSCora}_1}{\partial \lambda(r \cap c)} = \frac{\partial^2 \text{CDS}}{\partial \lambda^2(r \cap c)} \qquad (11.15)$$

Equation (11.15) reads: How much does the Cora of a CDS change if the default intensity correlation between the reference asset r and the counterparty c, $\lambda(r \cap c)$, changes by a infinitesimally small amount? From the last term in equation (11.15) we see that CDSGora_1 is the curvature of the original CDS function with respect to the default intensity correlation $\lambda(r \cap c)$. CDSGora tells us how stable the correlation hedge of the CDS is. The higher CDSGora, the higher is the change of Cora and the more often we have to adjust the correlation hedge.

There is no closed-form solution for the CDSGora_1. However, we can easily simulate it by numerically differentiating the Cora

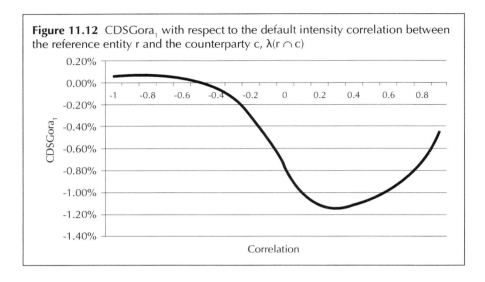

Figure 11.12 CDSGora$_1$ with respect to the default intensity correlation between the reference entity r and the counterparty c, $\lambda(r \cap c)$

function, which had displayed in Chapter 1, Figure 1.2. Doing so, we derive Figure 11.12.

From Figure 11.12, we observe that CDSGora$_1$ is slightly positive and slightly decreasing for correlation values from –0.9 to about –0.55. This means that in this area the necessity to change the hedge reduces (see Chapter 12 for hedging correlation risk). At about a correlation value of –0.55, the value of the CDSGora$_1$ is close to zero, so the investor does not have to adjust the correlation hedge much. For a correlation of –0.55 to +0.3, we observe that CDSGora$_1$ decreases. This means that the investor is more exposed to changes in the reference asset–counterparty correlation and has to adjust their hedge often. For an increasing correlation in the range of about +0.2 to +1, GoraCDS$_1$ increases and approaches zero. This means that the investor is less exposed to changes in correlation and has to adjust their correlation hedge less often for changes in correlation.

There are also the CDSGoras resulting from the CDSCoras in equations (11.12) to (11.14). From equation (11.12), we derive

$$\text{CDSGora}_2 = \frac{\partial \text{CDSCora}_2}{\partial \lambda(r \cap i)} = \frac{\partial^2 \text{CDS}}{\partial \lambda^2(r \cap i)} \tag{11.16}$$

Equation (11.16) reads: How much does the Cora of a CDS change if the default intensity correlation between the reference asset *r* and the investor i, $\lambda(r \cap i)$, changes by a infinitesimally small amount? From the last term in equation (11.16) we see that CDSGora$_2$ is the curvature of the original CDS function with respect to the default intensity correlation $\lambda(r \cap i)$. We have displayed the CDSCora$_2$ in Figure 11.11. We observe that CDSCora$_2$ decreases for increasing correlation. Therefore, the counterparty has to increase his correlation hedge if the default intensity correlation $\lambda(r \cap i)$ increases. Since the CDSCora$_2$ function in Figure 11.11 is quite monotonously decreasing (ie, has fairly low curvature), the counterparty does not have to change the degree of their correlation hedge much if the default intensity correlation $\lambda(r \cap i)$ increases.

In the previous section we concluded in the CDSCora$_3$ function that there is no significant influence of the correlation $\lambda(r \cap i)$ on the CDS spread, ie, the CDSCora$_3$ function is close to horizontal. Therefore, the CDSGora$_3$ function is close to zero.

With respect to CDSCora$_4$, we concluded that its numerical values are complex and depend on the default intensity input parameter values $\lambda(r)$, $\lambda(c)$, $\lambda(i)$, the volatilities of $\lambda(r)$, $\lambda(c)$, $\lambda(i)$ and the correlation $\lambda(r \cap c \cap i)$. Different combinations of input parameters result in sensitivities. Therefore, CDSGora$_4$ values are also complex and give different results for different input parameter values.

CORRELATION RISK IN A CDO

In Chapters 6 and 7, we discussed the valuation of CDOs in detail. Here we will derive the correlation risk parameters Cora and Gora in a one-factor Gaussian copula (OFGC) framework. The underlying CDO will be a synthetic CDO. The tranches are the same as in the US CDX index.

In Figure 11.13, we recognise the three parties in a CDO: the protection buyer who buys CDSs to typically hedge credit exposure; the SPV (special-purpose vehicle) is an intermediary, who manages the CDO; the investor, who invests in a particular tranche and assumes the credit risk.

Types of risk in a CDO

There are two main factors that determine the value of a CDO: the default probability of assets in the CDO and the default correlation between the assets. Consequently, the two main risks when

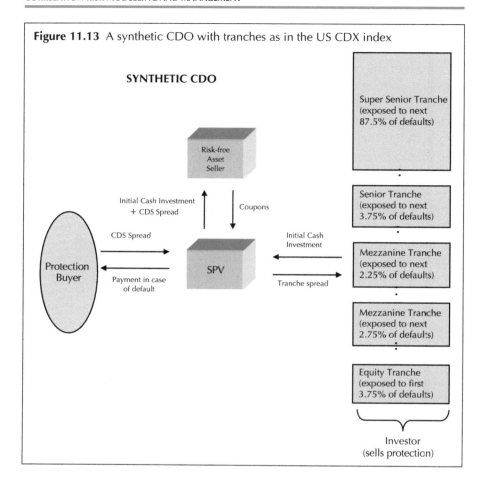

Figure 11.13 A synthetic CDO with tranches as in the US CDX index

hedging CDOs are credit risk and correlation risk, as shown in Figure 11.14.

Correlation risk in a CDO tranche is the risk that the correlation between the assets in said CDO tranche and consequently the value of the CDO tranche change unfavourably. We will now discuss correlation risk, which is measured by Cora and Gora.

Cora of a CDO

We have already displayed the dependency of the tranche spreads in a CDO with respect to correlation in Chapter 1, Figure 1.7. We will display it here again.

From Figure 11.15, we observe that the investor in the 0–3%

QUANTIFYING CREDIT CORRELATION RISK

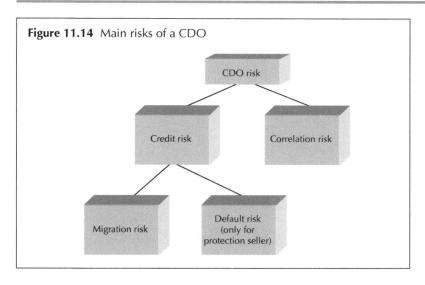

Figure 11.14 Main risks of a CDO

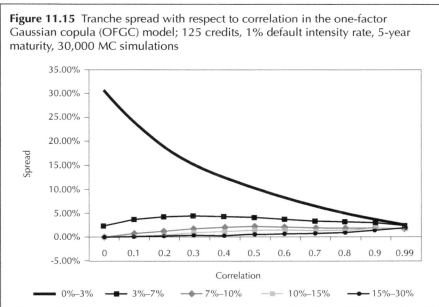

Figure 11.15 Tranche spread with respect to correlation in the one-factor Gaussian copula (OFGC) model; 125 credits, 1% default intensity rate, 5-year maturity, 30,000 MC simulations

equity tranche investor is long correlation. This means that, as the correlation between the assets increases, so does the present value of the equity tranche for the investor. This is because the investor receives a fixed spread of the tranche, eg, 500 basis points. When the market equity tranche spread decreases with increasing correlation, the investor then receives a spread that is higher than the market spread.

Formally, the Cora of a tranche x in a CDO is displayed in Equation 11.17:

$$\text{Cora}(\text{Tranche } x) = \frac{\partial s(\text{Tranche } x)}{\partial \rho} \qquad (11.17)$$

Equation (11.17) reads: How much does the spread s of Tranche x change, if the correlation between all assets ρ in the CDO changes by an infinitesimally small amount?

Differentiating the functions in Figure 11.15 gives the Cora of the tranches in a CDO, which is displayed in Figure 11.16.

From Figure 11.16 we observe that Cora is fairly constant and close to zero for the 3–7%, 7–11%, 11–15% and 15–30% tranches. Therefore the investor in these tranches has only little correlation risk and consequently does not have to hedge such risk much. However, the 0–3% equity tranche is highly sensitive to correlation changes: if correlation increases, the value of Cora decreases (on an absolute basis), and the investor can reduce their correlation hedge. Conversely, if correlation decreases, the value of the Cora increases (on an absolute basis), and the investor has to increase the correlation hedge.

Gora of a CDO

Differentiating the tranche functions in Figure 11.16, gives the Gora for tranches in the CDO. Formally,

$$\text{Gora}(\text{Tranche } x) = \frac{\partial \text{Cora}(\text{Tranche } x)}{\partial \rho} = \frac{\partial^2 (\text{Tranche } x)}{\partial \rho^2} \qquad (11.18)$$

Equation (11.18) reads: How much does the Cora of a Tranche x change if the correlation between all assets ρ in the CDO changes by an infinitesimally small amount? From the last term in equation (11.18) we see that the Gora of a tranche is the curvature of the original tranche functions (displayed in Figure 11.15) with respect to the correlation coefficient ρ. Graphically, the Goras of the tranches in the CDO are displayed in Figure 11.17.

From Figure 11.17, we observe that the Gora of the tranches 3–7%, 7–11%, 11–15% and 15–30% is close to zero. Therefore, the

QUANTIFYING CREDIT CORRELATION RISK

investor does not have to change their correlation hedge much. This is sensible since in Figure 11.16 we observed a Cora of close to zero for these tranches, hence there is little need to hedge correlation risk at all. However, the 0–3% equity tranche shows a high

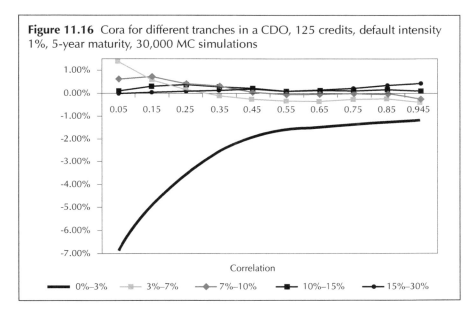

Figure 11.16 Cora for different tranches in a CDO, 125 credits, default intensity 1%, 5-year maturity, 30,000 MC simulations

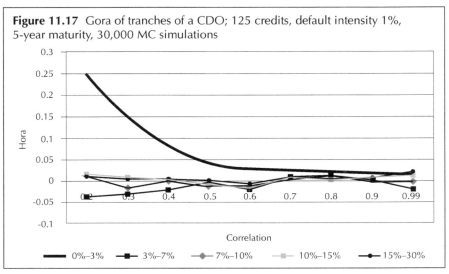

Figure 11.17 Gora of tranches of a CDO; 125 credits, default intensity 1%, 5-year maturity, 30,000 MC simulations

Gora, which means a high necessity to change the hedge amount Cora. In particular, Gora is high for low correlation levels. This means that for low correlation levels the investor has to adjust their correlation hedge often for changes in the level of correlation.

SUMMARY
In this chapter, we discussed how to quantify credit correlation risk. Credit risk is the risk of financial loss due to an adverse change in the credit quality of a debtor. There are two main types of credit risk: (1) migration risk, which is the risk of an unfavourable change in the credit quality of a debtor, and (2) default risk, which is a special case of migration risk and occurs only if an investor is long credit (ie, has bought a bond or is receiving fixed in a CDS).

Credit correlation risk is the risk that credit quality correlations between two or more counterparties change unfavourably.

All loan portfolios of financial institutions as well as all structured products such as CDOs, MBSs and so forth are exposed to credit correlation risk. In addition, all derivatives used as a hedge also include credit correlation risk. For example, a CDS used as a hedge includes three parties: (1) the CDS buyer, (2) the CDS seller (counterparty and (3) the underlying asset.

Therefore, there are three types of credit correlation risk in a CDS: (a) if the default correlation between the counterparty and the reference asset increases, the CDS value will decrease with a paper loss for the investor; (b) if the default intensity of the underlying asset decreases and the default intensity of the investor increases, the counterpart will have higher credit risk exposure; and (c) the default intensity correlation between the investor and the counterparty is of minor importance because the investor or the counterparty do not care too much if they default and at the same time their counterparty defaults.

Models that value a CDS, including the reference asset and counterparty default correlation risk in a rigorous way, can be derived. In addition, models that include the default intensity correlation of all three entities in a CDS are available.

Formally, the Cora and Gora of a CDS measure the sensitivity of a CDS value change with respect to changes in correlation between two entities in the CDS. Since we have three entities in a CDS, principally three Coras and Goras for the CDS exist. We can also derive the Cora and Gora of a CDS for the default intensity correlation of all three entities in the CDS.

The correlation risk of CDOs received great attention during the global financial crisis in 2007 to 2009. CDOs and their correlation properties were called "toxic". However, once understood, the correlation risk in a CDO is quite intuitive. In addition, the correlation risk can be quantified with Cora and Gora and hedged accordingly.

Questions for Chapter 11

Answers to these questions can be found at the end of this book.

1. What is credit risk?
2. Which two types of credit risk exist? What is the relationship between these two types of credit risk?
3. What is credit correlation risk?
4. Name three financial products that are exposed to credit correlation risk.
5. A CDS, which is used as a hedge has three parties: (1) the investor (CDS buyer); (2) the counterparty (CDS seller); and (3) the underlying asset. The default correlation between which two entities is the most significant for the valuation of a CDS?
6. For the counterparty, the default correlation between the investor and the underlying asset is also of importance. Which is the worse-case scenario for the counterparty from a risk perspective?
7. When valuing a CDS, we can also include the default intensity correlation between all three entities. Draw a Venn diagram that displays the default intensity correlation's properties.
8. What information does the Cora of a CDS give us?
9. Since there are three entities in a CDS, there are principally three Coras. Name them and interpret them. Which one is the most critical?
10. What does the Gora of a CDS tell us?

11. What are the two main risks in a CDO?
12. The value of a CDO and its tranches depends critically on the correlation of the assets in the CDO. Draw a graph showing the equity tranche's value, mezzanine tranche's value and a senior tranche's value with respect to correlation.
13. What does the Cora of a tranche in a CDO tell us?
14. Which tranche in a CDO has the highest correlation risk, ie, the highest Cora?
15. CDOs and their correlation properties are sometimes termed "toxic". Do you agree with this view?

1   We see from Figure 11.2 that the accrued interest $RR_r a$ is deducted from the settlement amount. This is because it is assumed that the coupon of the reference bond will be paid from the reference entity at the next coupon date. This may not happen though since the reference asset is in state of default. Hence, in some CDS contracts, the accrued interest is excluded.
2   The following is a short version of the paper "The impact of different correlation approaches on pricing CDS with counterparty credit risk"; see Meissner, Rooder and Fan (2013).
3   For an intuitive explanation of the LMM model, see Hull (2012), Chapter 31.
4   An exception is the Student-t. Here, tail dependence exists, even for $\rho = 0$.
5   In Chapter 5, we used the notation of Lucas, where $P(XY)$ is the joint default probability of X and Y. In this chapter, we use a more statistical notation, ie, is the joint default probability of r and c.
6   We will present a short version of the paper G. Meissner, D. Mesarch and O. Olkov, "The Valuation of Credit Default Swaps (CDSs) including Investor – Counterparty – Reference Entity Default Correlation", *Journal of Risk*, December 2013.
7   There is one exception though. If the default intensity of the counterparty c is smaller than the default intensity of the counterparty c, $\lambda(c) < \lambda(r)$, even in the case of perfect default intensity correlation, some Monte Carlo simulations will result in the reference entity defaulting, but the counterparty surviving. (The reader should keep in mind that we are correlating default intensities, not actual defaults.) In this case, the CDS has some value. This is especially the case of high default intensity volatility. The reader can verify this at www.dersoft.com/cdswithdefaultcorrelation.xlsm.

12
Hedging Correlation Risk

"Only if it was possible to delta-hedge correlation risk ... would it make sense to use a full-blown stochastic correlation model"
– Lorenzo Bergomi

In this chapter, we will discuss why hedging financial correlation risk is more challenging than hedging other financial risks such as market risk and credit risk. However, we will show two methods that can be applied to hedge financial correlation risk. At the end of the chapter, we will discuss in which situations it is better to hedge with options and in which it is better to hedge with futures.

WHAT IS HEDGING?

Let us first clarify what hedging is. Hedging is entering into a second trade to reduce the risk of an original trade. If the original trade is a simple transaction such as being long a bond, there are three main ways to hedge the market risk (risk of an unfavourable change in the price) and the credit risk (migration risk and default risk; see Figure 11.1 in the previous chapter). Let us assume an investor had bought a Greek government bond. To hedge the risk, they can perform one of the following.

(a) Simply sell the bond. This is beneficial since all types of risk, such as market risk, credit risk, operational risk, liquidity risk and correlation risk with other assets, are eliminated. The severe drawback, though, is that the investor often has to sell at a low price. Hence, a paper loss is realised and will not be recovered if the Greek bond price improves at a later point in time.

(b) Hedge the bond with a derivate such as a forward, future, swap[1] or with an option. Let us look at an example of a

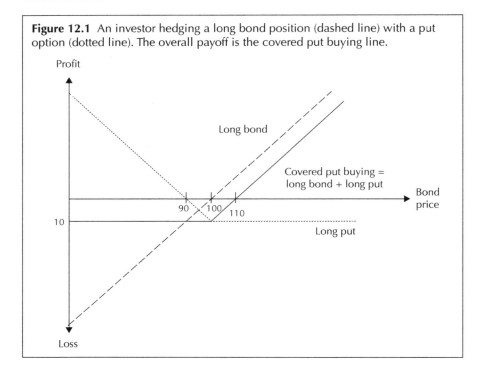

Figure 12.1 An investor hedging a long bond position (dashed line) with a put option (dotted line). The overall payoff is the covered put buying line.

hedge for the long bond position with a put option. The investor has bought a bond at US$100. They are now worried about a possible price deterioration and buys a put option with a strike of US$100 and a premium of US$10 as insurance. This is also referred to as "Covered Put buying" or "Married puts". The overall payoff is displayed in Figure 12.1.

The investor has now limited their downside risk to a loss of US$10. The catch is the reduced upside potential, which is lowered by the put premium of US$10.

(c) The investor can also hedge the long Greek bond position by selling a product that is negatively correlated to the price movement of the Greek bond. For example, let us assume that historically the correlation between Spanish bonds and Greek bonds was positive. The investor decides to sell a Spanish government bond in to offset the price risk of their long Greek bond. However, in this case, the investor has correlation risk, in particular the risk that the correlation between Greek bonds and Spanish bonds is not positive in the future. It could happen that the Greek bond declines in price and the Spanish bond increases, leading to a loss in both the underlying and the hedge.

In case (b), we applied a derivate, ie, an option to hedge a non-derivate, a bond position. In trading practice, the reverse operation of case (b) is also applied. We can hedge the risk of an option using a non-derivative. Let us discuss this case.

Typically, when hedging a derivative such as an option, the underlying asset is bought or sold to offset an unfavourable change in the option value. For example if a trader has bought a call option on the Apple stock (AAPL), the trader is vulnerable to a price decline in that stock, since in this case the call value decreases. To hedge this risk, the trader typically sells the underlying AAPL stock, or, more precisely, the trader sells the delta-amount of call on AAPL. This delta is given from a model. For example, the Black–Scholes–Merton option pricing model. Let us look at an example of a delta-hedge:

Example 12.1
An option trader at Goldman Sachs buys a call on IBM. The call option premium is US$10,000 (eg, the trader bought 1,000 calls with a call premium of C_0 =US$10). IBM trades at S_0 = 100. The trader decides to delta-hedge the IBM price risk of the option. The delta, derived from an option pricing model as the Black-Scholes-Merton model, comes out to 51%. Formally,

$$\Delta_C = \frac{\partial C}{\partial S} \approx \frac{0.51}{1} \qquad (12.1)$$

where

Δ_C : Delta of the call
C : Call price
S : Price of the underlying stock IBM
∂ : Partial derivative operator

Equation (12.1) reads: How much does the call price C change, if S changes by an infinitesimally small amount, assuming all other variables influencing the call price are constant? For practical purposes, the change in S can be approximated by a change of 1 unit, as done in equation (12.1).

How much IBM stocks does the option trader have to sell to stay delta-neutral, meaning the option trade has no price risk with respect to IBM?

The option trader has to sell IBM stocks in the delta amount, hence 51% of the option premium of US$10,000. Therefore the option trader sells 51 shares at US$100 each and receives US$5,100. The option trader now has no IBM price risk.[2] Let us show this.

If IBM increases by 1%, following equation (12.1) the call price increases by 0.51%. Therefore, the profit on the call is

$$C_1 \times 1,000 - C_0 \times 1,000 = US\$10.051 \times 1,000 - US\$10 \times 1,000 = US\$51$$

The loss on the hedge is

$$S_1 \times 51 - S_0 \times 51 = US\$101 \times 51 - US\$100 \times 51 = US\$51$$

Hence, the option trade is hedged against price risk of IBM. What the option trader gains on the call is lost on the hedge and vice versa.

WHY IS HEDGING FINANCIAL CORRELATIONS CHALLENGING?

Hedging correlation risk is more difficult than hedging a bond, a stock, or an option, for two main reasons:

1. hedging correlation risk involves two or more assets, since the correlation is measured between at least two assets; and
2. there is principally no underlying instrument that trades in the market and that can be bought or sold as a hedge.

However, the correlation market is evolving. We have already discussed four ways to trade correlation in Chapter 1, and this second book edition has devoted the entire Chapter 13 to correlation trading. We will now discuss how to use the correlation products that already exist in financial practice, to hedge correlation risk.

TWO EXAMPLES TO HEDGE CORRELATION RISK

In the following, we present two methods for hedging financial correlation risk. The first method is to hedge with correlation-dependent options; the second is to hedge with a correlation swap.

Hedging credit-default-swap (CDS) counterparty risk with a correlation-dependent option

Any financial product can be used for two main purposes:

(a) speculation, ie, trying to generate a profit; and
(b) hedging, ie, reducing risk.

In Chapter 1, in the section called "Trading and correlation", we discussed the speculative aspect of correlation options and showed how the correlation influences the price of certain assets as exchange options and quanto options. These correlation-dependent options can also be used to hedge correlation risk. Let us show how the counterparty credit risk in a CDS can be hedged with an option whose value depends on correlation.

Example 12.2
Let us start with an investor who has invested in a Spanish bond and has decided to hedge the default risk of Spain with a CDS from BNP Paribas. We had already discussed this CDS in Chapter 1, and a similar CDS in Chapter 11.

The investor in the CDS of Figure 12.2 has default correlation risk between the reference entity (Spain) and the CDS seller (BNP Paribas). As discussed in Chapter 1, the higher the default correlation between the reference entity and the CDS seller, the lower the CDS spread s for the investor. The worst-case scenario for the investor is the default of both the reference entity and the counterparty. In this case the investor loses their entire investment. The higher the default correlation, the more likely it is that the reference entity and the counterparty default together, hence the lower is the CDS spread. This is displayed in Figure 12.3.

A model that derives the CDS spread s, including reference–entity–counterparty default correlation can be found at www.dersoft.com/cdswithdefaultcorrelation.xlsm.

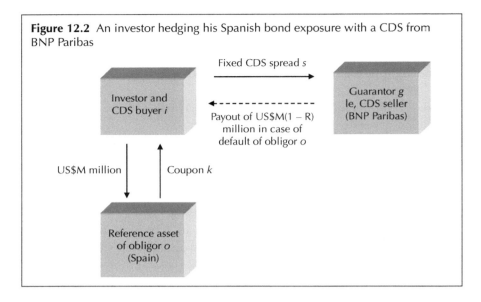

Figure 12.2 An investor hedging his Spanish bond exposure with a CDS from BNP Paribas

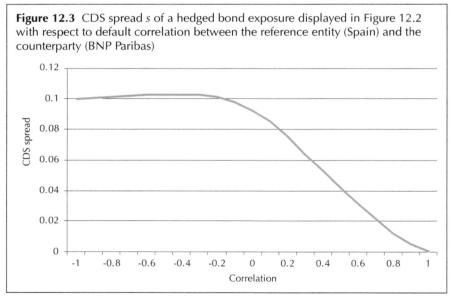

Figure 12.3 CDS spread s of a hedged bond exposure displayed in Figure 12.2 with respect to default correlation between the reference entity (Spain) and the counterparty (BNP Paribas)

How can we hedge this correlation risk? We could use one of many existing correlation-dependent options, such as:

❑ option on the better of two: payoff = $\max(S_1, S_2)$;

- option on the worse of two: payoff = min(S_1, S_2);
- call on the maximum of two: payoff = max[0, (max(S_1, S_2)) − K];
- exchange option (as a convertible bond): payoff = max(0, S_2 − S_1);
- spread call option: payoff = max[0, (S_2 − S_1) − K];
- option on the better of two or cash: payoff = max(S_1, S_2, cash);
- dual-strike call option: payoff = max(0, S_1 − K_1, S_2 − K_2); and
- portfolio of basket option:

$$\text{Payoff} = \left[\sum_{i=1}^{n} n_i S_i - K, 0 \right]$$

where n_i is the weight of assets i.

All of these options are candidates for hedging correlation risk, since their values are dependent upon the correlation between the underlying variables. Let us look at an "option on the better of two", with a payoff of max (S_1, S_2). As the payoff shows, in this option the investor can choose to receive either the underlying S_1 or S_2 at maturity. The lower the correlation between S_1 and S_2, the more valuable is an option on the better of two. If the correlation between S_1 and S_2 would be 1, this would just be a zero-strike call

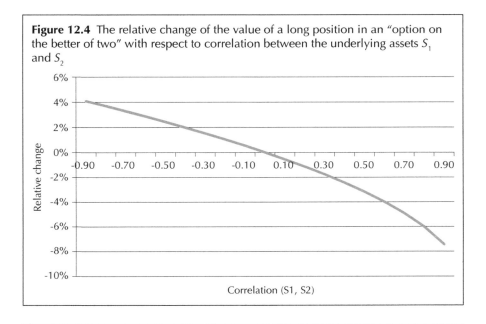

Figure 12.4 The relative change of the value of a long position in an "option on the better of two" with respect to correlation between the underlying assets S_1 and S_2

option on the underlying with the higher starting value. A model that derives the value of an "option on the better of two" can be found at www.dersoft.com/optiononthebetteroftwo.xlsm. Figure 12.4 shows the value of a long option on the better of two.

In Figure 12.4, the option price is standardised, ie, a zero correlation is set to a zero option value. This figure shows the strong impact of correlation on the option price. The option price fluctuates by about 12% for correlation levels from –0.9 to +0.9. The figure shows a long position of an "option on the better of two". In this case, the trader is "short correlation", ie, benefits if correlation decreases. If a trader wants to be "long correlation", they have to sell an "option on the better of two". In this case, the payoff reverses and we have an option function as displayed in Figure 12.5.

From Figures 12.4 and 12.5, we observe that the profit of the option buyer is the loss of the option seller with respect to correlation changes, and vice versa.

We can now use the short option position in Figure 12.5 to hedge the long correlation risk of the CDS displayed in Figure 12.3. Ideally, S_1 and S_2 in the short "option on the better of two" are the default probabilities of Spain and Greece. These could quite well be

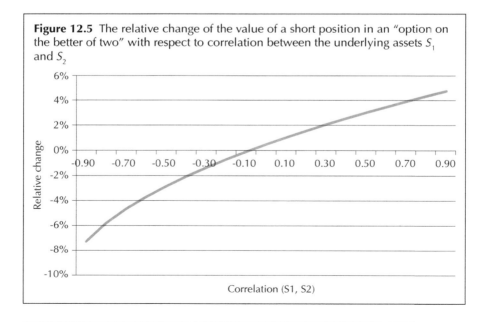

Figure 12.5 The relative change of the value of a short position in an "option on the better of two" with respect to correlation between the underlying assets S_1 and S_2

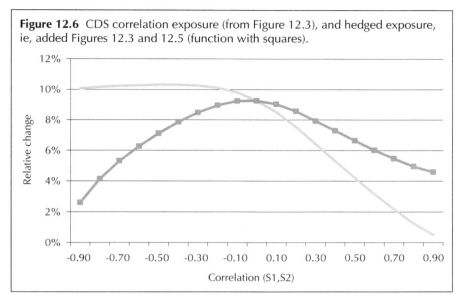

Figure 12.6 CDS correlation exposure (from Figure 12.3), and hedged exposure, ie, added Figures 12.3 and 12.5 (function with squares).

approximated with the CDS spread of Spain and BNP Paribas. If we combine Figures 12.3 and 12.5, we derive Figure 12.6.

From Figure 12.6, we observe that one of the main objectives is achieved. The high value of the original position (graph with no squares in Figure 12.6) for low correlation is lowered. However, there are very few free lunches in finance.[3] The cost of the hedge is the higher value of the hedged position (graph with squares) for positive correlation values.

If the investor wants to further increase the overall value for high correlation, they can increase the notional amount of the "option on the better of two" hedge. This leads to an overall position as displayed in Figure 12.7.

From Figure 12.7, we observe that, for high correlation values, the value of the overall hedged position (graph with triangles) is higher than in Figure 12.6, which is not desired, since ideally, the relative change with respect to correlation should be zero. The benefit is the now lower value of the overall hedged position for negative correlation compared with Figure 12.6.

Hedging Value at Risk (VaR) correlation risk with a correlation swap

We discussed correlation swaps in Chapter 1 (see equations (1.6) and (1.7)). Let us now apply correlation swaps to hedge VaR

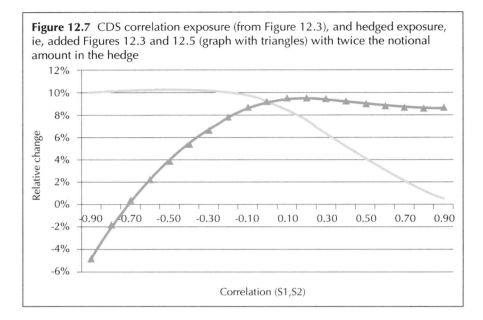

Figure 12.7 CDS correlation exposure (from Figure 12.3), and hedged exposure, ie, added Figures 12.3 and 12.5 (graph with triangles) with twice the notional amount in the hedge

correlation risk. We analysed VaR correlation risk in Chapter 1 and in more detail in Chapter 10. Let us hedge the VaR correlation risk of the 10-asset portfolio in example 10.1. We derived VaR as a function of pairwise correlation of the assets in the portfolio in Figure 10.1.

We can now hedge this VaR correlation risk with a correlation swap. The dependence of a correlation swap with respect to the pairwise change in correlation of the assets is displayed in Figure 12.8.

The fixed rate in the correlation swap in Figure 12.8 is set at 23.14%. This is the actual correlation of the assets in the portfolio following equation (1.6)

$$\rho_{realised} = \frac{2}{n^2 - n} \sum_{i>j} \rho_{i,j} \qquad (1.6)$$

and example 10.1. A simple spreadsheet showing the present value of a correlation swap can be found at www.dersoft.com/correlationswap.xlsx. A model valuing interest rate swaps, which can be applied to correlation swaps if a correlation term structure is available, can be found at www.dersoft.com/interestrateswap.xls.

HEDGING CORRELATION RISK

Figure 12.8 Change in value of a long correlation swap (pay fixed and receive realised; see Figure 1.5 for details) with respect to pairwise change in the correlation between all assets in a 10-asset portfolio; the returns and consequently the correlation between the returns of the 10 assets in the portfolio are the same as in the VaR example 10.1

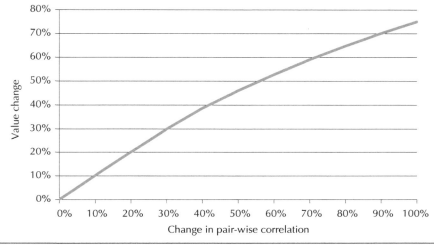

Figure 12.9 Change in value of a short correlation swap (receive fixed and pay realised; see Figure 1.5 for details) with respect to pairwise change in the correlation of a 10-asset portfolio; the returns and consequently the correlation between the returns of the 10 assets in the portfolio are the same as in the VaR example 10.1

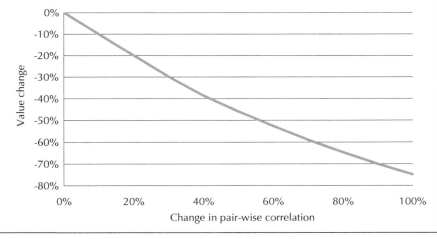

295

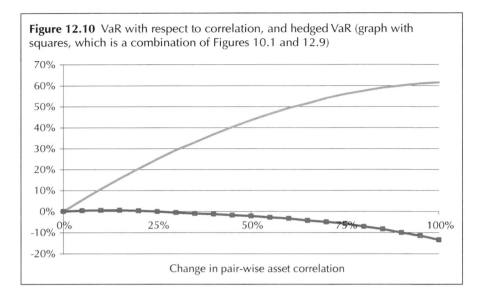

Figure 12.10 VaR with respect to correlation, and hedged VaR (graph with squares, which is a combination of Figures 10.1 and 12.9)

In order to hedge the VaR correlation risk in Figure 10.1 in the previous chapter, we have to reverse the swap in Figure 12.8, ie, receive fixed and pay realised. This is displayed in Figure 12.9.

From Figures 12.8 and 12.9, we observe that the present values of the long correlation swap and short correlation swap are reversed. Hence, what the correlation buyer (long correlation) gains, the correlation seller loses for a change in correlation, and vice versa.

We can now hedge the VaR correlation risk in Figure 10.1 with the short correlation swap in Figure 12.9. We derive Figure 12.10.

From Figure 12.10, we see that VaR correlation risk is eliminated for small changes in the all-pairwise correlations of the assets in the portfolio. For larger changes, the hedged VaR now has a negative dependence on correlation. This means that, as correlations increase strongly, the hedged VaR actually decreases. This hedge can be fine-tuned: a lower or higher notional can be applied in the correlation swap hedge or a different strike can be used. This will lead to a slightly different overall hedge function.

WHEN TO USE OPTIONS: WHEN TO USE FUTURES TO HEDGE?

Two key aspects have to be considered when choosing whether to hedge with an option or a futures contract.[4]

(a) We have to analyse which contract matches the price function of the underlying instrument. For example, in Figure 12.9 we observed that hedging VaR correlation risk can be achieved well with a correlation swap. The overall correlation risk function is close to zero and decreases only for high correlation levels. Therefore, a correlation swap is a good hedging instrument for VaR correlation risk, at least in our given, real-world example.

(b) In contrast to an option, which has an option premium, a futures contract has no upfront premium. One benefit of a long option position is that the loss is limited to the option premium, which is typically quite low. However, in a futures contract the loss can be significant if the underlying has moved strongly in the undesired direction. Let us look at the implication of this in an example. Let us assume an investor wants to hedge a long Greek bond position. When should the investor use a swap as a CDS? When should the investor use a put option?

(b1) If the investor is quite certain that the Greek bond will decline further (but does not want to sell and realise a loss), they can hedge with a swap or a future. This way no option premium is wasted.

(b2) The investor wants to hedge their Greek bond price risk, but is somewhat uncertain whether the Greek bond price will actually decline. In this case a long put option is warranted, since a profit is generated if the Greek bond price increases; see Figure 12.1.

In conclusion, the more confident an investor is that the undesirable event (a price decline of the Greek bond in the above example) will occur, the more appropriate it is to hedge with a future or a swap. The less confident an investor is that the undesirable event will occur, the more appropriate it is to hedge with an option.

SUMMARY

In finance, hedging means reducing risk or, more precisely, entering into a second trade to reduce the risk of an original trade. In this chapter we discussed ways to hedge correlation risk. Hedging can be principally done in three ways.

(a) Close the original position, eg, if a bond was purchased, sell the bond. The drawback is that, if the position has created a paper loss, this paper loss is realised.
(b) Use a derivative to hedge the position. This is an efficient way to hedge. Typically, the hedge amount has to be adjusted when the underlying price changes – called dynamic delta hedging.
(c) Enter into a position that is negatively correlated with the original trade. Here the investor has correlation risk, though, ie, the risk that both the original trade and the hedge create a loss.

Hedging correlation risk is more difficult than hedging equity risk, bond price risk or the risk of a derivatives position, for two reasons: (a) hedging correlation risk involves two or more assets, since the correlation is measured between at least two assets, and (b) there is principally no underlying instrument that trades in the market and that can be bought or sold as a hedge.

However, the correlation market is evolving. There are numerous products that are sensitive to correlation such as correlation options, correlation swaps and options on correlation swaps. Each of them can be used to hedge correlation risk. An investor who wants to hedge their correlation risk will have to find the correlation hedge that matches the correlation exposure of the original trade best.

A general question with respect to hedging is when to use a future or forward (or swap, which is just a series of forwards) and when to use options. Let us assume an investor has a CDS and is exposed to correlation-risk with respect to the reference entity and the counterparty. The investor should use a forward (or a swap such as a correlation swap) if they are very certain – as certain as they can be – that the hedge is needed. This way no option premium is wasted. However, the investor should use options in the hedge, such as an option on a correlation swap, if the investor wants to hedge the correlation risk, but is not that certain that the correlation risk will occur. If the correlation risk does not occur, the loss on the hedge is just the option premium.

Questions for Chapter 12

Answers to these questions can be found at the back of this book.

1. What is hedging?
2. Name the three main ways to hedge.
3. Name two reasons why it is more difficult to hedge correlation risk compared with equity risk or currency risk.
4. Can it be a good idea not to hedge an exposure as a correlation exposure?
5. In a delta hedge, the delta amount of the exposure is sold or bought. Give an example of delta hedging.
6. Delta hedges are typically not constant. Give an example of dynamic delta hedging.
7. Name several instruments that can hedge correlation risk.
8. How can we determine whether a certain correlation hedge is a "good" hedge?
9. When an investor has a "perfect" hedge, doesn't this mean that the profit potential is zero?
10. Generally, when should we hedge with forwards, futures, and swaps, and when should we hedge with options?

---

1 Forwards, futures and swaps are closely related. A forward is the agreement between two parties to conduct a trade at a certain price in the future. A swap is just a series of forward contracts. Forwards and swaps are typically traded OTC (over the counter), so not on an exchange. A future trades on an exchange and is just a standardised forward, ie, the maturity date, notional amount, underlying, etc, are standardised. See Hull (2012) for more on derivatives.
2 This is true for small changes in the IBM price. If the IBM changes by a large amount, the delta changes and has to be adjusted.
3 One of these free lunches is diversification, which is related to a low correlation of the assets in a portfolio. This increases the return/risk ratio, as discussed in Chapter 1.
4 See endnote 1, above, for the close relationship between futures, forwards and swaps.

13

Correlation Trading Strategies – Opportunities and Limitations

"The best investment one can make is to invest in your own abilities."

– Warren Buffett

In this chapter, we give an overview and analyse the most popular correlation trading strategies in financial practice. Six correlation strategies are discussed: (1) empirical correlation trading; (2) pairs trading; (3) multi-asset options; (4) structured products; (5) correlation swaps; and (6) dispersion trading.

EMPIRICAL CORRELATION TRADING

Empirical correlation trading attempts to exploit historically significant correlations within or between financial markets. Numerous financial correlations can be investigated. One area of interest is the autocorrelation between stocks or between indices. Figure 13.1 shows the autocorrelation of the Dow Jones Industrial Index (Dow) from 1920 to 2017.

From Figure 13.1, we observe that autocorrelation since the start of World War Two in 1939 until the mid-1970s was mostly positive. However, since the mid-1970s, autocorrelation has been declining and has mostly been in range with a mean of zero until 2014. We also observe the high negative autocorrelation in bad economic times as in the Great Depression and the Great Recession. Altogether, Figure 13.1 verifies that the Dow is trending less in recent times. This can be interpreted as an increase in the efficiency of the Dow and a demise of technical analysis trend-following strategies.

A further interesting association is the correlation between international equity markets. Numerous studies on this topic exist, such as Hilliard (1979), Ibbotson (1982), Schollhammer and Sand (1985),

CORRELATION RISK MODELLING AND MANAGEMENT

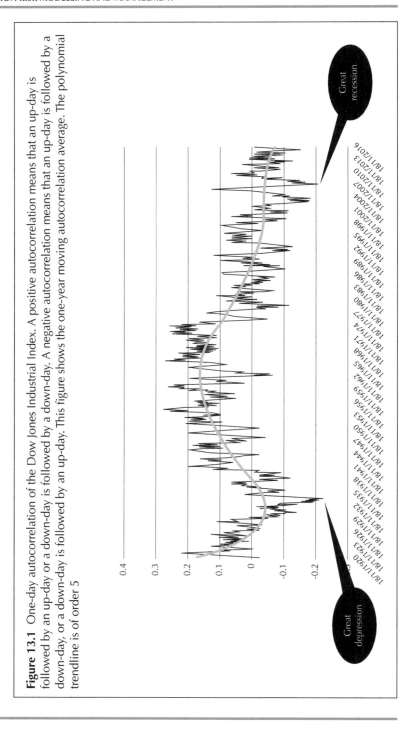

Figure 13.1 One-day autocorrelation of the Dow Jones Industrial Index. A positive autocorrelation means that an up-day is followed by an up-day or a down-day is followed by a down-day. A negative autocorrelation means that an up-day is followed by a down-day, or a down-day is followed by an up-day. This figure shows the one-year moving autocorrelation average. The polynomial trendline is of order 5

Eun and Shim (1989), Koch (1991), Martens and Poon (2001), Johnson and Soenen (2009) and Vega and Smolarski (2012). Most studies find a positive correlation between international equity markets. This is confirmed by Meissner *et al* (2018), whose results are displayed in Table 13.1.

From Table 13.1, we observe that the US market follows the European market quite closely. For example, if the European market was up or down more than 2%, the US market would have had the same directional change in 76.08% of all cases the following day. The degree of the change was 0.91% on average.

We also observe from Table 13.1 that, except for one case (the European market following the US market if the US market has changed by more than 2%), all dependencies are higher than 50%. This confirms the high interdependences between international equity markets.

PAIRS TRADING

A popular correlation trading strategy in the financial markets is pairs trading. Pairs trading, a type of statistical arbitrage or convergence arbitrage, was pioneered in the quant group of Morgan Stanley in the 1980s. The idea is to find two stocks, whose prices[1] are highly correlated. Once the price correlation weakens, the stock that has increased is shorted and the stock which has declined is bought. Presumably the spread will narrow again and a profit is realised. In today's market, pairs trading is often combined with Algorithmic and High Frequency trading. Preprogrammed mathematical algorithms find the pairs and execute the trade in the fastest time possible.

The three critical elements of pairs trading are (a) selection of the pairs, (b) timing of trade execution and (c) timing of trade closing. In this chapter, we will concentrate on point (a) selection of the pairs. For an empirical paper on timing and closing of pairs, see Gatev, Goetzman and Rouwenhorst (2006).

Several statistical concept can be applied to identify potentially interesting pairs.

Applying Correlations to determine the Pairs

A simple Pearson correlation model could be used to identify the pairs. First we screen for pairs whose prices have highly correlated,

Table 13.1 Relationship between the US equity market (the Dow Jones Industrial Average), Europe (an average of the DAX, FTSE and CAC), and Asia (an average of the Nikkei, *Straits Times* and Hang Seng) from 1991 to 2000. For example, the bold number 87.21% means: if the US market has changed (up or down) by more than 2.5%, in 87.21% of these cases, the Asian market has the same change the following day. The number 2.18% represents the degree of the percentage change.

Leading market		Lagging market							
		Success US	Change US	Success Europe	Change Europe	Success Asia	Change Asia	Limit
US				51.25	0.71	60.50	1.12	> 0.5
				52.45	0.75	65.86	1.31	> 0.1
				51.78	0.78	69.66	1.22	> 1.5
				47.26	0.81	75.74	1.60	> 2.0
				56.30	0.87	**87.21**	**2.18**	> 2.5
				53.61	1.02	74.65	2.86	> 3.0
Europe		64.10	0.74			57.07	1.07	> 0.5
		67.84	0.84			58.24	1.14	> 1.0
		70.75	0.92			61.55	1.2	> 1.5
		76.03	0.91			58.83	1.24	> 2.0
		64.01	1.15			68.29	1.49	> 2.5
		84.62	1.33			69.90	1.56	> 3.0
Asia		52.33	0.67	54.95	0.73			> 0.5
		53.74	0.70	56.66	0.75			> 1.0
		54.86	0.68	56.86	0.79			> 1.5
		56.72	0.71	58.62	0.83			> 2.0
		61.38	0.73	61.83	0.92			> 2.5
		60.11	0.71	59.94	0.95			> 3.0

ie, have a high correlation coefficient. If the correlation weakens, the pair's trade is executed, ie, the stock that has increased is sold and the stock that has decreased is purchased. Note that an increase in price correlation after executing the pairs trade does not necessarily mean that the price spread narrows. The stocks can move highly correlated without the spread narrowing. Hence we are only discussing the application of the Pearson correlation to identify potential pairs to trade. It is not feasible to apply the Pearson correlation model to evaluate the narrowing of the spread after trade execution.

Generally, we have to be cautious when applying the Pearson correlation model, since it suffers from a variety of limitations as we discussed in Chapter 3.

(a) The Pearson model evaluates the strength of the linear association between two variables. However, most dependencies in finance, in particular stock price movements, are nonlinear.

(b) In particular, linear correlation measures are natural dependence measures only if the joint distribution of the variables is elliptical.[2] However, only few distributions such as the multivariate normal distribution and the multivariate student-t distribution are special cases of elliptical distributions, for which a linear correlation measure can be meaningfully interpreted. See Embrechts, McNeil, and Straumann (1999) and Binghma and Kiesel (2001) for details.

(c) As a consequence of point (a), zero correlation derived by the Pearson model does not necessarily mean independence. For example, the parabola $Y = X^2$ will lead to a correlation coefficient of 0, which is arguably misleading.

(d) Pearson correlations are non-robust, ie, highly timeframe-sensitive. Shorter timeframes can lead to a highly positive (negative) correlation, whereas longer timeframes can display a negative (positive) correlation. See Wilmott (2009) and Meissner (2015a) for details.

(e) Pearson himself mentioned a limitation of his model with respect to "spurious correlations". Spurious correlations occur when the absolute values of variables show no pairwise correlation, even though the relative values show a non-zero correlation.

(f) Correlation analysis can also result in "spurious relationships". A spurious relationship (also termed "nonsense correlation" or "correlation does not imply causation") refers to the fact that two variables may be highly correlated without causation. This may occur if we see the following.
  1. The two variables both change together in time. For example an increase in organic food consumption will be highly correlated with an increase in autism even though the two are not causally related. In finance, stocks often trend upwards. Hence, two upward-trending stocks can be correlated without causation simply because they both increase in time.
  2. A third (lurking) factor impacts on the two variables. For example, a heat wave increases ice-cream consumption and death in older people. The correlation between ice-cream consumption and death in older people will be highly correlated without direct causation.

For a list and detailed discussion of the limitations of the Pearson model, see Chapter 3. We conclude that, due to the severe limitations of the Pearson correlation model, it is not well suited for the application in finance. In particular it is not well suited to identify potentially interesting pairs.

Mean-reversion techniques

Pairs trading assumes that a spread (eg, the difference between the returns of two stocks) that has widened will revert to its long-term mean. Therefore, mean-reverting techniques can be applied to find potentially interesting stock pairs. We discussed mean reversion in detail in Chapter 2, but will apply the core elements to pairs trading here. Formally, mean reversion exists if

$$\frac{\partial(S_t - S_{t-1})}{\partial S_{t-1}} < 0 \qquad (13.1)$$

where S_t, S_{t-1}: spread (the difference between the return of two assets) at time t and time $t-1$ respectively.

The idea of equation (13.1) is that if S_{t-1} has increased (in the denominator), in the next time period t, $S_t - S_{t-1}$ will decrease, preventing S from diverging further, and vice versa. Conversely, if S_{t-1} has decreased (in the denominator), in the next time period t, $S_t - S_{t-1}$ will increase, preventing S from diverging further, and vice versa.

We can apply the Ornstein–Uhlenbeck 1930 model – also known as the Vasicek 1977 model – to quantify the degree of mean reversion that a certain spread S exhibits. The discrete version of the Ornstein–Uhlenbeck process is

$$S_t - S_{t-1} = a(\mu_S - S_{t-1})\Delta t + \sigma_S \varepsilon_t \sqrt{\Delta t} \qquad (13.2)$$

where

S_t, S_{t-1}: Spread at time t and time $t-1$ respectively
a: Degree of mean reversion, also called mean-reversion rate or gravity, $0 \le a \le 1$
μ_S: Long-term mean of S
σ_S: Volatility of S
ε: White noise, ie, ε is *iid* and $n(0, 1)$.

We are currently interested only in mean reversion, so we will ignore the stochasticity part in equation (13.2) $\sigma_S \varepsilon \sqrt{\Delta t}$. For ease of exposition let us also assume $\Delta t = 1$. Hence equation (13.2) simplifies to

$$S_t - S_{t-1} = a\mu_S - aS_{t-1} \qquad (13.3)$$

To find the degree of mean-reversion "a", we can run a standard regression analysis of equation (13.3) of the form $Y = \alpha + \beta X$, where Y corresponds to $S_t - S_{t-1}$, α corresponds to $a\mu_S$ and, importantly, the regression coefficient β corresponds to the negative of the mean-reversion rate "a".

The approach of equations (13.1) to (13.3) is a reasonable approach to quantify mean reversion of the spread between two stocks. The higher the mean-reversion rate $-a = \beta$, the more promising a spread trade is once the spread has diverted from its long-term mean μ_S. However, the approach (13.1) to (13.3) applies the Pearson regression model to quantify the mean-reversion rate $-a$. Therefore, the limitations mentioned in Chapter 3 apply. For a model explaining mean reversion, see www.dersoft.com/meanreversioncalculation.xlsx.

Cointegration

We discussed the concept of cointegration in detail in Chapter 4. We will apply the cointegration concept to pairs trading now. Cointegration is a natural and mathematically rigorous model to find potentially interesting pairs. The idea is to identify a linear combination of two stocks that are cointegrated. A linear combination, ie, the spread of two stocks, is $S_1 - a\, S_2$, where S_1 and S_2 are stock returns and "a" is a constant. Formally, this spread is cointegrated if S_1 and S_2 are individually integrated but the spread $S_1 - a\, S_2$ has a lower order of integration. In particular, we are looking for a spread that is integrated to the order 0, $I(0)$. In this case, the spread is stationary.[3] A stationary process is defined by three criteria:

1. a constant drift;
2. a constant variance, and sometimes additionally; and
3. constant autocorrelation.

If we can verify that our spread $S_1 - a\, S_2$ is stationary, this means that the spread will never divert too far from its mean. Once it has diverted from its mean, it can be expected to revert to its mean due to the constant mean, variance and autocorrelation. Hence stationary spreads are promising candidates for Pairs trading!

Typically we apply the Dickey–Fuller test to find critical *t*-values for the degree of stationarity of our spread. Dickey and Fuller tabulated the asymptotic distribution of the *t*-statistic of our null-hypothesis of a unit root process to determine the degree of stationarity in a time series.

So why can cointegration be seen as superior to the correlation when identifying pairs? The answer is that cointegration, besides being mathematically more rigorous (see "Applying correlations to determine the pairs", above), is "better suited" for financial markets. Most stocks trend upwards, ie, they are not stationary, but integrated to the order 1, $I(1)$.

Cointegration naturally applies $I(1)$ stock processes and evaluates if a combination, ie, a spread of the $I(1)$ processes, is stationary $I(0)$. In addition, the Granger causality concept, which includes an autoregressive process augmented by independent lagged variables, tries to determine the direction and degree of the causal relationships $Y(X)$ and $X(Y)$.[4]

In summary, the benefits of pairs trading are a high degree of market neutrality (β close to zero) and largely self-funding, since one asset is shorted and the other purchased. Pairs can best be identified using cointegration techniques. As with all risk-arbitrage strategies, the limitations are that profits are arbitraged away (or, as it is often said, "arbed away"), ie, the more the strategy is applied, the fewer pairs exist that can be exploited. For example, the originators of pairs trading at Morgan Stanley were very successful at first, but after a few years abandoned the strategy. In today's market, traders try to generate profits from pairs trading using efficient mathematical algorithms combined with high-frequency trading.

MULTI-ASSET OPTIONS

A further way to trade correlation are multi-asset options, also called correlation options or rainbow options. Multi-asset options are options whose payoff depends at least partially on the correlation between two or more underlying assets in the option.

The following list displays popular multi-asset options, which started trading in the 1990s.

Table 13.2 List of popular multi-asset options

	Payoff at option maturity
Option on the better of two	max (S_1, S_2)
Option on the worse of two[5]	min (S_1, S_2)
Call on the maximum of two	max $[0, (S_1, S_2) - K]$
Exchange option	max $(0, \max(S_2 - S_1))$
Spread option	max $[0, (S_2 - S_1) - K]$
Option on better of two or cash	max (S_1, S_2, Cash)
Dual strike option	max $(0, S_1 - K_1, S_2 - K_2)$
Basket option[6]	$\max\left(\sum_{i=1}^{n} n_i S_i - K, 0\right)$ n_i: weight of asset S

Let V be the value of a multi-asset option and ρ the Pearson correlation coefficient between the prices of the underlying assets in the option. Interestingly, for all of the options except two in Table 13.1 we have $\frac{\partial V}{\partial \rho} < 0$, ie, the more negative the correlation, the higher the options price. The two options for which $\frac{\partial V}{\partial \rho} > 0$ applies are options on the worse of two, and basket options.

In an option on the worse of two, the options buyer will receive the underlying with the lower price. Hence if the correlation between the underlying assets is positive, they will both on average go up or down together, minimising the chance of a high S_1 and a low S_2 and the change of a low S_1 and a high S_2, which are both negative for the option buyer.

For a basket option, also termed "portfolio option", the higher the correlation between the assets in the basket, the higher the probability of a high payoff, since the assets have a high probability of increasing together. For a high correlation, the probability of the assets in the portfolio decreasing together is also higher; however, the loss of the option for the option buyer is floored at the typically low option premium.

Investment banks, also referred to as the dealer, are typically sellers of multi-asset options. While from a seller's perspective only two of the eight options mentioned are short-correlation – the option on the worse of two and the basket option – these two options comprise most of the multi-asset option market. Therefore, the equity portfolio of investment banks typically has a short-correlation position.

The quanto option is another popular option that depends critically on correlation. However, it is technically not a multi-asset option since it does not include two or more assets. A quanto option allows a domestic investor to exchange their potential payoff in a foreign currency back into their home currency at a fixed exchange rate. A quanto option therefore protects an investor against currency risk: eg, an American believes the Nikkei will increase, but is worried about a decreasing yen. The investor can buy a quanto call on the Nikkei with the yen payoff being converted into dollars at a fixed (usually the spot) exchange rate. The term "quanto" comes from "quantity", meaning that the amount that is re-exchanged to the home currency is unknown because it depends on the payoff of the option.

Let S' be the price of the foreign underlying (eg, the Nikkei), and let the investor be American, ie, the investor wants to exchange their potential payoff in yen into US$ at the rate $X = $ US\$/yen. The payoff of the quanto call then is $X \max [S' - K', 0]$. The value of a quanto call option is highly sensitive to the correlation between S' and X, $\rho(S', X)$. We have $\frac{\partial Q}{\partial \rho(S',X)} < 0$, where Q is the value of the quanto call. This is intuitive since a negative correlation $\rho(S', X)$ implies a hedge: if S' increases as X decreases, the quanto call seller (typically the investment bank) faces a high payoff but has to convert less in yen to US$ to satisfy the payoff. Conversely, if S' decreases and X increases, the quanto call seller has to convert more in yen into US$, but the amount of yen is low since S' is low.[7]

Most investment banks are short options, since many of their counterparts such as individual investors prefer to purchase options due to the high (unlimited for calls) profit potential and limited loss potential for long options. The same applies for quanto options, therefore most investment banks are short quantos. Since the quanto option value has a negative relationship to correlation, $\frac{\partial Q}{\partial \rho(S',X)} < 0$, investment banks in a quanto option are short-correlation, adding to the already short-correlation position of multi-asset options.

Interestingly, the sensitivity of the quanto option value, Q, to the volatility of the exchange rate, $\sigma(X)$, depends on the absolute value of the correlation $\rho(S', X)$. We have

$$\frac{\partial Q}{\partial \sigma(X)} < 0 \text{ if } \rho(S',X) > 0 \qquad (13.4)$$

and

$$\frac{\partial Q}{\partial \sigma(X)} > 0 \text{ if } \rho(S',X) < 0 \qquad (13.5)$$

Typically, an increase in volatility leads to an increase in an option value. However, equation (13.4) shows that an increase in the volatility of the exchange rate $\sigma(X)$ lowers the value of the quanto call Q if the correlation coefficient $\rho(S', X)$ is positive. The reason is that the negative impact of the positive correlation $\rho(S', X)$ on Q is reduced by the higher volatility of the correlation $\sigma(X)$, hence the option value is lowered. However, if the correlation $\rho(S', X)$ is negative as in equation (13.5), a higher volatility of the exchange rate $\sigma(X)$ increases the option price Q, since the built-in hedge of the negative correlation is reduced by the higher volatility of $\sigma(X)$, hence increasing the option value Q. This effect is similar to a binary option, which has a positive vega if it is out-of-the-money and a negative vega if it is in-the-money.

Generally, the sensitivity of an option, a structured product such as a CDO or CMO, or any financial value such as value-at-risk (VaR) or expected shortfall (ES) to correlation can be quantified with mathematical derivatives, the first order termed Cora and the second order termed Gora. For an option value V, we have

$$\text{Cora} = \frac{\partial V}{\partial \rho(x_{i=1,\ldots,n})} \tag{13.6}$$

where $x_{i=1,\ldots,n}$ are independent variables, in the case of the Quanto option $x_1 \equiv S'$ and $x_2 \equiv X$.

The sensitivity of Cora to correlation can be quantified with Gora,

$$\text{Gora} = \frac{\partial \text{Cora}}{\partial \rho(x_{i=1,\ldots,n})} = \frac{\partial^2 V}{\partial \rho^2(x_{i=1,\ldots,n})} \tag{13.7}$$

For an exchange option E with a payoff max $(0, \max(S_2 - S_1))$, the pricing equation in the Black-Scholes-Merton environment is

$$E = S_2 e^{-q_2 T} N\left(\frac{\ln\left(\frac{S_2 e^{-q_2 T}}{S_1 e^{-q_1 T}}\right) + \frac{1}{2}(\sigma_1^2 + \sigma_2^2 - 2\rho\sigma_1\sigma_2)T}{\sqrt{\sigma_1^2 + \sigma_2^2 - 2\rho\sigma_1\sigma_2}\sqrt{T}}\right)$$

$$- S_1 e^{-q_1 T} N\left(\frac{\ln\left(\frac{S_2 e^{-q_2 T}}{S_1 e^{-q_1 T}}\right) + \frac{1}{2}(\sigma_1^2 + \sigma_2^2 - 2\rho\sigma_1\sigma_2)T}{\sqrt{\sigma_1^2 + \sigma_2^2 - 2\rho\sigma_1\sigma_2}\sqrt{T}}\right) \tag{13.8}$$

where

S_1: asset to be given away
S_2: asset to be received
q_2: return of asset 2
q_1: return of asset 1
σ_1: volatility of asset S_1
σ_2: volatility of asset S_2
ρ: correlation coefficient for assets S_1 and S_2
T: option maturity in years
$N(x)$: the cumulative standard normal distribution of x.

Differentiating equation (13.8) partially with respect to ρ, we derive the Cora of an exchange option E

$$\text{Cora}_E = \frac{\partial E}{\partial \rho} = -\frac{e^{-q_2 T}\sqrt{T}S_2\sigma_1\sigma_2 n\left[\dfrac{\ln\left[\dfrac{S_2 e^{-q_2 T}}{S_1 e^{-q_1 T}}\right] + \dfrac{1}{2}T(\sigma_1^2 - 2\rho\sigma_1\sigma_2 + \sigma_2^2)}{\sqrt{T}\sqrt{\sigma_1^2 - 2\rho\sigma_1\sigma_2 + \sigma_2^2}}\right]}{\sqrt{\sigma_1^2 - 2\rho\sigma_1\sigma_2 + \sigma_2^2}} \quad (13.9)$$

Differentiating equation (13.9) partially with respect to ρ, we derive the Gora

$$\text{Gora}_E = \frac{\partial \text{Cora}_E}{\partial \rho}$$

$$= -\left(\frac{e^{-q_2 T}S_2\sigma_1^2\sigma_2^2\left(-4\ln\left[\dfrac{S_2 e^{-q_2 T}}{S_1 e^{-q_1 T}}\right]^2 + T(\sigma_1^2 - 2\rho\sigma_1\sigma_2 + \sigma_2^2)(4 + T\sigma_1^2 - 2T\rho\sigma_1\sigma_2 + T\sigma_2^2)\right)}{n\left[\dfrac{\ln\left[\dfrac{S_2 e^{-q_2 T}}{S_1 e^{-q_1 T}}\right] + \dfrac{1}{2}T(\sigma_1^2 - 2\rho\sigma_1\sigma_2 + \sigma_2^2)}{\sqrt{T}\sqrt{\sigma_1^2 - 2\rho\sigma_1\sigma_2 + \sigma_2^2}}\right]}\right) \Big/ \left(4\sqrt{T}(\sigma_1^2 - 2\rho\sigma_1\sigma_2 + \sigma_2^2)^{5/2}\right) \quad (13.10)$$

In summary, multi-asset option allow an investor to trade correlation between desired assets. Multi-asset options which contain only two assets are typically priced in the Black–Scholes–Merton environment, ie, have a closed-form solution. As a consequence, conveniently, the correlation risk parameters Cora and Gora can also be derived closed form. The pricing of multi-asset options, which contain more than two assets, require Monte Carlo simulations. Typically, the assets follow correlated geometric Brownian motions; see Zhang (1997) and Linders and Schoutens (2014) for details.

STRUCTURED PRODUCTS

Structured products are customised instruments, designed to provide the investor with a relatively high return and – due to diversification – relatively low risk. Typically, a structured product:

(a) contains multiple assets;
(b) often includes a derivative; and
(c) is sometimes tranched.

Structured products comprise a wide range of instruments. CDOs and a CMOs comprise all criteria above. The multi-asset options, which we have discussed, are simple structured products, most containing just two assets. Pension funds, mutual funds and cost-efficient exchange-traded funds (ETFs) can also be considered structured products, satisfying only criterion (a) above, however.

Especially tranched structured products are highly sensitive to correlation between the assets in the structure and the correlation between the tranches. We will show this with the example of a cash CDO.

A cash CDO is a structured product, referencing typically 125 bonds. The default risk of these bonds is tranched. The equity tranche holder is exposed to the first 3% of defaults, the mezzanine tranche holder is exposed to the 3–7% of defaults and so on. Figure 13.2 shows the relationship of the tranche spread with respect to the degree of correlation between the assets in the CDO, when the Gaussian copula correlation model is applied.[8]

The correlation properties of a CDO, displayed in Figure 13.2, led to huge hedge fund losses in 2005. Hedge funds had invested in the equity tranche (0–3% in Figure 13.2) to collect the high-equity tranche spread. They had then presumably hedged the risk by going short the mezzanine tranche (3–7% in Figure 13.2). However, as we can see from Figure 13.2, this "hedge" is flawed.

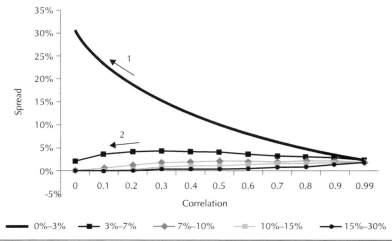

Figure 13.2 Tranche spread with respect to correlation between the assets in the CDO. The equity tranche investor (0–3% tranche), is "long correlation", since, when the correlation between the assets in the CDO increases, the equity tranche spread decreases, and the investor now receives an above market spread

When the correlations of the assets in the CDO decreased in 2005 due to the downgrade of Ford and General Motors, the hedge funds lost on both positions: (1) the equity tranche spread (0–3%) increased sharply (see arrow 1), hence the fixed spread that the hedge fund received in the original transaction was now significantly lower than the current market spread, resulting in a paper loss; (2) in addition, the hedge funds lost on their short mezzanine tranche position, since a lower correlation lowers the mezzanine tranche spread (see arrow 2), hence the spread that the hedge fund paid in the original transactions was now higher than the market spread, resulting in another paper loss. As a result of the huge losses, several hedge funds such as Marin Capital, Aman Capital and Baily Coates Cromwell filed for bankruptcy.

Correlation properties of a CDO had a critical impact on the global financial crisis of 2007–9. When default probabilities and, with them, default correlations increased, the correlation between the tranches also increased, providing less protection of the lower tranches for the higher tranches. Especially, the default probability of AAA-rated super-senior tranches increased sharply due to the decreased protection of the lower tranches. When losses mounted, many investors unwound their super-senior tranches' positions at significantly higher spreads, realising big losses and increasing the spread even further. The issuers of the CDOs containing super-senior tranches realised large gains.

In conclusion, the value of structured products depends critically on the correlation between the assets in the structured product. The correlation properties of the assets in a structured product can be fairly complex. Investors should well understand the correlation properties before investing in a structured product.

CORRELATION SWAPS

Correlation swaps are pure correlation plays, ie, contrary to the previously discussed correlation trading strategies, no price or volatility components of an underlying instrument are involved. In a correlation swap, one party pays a fixed correlation rate in exchange for a realised, stochastic correlation rate. The fixed-rate payer is "buying correlation", since they benefit from an increase in correlation, and the fixed-rate receiver is "selling correlation". Figure 13.3 displays a correlation swap.

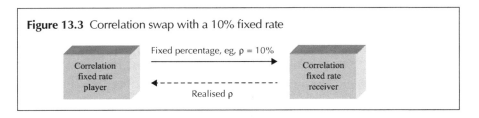

Figure 13.3 Correlation swap with a 10% fixed rate

The payoff of a correlation swap for the fixed-rate payer is N $(\rho_{realised} - \rho_{fixed})$, where N is the notional amount. $\rho_{realised}$ is the average correlation between the assets in the correlation swap, which is realised during the time period of the swap. Formally, we have

$$\rho_{realised} = \frac{\sum_{i>j} w_i w_j \rho_{ij}}{\sum_{i>j} w_i w_j} \qquad (13.11)$$

where $\rho_{i,j}$ is the Pearson correlation coefficient between assets i and j. In trading practice, we typically have identical weights $w_i = w_j$. In this case, equation (13.11) reduces to

$$\rho_{realised} = \frac{2}{n^2 - n} \sum_{i>j} \rho_{i,j} \qquad (13.12)$$

The critical question is how to value correlation swaps, ie, how to derive $\rho_{realised}$. A first thought is to use interest-rate swap-valuation techniques. In an interest-rate swap, forward interest rates are derived by arbitrage arguments from the term structure of spot interest rates.[9] However, in 2018, a correlation term structure still did not yet exist. We can derive implied correlations from option prices on indices (see later for details). However, often the implied correlations differ quite strongly from the zero-cost, correlation-swap fixed rate in the correlation-swap market.

One approach to derive the forward correlation rate $\rho_{realised}$ is to model correlation with a stochastic process, just as we model stocks, bonds, interest rates, exchange rates, commodities, volatility and other financial variables with a stochastic process. Quite a bit of research has recently been done in stochastic correlation modelling; see Engle (2002), Emmerich (2006), Düllmann, Küll and Kunisch (2008), Ma (2009a, 2009b), Da Fonseca, Grasselli and Ielpo (2007), Buraschi, Porchia and Trojani (2010) and Lu and Meissner (2012).

When modelling a financial variable, a critical question is whether to include mean reversion. Except for stocks, which have increased on average annually by about 7.9% (including dividends) each year since 1920, we typically model other financial variables as bonds, interest rates, exchange rates, commodities and volatility with a mean reverting process.

Empirical studies find that correlation exhibits strong mean reversion. The monthly mean reversion of stocks in the Dow Jones industrial average from 1972 to 2012 was 77.51% (meaning the average monthly Dow correlation reverted each month to its long-term mean by 77.51%); see Meissner 2014. Hence, we should definitely include a mean-reversion component in a stochastic correlation process.

In addition, when modelling Pearson correlations, we should limit the stochastic process to between −1 and +1.[10] The bounded Jacobi process includes mean reversion and bounds:

$$d\rho = a(m_\rho - \rho_t)dt + \sigma_\rho \sqrt{(h - \rho_t)(\rho_t - f)} \varepsilon_t \sqrt{dt} \qquad (13.13)$$

where

ρ: Pearson correlation coefficient
a: degree of mean reversion (gravity), $0 \leq a \leq 1$
m_ρ: long term mean of the correlation ρ
σ_ρ: volatility of correlation ρ
h: upper boundary level, f: lower boundary level, ie, $h \geq \rho \geq f$
ε: Brownian motion ε is *iid* and $\varepsilon = n(0, 1)$

For bounds of $h = 1$ and $f = -1$, equation (13.13) reduces to

$$d\rho = a(m_\rho - \rho_t)dt + \sigma_\rho \sqrt{(1 - \rho_t^2)} \varepsilon_t \sqrt{dt} \qquad (13.14)$$

Equation (13.14) is a good candidate for modelling correlations since it includes mean reversion and bounds, which can be set between −1 and 1. Buraschi *et al* (2010) extend equation (13.14) and apply an *n*-dimensional stochastic process for a correlation matrix Σ_t, which includes bounds and mean reversion. The stochastic process for the correlation matrix is then correlated with an n-dimensional vector for the underlying price process, applying the Heston 1993 correlation identity. The model can replicate the negative relationship between returns and volatility (sometimes called "leverage") and the higher correlation in a recession (sometimes referred to as "asymmetric correlation"). In addition, volatility skews (ie, higher volatility when returns are negative) and the right balance between correlation persistence and correlation mean-reversion can be modelled.

For further research on stochastic correlation modelling, see Engle (2002), Emmerich (2006), Da Fonseca *et al* (2007), Düllmann *et al* (2008), Ma (2009a, 2009b), Hull and White (2010) and Lu and Meissner (2015).

While correlation swaps can be applied as a speculation tool, their value lies in the convenient hedging of correlation risk. Most clients of investment banks go long correlation in a multi-asset option (see "Multi-asset options" above), or a structured product (see "Structured products" above). Consequently, investment banks find themselves typically with a short-correlation portfolio and a correlation swap provides a direct hedge for this short-correlation position.

In conclusion, correlation swaps are a direct way to trade correlation and hedge correlation risk. However, in 2018, no agreed valuation procedure existed. Option-implied correlations (see "Dispersion trading" below for details) often differ quite strongly from zero-cost fixed rates in a correlation swap and are therefore not applicable to derive the realised swap rate. Stochastic correlation models are developing, which seem to be a promising approach to model the stochastic correlation in a correlation swap.

DISPERSION TRADING

Dispersion trading emerged in the late 1990s from index arbitrage. In a long-index arbitrage trade, the trader buys certain components (eg, stocks) of an index (eg, the S&P 500) and shorts the whole index. The index components are expected to outperform the index, so that $\sum_{i=1}^{n} w_i r_i > r_I$, where w_i are the component weights, r_i is the return of the index components and r_I is the return of the index.

Dispersion trading applies the same idea, just with respect to component volatility and index volatility. The strategy can be well implemented with options. Three types of dispersion trades can be employed.

(a) Directional dispersion trading. Here call options on index components can be bought and call options on the index[11] sold in the expectation that

$$\sum_{i=1}^{n} w_i \max(S_i - K_i) > \max(S_I - K_I) \qquad (13.15)$$

where S_i are prices of the index components, S_I is the price of the index and K_i and K_I are the strike prices of the ith component and index respectively.

The key is to find index components $S_{i'}$ which outperform relative to the index. Naturally directional dispersion trading can also be implemented with put options, if a trader believes they can identify index components that will underperform relative to the index.

(b) Non-directional dispersion trading. If the trader primarily wants to trade volatility and not the direction of the components or the index, dispersion trading can be implemented with straddles. In a long dispersion trade, the trader would purchase straddles on individual index components and sell straddles on the index in the expectation that

$$\sum_{i=1}^{n} w_i St_i > St_I \qquad (13.16)$$

where St_i is the payoff of the straddle on the ith components and St_I is the payoff of the straddle on the index.[12] Equation (13.16) can be well approximated with the volatilities

$$\sum_{i=1}^{n} w_i \sigma_i > \sigma_I \qquad (13.17)$$

where σ_i is the volatility of ith price component, w_i is the weighting of the ith component and σ_I is the volatility of the index.

(c) Non-directional dispersion trading can also be implemented by buying call or put options on individual components and selling call or put options on the index and delta-hedging both legs. In this case the expectation is that the volatility of the index components is bigger than the volatility of the index, therefore the gamma–theta difference of the index components is bigger than gamma–theta difference of the index:[13]

$$\sum_{i=1}^{n} w_i (\text{gamma}_i - \text{theta}_i) > \text{gamma}_I - \text{theta}_I$$

The three dispersion trading strategies are also termed "standard dispersion" or "vanilla dispersion".

Why is dispersion trading a play on correlation?
To derive why dispersion trading is a play on correlation, let us start with the variance equation for two assets i and j:

$$Var_{ij} = Var_i + Var_j + 2Cov_{ij} \qquad (13.18)$$

where Var_{ij} is the variance of the assets i and j and Cov_{ij} is the covariance of i and j.

Generalising for $n = \{i, j = 1, ..., n\}$ assets which comprise the index I, and using financial notation, ie, $Var \equiv \sigma^2$, equation (13.18) becomes

$$\sigma_I^2 = \sum_{i=1}^{n} w_i^2 \sigma_i^2 + 2 \sum_{i=1}^{n-1} \sum_{j>i}^{n} w_i w_j \sigma_i \sigma_j \rho_{ij} \qquad (13.19)$$

where σ_I^2 is the implied variance of the index, ie, the variance implied by option prices on the index, and σ_i^2 is the implied variance of an option on the component i, and w_i and w_j are weighting factors. Solving equation (13.19) for the average pairwise correlation coefficient between assets i and j, ρ_{ij}, we derive

$$\rho_{ij} = \frac{\sigma_I^2 - \sum_{i=1}^{n} w_i^2 \sigma_i^2}{2 \sum_{i=1}^{n-1} \sum_{j>i}^{n} w_i w_j \sigma_i \sigma_j} \qquad (13.20)$$

Equation (13.20) shows the general concept of dispersion trading. The correlation between the components i and j, ρ_{ij}, is not derived by data points in a two-dimensional coordinate system as in the Pearson model, but by the relationship between the index-implied volatility σ_I and component-implied volatility σ_i. For a model explaining equations (13.19) and (13.20) see www.dersoft.com/Dispersion.xlsx.

A trader can now assess the value of ρ_{ij} derived by equation

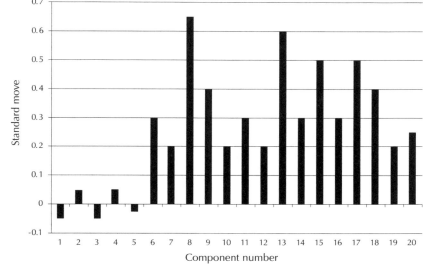

Figure 13.4 Example of a high positive correlation ρ_{ij} of the index components and consequently high standard move of the index. In the scenario of Figure 13.4, a short dispersion trade, eg, selling straddles on the index components 1 to 5, and buying a straddle on the index would have been warranted. For a model-displaying feature of Figure 13.4, see www.dersoft.com/Dispersion.xlsx

(13.20) and possibly compare it with the historical values of ρ_{ij} or with the trader's views on future values of ρ_{ij}. From equation (13.20), we observe that $\frac{\partial \sigma_I^2}{\partial \rho_{ij}} > 0$ and $\frac{\partial \sigma_i^2}{\partial \rho_{ij}} < 0$. So, if a trader believes in an increase of correlation, they will buy index volatility (eg, buy straddles on the index) and sell component volatility (eg, sell straddles on index components), termed short dispersion. As an example, let us assume the trader sells straddles on index components 1 to 5 and buys a straddle on the index. This would be a successful trade if the components and the index volatility behave as in Figure 13.4.

From Figure 13.4, we observe that the loss of the trader from selling straddles on the components 1 to 5 is low, but the profit from buying an index straddle is high (since the calls produce a high payoff). Conversely, if the components behave as in Figure 13.5, the strategy of selling straddles on components 1 to 5 and buying a straddle on the index is now a disaster.

From Figure 13.5, we observe that the loss of the trader from

CORRELATION RISK MODELLING AND MANAGEMENT

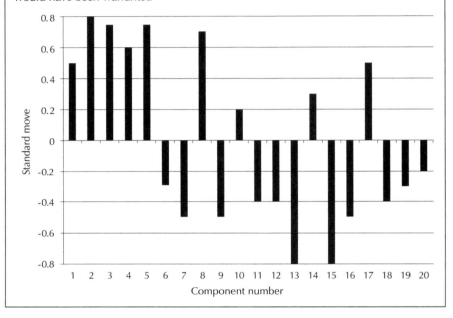

Figure 13.5 Example of a low-correlation ρ_{ij} of index components and consequently a low index standard move; in fact in Figure 13.4 the sum of the standard moves of the index components = 0,

$$\sum_{i=1}^{n} \sigma_i = 0$$

resulting in a constant index. In the scenario of Figure 13.5, a long dispersion trade, ie, buying straddles on the components 1 to 5 and selling a straddle on the index would have been warranted

selling an index straddle is zero, since the index has not moved, and the profit from buying straddles on the components 1 to 5 is high, since the calls are in-the-money.

> "Correlations always increase in distressed markets"
> John Hull

The critical questions with respect to dispersion trading are:

1. when to go long dispersion, ie, buying volatility on index components and selling volatility on the index; when to go short dispersion, ie, selling volatility on index components and buying volatility on the index;

2. how many and which components of the index to trade; and
3. which type of dispersion trade to implement; see points (a) to (c) in "Dispersion trading", above.

With respect to point (1), empirical studies show that correlations levels and correlation volatility are higher in recessions and lower in normal economic periods and expansionary periods; see Chapter 2. Hence, in anticipation of a recession, a short dispersion trade is warranted (ie, buying volatility on the whole index and selling volatility on index components); in anticipation of a normal economic period or an expansion, a long dispersion trade (ie, buying volatility on index components and selling volatility on the whole index) may be implemented. Component selection is a matter of the trader's skill, possibly enhanced by algorithmic and high-frequency trading techniques.

Should we have a bias towards long dispersion?

To analyse whether a long dispersion trade typically leads to a higher payoff, let us start with equation (13.19), which rearranged, is

$$\sigma_I = \sqrt{\sum_{i=1}^{N}\sum_{j=1}^{N} w_i w_j \sigma_i \sigma_j \bar{\rho}_{ij}} \qquad (13.21)$$

where $\bar{\rho}_{ij}$ is the historical (not option-implied) average correlation coefficient between the components i and j, and σ_i and σ_j are, as in equation (13.19), the option implied volatilities of the components i and j. The σ_I of equation (13.21) is referred to as the MIV, or Markowitz-implied volatility. The MIV is the theoretical value, based on implied component volatility and historical correlation, at which the index volatility σ_I should trade. However, MIV often differs from the IOIV (the index-option-implied volatility), at which the index actually trades. Most existing studies find that IOIV > MIV; see Lozovaia and Hishniuakova (2005), Marshall (2009), Maze (2012) or Bossu (2014). The reasons for the option-implied volatility IOIV to be higher than Markowitz-implied volatility MIV may be due to the following.

(a) The risk-aversion of investors. In virtually every market we have a risk-premium:

❏ in the bond market the credit spread, which reflects default probability of traded bonds, is significantly higher than the historical default probability, which Altman (1989) pointed out;
❏ in the equity market, the equity risk premium is $r_s > r_f$, where r_s is the return of a stock and r_f is the risk-free interest rate, accounting for higher stock volatility; and
❏ in the option market the implied volatility, reflecting option prices, is typically higher than historical option volatility.

Therefore, we can also expect the option-implied volatility IOIV to be higher than the Markowitz-implied volatility MIV, due to risk-averse investors buying protection on the whole index.

(b) Related to point (a) is the perception of systemic risk, ie, the possibility of a significant downturn of several major markets as in the 2007-to-2009 crisis, which investors want to protect against by buying protection on the whole index, hence increasing IOIV.

(c) Liquidity is a further reason for option-implied volatility IOIV being higher than Markowitz-implied volatility MIV. Most investors buy protection on the more liquid index option market, driving up option-implied volatility IOIV.

(d) Risk-taking professionals often sell individual option volatility, driving down Markovitz-implied volatility MIV.

In conclusion, there is theoretical, rational and empirical evidence that the option-implied volatility IOIV is typically higher than the Markowitz-implied volatility MIV. In the long run this can be exploited by traders by going short IOIV and long MIV. Traders should be aware of a systemic downturn though, in which IOIV is expected to increase sharply due to increased correlation.

Risk-managing dispersion trades

In trading practice, traders often take a position in the Cora, the correlation exposure, introduced earlier, and in detail discussed in Chapter 12, and hedge the delta, vega, gamma and theta risk. These risks are typically quite small at inception of the dispersion trade, since options are bought in one leg of the dispersion trade and sold in the other. For example, in a long dispersion trade, straddles can be bought on index components, and a straddle is sold on the index, netting some of the initial risks.

However, once the underling components diverge from their initial values, the risk parameters can become quite large. This is especially the case if only some of the index components are traded: the index may have diverged strongly from its initial value, resulting in a change of the index risk parameters. However, the partial components may have a low correlation, resulting in only a modest change of the risk parameters as we displayed in Figure 13.4 (components 1–5). Conversely, the risk parameters of the partial index components can change strongly if they are highly correlated, but the index standard move may be small due to a low correlation of all components.

The derivation of an index option value and its risk parameters is occasionally done by treating the basket as a single underlying variable and applying a Black–Scholes–Merton approach. However, this is an overly simplistic approximation for two main reasons:

1. the sum of the lognormal distributed components is not lognormally distributed; and
2. the critical factor correlation between the components is not incorporated.

To derive index option values and its risk parameters, typically Monte Carlo simulation is applied, assuming the components follow correlated geometric Brownian motions. For more details, see Zhang (1997), Linders and Schoutens (2014) and, for a useful overview paper, Krekel *et al* (2004).

Risk-managing dispersion trades is also costly, computationally intensive and quite complex. If all options of the S&P 500 are traded, the bid–ask spread has to be paid for each trade and additionally transaction costs occur. The options have to be risk-managed continuously, especially the pairwise correlation matrix of the positions, which can become operationally and computationally intensive: trading 500 S&P options results in $n(n-1)/2$, so $500(499)/2 = 124{,}750$ pairwise correlations, which have to be implied by option prices and their impact on the dispersion value has to be derived. In addition, the risk parameters can become quite large. Therefore dispersion desks typically demand high-risk limits to manage the exposure. The dispersion risk-parameters can also be quite complex. The greeks (delta, gamma, vega, theta) are typically highly interdependent. For example, dispersion trades include a "hidden vega risk": changes in the implied component volatility σ_i can have a significant impact on the index volatility–component volatility ratio σ_I/σ_i, but, depending on parameter constellations, can also have very little impact; see Avellaneda and Kim (2002) and Bossu (2014).

In summary, the high cost, high computational intensity and fairly high mathematical complexity of continuously hedging dispersion trades limits the application of actively hedged dispersion trading in practice.

Variance dispersion trading
If dispersion trading is executed via straddles, as we have discussed, the trader has to deal with the price and volatility of the underlying components and the index. If the dispersion trade is hedged, the trader has to deal additionally with the risk parameters, delta, vega, gamma, theta, vanna, volga and rho, which, as we have seen, are complex and correlated. An easier and more direct way to trade correlation is variance dispersion trading, which is a combination of a standard dispersion trade and variance swaps. The payoff of a short variance dispersion trade is

$$\sigma_I^2 - \sum_{i=1}^{n} w_i \sigma_i^2 \qquad (13.22)$$

where σ_I^2 is the realised variance of the index for the time period of the trade, σ_i^2 is the realised variance of the index components for the time period of the trade and w_i is the weighting of the ith component. Hence, in a short-variance dispersion trade, the trader is anticipating that the index volatility is higher than the component volatility during the time period of the trade and the payoff is as in equation (13.22). Naturally, for a long-variance dispersion trade, the payoff is equation (13.22) multiplied with –1

Note that equation (13.22) is the square of equation (13.17), which is an approximation of the standard dispersion trade via straddles. Applying a variance dispersion trade with the payoff of equation (13.22) enables investment banks to take a position in variances directly without the hassle of having to trade and hedge the underlying options. This is convenient for investment banks, who, as we explained above, typically have short-correlation portfolios and can hedge this short-correlation position directly by going long-correlation via a short-variance dispersion trade. The other product, which allows a direct trading and hedging of correlation risk, is correlation swaps, which we have already discussed.

Mathematically, it can be shown that the payoff of a short-variance dispersion trade can be approximated by

$$\sum_{i=1}^{n} w_i \sigma_i^2 \left(\rho_{ij} - \bar{\rho}_{ij} \right)$$ (13.24)

where is the realised variance of the index components for the time period of the trade, ρ_{ij} is the option implied correlation and $\bar{\rho}_{ij}$ is the realised correlation; see Bossu (2006) and Jacquier and Slaoui (2010). As we discussed earlier, there is a risk premium in the correlation market. It follows that the implied correlation is typically higher than the realised correlation, ie, $\rho_{ij} > \bar{\rho}_{ij}$. Hence a short-variance swap trade, ie, receiving σ_i^2 and paying $\sum_{i=1}^{n} w_i \sigma_i^2$ with a payoff, as in equation (13.22), is typically a promising trade. However, the trader should be aware of systemic risk: in a downturn of several markets and its components, the realised correlation $\bar{\rho}_{ij}$ will increase sharply, leading to losses of the short-variance dispersion trade.

SUMMARY
In this chapter, we gave an overview of the most popular correlation-trading strategies in practice, which comprise (1) empirical correlation trading, (2) pairs trading, (3) multi-asset options, (4) structured products, (5) correlation swaps and (6) dispersion trading. Most strategies involve trading an underlying asset, ie, levels and volatilities of the underlying have to be managed. However, pairs trading and variance dispersions are pure correlation plays, which simplify correlation trading. Correlation levels and volatility display expected properties, ie, they are low in economic expansions and higher in economic downturns, as also discussed in Chapter 2. This facilitates correlation trading.

It can be expected that, with growing mathematical

sophistication and computer power, correlation trading will be an integral part of algorithmic and high-frequency trading.

Correlation products can also be applied in risk management to reduce correlation exposure in portfolio risk measures as value-at-risk (VaR), expected shortfall (ES), enterprise risk management (ERM) and extreme value theory (EVT). In addition, there is a strong negative correlation between equity prices and equity correlation, as discussed in Chapter 2. Therefore, correlation products can also be applied to hedging systemic equity risk.

Questions for Chapter 13
Answers to these questions can be found at the end of this book.

1. What is correlation trading?
2. Give an example of empirical correlation trading.
3. What is pairs trading?
4. Name the three critical elements of pairs trading.
5. How can potentially successful pairs be determined?
6. How does a quanto option work?
7. Which correlation is critical in a quanto option?
8. What do Cora and Gora tell us?
9. In a CDO, why is the equity tranche investor "long correlation"?
10. Is it a good idea to hedge a long equity tranche position with a short mezzanine tranche position?
11. What is the main advantage of a correlation swap compared with other correlation products?
12. Why is dispersion trading correlation trading?
13. What are long dispersion trading and short dispersion trading?
14. In which economic situation should a trader go "short dispersion", ie, sell straddles on individual stocks and buy volatility on the index?
15. Can correlation products be used to hedge systemic equity risk?
16. What is the advantage of variance dispersion trading?

1 We will discuss price correlations here. Equivalent arguments apply to return correlations.
2 An elliptical distribution is a generalisation of multivariate normal distributions.
3 See Chapter 4 for details.
4 See Chapter 4 for details
5 In 1998, Société Générale marketed an extension of the worse of two, termed Everest Option. The payoff is on the worst performer of typically 10 to 15 asset at maturity T: $\min_{i=1,\ldots,n} \frac{S_i(T)}{S_i(0)}$, where S_i is the price of the ith asset and n is the number of assets.
6 A variation of the basket option is Société Générale's Himalayan option. At multiple points in time t_i, the payoff of the best-performing asset S_b in a basket $\max\left(\frac{S_b(t_i) - S_b(t_0)}{S_b(t_0)}, 0\right)$ is paid out and this asset is then removed until the basket is empty.
7 If the underlying in a quanto is a basket as the Nikkei, another correlation exposure exists: the volatility of the Nikkei depends on the correlation of its components. The higher the correlation of the components, the higher the volatility (see the section called "Dispersion trading" for details).
8 For details on the copula model, see Chapters 6 and 7.
9 See Hull 2011 or Meissner 1998 for details.
10 For an extension of the correlation coefficient above 1 and below −1, see Burgin and Meissner 2016.
11 Index options are identical with basket options, which we discussed earlier.
12 More precisely, equation (13.16) is $\sum_{i=1}^{n} \max(S_i^T - K) \cup \max(K - S_i^T) > \max(S_I^T - K) \cup \max(K - S_I^T)$, where S_i^T is the price of the ith component at maturity T, and S_I^T is the price of the index I at maturity T.
13 In a long option position, the trader gains on the delta hedge measured by the gamma, and loses time value, measured by the theta, and vice versa. So, in a long dispersion trade, the trader would generate profits from the individual components gamma, lose money on the individual components theta, gain on the index theta and lose on the index gamma.

14

Credit Value at Risk under Basel III – Too Simplistic?

> "Bank supervisors play an important role in encouraging the proper balance of risk-taking by developing prudent standards and enforcing sound practices at banks"
>
> – Alan Greenspan

In this chapter, we will discuss the counterparty-credit-risk approach of the Basel II accord, which was envisioned to be part of Basel III. We will see that the approach applies the one-factor Gaussian copula (OFGC) model, which we analysed in Chapter 7. To clarify, credit value-at-risk (CVaR) is a concept that quantifies correlated counterparty credit risk in standard portfolios with bonds and loans. In Chapters 15 and 16, we will discuss Basel III's approach of credit value adjustment (CVA). CVA also quantifies correlated counterparty credit risk, however, in derivatives portfolios. While CVaR is derived by the value-at-risk (VaR) concept, Basel III applies the expected shortfall (ES) concept to calculate CVA.

First, let us look at some basics.

WHAT ARE THE BASEL I, II AND III ACCORDS? WHY DO MOST SOVEREIGNS IMPLEMENT THE ACCORDS?

We briefly introduced the Basel accords in Chapter 1. We will expand the discussion in this chapter, especially the correlation aspects of the accords.

The Basel accords are developed by the Basel Committee for Banking Supervision (BCBS), which is a subcommittee of the Bank for International Settlements (BIS). The Basel I accord was implemented in 1988; the Basel II started in 1999 and was implemented in 2006; the Basel III accord was initiated in 2008 and is intended to be implemented by 2019. Basel III is designed to particularly address the banking failures in the global financial crisis of 2007 to 2009. The objective of the accords is to "improve the banking sector's ability to absorb shocks arising from financial and economic stress" and "to reduce the risk of spillover from the financial sector to the real economy" (BCBS 2011).

The Basel accords do not have international legal authority. However, most sovereigns (about 100 for Basel II) have implemented legislation to enforce them. The reason for the implementation of the accords is simple: they increase the creditworthiness of the sovereign and its banking system, which leads to a higher credit rating by the agencies Moody's, Standard & Poor's and Fitch. This in turn leads to an increase in international trade and capital flow at a lower cost of capital.

One of the most critical aspects of the new Basel III accord is the way CVaR is calculated, since sharp increases in credit risk and consequently defaults were one of the main reasons for the 2007–9 crisis. Correlations play a key role in the derivation of portfolio credit risk. Let us discuss how the Basel accords' quantify portfolio credit risk and which correlation concept the Basel accord applies.

BASEL II AND III'S CREDIT-VALUE-AT-RISK APPROACH

In Chapters 1 and 10, we have defined market VaR. It measures the maximum loss of a portfolio with respect to market risk with a certain probability for a certain timeframe. Analogously, we can define CVaR: it measures the maximum loss of a portfolio due to credit risk with a certain probability for a certain time frame.

Credit risk can be considered the most critical of all types of risk. It is estimated that financial institutions allocate about 60% of their regulatory capital to credit risk, about 15% to market risk and about 25% to operational risk.

We defined credit risk in Chapter 11 as "the risk of financial loss due to an adverse change in the credit quality of a debtor" and mentioned the two types of credit risk: (1) migration risk; and (2) default risk.

To value CVaR it is tempting just to take the market VaR equation (1.8) $VaR_p = \sigma_p \alpha \sqrt{x}$ and transfer it to CVaR. However, there are two main problems when using equation (1.8) for CVaR:

CREDIT VALUE AT RISK UNDER BASEL III – TOO SIMPLISTIC?

1. The portfolio variance defined in equation (1.9) $\sigma_p = \sqrt{\beta_h C \beta_v}$ would require input data as standard deviations of relative credit-rating changes, and the correlation coefficient between the changes. However, these data for credit risk are rare, since credit-rating changes for most entities rarely occur, often only once a year or not even at all.
2. The value for α in equation (1.8) would assume a normal distribution of relative credit-rating changes. However, credit-rating changes are typically not normally distributed and depend on the current credit-rating, past credit-rating changes, country, sector, seniority, coupon, yield etc. See Meissner (2005) for a further discussion.

Since credit data are much scarcer than market data, in practice a much more granular approach is used to derive CVaR. Basel II uses the one-factor Gaussian copula (OFGC) model, which we discussed in detail in Chapter 7 for valuing CDO tranches. Let us apply the OFGC to value CVaR.

We start with the core equation of the OFGC, which we had discussed in Chapter 7:

$$x_i = \sqrt{\rho}M + \sqrt{1-\rho}Z_i \qquad (14.1)$$

ρ: Default correlation parameter for the companies in the portfolio, $0 \le \rho \le 1$. ρ is assumed identical and constant for all company pairs in the portfolio.

M: Systematic market factor, which impacts on all companies in the portfolio. M can be thought of as the general economic environment – for example, the return of the S&P 500. M is a random drawing from a standard normal distribution, formally $M = n \sim (0, 1)$. M is the same as ε in Chapter 5, section "Correlating Brownian motions". See spreadsheet www.dersoft.com/epsilon.xlsx for details.

Z_i: Idiosyncratic factor of asset i. Z_i expresses i-th company's individual strength, possibly measured by company i's stock price return. As M, Z_i is also a random drawing from a standard normal distribution

x_i: Results from equation (14.1) are interpreted as a "Default indicator variable" for company i. The lower i, the earlier is the default time T for company i. x_i is by construction standard normal.

Solving equation (14.1) for Z_i, we derive

$$Z_i = \frac{x_i - \sqrt{\rho}M}{\sqrt{1-\rho}}$$

Taking cumulative values, we get

$$N(Z_i) = N\left(\frac{x_i - \sqrt{\rho}M}{\sqrt{1-\rho}}\right) \qquad (14.2)$$

where $N(x)$ is the cumulative standard normal distribution at x. Since we use the standard normal cumulative distribution N, this approach is called Gaussian copula.

We now equate the individual default probability of entity i at time T, $PD_i(T)$, which is given or estimated from the market data with the model-simulated barrier $N(x_i)$, which includes the default correlation via the x_i: $PD_i(T) = N(x_i)$. Solving for x_i, we derive $x_i = N^{-1}(PD_i(T))$, where N^{-1} is the inverse of N. See chapter 5, Figure 5.3 for details of the mapping procedure $N^{-1}(PD_i(T))$.

Inputting $x_i = N^{-1}(PD_i(T))$ into equation (14.2), we get

$$N(Z_i) = N\left(\frac{N^{-1}[PD_i(T)] - \sqrt{\rho}M}{\sqrt{1-\rho}}\right) \qquad (14.3)$$

Now the strong assumption is made that all entities i have the same default probability PD at a certain time T. Hence we can drop the index i and get

$$N(Z) = N\left(\frac{N^{-1}[PD(T)] - \sqrt{\rho}M}{\sqrt{1-\rho}}\right) \qquad (14.4)$$

For a large homogeneous portfolio (LHP) with identical pairwise correlation ρ and identical default correlation $PD(T)$, the right side of equation (14.4) is approximately the percentage of entities in the portfolio defaulting at T. For example, if there is no correlation between the entities, ie, $\rho = 0$, then equation (14.4) reduces to $N[N^{-1}(PD(T))] = PD(T)$. In this case, if the individual default probability is $PD(T) = 10\%$, we can assume that approximately 10% of the entities will default by T.

We now replace the market factor M with a confidence level X. M is standard normal. Therefore, for a certain abscise value $N^{-1}(Y)$ of M, we have

$$\Pr(M \le N^{-1}(Y)) = \int_{-\infty}^{N^{-1}(Y)} n(M)dM = N(N^{-1}(Y)) = Y \qquad (14.5)$$

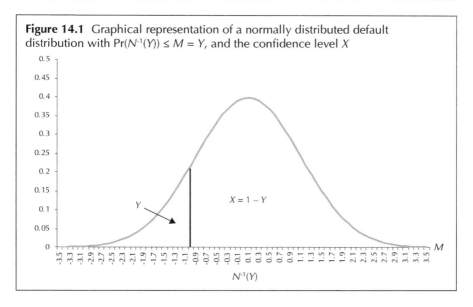

Figure 14.1 Graphical representation of a normally distributed default distribution with $Pr(N^{-1}(Y)) \leq M = Y$, and the confidence level X

Equation (14.5) reads: The probability of M being smaller equal than $N^{-1}(Y)$ is the surface of a normal distribution from $-\infty$ to $N^{-1}(Y)$, where $n(M)$ is the normal distribution of M. This can be written as $N(N^{-1}(Y))$, since $N(N^{-1}(Y))$ is the cumulative normal distribution from $-\infty$ to $N^{-1}(Y)$. N is the inverse of N^{-1}, therefore $N(N^{-1}(Y)) = Y$.

Graphically, we can express this as in Figure 14.1.

Replacing M in equation (14.4) with $N^{-1}(Y)$, we get

$$N\left(\frac{N^{-1}[PD(T)]-\sqrt{\rho}N^{-1}(Y)}{\sqrt{1-\rho}}\right) \qquad (14.6)$$

The term (14.6) tells us the probability Y of the percentage of defaults in the portfolio being bigger than

$$N\left(\frac{N^{-1}[PD(T)]-\sqrt{\rho}N^{-1}(Y)}{\sqrt{1-\rho}}\right)$$

We are interested in the probability of defaults smaller than Y. This is $1 - Y$. Let us set $1 - Y = X$, where X is a certain confidence level. Replacing Y with $1 - X$, and using $N^{-1}(1-X) = -N^{-1}(X)$, we derive

$$CVaR(X,T) = N\left(\frac{N^{-1}[PD(T)]-\sqrt{\rho}N^{-1}(X)}{\sqrt{1-\rho}}\right) \qquad (14.7)$$

where

CVaR(X, T): Credit value at risk for the confidence level X for the time horizon T
N: cumulative normal distribution
N^{-1}: inverse of the cumulative normal distribution
PD(T): average probability of default of the assets in the portfolio for the time horizon T
ρ: pairwise correlation coefficient of the assets in the portfolio; ρ is assumed constant for all asset pairs.

Equation (14.7) reads: We are X% certain that regarding our loan portfolio we will not lose more than

$$N\left(\frac{N^{-1}[PD(T)] - \sqrt{\rho}N^{-1}(Y)}{\sqrt{1-\rho}}\right)$$

due to (correlated) default risk, for the time horizon T.

Equation (14.7) is an important result, which was first published by Vasicek (1987/2002). It is derived from the OFGC model of equation (14.1); see above. Equation (14.7) is currently used in the Basel II accord as the basis to value credit risk in a portfolio. It takes into consideration default risk, not migration risk. CVaR is also called "credit at risk" or "worst-case default rate" (WCDR).

Example of equation (14.7)
Example 14.1: JP Morgan has given loans to several companies in the amount of US$100,000,000. The average one-year default probability of the companies is 1%. The copula default correlation coefficient between the companies is 5%. What is the one-year CVaR on a 99.9% confidence level?
It is

$$CVaR(0.999, 1) = N\left(\frac{N^{-1}[PD(0.01)] - \sqrt{0.05}N^{-1}(0.999)}{\sqrt{1-0.05}}\right) = 4.67\%$$

We can derive $N^{-1}(x)$ via Excel's =normsinv(x) or MATLABs norminv(x) function. $N(x)$ is =normsdist(x) in Excel and normdist(x) in MATLAB.

Interpretation: JP Morgan is 99.9% sure that it will not lose more than 4.67% of is loan exposure of US$100,000,000 due to (correlated) default risk of its debtors for a one-year time horizon. In dollar amounts and including a recovery rate of 40%, we derive that JP Morgan is 99.9% sure that it will not lose more than US$100,000,000 × 0.0467 × (1−0.4) = US$2,802,000.

Properties of equation (14.7)
Equation (14.7) has some interesting properties.

(a) We observe that for zero default correlation between the debtors in the portfolio $\rho = 0$, it follows that $CVaR = PD(T)$. So for a 99.9% confidence level, we are 99.9% sure that we will not lose more than the average default rate $PD(T)$. This is reasonable because there is no effect from correlation and the maximum loss is just the average default probability of the debtors.

(b) CVaR is a function of the default probability PD for the time horizon T, the confidence level X and the pairwise default correlation ρ. T is typically set to one year and the confidence level used is typically 99.9%. In this case we get a relationship between $CVaR$, $PD(T)$ and ρ as displayed in Figure 14.2.

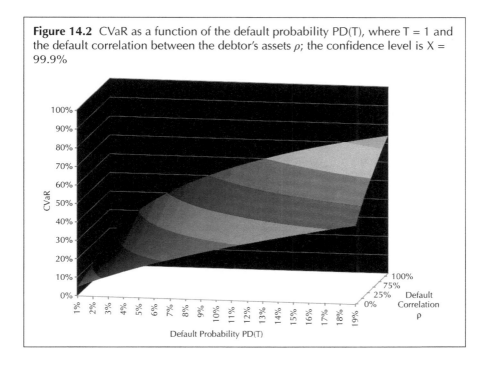

Figure 14.2 CVaR as a function of the default probability PD(T), where T = 1 and the default correlation between the debtor's assets ρ; the confidence level is X = 99.9%

337

From Figure 14.2, we observe that CVaR is a positive function with respect to $PD(T)$ and ρ. The positive relationship between CVaR and $PD(T)$, $\frac{\partial CVaR}{\partial PD(T)} > 0$ is obvious: the higher the default probability $PD(T)$, the higher is the maximum-loss CVaR. The positive relationship between CVaR and the default correlation between the debtors ρ, $\frac{\partial CVaR}{\partial \rho} > 0$, is also plausible: the higher the default correlation, the higher is the probability that many debtors default and the higher is the maximum-loss CVaR. This is especially the case for high-default probability $PD(T)$. For values of $PD(T)$ higher than 20% and ρ higher than 80%, the maximum-loss CVaR is close to 100% of the total loan exposure; see Figure 14.2.

A model, which displays the CVaR, can be found at www.dersoft.com/CVaR.xlsm.

BASEL-REQUIRED CAPITAL FOR CREDIT RISK

Basel uses equation (14.7) as a basis to calculate the capital charge for credit risk. However, the capital charge is reduced by the expected loss, which is measured by PD(T). The rationale is that banks cover the expected loss with their own provisions such as the interest rate that they charge. (Naturally low-rated debtors have to pay a higher interest rate on their loans than highly rated debtors.) Therefore, the required capital (RC) for credit risk in the Basel II accord is

$$RC = EAD \times (1-R) \times [CVaR - PD(T)] \qquad (14.8)$$

where

RC: Required capital by Basel II for credit risk in a portfolio
EAD: Exposure at default (for loans EAD is equal to the loan amount)
R: Recovery rate (rate that is recovered from the defaulted loan)
CVaR: Credit value at risk derived by equation (14.7)
PD(T): Average probability default of the debtors in the portfolio for time horizon T

Let us look at equation (14.8) in an example. Let us expand Example 14.1:

Example 14.2: JP Morgan has given loans to several companies in the amount of US$100,000,000. The average one-year default probability PD of the companies is 1%. The copula default correlation coefficient between the companies is 5%. What is the one-year capital charge of Basel II on a 99.9% confidence level assuming the recovery rate is 40%?

Answer: We had already derived CVaR in example 14.1 as CVaR = 4.67%. Following equation (14.8), the required capital charge of Basel II is

$$RC = US\$100{,}000{,}000 \times (1-0.4) \times (4.67\% - 1\%) = US\$2{,}202{,}000$$

Credit value at risk (CVaR) is typically calculated for a one-year time horizon. If a different time horizon is used, Basel II adds a maturity adjustment (MA). In this case equation (14.8) changes to

$$RC = EAD \times (1 - R) \times [CVaR - PD(T)] \times MA \qquad (14.8a)$$

where $MA = \frac{1+(M-2.5) \times b}{1-1.5 \times b}$ and M is the maturity date; b is a constant set at $b = [0.11852 - 0.05478 \times \ln(PD(T))]^2$.

The default probability–default correlation relationship

Interestingly, the correlation coefficient ρ is not an exogenous input in equation (14.8) or (14.8a), but ρ is a function of the default probability $PD(T)$, $\rho = f(PD(T))$. In particular, the Basel accord (BCBS 2011) sets

$$\rho = 0.12 \frac{1-\exp(-50 \times PD(T))}{1-\exp(-50)} + 0.24 \left(1 - \frac{1-\exp(-50 \times PD(T))}{1-\exp(-50)} \right) \qquad (14.9)$$

Equation (14.9) can be approximated well with equation (14.9a) as Hull (2012) points out

$$\rho = 0.12 \left[1 + \exp(-50 \times PD(T)) \right] \qquad (14.9a)$$

Indeed, equations (14.9) and (14.9a) are identical to at least 4 decimal points for any value of PD(T).

Equation (14.9) or (14.9a) are represented in Figure 14.3.

What is the rationale for making correlation ρ a function of the default probability PD(T) as displayed in Figure 14.3? It is assumed that highly rated companies with a low default probability have a higher correlation of default, since they are mostly prone to such systematic factors as a recession, in which they default together. However, companies with a high default probability are more affected by their own idiosyncratic factors and less by systematic

Figure 14.3 Correlation between the debtors in a portfolio ρ as a function of the average default probability of the debtors in the portfolio PD(T) in the Basel II accord

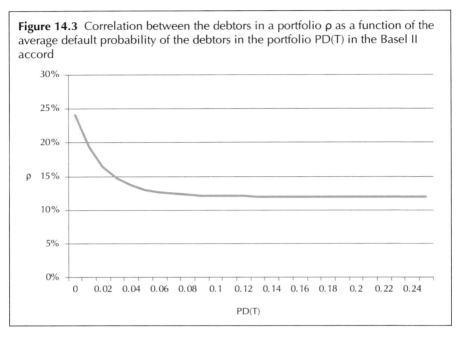

risk, hence are assumed to be less correlated. This is replicated in equations (14.9) and (14.9a) and Figure 14.3.

CVAR AND DOUBLE DEFAULTS

The Basel accord recognises the credit-risk reduction when a credit default swap (CDS) is used as a hedge, as displayed in Figure 14.4.

As seen in Figure 14.4, the investor will lose their investment to the obligor only if both the obligor and the guarantor default. Under the Basel accord, banks may use two approaches: the substitution approach and the double-default approach to address double default. Let us discuss them.

Substitution approach

For hedged credit exposures as in Figure 14.4, the Basel II accord allows that the exposure to the original obligor is substituted with the exposure of the guarantor. Hence, rewriting equation (14.7), we derive

$$CVaR_{hs}(X,T) = N\left[\min\left(\frac{N^{-1}(PD_o) + \sqrt{\rho_o}N^{-1}(X)}{\sqrt{1-\rho_o}}\right), \left(\frac{N^{-1}(PD_g) + \sqrt{\rho_g}N^{-1}(X)}{\sqrt{1-\rho_g}}\right)\right] \quad (14.10)$$

CREDIT VALUE AT RISK UNDER BASEL III – TOO SIMPLISTIC?

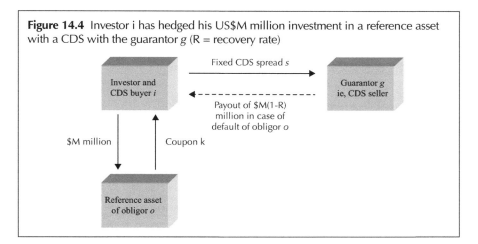

Figure 14.4 Investor i has hedged his US$M million investment in a reference asset with a CDS with the guarantor g (R = recovery rate)

where

$CVaR_{hs}(X,T)$: Credit value at risk for hedged exposures using the substitution approach in the Basel accord for the confidence level X time horizon T; X is set at 99.9% in the Basel II approach; compare with equation (14.7) for unhedged exposures

PD_o: probability of default of obligor

PD_g: probability of default of guarantor

ρ_o: Copula correlation coefficient between all assets in the portfolio of the obligor

ρ_g: Copula correlation coefficient between all assets in the portfolio of the guarantor

X: confidence level; X is set at 99.9% in the Basel II accord

Other variables defined as in equation (14.7).

In most cases, the guarantor g has a higher credit rating than the obligor o and therefore the guarantor g has a lower CVaR

$$N\left(\frac{N^{-1}[PD(T)]+\sqrt{\rho}N^{-1}(X)}{\sqrt{1-\rho}}\right)$$

Therefore, the term

$$N\left[\min\left(\frac{N^{-1}(PD_o)+\sqrt{\rho_o}N^{-1}(X)}{\sqrt{1-\rho_o}}\right),\left(\frac{N^{-1}(PD_g)+\sqrt{\rho_g}N^{-1}(X)}{\sqrt{1-\rho_g}}\right)\right]$$

is typically

$$N\left(\frac{N^{-1}(PD_g) + \sqrt{\rho_g} N^{-1}(X)}{\sqrt{1-\rho_g}}\right)$$

The Basel accord interprets ρ_o in equation (14.10) as "the sensitivity of the obligor to the systematic risk factor [M]". Strictly speaking, ρ_o is the default correlation coefficient between all asset pairs in the portfolio of the obligor o. As discussed above, this is a conditional correlation on the market factor M, as seen in the core equation (14.1) $x_i = \sqrt{\rho} M + \sqrt{1-\rho} Z_i$ of the one-factor Gaussian copula model. It is reasonable to approximate the conditional correlation between the obligor's assets on the market factor M as the correlation of the obligor to the market factor M. The same logic applies to ρ_g.

Importantly, ρ_o in equation (14.10) is derived in the Basel accord with equation (14.9) and therefore takes values between 12% and 24%, as shown in Figure 14.3. From equation (14.10) we also observe that the substitution approach is the more valuable the lower the CVaR of the guarantor (second term in the min-function) compared with the CVaR of the obligor (first term in the min-function). Since in reality the default probability of the guarantor PD_g is typically lower than the default probability of the obligor PD_o, regulatory capital relief is often achieved when the substitution approach is applied.

Double-default approach
The Basel II accord also allows banks to address credit risk that is hedged with a credit derivative, as displayed in Figure 14.4, with the double-default approach. This approach is quantified with the bivariate normal distribution M_2. We have already discussed the bivariate normal distribution in Chapter 5 (see Figure 5.4). A bivariate normal distribution has three input parameters: the variables X and Y and the correlation parameter between X and Y, ρ:

$$M_2 = f(X, Y, \rho) \qquad (14.11)$$

To reduce the capital charge for hedged exposures, the Basel accord defines the variables X and Y as the credit value at risk (CVaR) values of the obligor o and the guarantor g, which we derived in equation (14.7). These are correlated with a correlation factor, which correlates the CVaR of the obligor and the guarantor and includes wrong-way risk. Let us have a look at this correlation factor.

From equation (14.1), earlier we derive the default indicator variable x for the obligor x_o and the guarantor x_g:

$$x_o = \sqrt{\rho_o} M + \sqrt{1-\rho_o} Z_o \qquad (14.1a)$$

$$x_g = \sqrt{\rho_g} M + \sqrt{1-\rho_g} Z_g \qquad (14.1b)$$

The correlation between x_o and x_g in equations (14.1a) and (14.1b) is $\sqrt{\rho_o \rho_g}$. This can be seen easily: if ρ_o and ρ_g both are 1, x_o and x_g are equal to M in every simulation and hence are perfectly correlated. If ρ_o and ρ_g both = 0, x_o and x_g are determined solely by their idiosyncratic variables Z_o and Z_g, hence are uncorrelated. Even if either ρ_o or ρ_g is 0, the correlation between x_o and x_g is 0. Let us assume ρ_o is zero. Hence, the obligor is uncorrelated to the systematic market factor M. Since all correlation is conditioned on M, there is also zero correlation between x_o and M, and therefore also zero correlation between x_o and x_g. For values of $0 < \sqrt{\rho_o \rho_g} < 1$, x_o and x_g are partially correlated.

Basel II now adds a correlation factor for wrong-way risk between the obligor and guarantor, $\rho^*(1-\rho_o)(1-\rho_g)$. Altogether, the correlation between the obligor o and the guarantor g is set to

$$\rho_{og} \equiv \sqrt{\rho_o \rho_g} + \rho^* \sqrt{(1-\rho_o)(1-\rho_g)} \qquad (14.12)$$

where

ρ_{og}: Correlation between the credit quality of the obligor o and the guarantor g
$\equiv$: "is set to" or "defined as"
$\sqrt{\rho_o \rho_g}$: Systematic correlation with respect to the market factor M, which follows from the one-factor Gaussian model of equations (14.1a) and (14.1b)
ρ^*: Correlation coefficient for wrong-way risk
$\rho^* \sqrt{(1-\rho_o)(1-\rho_g)}$: correlation term to address wrong-way risk.

Equation (14.12) reminds us of the Pearson correlation approach. From equations (A4) and (A5) in the appendix of Chapter 1, we have

$$E(XY) = E(X)E(Y) + \rho\, \sigma(X)\sigma(Y) \qquad (A5a)$$

However, equations (14.12) and (A5a) are fundamentally different. From $\rho = 0$ in equation (A5a) it follows that $E(XY) = E(X)E(Y)$, which means that X and Y are uncorrelated. From $\rho^* = 0$ in equation (14.16) it follows that $\rho_{og} \equiv \sqrt{\rho_o \rho_g}$. However, this is not a case of uncorrelatedness. The correlation between the obligor o and the guarantor g, ρ_{og} will only be zero is either ρ_o or ρ_g is zero, since from equations (14.1a) and (14.1b), ρ_o and ρ_g are the correlation parameters that conditionally correlate on the common factor M.

We are now ready to derive the double-default approach for hedged credit exposures in the Basel accord. We apply the bivariate equation (14.11) and define the variable X as the CVaR of the obligor o and Y as the CVaR of the guarantor g (see equation (14.7) for CVaR). We solve equation (14.16) for the correlation coefficient

$$\rho^* = \frac{\rho_{og} - \sqrt{\rho_o \rho_g}}{\sqrt{(1-\rho_o)(1-\rho_g)}}$$

Hence we derive

$$CVaR_{hDD}(X,T) = M_2\left(\frac{N^{-1}(PD_o) + \sqrt{\rho_o} N^{-1}(X)}{\sqrt{1-\rho_o}}, \frac{N^{-1}(PD_o) + \sqrt{\rho_g} N^{-1}(X)}{\sqrt{1-\rho_g}}; \frac{\rho_{og} - \sqrt{\rho_o \rho_g}}{\sqrt{(1-\rho_o)(1-\rho_g)}}\right) \quad (14.13)$$

where

$CVaR_{hDD}(X, T)$: Credit value at risk for hedged exposures using the double-default approach in the Basel accord for a confidence level of X and time horizon T; X is set at 99.9% in the Basel accord

M_2: Bivariate cumulative normal distribution

ρ_o: Copula correlation coefficient between all assets in the portfolio of the obligor, derived by equation (14.9). Hence ρ_o takes values between 0.12 and 0.24.

ρ_g: Copula correlation coefficient between all assets in the portfolio of the guarantor; ρ_g is set to 0.7 in the Basel accord

ρ_{og}: Copula correlation between the obligor and the guarantor; ρ_{og} is set to 0.5 in the Basel accord.

Other variable defined as in equation (14.10)

From equation (14.13) we can expect a much lower CVaR compared with an unhedged exposure of equation (14.7) since a joint probability M_2 is typically much lower than a single probability N.

Let us compare three scenarios with respect to credit value at risk (CVaR).

(a) Unhedged capital charge CVaR for credit risk derived in equation (14.7). CVaR is the basis for calculating the required capital of equation (14.8).
(b) A hedged CVaR, displayed in Figure 14.5, applying the substitution approach of equation (14.10), which reduces CVaR.
(c) A hedged capital charge CVaR, displayed in Figure 14.6, applying the double-default approach of equation (14.13), which also reduces CVaR.

Figures 14.5 and 14.6 compare the scenarios.

From Figure 14.5 and 14.6, we observe the significant capital charge reduction in the Basel accord when a credit exposure is hedged. Comparing Figures 14.5 and 14.6, we also see that the double-default approach typically allows a lower capital charge than the substitution approach does.

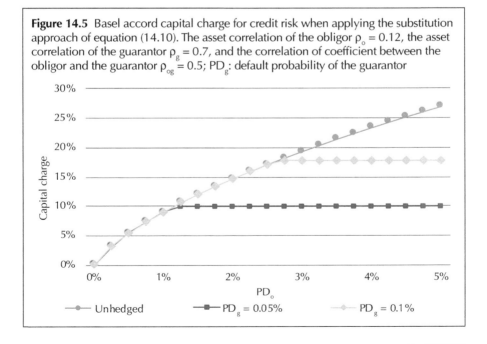

Figure 14.5 Basel accord capital charge for credit risk when applying the substitution approach of equation (14.10). The asset correlation of the obligor $\rho_o = 0.12$, the asset correlation of the guarantor $\rho_g = 0.7$, and the correlation of coefficient between the obligor and the guarantor $\rho_{og} = 0.5$; PD_g: default probability of the guarantor

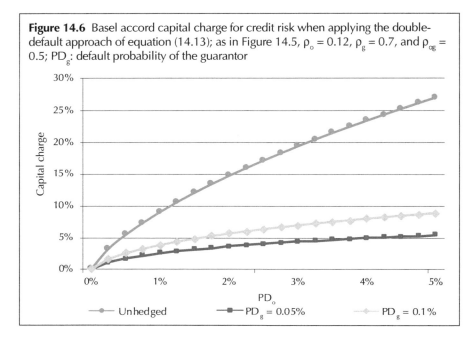

Figure 14.6 Basel accord capital charge for credit risk when applying the double-default approach of equation (14.13); as in Figure 14.5, $\rho_o = 0.12$, $\rho_g = 0.7$, and $\rho_{og} = 0.5$; PD_g: default probability of the guarantor

The substitution approach has been criticised for its lack of mathematical foundation and a lack of sensitivity to high risk exposure (since the high risk exposure is substituted for the guarantor's risk exposure). The double-default approach, also called ASRF (asymptotic single-risk factor) approach following a paper by Gordy (2003), has a more rigorous mathematical foundation and is sensitive to both high risk (obligor) and low risk (guarantor) debtors.

For a spreadsheet, which derives the Basel III capital charge for hedged credit exposure with equations (14.10) and (14.13), see www.dersoft.com/Baseldoubledefault.xlsm.

SUMMARY

In this chapter, we discussed the way correlation risk is addressed in the Basel II and Basel III frameworks. The Basel Committee has recognised the significance of correlation risk and has suggested several approaches to manage correlation risk.

In the Basel II and III accords, credit risk of a portfolio is quantified with the credit value-at-risk (CVaR) concept. CVaR measures the maximum loss of a portfolio due to credit risk with a certain probability for a certain timeframe. Basel II and Basel III derive

CVaR on the basis of the one-factor Gaussian copula (OFGC) correlation model, which we discussed in Chapter 7.

The required capital to be set aside for credit risk is the CVaR minus the average probability of default of the debtors in the portfolio. This is because the Basel Committee assumes that banks cover the expected loss (approximated as the average probability of default) with their own provisions such as the interest rate that they charge.

Interestingly, the Basel Committee requires an inverse relationship between the default correlation of the debtors in a portfolio with respect to the default probability of the debtors: the lower the default probability of debtors in a portfolio, the higher is the default correlation between the debtors. This is reasonable, since debtors with a high default probability are more prone to default for systematic reasons, ie, more often default together in a recession. Conversely, highly rated debtors with a low default probability are more affected by their own idiosyncratic factors and less by systematic risk. Hence the default risk of highly rated debtors is assumed to be less correlated. This is supported by empirical data.

The Basel Committee also realises the risk reduction, which is achieved when a credit exposure is hedged with a credit default swap (CDS). The Basel Committee allows banks to address the credit-risk reduction of a CDS in two ways: (1) the substitution approach, which allows banks to use the typically lower default probability of the guarantor (CDS seller) in the credit exposure calculation and (2) the double-default approach, which derives the joint probability of the obligor and the guarantor defaulting. This joint default probability is typically much lower than the individual default probability of the obligor, lowering the overall credit exposure value.

The Basel II and most likely Basel III applies the OFGC (one-factor Gaussian copula) model to derive CVaR. As discussed in Chapter 7, this model assumes (1) identical probabilities of default for all bonds and loans in a bank's portfolio and (2) principally identical default correlation between all bonds and loans. As mentioned, the Basel Committee has altered the second assumption and has made default correlation a function of the probability of default (Figure 14.3), which adds realism to the model. However,

347

the model is simplistic and should be applied only to homogeneous banks' loan and bond portfolios or sub-portfolios, ie, with similar properties such as similar default probabilities, similar pairwise default correlation, similar recovery rates, interest rates, and maturities.

Questions for Chapter 14

Answers to these questions can be found at the end of this book.

1. What information does credit value-at-risk (CVaR) give us?
2. Why don't we just apply the market value-at-risk (VaR) concept to value credit risk?
3. Which correlation concept underlies the CVaR concept of the Basel II and III approaches?
4. In the Basel Committee CVaR approach, what follows for the relationship between the CVaR value and the average probability of default, if we assume the correlation between all assets in the portfolio is zero?
5. Deutsche has given loans to several companies in the amount of US$500,000,000. The average one-year default probability of the companies is 2%. The copula default correlation coefficient between the companies is 3%. What is the one-year CVaR on a 99.9% confidence level?
6. In the Basel Committee CVaR model, the default correlation is an inverse function of the average probability of the default of the assets in the portfolio. Explain the rationale for this relationship.
7. In the Basel Committee approach, the required capital to be set aside for credit risk is the CVaR minus the average probability of default. Explain why.
8. Which two approaches does the Basel Committee allow banks to quantify double defaults?
9. Which of the two approaches typically results in a lower capital requirement?
10. What is the main criticism of the substitution approach?

15
Basel III and XVAs

"I'm very close to thinking the United States shouldn't be in Basel anymore"

– Jamie Dimon

In this chapter, we will discuss the Basel Accord's view on the adjustments to the no-default value of a derivatives portfolio, collectively called XVAs. There is no shortage of XVAs. We have the following.

1. CVA: credit value adjustment. Addresses counterparty credit risk in a derivatives portfolio.
2. DVA: debt value adjustment. Also addresses counterparty credit risk in a derivatives portfolio. However, it addresses an entity's own credit risk. If allowed, DVA will increase the no-default value of the derivatives portfolio.
3. FVA: funding value adjustment. An adjustment to the price of a transaction due to the cost of funding the transaction or the related hedge.
4. ColVA: collateral value adjustment. Also termed IOS (index overnight swap) adjustment. Is an adjustment for the cost of funding the collateral in a derivatives transaction or the related hedge. ColVA can increase or decrease the value of a derivatives portfolio.
5. KVA: regulatory capital adjustment. An adjustment for holding regulatory capital during the life of the derivative.
6. MVA: adjustment for the cost of an initial margin and a variation margin for non-centrally cleared derivatives.[1]

CVA APPROACH WITHOUT WRONG-WAY RISK IN THE BASEL ACCORD

CVA has become an important part of correlated credit-risk modelling in the recent past. Most investment and commercial banks have CVA quant groups, which analyse CVA risk, and CVA desks, where CVA risk is traded and hedged. The importance of CVA is highlighted by Basel II, which reports that two-thirds of the credit-risk losses during the global financial crisis were caused by CVA volatility rather than actual defaults. In addition, the derivatives' portfolios of investment banks are typically quite large. When Lehman defaulted in September 2008, it had 1.5 million derivative transactions with 8,000 different counterparties, stressing the importance to manage derivatives credit risk. What is CVA? Here is a broad definition: CVA is an adjustment to address counterparty credit risk.

The focus of CVA is typically narrower than the definition above, referring to counterparty credit risk in a derivatives transaction. This narrower CVA framework is applied in the Basel Accord (BCBS 2011a):

> In addition to the default risk capital requirements for counterparty credit risk determined based on the standardized or internal ratings-based (IRB) approaches for credit risk, a bank must add a capital charge to cover the risk of mark-to-market losses on the expected counterparty risk (such losses being known as credit value adjustments, CVA) to OTC derivatives.

We will concentrate on this derivatives aspect of CVA here. With respect to a derivative, CVA is the difference between the price of a credit-risky derivative and the price of a default-free derivative as displayed in equation (15.1).

$$\text{Credit-risky derivative} = \text{Default-free derivative} - \text{CVA} \qquad (15.1)$$

If CVA > 0, we see from Equation (15.1) that a credit-risky derivative has a lower price than a derivative without credit risk. This is because the buyer of the credit-risky derivative (often referred to as "the dealer"), lowers the price of the derivative since they assume the credit risk of the counterparty (the derivatives seller). In particular, if the counterparty defaults, the buyer of the derivative

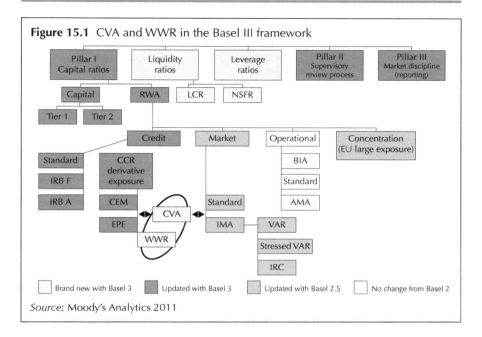

Figure 15.1 CVA and WWR in the Basel III framework

Source: Moody's Analytics 2011

will not receive the payout of the derivative. CVA is called an adjustment, since the derivatives buyer adjusts (lowers) the price of the derivative due to credit risk.

CVA is an integral part of the Basel III accord. Figure 15.1 shows CVA, and the associated wrong-way risk (WWR), which will be discussed below.

From Figure 15.1 we observe that CVA has a market-risk component and a credit-risk component. We formalise this in equation (15.2).

$$CVA_{a,c} = f\left(\underbrace{D^+_{a,c}}_{\text{Market risk}} , \underbrace{PD_c}_{\text{Credit risk}} \right) \qquad (15.2)$$

where

$CVA_{a,c}$: Credit value adjustment of entity 'a' with respect to the counterparty c
$D^+_{a,c}$: Netted, positive derivatives portfolio value of entity 'a' with counterparty c
PD_c: Default probability of counterparty c

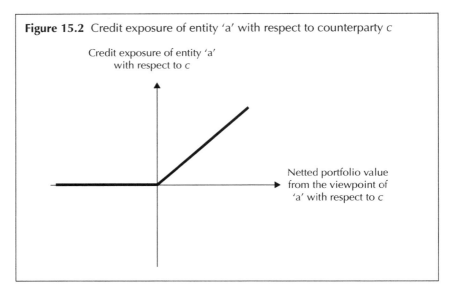

Figure 15.2 Credit exposure of entity 'a' with respect to counterparty c

In equation (15.2), the term $D^+_{a,c}$ – the netted, positive derivatives portfolio value of entity 'a' with counterparty c – constitutes the market-risk component, since market prices and the volatility of the underlying instrument determine the value of $D^+_{a,c}$. In equation (15.2), we only take the positive netted derivative portfolio value, $D^+_{a,c} = \max\left(\sum D_{a,c}, 0\right)$ into consideration. This is because entity 'a' has credit exposure only if netted derivatives portfolio between 'a' and c is positive for 'a'. (In simple terms, 'a' has credit exposure with respect to c only if c is the debtor of 'a'). Figure 15.2 shows this property.

Figure 15.2 shows that, for positive credit exposure, the credit exposure is identical with the netted portfolio value, also called portfolio MtM (mark-to-market) value. This is reasonable since an increase in the MtM value of the netted portfolio value of entity 'a' with a counterparty c by US$1, increases the credit exposure of 'a' with respect to c by US$1.

Equation (15.2) shows that CVA can be viewed as a derivative itself. It is a complex derivative since it has two underlyings, D^+ and PD_c, which may be correlated! If they are not correlated, we can multiply the market-risk component and the credit-risk component. Adding a recovery rate of the counterparty c, R_c, we can write

$$CVA_{a,c} = \left(D_{a,c}^+ \times PD_c\right)\left(1 - R_c\right) \tag{15.3}$$

Let us look at an example of equation (15.3).

Example 15.1: Entity 'a' has a derivatives portfolio with counterparty c, which has a present value of +US$100,000,000 for 'a'. The default probability of c for a 1-year time horizon is 5%. The recovery rate of counterparty c in case of default of c is expected to be 30%. What is the CVA from the viewpoint of 'a' with respect to counterparty c for a 1-year time horizon? Following equation (15.3) it is

$CVA_{a,c}$ = US$100,000,000 × 0,05 × (1 − 0.3) = US$3,500,000.

Equation (15.3) is the basis for calculating CVA in the Basel III Accord, when the correlation between market risk and credit risk is assumed to be zero. However, this is a simplistic assumption, which we will alter in the next section.

CVA WITH WWR IN THE BASEL ACCORD

As mentioned above, equations (15.2) and (15.3) assume that market risk of the derivative D and PD (probability of default) are not correlated. However, this is not a realistic assumption. Market risk and credit risk are clearly related. For example, if the equity market declines (maybe due to a recession), the default probabilities of companies typically increase (since debt-to-equity ratios increase). Conversely, if the default probability of a company increases (maybe due to bad management or increased competition), the stock price of the company will decline.

The Basel Accord recognises the correlation between market risk and credit risk. The Basel Accord defines two types of WWR: general and specific. Let us look at general wrong-way risk first.

Definition: General wrong-way risk exists when the probability of default of a counterparty is positively correlated with general market risk factors (BCBS 2011b).

Following the Basel II accord "general market-risk factors" are interest rates, equity prices, foreign exchange rates, commodity prices, etc.

Let us discuss an example of general WWR regarding the market-risk-factor interest rates, which can be positively correlated

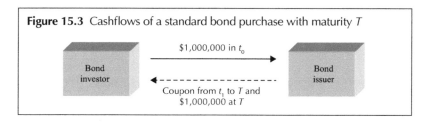

Figure 15.3 Cashflows of a standard bond purchase with maturity T

with default probability. We will explain general WWR with the practical example of a long bond position, which is displayed in Figure 15.3.

In Figure 15.3 only the bond investor has credit risk with respect to bond issuer. This is because, in case of default of the issuer, the bond investor will not receive the coupon payments, and, most importantly, just receive the recovery rate of the principal investment of US$1,000,000. The bond issuer does not have credit exposure to the bond investor, since the bond issuer has received all contractual payments, ie, the initial investment of US$1,000,000 at t_0.

A bond price B is mainly a function of the market interest rate level i and the default probability of the issuer PD_c, hence $B = f(i, PD_c, ...)$. There is a negative relationship between the bond price B and market rates i: the higher the market interest rates i, the lower is the bond price B, since the coupon of the bond price is now lower compared with the market interest rate i, formally: $\frac{\partial B}{\partial i} \leq 0$. There is also a negative relationship between the bond price B and the default probability of the issuer PD_c: $\frac{\partial B}{\partial PD_c} \leq 0$.

The relationship between B, i and q_c constitutes general wrong-way risk: in a weakening economy, typically interest rates i decrease and default probabilities q_c increase. However, from the relationship $\frac{\partial B}{\partial i} \leq 0$, decreasing interest rates also mean a higher bond price, ie, higher credit exposure of the bond buyer with respect to the bond issuer. But a higher default probability PD_c also means a lower probability that the issuer will be able to pay the coupons and the principal amount. Hence the higher the credit exposure, the more likely it is that the bond issuer can't pay coupons and principal, which constitutes general WWR. Graphically this is displayed in Figure 15.4.

Figure 15.4 General WWR: Decreasing interest rates i lead to higher credit exposure via a higher bond price B. Decreasing interest rates i in a recession also mean increasing default probability PD_c of the bond issuer. Hence the higher the credit exposure, the higher is the credit risk, ie, the higher the risk that the issuer can meet their obligation to pay coupons and principal.

Definition: A bank is exposed to specific WWR if future exposure to a specific counterparty is positively correlated with the counterparty's probability of default (BCBS 2011a).

We can formalise specific WWR with equation (15.4),

$$\frac{\partial PD}{\partial D^+} > 0 \qquad (15.4)$$

Equation (15.4) reads: If the credit exposure, expressed by the netted positive derivatives value D^+, increases, credit risk, expressed as the default probability PD, also tends to increase. This is clearly not a good situation to be in. In simple words, the higher the credit exposure, the higher is the credit risk, ie, the risk that the debtor cannot meet their obligations.

Let us look at an example of specific WWR. We had already briefly mentioned an example of specific WWR in Chapter 1 in Figure 1.1. Let us discuss it in detail now.

Figure 15.5 shows the cashflows between the three entities in a CDS.

In Figure 15.5, the terminology and notation of the Basel Accord is applied. In most literature the guarantor g is called counterparty c and the obligor o is called reference entity r.

In Figure 15.5, the investor has specific WWR, if there is a positive correlation between the default probability of the obligor o and the guarantor g (ie, the CDS seller). This means, the higher the default probability of the obligor PD_o, the higher is also the default probability of the guarantor PD_g.

In particular, if the default probability of the obligor increases, the market spread of the CDS increases. Therefore, the present

Figure 15.5 Cashflows of an investor i, who has credit exposure to an obligor o, which is hedged with credit default swap (CDS) with the guarantor g; R: recovery rate

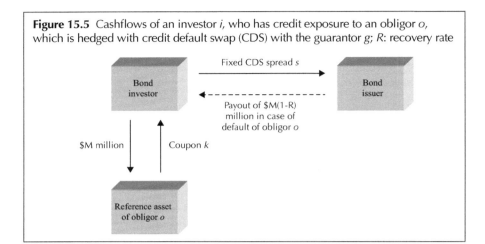

value for the CDS buyer increases, since their fixed spread s is now lower than the market spread. If the CDS is market-to-market, this is good from a profit perspective, but from a risk perspective it means that the credit exposure for the CDS buyer i increases.

Also, with increasing default probability of the guarantor, the credit risk increases, since it is less likely that the guarantor can pay the payoff in default. Hence we have increased credit exposure together with increased credit risk, constituting specific WWR. Figure 15.6 shows the WWR dilemma.

A further example of specific WWR is if a company sells put options on its own stock (BCBS 2011a). This is displayed in Figure 15.7.

Figure 15.6 Specific WWR in a CDS if the default correlation between the obligor PD_o and the guarantor PD_g is positive. Let us assume PD_o and PD_g both increase, ie, $(PD_o \cap PD_g)\uparrow$. Hence the present value of the CDS, PV(CDS) for i increases, which means higher credit exposure for i. In addition, the increasing probability of default of the guarantor means that the probability P of the future payoff from the guarantor decreases. Hence we have increasing credit exposure together with increasing credit risk, constituting specific wrong-way risk WWR.

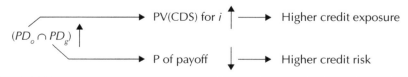

Figure 15.7 Example of specific WWR: Deutsche Bank selling a put on its own stock

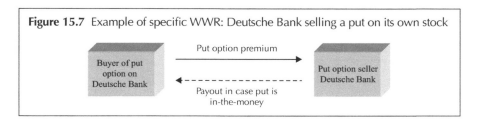

Selling a put on its own stock constitutes specific WWR, since the lower the stock price the more the put is in-the-money, ie, the higher is the credit exposure for the put option buyer with respect to the put option seller Deutsche Bank. But the lower the Deutsche Bank stock price, the higher is typically also the default probability of Deutsche Bank. This means the higher the credit exposure (when the put is deeper in-the-money), the higher is the credit risk (the probability that Deutsche Bank defaults), constituting specific WWR.

How do Basel II and III quantify WWR?

Basel II and III have a simple approach to address both general and specific WWR. A multiplier α is applied to increase the derivatives exposure $D_{a,c}^+$. The multiplier α is set to 1.4, which means the credit exposure $D_{a,c}^+$ is increased by 40% compared with assuming credit exposure $D_{a,c}^+$ and credit-risk PD_c are independent, as was expressed in equation (15.3). Banks that use their own internal models are allowed to use an α of 1.2, meaning the credit exposure is increased by 20% to capture WWR. Banks report an actual alpha of 1.07 to 1.1, hence the α of 1.2 to 1.4 that Basel III requires is conservative.

Currently, models are developed to quantify WWR in a more rigorous way. See for example Cepedes *et al* (2010) or Hull and White (2014).

DVA: IF SOMETHING SOUNDS TOO GOOD TO BE TRUE...

Let us first clarify: Credit value-at-risk (CVaR), derived in the previous chapter with equation (14.7), addresses counterparty credit risk in a portfolio with relatively fixed exposures such as bonds and loans. Credit value adjustment (CVA) derived in equations (15.2) and (15.3) is a specific capital charge, which typically addresses counterparty credit risk in a derivatives transaction.

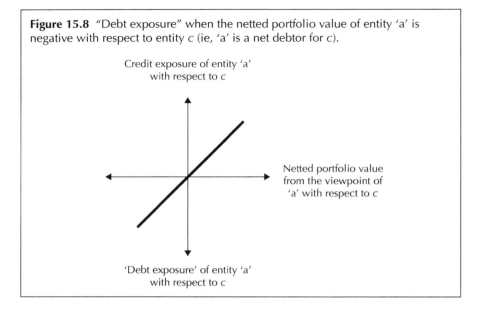

Figure 15.8 "Debt exposure" when the netted portfolio value of entity 'a' is negative with respect to entity c (ie, 'a' is a net debtor for c).

As with CVA, DVA also addresses counterparty credit risk, in a derivatives portfolio, however – an entity's own credit risk.

Definition: DVA adjusts the value of a derivatives portfolio by taking the entity's own default probability into consideration.

The Basel Accord prefers the term "CVA liability" instead of DVA. However, we will refer to DVA as DVA.

In Figure 15.2, we displayed credit exposure and concluded that credit exposure can only be bigger or equal zero. Credit exposure for entity 'a' with counterparty c exists if the counterparty c is a net debtor to 'a'. If we allow recognising negative credit exposure or "debt exposure", Figure 15.2 would change to Figure 15.8.

This "debt exposure" of 'a' with respect to c could theoretically be taken into consideration when evaluating a portfolio. In particular, "debt exposure" could be recognised in derivatives transactions. This debt exposure in derivatives transactions is the netted negative derivatives portfolio of entity 'a' with respect to c, This is weighted, ie, reduced by the probability of default of entity 'a'. Including a recovery rate of 'a', we derive in analogy to equation (15.3) for CVA, which is $CVA_{a,c} = (D^+_{a,c} \times PD_c)(1-R_c)$,

$$DVA_{a,c} = (D^-_{a,c} \times PD_a)(1-R_a) \qquad (15.5)$$

where

$DVA_{a,c}$: Debt value adjustment of entity 'a' with respect to entity c
$D^{-}_{a,c}$: Netted negative derivatives portfolio value of 'a' with respect to c (ie, 'a' is a debtor to c)
PD_a: Default probability of entity 'a'
R_a: Recovery rate of entity 'a'.

Importantly, let us now consider that in the event of default of entity 'a', only the recovery rate of 'a's debt is paid out. If this is accounted for, this decreases 'a's debt and increases the book value (defined as assets – debt) of 'a'. If we apply this concept to a derivatives portfolio, the derivatives portfolio value increases and equation (15.1) expands to (15.6)

$$\text{Value of derivatives portfolio} = \text{Default-free value} - \text{CVA} + \text{DVA} \qquad (15.6)$$

However, there are two critical problems with DVA.

(a) An entity 'a' would benefit from its own increasing default probability PD_a, since a higher default probability would increase DVA (via equation (15.5)), which in turn increases the value of the derivatives portfolio (via equation (15.6))!
(b) Entity 'a' could realise the DVA benefit only if it actually defaults!

Both (a) and (b) defy financial logic.

DVA in 2011 and 2012

On 8 August 2011, the United States lost its triple-A credit rating from S&P due to the gridlock in Washington and major implications to the nation's budget and debt problems. With it, many financial institutions received a credit downgrade.

In fixed-income accounting, debt is essentially a liability. In turn, trading performance is measured as the change in assets minus the change in liabilities. Hence, in 2011, many financial institution applied equation (15.5) and reported huge "trading profits" since the value of their own debt had increased. Table 15.1 shows that especially Morgan Stanley reported huge profits in 2011, which

Table 15.1 Trading profits in 2011 mainly due to DVA increases, and trading losses in 2012 mainly due to DVA declines

Trading Profits	2011	2012
Morgan Stanley	3,681	−4,401
Citigroup	1,732	−2,487
Bank of America	1,001	−2,448
JP Morgan	1,452	−920
Goldman Sachs	596	−714

Source: http://www.nasdaq.com/article/banks-debt-valuation-accounting-rules-need-a-revision-cm218588

were mainly due to DVA increases and huge losses in 2012, which were mainly due to DVA declines.

A solution to the artificial trading profits from DVA would be to separate trading profits into those due to (1) market factors and those due to (2) DVA changes.

Basel Accord and DVA

Starting in 2010, the Basel Accord has stated its views on the question of allowing DVA in the accounting and regulatory environment in several papers. Paragraph 75 of the critical 2011 paper states to "Derecognise in the calculation of Common Equity Tier 1, all unrealised gains and losses that have resulted from changes in the fair value of liabilities that are due to changes in the bank's own credit risk" (BCBS 2011c).

Though for derivatives the BCBS states: "However, the application of paragraph 75 to derivatives is not straightforward since their valuations depend on a range of factors other than the bank's own creditworthiness, such as interest rates and other market factors that can affect the exposures value. It is not easy to separate out changes in value that are only due to changes in a bank's own credit risk" (BCBS 2011c). In the same document the BCBS concludes that DVA for derivatives is allowed: "Therefore, after considering various alternatives, the Basel Committee is of the view that all DVAs for derivatives should be fully deducted in the calculation of CET1 [Common Equity Tier 1]".

However, in the critical 2015 paper on the FRTB (Fundamental Review of the Trading Book), which we will discuss in the next chapter, BCBS has not allowed DVA in the derivatives valuation: "... the Debt Valuation Adjustment (DVA) component of bilateral CVA will not be recognised in the proposed framework" (BCBS 2015a).

Whether to recognise DVA in an accounting and regulatory framework will be an ongoing discussion. The author of this book is of the opinion that, in an accounting framework, profits should be separated into (1) profits from market factors and (2) DVA changes, to increase information clarity for the investor. For derivatives, DVA is more complex. However, the facts that (1) an increase in the probability of default of an entity increases the value of the derivatives portfolio for that entity, and (2) an entity can realise the DVA benefit only if it actually defaults, defy financial logic. Therefore DVA should not be allowed in derivatives trading and valuation.

FUNDING VALUE ADJUSTMENT

A further recent development relating to CVA and DVA is funding value adjustment (FVA). What is FVA?

Definition: FVA, funding value adjustment, is an adjustment to the price of a transaction due to the cost of funding for the transaction or the related hedge.

Funding cost had not been a major issue in derivatives pricing in the past. However, in 2008, when interest rates, especially for poor credits, increased sharply, funding cost could no longer be ignored.

There was quite a spirited debate in 2012 as to whether the cost of funding should be taken into consideration when pricing a derivative. Professors Hull, White and Duffie argue that adding funding costs violates the risk-neutral derivatives pricing principle. It would lead to arbitrage opportunities, since the same derivative would have different prices. However, derivatives traders argue their treasury department charges them the funding cost. Hence funding costs exist in reality and cannot just be ignored. Funding cost should be priced in and passed through to the end-user (*Risk* 2012a, 2012b).

Let us look at the issue of cost of funding. The cost of funding of an entity is mainly a function of the default probability of the entity. Hence, we have

$$FVA_a = f(PD_a,...) \tag{15.7}$$

There is a positive relationship between FVA and PD, since the higher the default probability, the higher is the cost of funding:

$$\frac{\partial FVA_a}{\partial PD_a} > 0 \tag{15.8}$$

If the cost of FVA is taken into account, the value of a derivatives portfolio is reduced. Hence equation (15.6) then changes to

$$\text{Value of derivatives portfolio} = \text{Default-free value} - \text{CVA} + \text{DVA} - \text{FVA} \tag{15.9}$$

As we see from equations (15.5) and (15.8), both DVA and FVA increase if the probability of default increases, hence credit quality decreases. In a 2017 response to the Basel proposal, the International Swaps and Derivatives Association (ISDA) has suggested that "CVA liability [ie, DVA] should be deducted only to the extent that it exceeds the increase in FVA" (ISDA 2017). In this case there would be no benefit, ie, no increase in the value of a derivatives portfolio if the default probability of an entity increases, as we can see from equation (15.9), since DVA is added only up to the amount that FVA is subtracted.

COLLATERAL VALUE ADJUSTMENT

Definition: Collateral value adjustment (ColVA), also abbreviated CRA, or termed OIS (overnight interest rate swap) adjustment is an adjustment to the no-default value of a derivatives portfolio for OTC (over-the-counter), so non-centrally cleared derivatives if collateral is posted.

In OTC derivatives trading practice, typically the credit support annex (CSA) is included in the transaction. The CSA regulates the terms under which collateral is posted, ie, what type of collateral is eligible, what currency the collateral may be posted in and what haircut may be applied.[2]

Let us look at ColVA in an example.

Example 15.2: Counterparty A has a derivatives position with counterparty B. The derivative is "in-the-money"[3] for B and therefore "out-of-the-money" for A. Hence B has credit risk with respect

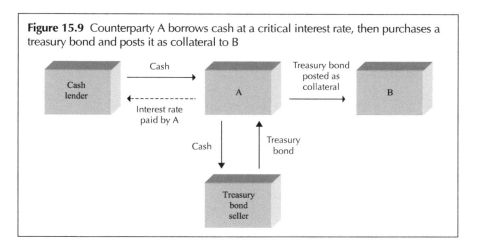

Figure 15.9 Counterparty A borrows cash at a critical interest rate, then purchases a treasury bond and posts it as collateral to B

to A and requires collateral from A. A borrows cash at a critical interest rate, then purchases a treasury bond and posts it as collateral to B. This is displayed in Figure 15.9.

Three scenarios with respect to a benefit or loss from collateralisation are possible.

1. If the interest rate paid by A to borrow cash is lower than the interest rate that is typically paid by A, then there will be benefit from the collateralisation, ie, ColVA will be positive. For example, A may be able to pay the OIS rate, which is typically relatively low.
2. If the interest rate paid by A to borrow cash is equal to the interest rate that is typically paid by A, then there will be no benefit or loss from the collateralisation, ie, ColVA will be zero.
3. If the interest rate paid by A to borrow cash is higher than the interest rate that is typically paid by A, then there will a loss from the collateralisation, ie, ColVA will be negative.

Collateralisation of OTC derivatives positions will most likely continue to increase in the future, since Basel regulations recognise the credit-risk reduction from collateralisation (BCBS 2012). In particular, collateralisation enables a regulatory capital reduction of CVA as well as DVA. Researchers have built models to quantify ColVA; see, for example, Duffie and Zhou (2011), Piterbarg (2012) and Hull and White (2014). Banks have employed these models and in addition developed sophisticated algorithms, typically using Monte Carlo simulations to determine the "cheapest to deliver" collateral.

REGULATORY CAPITAL ADJUSTMENT

Definition: Regulatory capital adjustment (KVA), is an adjustment for the regulatory capital requirement of a derivatives portfolio during the life of the derivative.

Currently banks are developing sophisticated models to minimise KVA. These models require complex Monte Carlo simulations, since:

(a) due to changing market factors, the present value of the derivatives portfolio is constantly changing, resulting in changing KVAs;
(b) the maturity of a derivative can be up to 30 years, requiring the KVA calculation going far into the future;
(c) KVA has to be calculated for each counterparty since netting sets with each counterparty determine the specific counterparty KVA;
(d) complex stress tests for correlated market risk, credit risk and operational risk at a portfolio level have to be performed, which will result in complex, stressed KVA level calculations;
(e) regulations regarding KVA are currently evolving[4] and can be hard to anticipate; and
(f) the implementation date of the KVA regulation is uncertain.

For these reasons, banks are employing sophisticated mathematical models and high computational power to minimise KVA.

MARGIN VALUE ADJUSTMENT

Definition: Margin Value Adjustment (MVA), is a requirement by the Basel committee to post initial margin and variation margin for non-centrally cleared derivatives.

In a 2013 paper, revised 2015 (BCBS 2015b), the committee, together with the International Organization of Securities Commissions (IOSCO), justified its decision that derivatives' counterparties post initial margin and variation margin for non-centrally cleared derivatives, citing: "These non-centrally cleared derivatives, totaling hundreds of trillions of dollars in notional amounts, pose the same type of systemic contagion and spillover risks that materialised in the recent financial crisis." Principally the BCBS is trying to reduce credit risk from derivatives by reducing the number of OTC, so not centrally cleared, derivatives. In a 2015 paper (BCBS 2015b), the Basel Committee proposes that:

1. all standardised OTC derivatives should be traded on exchanges or electronic platforms, where appropriate;
2. all standardised OTC derivatives should be cleared through central counterparties (CCPs);
3. OTC derivatives' contracts should be reported to trade repositories; and
4. non-centrally cleared derivatives contracts should be subject to higher capital requirements.

However, only standardised derivatives can be centrally cleared. For non-standardised, OTC derivatives, the following initial margins must be posted.

Table 15.2 Initial margin for non-centrally cleared derivatives

Asset Class	Initial Margin Requirement (% of notional)
Credit derivatives: 2–5-year duration	5
Credit derivatives: 2–5-year duration	5
Credit derivatives 5+-year duration	10
Commodity derivatives	15
Equity derivatives	15
Foreign-exchange derivatives	6
Interest-rate derivatives: 0–2-year duration	1
Interest-rate derivatives: 2–5-year duration	2
Interest-rate derivatives: 5+-year duration	4
Other	15

Variation margins are more complex in nature since they depend on market variables and therefore change in time. Hence, they can

Table 15.3 Timetable for the MVA implementation

	September 2013 framework	March 2015 revisions
	Initial margin	
Covered entities belonging to a group whose aggregate month-end average notional amount of non-centrally cleared derivatives exceeds:		
€3.0 trillion	1 December 2015 to 30 November 2016 (based on average notional amounts for June, July and August 2015)	1 September 2016 to 31 August 2017 (based on average notional amounts for March, April and May 2016)
€2.25 trillion	1 December 2016 to 30 November 2017 (based on average notional amounts for June, July and August 2016)	1 September 2017 to 31 August 2018 (based on average notional amounts for March, April and May 2017)
€1.5 trillion	1 December 2017 to 30 November 2018 (based on average notional amounts for June, July and August 2017)	1 September 2018 to 31 August 2019 (based on average notional amounts for March, April and May 2018)
€0.75 trillion	1 December 2018 to 30 November 2019 (based on average notional amounts for June, July and August 2018)	1 September 2019 to 31 August 2020 (based on average notional amounts for March, April and May 2019)
Covered entities belonging to a group whose aggregate month-end average notional amount of non-centrally cleared derivatives exceeds €8 billion	From 1 December 2019 onwards (based on average notional amounts for June, July and August of that year)	From 1 September 2020 onwards (based on average notional amounts for March, April and May that year)
	Variation margin	
Covered entities belonging to a group whose aggregate month-end average notional amount of non-centrally cleared derivatives exceeds €3 trillion	1 December 2015	1 September 2016
All other covered entities		1 March 2017

Source: http://www.bis.org/bcbs/publ/d317_summarytable.pdf

be subject to dispute by one or both counterparties. This may be especially the case for illiquid derivatives. The BCBS requires that the counterparties have a "rigorous and robust dispute resolution procedures in place with their counterparty before the onset of a transaction" (BCBS 2015b). The BCBS requires all entities to exchange, on a daily basis, the full amount of variation margin.

The timetable of the MVA implementation can be found in Table 15.3.

Expanding equation (15.9) by including ColVA, KVA, and MVA, we get:

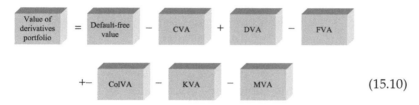 (15.10)

From equation (15.10) we realise that altogether XVAs reduce the value of a derivatives portfolio significantly.

SUMMARY

In this chapter, we discussed XVAs, which are adjustments to the no-default value of a derivatives portfolio, in particular the Basel Accords views on the XVAs.

Credit value adjustment (CVA) is a capital charge to address credit risk in derivatives transactions. CVA has a market-risk component, the netted derivatives value and a credit-risk component, the probability of default of the counterparty. Importantly, these market-risk and credit-risk components are typically correlated! This results in the correlation concepts of wrong-way risk (WWR). The Basel Committee defines two types of WWR:

(a) general WWR, which arises when the probability of default of counterparties is positively correlated with general market-risk factors; and
(b) specific WWR, which exists if the future exposure to a specific counterparty is highly correlated with the counterparty's probability of default.

The Basel Committee requires financial institutions to address WWR: financial institutions have to increase their credit exposure value (calculated without WWR) by 40%. Financial institutions that use their own internal models can apply a 20% increase. This is conservative, since banks report a numerical value for WWR of 1.07 to 1.1.

As CVA, debt value adjustment (DVA) is a capital charge to address credit risk in derivatives transactions. However, it addresses a counterparty's own credit risk. If a counterparty applies DVA, this reduces the credit exposure of the counterparty and leads to an increase in the no-default derivatives portfolio. Applying DVA is highly controversial and has been banned by the Basel Committee in a regulatory environment.

Funding value adjustment (FVA) is an adjustment to the price of a derivative due to the cost of funding the transaction or the related hedge. FVA was quite controversially debated in 2012 and 2013. Finance professors have argued that it creates arbitrage opportunities, since different FVA values lead to different derivatives' prices. However, traders argue, the FVA is a substantial cost and has to be included in the transaction price.

Collateral value adjustment (ColVA) is an adjustment to the no-default value of a derivative for over-the-counter (OTC) – so non-centrally cleared derivatives – if collateral is posted. Depending on what interest rate the counterparty pays on financing the collateral, ColVA can increase or decrease the no-default value of a derivatives portfolio. Collateralisation of OTC derivatives positions will most likely continue to increase in the future, since Basel regulations recognise the credit-risk reduction from collateralisation.

Regulatory capital adjustment (KVA) is an adjustment for the regulatory capital requirement of a derivatives portfolio during the life of the derivative. Regulations regarding KVA are evolving and are hard to anticipate. Stay tuned.

Margin value adjustment (MVA) is an adjustment proposed by the Basel Committee, which requires derivatives' counterparties to post initial margin and variation margin for non-centrally cleared derivatives. The initial margin ranges from 5% to 15%, depending on the type of derivative. The full amount of variation margin has to be exchanged between the counterparties on a daily basis.

Collectively, these adjustments are known as XVAs. They can add up to millions of dollars and are labour- and cost-intensive. They reduce the non-default value of a derivatives portfolio significantly.

Questions for Chapter 15

Answers to these questions can be found at the end of this book.

1. CVA is an important concept of credit risk. What is CVA? Why is it important?
2. Why can CVA be considered a complex derivative?
3. How can CVA without correlation between market risk and credit risk be calculated?
4. Including the correlation between market risk and credit, the concept of WWR arises. What is general WWR? What is specific WWR?
5. Name two examples of specific WWR.
6. How does the Basel Committee address WWR?
7. What is DVA? Should DVA be allowed to be applied in financial practice?
8. What is FVA? Should FVA be included into the pricing of derivatives?
9. Why does the Basel not require to have all derivatives centrally cleared?
10. Explain why ColVA can increase or decrease the value of a derivatives portfolio.
11. Why is KVA one of the most complex XVAs?
12. The variation margin of MVA can be a source of dispute between counterparties. Why?

---

1 Even more XVAs are in the making. An economic value adjustment to address potential economic capital loss, TVA (tax value adjustment) and RVA (replacement value adjustment) for replacing a derivative are currently being discussed.
2 A haircut is the difference between the current market value of an asset and the lower value of that asset when used as collateral. The haircut reflects the potential loss in value of the asset when it is pledged in the event of default.

3 In-the-money means that the present value of the derivative is positive. Out-of-the-money means that the present value of the derivative is negative.
4 See the critical Basel paper "Fundamental review of the trading book [FRTB]: A revised market risk framework" from October 2013, as well as a mathematical paper on the FRTB-CVA framework: "Review of the Credit Valuation Adjustment Risk Framework" from July 2015. We will discuss the FRTB in the next chapter.

16

Fundamental Review of the Trading Book

"There is no such thing as free regulation"
– John Hutton

Starting in May 2012, the Basel Committee on Banking Supervision (BCBS) published several papers on the Fundamental Review of the Trading Book (FRTB) proposing major changes to capital requirements for market risk. In 2015 the FRTB was enhanced with the "FRTB-CVA [credit value adjustment] framework" (BCBS 2015). We will discuss this latest version here. The key issues of the FRTB-CVA framework are as follows.

(a) After about 20 years of applying VaR (value-at-risk) with a 99% confidence level and a 10-day horizon, now the expected shortfall (ES) on a 97.5% confidence level for different liquidity time horizons is applied. We will discuss this change in detail below.

(b) Six risk types are determined: (1) equity risk (2) interest-rate risk, (3) foreign-exchange risk (FX), (4) counterparty credit spread risk, (5) reference credit spread risk and (6) commodity risk. For each risk type ES (expected shortfall) has to be derived daily on a 97.5% one-tailed confidence level for different time horizons. ES also has to be derived for a period of significant stress.

(c) The FRTB-CVA framework addresses the credit exposure part of CVA. Future potential volatility (termed "variability") of the credit exposure is newly implemented, which is directly related to market prices.[1] Volatility of the credit exposure is critical because in 2008 major losses came from adjustments to derivatives values, not counterparty defaults. We will also discuss this below.

(d) Since the increase in correlation within and between markets was highly underestimated in the 2007–9 crises, the FRTB includes numerous correlations within the risk-type buckets, between the risk types, correlations between credit spread of a counterparty and systematic factor, and correlations between the credit spread of a counterparty and the associated hedge, see equation (16.7) below.

(e) Hedges are recognised in the calculation of CVA, encouraging banks to hedge their credit exposure; see equation (16.7) below.

(f) As in previous versions, two approaches to calculate CVA are available: (i) an internal model approach (IMA-CVA) for sophisticated banks and (ii) the standardised approach (SA-CVA) for typically smaller, less sophisticated banks.

(g) Delta and vega risk of an option are part of CVA in the FRTB, however not the gamma of an option in order to reduce computational complexity.[2] In addition, default risk is not explicitly part of the CVA calculation since it is accounted for in the credit value-at-risk (CVaR); see Chapter 14. Default risk is also accounted for with an additional default risk charge (BCBS 2016). Not recognised in the FRTB is DVA (debt value adjustment), which we discussed in Chapter 15.

(h) The FRTB envisions clearer and less arbitrary boundaries between the trading book[3] and the banking book. Banks had previously engaged in "regulatory arbitrage", often putting positions into the trading book since it requires less regulatory capital.

(i) The implementation of the FRTB is scheduled for 2019. However, several banks have commented that they not ready to comply with the FRTB by 2019, so a delay is possible.

REPLACING VAR WITH ES – A GOOD IDEA?

The Basel Committee had quantified market risk for the last 20 years with the VaR concept, which we discussed in Chapter 1. In the FRTB, the Basel Committee is now requiring banks to use the expected shortfall (ES) measure. Let us discuss if this is a good idea. What is ES? ES can be defined as the average loss when exceeding value-at-risk (VaR).

Hence, we have

$$ES = E(L|L > VaR) \tag{16.1}$$

where E: Expected value and L: Loss.

Equation 16.1 reads: ES is the expected loss, given that the loss is bigger than VaR.

Let us look at VaR and ES in an example in Figure 16.1.

As we discussed in Chapter 1,

$$VaR_p = \sigma_p \alpha \sqrt{x} \tag{16.2}$$

where VaR_p is the portfolio VaR, α is the x-axis value representing a certain confidence level and x is time in days. Correlations between the asset returns in the portfolio are incorporated in the portfolio standard deviation σ_p; see Chapter 1.

Conveniently, for a standard normal distribution the x-axis units are in standard deviations σ. Assuming $x = 1$, if follows from equation (16.2) that in the ideal case of a standard normally distributed profit and loss, $VaR_p = \alpha$.

From equation (16.1) we see that ES is the average loss exceeding VaR. Hence it is the area exceeding VaR. So we can write

$$ES = \frac{1}{n} \sum_{i=1}^{n} l_i f_i \quad \text{with } |l_i| > VaR \tag{16.3}$$

where l_i is the i-th loss, and f_i is the frequency of the i-th loss

So for the example of Figure 16.1 we have

$$ES = 1/10 \times (5 \times 5 + 6 \times 4 + 8 \times 2) = 6.5$$

So how do we interpret VaR = 4 and ES = 6.5 in our example 16.1? Let us assume $\alpha = 2.33$, which represents a 99% confidence level for a normal distribution (assuming x =1, then VaR = $\alpha \sigma$, so VaR = 2.33 × 1.7167 = 4, as in Figure 16.1). Let us also assume the units in example 16.1 are in millions of US$ and $x = 1$.

Since VaR is the maximum we can lose for a certain confidence level, we conclude that we are 99% sure that on average we will not lose more than US$4 million a day. Since ES is the average loss exceeding VaR, we conclude that, whenever we have a loss exceeding VaR, on average this loss will be US$6.5 million. Note that ES will always be bigger or equal than VaR.

Figure 16.1 VaR as the distance (not area) from the mean 0 to –4 for a certain confidence level. ES is the average loss exceeding VaR, ie, the average of the black losses (calculated below).

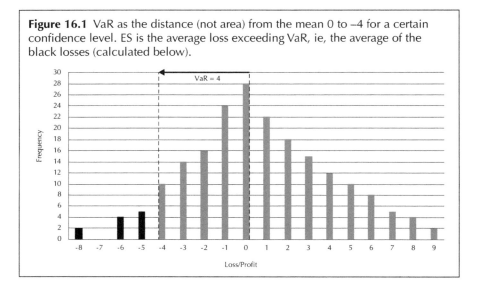

Loosely speaking, VaR tells us: "How bad it will get in good times" and ES tells us: "How bad it will get in bad times". Since the Basel Accord is interested in minimising extreme losses, we can say that it is a good idea that Basel switched from the VaR concept to ES.

More mathematically, ES has a number of advantages over VaR. Most importantly, it satisfies subadditivity. This means that the risk of a portfolio R must be smaller than or equal to the risk of the individual positions, ie, $R(A + B) \leq R(A) + R(B)$. It can be shown that VaR does not necessarily satisfy subadditivity. We recommend the original articles by Artzner *et al* (1997) and (1999) and a good educational paper by Yamai and Yoshiba (2002) for details.

Converting VaR into ES

For a normal distribution, conveniently, ES is just a scalar multiple of VaR see Figure 16.2.

How can we derive VaR-α levels and their corresponding ES α-levels? For VaR, the α-level can be derived by inverting the (cumulative) standard normal distribution (finding x-axis values ie, α-values for given y-axis confidence values).[4] This can be done with =normsinv(confidence level) in Excel or norminv(confidence level) in MATLAB. For example, =normsinv(0.95) = 1.6449;

Figure 16.2 ES as a scalar multiple of VaR. For a confidence level of 95%, hence a significance level s = 5%, α (VaR) = 1.65. The corresponding α (ES) = 2.06. Table 16.1 shows corresponding α-levels for critical confidence levels with four decimals.

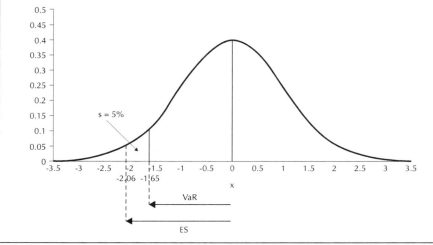

Table 16.1 Corresponding VaR-α and ES-α levels for certain confidence levels.

	VaR	ES
α(95%) =	1.6449	2.0627
α(97.5%) =	1.9600	**2.3378**
α(99%) =	**2.3263**	2.6652
α(99.9%) =	3.0902	3.3673

compare Table 16.1 or Figure 16.2. See the spreadsheet www.dersoft.com/epsilon.xlsx for details.

ES is the average loss when exceeding VaR. So to derive ES α-levels from certain VaR α-levels, we have to take all the VaR α-levels that exceed a specific significance level, and average them. The result is in Table 16.1 and the derivation can be found in the spreadsheet www.dersoft.com/VaRESconversion.xlsx (case-sensitive).

To quantify market risk, the Basel Committee is moving from a 99% VaR confidence level to a 97.5% ES confidence level (BCBS 2013). On first sight, this does not seem like a big change, since, for normal distributions, a 99% VaR confidence level corresponds to an

$\alpha = 2.3263$, and a 97.5% ES confidence level corresponds to an $\alpha = 2.3378$; see bold numbers in Table 16.1. However, for distributions with fatter tails, ES α-levels of 2.3378 can result in much higher loss derivations than VaR α-levels of 2.3263.

BASEL'S NEW LIQUIDITY-ADJUSTED ES CALCULATION FOR MARKET RISK

In December 2014, the BCBS outlined a new liquidity time-horizon-based method to calculate ES for banks (BCBS 2014).

The BCBS defines five risk categories $j = 1 \ldots 5$, each having a different liquidity time horizons (Column 3 in Table 16.2). Also, five risk factors are defined: (1) equity risk, (2) interest-rate risk, (3) credit-spread risk, (4) FX risk and (5) commodity risk. Each risk factor has subsets, ie, risk-factor variables (see Column 2 in

Table 16.2 Risk categories j and their associated risk factors variables and time horizon

Risk Categories $j = 1 \ldots 5$	Risk-factor variables	Liquidity time horizon (in days)
j = 1	Equity price (large cap) Interest rate – domestic currency of bank FX rate – liquid currency pairs	10
j = 2	Equity price (small cap) Equity price (small cap) volatility Credit spread – sovereign (IG) FX rate (other currency pairs) Precious-metal price	20
j = 3	Interest rate ATM volatility Interest rate (other than yields and ATM volatility) Credit spread – sovereign (HY) Credit spread – corporate (IG) FX volatility FX (other) Energy price volatility Precious-metal price volatility Other commodities price	60
j = 4	Equity (other) Equity price (small cap) volatility Credit spread – corporate (HY) Other commodities price volatility Commodity (other)	120
j = 5	Credit spread – structured (cash and CDS) Credit (other)	250

Table 16.2). Each risk-factor variable is associated with a certain liquidity time horizon, hence falls into a certain risk category. Table 16.2 clarifies this concept.

Banks now have to find a historically stressed time period, and perform five simulations from data of the stressed period. Each simulation will result in an $ES_j j = 1 \ldots 5$. This gives equation (16.4):

$$ES = \sqrt{(ES_1)^2 + \sum_{j=1}^{5}\left(ES_j \sqrt{\frac{LH_j - LH_{j-1}}{T}}\right)^2} \qquad (16.4)$$

where LH_j is the liquidity time horizon of risk category j and T is set by the Basel Accord to 10 days.

The five expected shortfalls ES_1 to ES_5 are derived by:

1. changing all risk-factor variables, each for a 10-day period from the historically stressed time period; this will be ES_1 (see equation (16.4));
2. keeping the risk factors variables in risk category $j = 1$ constant and changing the risk factors in risk categories $j = 2$ … 5, for a 20-day period from the historically stressed time period; this will be ES_2 (see equation (16.4));
3. keeping the risk factors' variables in risk category $j = 1$ and 2 constant and changing the risk factors in risk categories $j = 3$ … 5, for a 60-day period from the historically stressed time period; this will be ES_3 (see equation (16.4));
4. keeping the risk factors' variables in risk category $j = 1, 2,$ and 3 constant and changing the risk factors in risk categories $j = 4$ and 5, for a 120-day period from the historically stressed time period; this will be ES_4 (see equation (16.4)); and
5. keeping the risk factors' variables in risk category $j = 1, 2, 3$ and 4 constant and changing the risk factors in risk category $j = 5$, for a 250-day period from the historically stressed time period; this will be ES_5 (see equation (16.4)).

While in the past, VaR and ES were calculated over consecutive one-day time horizons, the Basel Accord now requires 10-day time horizons that are overlapping. The first time horizon is day 0 to day 10, the second is from day 1 to day 11, the third is from day 2 to day 12 and the last is from day 249 to day 259. A spreadsheet-deriving

ES of equation (16.4) can be found at www.dersoft.com/ESinFRTB.xlsm (case-sensitive).

Properties of the ES concept
- If the first day is noted as day 0, then the last day for a simulation for ES is day 249. Since ES5 has to be calculated for 250 days forward, roughly two years of stressed data is necessary to derive ES.
- Risk-factor variables with a long liquidity time horizon are mathematically overweighted in equation (16.4), since $LH_j - LH_{j-1}$ is higher eg, for a risk-factor variable in risk category $j = 5$, $LH_j - LH_{j-1} = 250$; for a risk variable in risk category $j = 1$, $LH_j - LH_{j-1} = 10$. In addition, risk-factor variables' changes in risk category 5 are incorporated in all simulations (1) to (5), whereas risk-factor variables in lower risk categories are not. However, this mathematical overweighting is compensated by the fact that risk-factor variables with a longer time horizon change less often. For example, the credit spread of a company may not change in months, whereas equity prices change every second.
- As mentioned above, the Basel Accords do not use a 1-day time horizon, but a 10-day horizons for calculating ES. These 10-day horizons are overlapping since the first simulation is between day 0 and day 10, the second between day 1 and day 11, the third between day 2 and day 12, etc. As a consequence, extreme changes in the risk-factor variables are amplified, resulting in high and volatile ES values.
- How do correlations enter the ES derivation? Conveniently, ES in equation (16.4) is derived by empirical data, not a mathematical model. Therefore, correlations between the risk-factor variables are implicitly incorporated in the ES derivation.
- Equation (16.4) outlines the general concept for deriving ES for the internal model approach (IMA). A simpler derivation of CVA is available for mostly smaller banks in the standardised approach (SA). Many other provisions exist. For example, banks are required to derive a partial ES for every risk category by shocking the risk-factor variables. These potential shocks can be found in the spreadsheet www.dersoft.com/ESinFRTB.xlsm (cells I11 to M11).

What to make of the new ES concept? Well, the overlapping 10-day time periods are conceptually somewhat inconsistent since, as mentioned, they lead to volatile ES values. Having the old-fashioned one-day time horizons is a more rigorous approach, since there is no overlapping.

Banks have complained about the computational complexity of the new ES approach. Indeed, ES has to be derived on a daily basis, shocked partial ES values have to be calculated, backtesting and stress-testing have to be performed, etc. The pendulum typically over-swings in both ways. While there was too little regulation before the 2007–9 global financial crises, the current Basel regulation seems like an overkill. In addition, US banks also have to deal with Dodd–Frank regulation. It is a 2,300-page paper with an additional roughly 20,000 pages of supporting content published by the regulatory agencies!

THE CAPITAL CHARGE K FOR CVA

In a 2015 paper, the Basel Committee outlined a new concept for the CVA in the FRTB framework and a precise derivation of the capital charge K for CVA (BCBS 2015). Let us first clarify. In Chapter 14, we discussed CVaR. Is it a VaR-based concept to measure the credit risk in standard exposures such as bonds and loans. The CVA is an ES-based concept that derives credit risk in a derivatives transaction.

Three key features in the new FRTB-CVA concept are as follows.

1. Basel defines CVA as "the risk of losses arising from changing CVA values in response to changes in counterparty credit spreads and market risk factors that drive market prices of derivative transactions" (BCBS 2015). The incorporation of changes to market risk factors (equity risk, interest-rate risk, FX risk, credit-spread risk and commodity risk) that drive the credit exposure volatility (termed "variability" in the Accord), is a new element in the calculation of CVA. We outlined the CVA composition in Chapter 15, equation (15.2):

$$CVA_{a,c} = f\left(\underbrace{D^+_{a,c}}_{\text{Market risk}} , \underbrace{PD_c}_{\text{Credit risk}} \right) \quad (15.2)$$

where $D^+_{a,c}$ is the netted positive derivatives value of counterparty 'a' with counterparty c, and PD_c is the default probability of counterparty c. Equations (16.5) to (16.8) below will show how exactly the capital charge for CVA is derived.

2. The Basel Accord recognises that the increase in correlations was underestimated in the Basel II accord: "As the recent crisis demonstrated, reliance on historical correlations … in the market risk metric may materially underestimate 'true' risk in certain cases" (BCBS 2013). Consequently, numerous Pearson correlations between the risk types (equity risk, interest-rate risk, FX risk, commodity risk, counterparty-credit-spread risk and reference asset credit-spread risk) and within the risk types, as well as correlations between credit spread of a counterparty and systematic factor, and correlations between the credit spread of a counterparty and the associated hedge, are part of the CVA capital charge.

3. Direct hedges and indirect hedges as well as index hedges (mostly credit default swaps (CDSs)) are for the first time recognised in the CVA derivation and reduce the CVA capital charge K.

These three components result in several equations:

$$K = \underbrace{K_{EE}}_{\text{Market risk}} + \underbrace{K_{spread}}_{\text{Credit risk}} \qquad (16.5)$$

where

K is the CVA capital charge
K_{EE} is the contribution to EE (expected exposure) variability (ie, the market risk component)
K_{spread} is the contribution of credit spread variability (ie, the credit risk component).

Equation (16.5) is related to equation (15.2), displayed above. Equation (15.2) outlines the components of CVA, whereas equation (16.5) will result, together with the following equations, in a precise derivation of the new capital charge K for CVA.

As already mentioned above, the Basel Accord recognises hedges when calculating the capital charge K for CVA. For banks which do not hedge CVA, the credit risk part of CVA, K_{spread} is derived by equation

$$K_{spread}^{unhedged} = \sqrt{\underbrace{\left(\rho \sum_c S_c\right)^2}_{\text{Systematic part}} + \underbrace{(1-\rho^2)\sum_c S_c^2}_{\text{Idiosyncratic part}}} \qquad (16.6)$$

where

S_c is the EAD, exposure at default, over all derivatives netting sets with counterparty c

ρ is the Pearson correlation between the credit spread of the counterparty c and the systematic factor. Hence as indicated in equation (16.6), the capital charge K for the unhedged credit spread includes a systematic and idiosyncratic part.

One key innovation in the new Basel Accord is that if the credit spread K_{spread} is hedged, banks can include the hedges in the derivation of K_{spread}. This results in a rather complicated equation (16.7).

$$K_{spread} = \sqrt{\underbrace{\left[\rho\sum_c\left(S_c - \sum_{h\in c} r_{hc}S_h^{SN}\right) - \sum_i S_i^{ind}\right]^2}_{\text{Systematic part}} + \underbrace{(1-\rho^2)\sum_c\left(S_c - \sum_{h\in c} r_{hc}S_h^{SN}\right)^2}_{\text{Idiosyncratic part}} + \underbrace{\sum_{h\in c}(1-r_{hc}^2)(S_h^{SN})^2}_{\substack{\text{Ensures that}\\ K_{spread}\text{ is} >0\\ \text{in case of}\\ \text{indirect hedges}}}} \qquad (16.7)$$

where S_c and ρ are defined as in equation (16.6)

$h \in c$: hedges with counterparty c

r_{hc}: Pearson correlation between the credit spread of counterparty c and the credit spread of a single-name hedge h of counterparty c.

S_h^{SN}: Price of a single name (SN) hedge, weighed by the Basel Accord with respect to the risk of sector, ranging from 4.1% to 10.2% for investment grade counterparts.

S_i^{ind}: Price of index hedge i.

Properties of equation (16.7)

1. As we can see from equation (16.7), hedges are deducted from the calculation of the capital charge K for CVA and therefore reduce K. In addition, the Basel Accord recognises the quality of the hedge: the correlations between the credit spread of the counterparty c and the credit spread of the hedge, ie, the ratios r_{hc}, determined by the Basel Accord, are:

❑ r_{hc} = 100% if the hedge references the counterparty c directly;
❑ r_{hc} = 80% if the hedge has legal relation to c; and
❑ r_{hc} = 50% if the hedges shares sector and region with the c.

2. If at least one of the hedges with the counterparty c is indirect (50% or 80%), this means that at least one correlation ratio r_{hc} is < 0. Then the third term on the right-hand side of equation (16.7) will be > 0 and K_{spread} will be > 0. This is desired, since in case of indirect hedges, K_{spread} should be > 0.
3. Following the Basel Accord, the price of an index hedge S_i^{ind} in equation (16.7) has to be multiplied by 0.7, which reduces the efficiency of the hedge by 30%, reflecting the lower correlation between the derivatives position and the index hedge.

The market risk part of the CVA capital charge K_{EE} (see equation 16.5) is simply a scaling of equation (16.6) with a factor β:

$$K_{EE} = K_{spread}^{unhedged} \beta = \left[\sqrt{\left(\rho \sum_c S_c\right)^2 + (1-\rho^2)\sum_c S_c^2} \right] \beta \qquad (16.8)$$

where β is set to 0.5 by the Basel Accord. For a model deriving the CVA capital charge K, see www.dersoft.com/CVAcapitalcharge.xlsx (case-sensitive).

COMPUTATIONAL COMPLEXITY

❑ Banks have to calculate ES of CVA on a daily basis on a 97.5th percentile.
❑ All five risk factors (equity risk, interest-rate risk, FX risk, credit-spread risk and commodity risk) have to be modelled including correlations within the risk factors and cross risk-factor correlations (ie, correlation between the risk factors).
❑ Partial expected shortfall values for every one of the six risk types (counterparty credit spread, interest rate, FX, reference credit spread, equity and commodity) have to be calculated.
❑ Banks' internal models must at least capture delta and vega risk.
❑ The market risk factors have to be simulated with stochastic processes for "an appropriate number of paths defined on an appropriate set of future time points" (BCBS 2015).

Assuming 100 daily market scenarios over two years of stress – across the six risk types for specific liquidity horizons, including correlations within and between risk factors, delta and vega simulations, calculated for a specific counterparty and on a portfolio level, including backtesting and stress-testing and collateral agreement with margining – simulations are in the billions, requiring high computer power.

SUMMARY
Starting in 2012, the BCBS (Basel Committee for Banking Supervision) published several papers on what is known as the fundamental review of the trading book (FRTB). Key elements include calculating market risk no longer on a VaR (value-at-risk) concept, but the ES (expected shortfall) concept. This is reasonable since the BCBS is concerned about worst case losses in a crisis, which ES derives.

A further key element of the FRTB is liquidity, which was also a critical problem in the 2007–9 crises. Therefore, ES has to be derived for six different liquidity horizons. Credit spreads of illiquid counterparties are estimated from liquid peers.

Another critical factor in the 2007–2009 crisis was the underestimation of the increase in correlation. Hence when deriving the capital charge K for CVA, numerous Pearson correlations are included: Equity risk, Interest-rate risk, FX risk, commodity risk, counterparty credit spread risk and reference asset credit-spread risk within the risk types, as well as correlations between credit spread of a counterparty and systematic factor, and correlations between the credit spread of a counterparty and the associated hedge.

Banks have complained about the computational complexity of the new FRTB. Indeed, the required stochastic simulations, including market scenarios, risk factors, volatilities, correlations, risk parameters (at least delta and vega), collateral effects and margining, backtesting and stress-testing, can easily go into the billions

Questions for Chapter 16

Answers to these questions can be found at the end of this book.

1. Name five key elements of the FRTB.
2. Explain the variables in $VaR_p = \sigma_p \alpha \sqrt{x}$.
3. Define ES in terms of VaR.
4. How are α-values, ie, x-axis values for a certain confidence levels, derived?
5. In a normal distribution, how can VaR-α values be converted into ES-α values?
6. Is it a good idea that the BCBS abandoned VaR in favour of ES?
7. Which five risk factors does the BCBS require as inputs to calculate market risk?
8. The BCBS applies 10-day overlapping time periods to derive ES. What is the consequence of this approach?
9. Name three critical differences between CVaR and CVA.
10. Name three critical elements in Basel III's new calculation of the capital charge K for CVA.
11. Which correlations are inputs to derive the capital charge K for CVA?

---

1 Let us assume company X buys a put option on Deutsche Bank from company Y. If the market price (stock price) of Deutsche Bank decreases, the put value will increase and with it the credit exposure of company X to company Y.
2 See BCBS 2015. The curvature (=gamma) risk is incorporated when deriving capital requirements for market risk; see also, BCBS 2016.
3 Principally, the trading book includes positions that are held for trading intent, whereas the banking book comprises positions that are expected to be held to maturity.
4 The α-values are derived in the same way we derived ε in Chapter 4 and Chapter 5; and M and Z_i in Chapter 7. See the spreadsheet www.dersoft.com/epsilon.xlsx, for a derivation of ε.

17
The Future of Correlation Modelling

"Solving the right problem numerically beats solving the wrong problem analytically every time"
— Richard Martin

In this chapter, we will discuss new developments and financial modelling, which can be extended to correlation modelling. We will address the application of GPUs (graphical processing units), which allow fast parallel execution of numerically intensive code without the need of mathematical solvency. We will also discuss some new artificial-intelligence approaches such as neural networks and genetic algorithms, as well as fuzzy logic, Bayesian mathematics and chaos theory.

NUMERICAL FINANCE: SOLVING FINANCIAL PROBLEMS NUMERICALLY WITH THE HELP OF GPUS
Some problems in finance are quite complex so that a closed-form solution is not available. For example, path-dependent options such as American-style options principally have to be evaluated on a binomial or multi-nominal tree, since we have to check at each node of the tree if early exercise is rational. In risk management, especially in credit risk management, thousands of correlated default risks have to be evaluated. While there are simple approximate measures to model counterparty risk in a portfolio such as the Gaussian copula model (see Chapters 6 and 7), it is more rigorous to model counterparty risk on a multifactor approach using numerical methods such as Monte Carlo simulation.

In the recent past, the increase of computer power has made "numerical finance" an alternative to analytical solutions. Let us define it. Numerical finance solves financial problems with numerical methods (such as Monte Carlo simulation), without the need of mathematical solvency. Other terms for numerical finance are "statistical finance", "computational finance" and also "econophysics". More narrowly defined, econophysics is the combination of physical concepts and economics. However, the economic concepts include stochastic processes and their uncertainty, which are also an essential part of finance.

> "Why waste good technology on science and medicine"
> – Light-hearted phrase of Gamers on GPU technology

GPU technology

GPU is a technology that alters memory in a parallel execution of commands to instantaneously produce high-resolution, three-dimensional images. The GPU technology was derived in the computer gaming industry, where gamers request high-resolution, instant response of their 3D activities at low cost. This had caught the attention of the financial industry, which is paying millions to receive real-time response for valuing complex financial transactions and risk-management sensitivities.

Hence, over time, financial software providers have started to rewrite their mathematical code to make it applicable for the GPU environment. Companies such as Murex, SciComp, Global Valuation Limited, Hanweck Associates, BNP Paribas and many others have implemented GPU-based infrastructures to numerically solve complex derivatives transactions and calculate risk parameters. The academic environment has also responded. More than 600 universities worldwide offer courses in GPU programming.

A GPU model for valuing portfolio counterparty risk

Albanese *et al* (2011) display a detailed approach, which applies GPU technology to model counterparty risk in a portfolio. These portfolios typically consist of thousands of counterparties whose default and transition probabilities are correlated. To evaluate this complex counterparty risk in a rigorous way, numerical methods are necessary. The model consists of the following steps.

1. The portfolio data, ie, the contracts of the loans, swaps, CDSs, FX contracts, options, futures and so forth, with each counterparty are netted[1] and input into the model.
2. The stochastic processes of the underlying input variables

THE FUTURE OF CORRELATION MODELLING

such as interest rates, exchange rates, default intensities and CDS contracts are generated.

3. Parallelised pricing of the contracts is done using multi-threading[2] technology in a GPU framework.
4. The model is calibrated using a large number of liquid assets and derivatives. It is tested whether backward induction or Monte Carlo forward induction gives the better calibration results.
5. Correlations are integrated in the model via dynamic multi-factor copulas; see Chapter 7, "Extensions of the OFGC".
6. GPU technology allows real-time 3D visualisation of the output.

Figure 17.1 shows the model in graphical form.

Benefits of GPUs
(a) Speed: The main benefit of the GPU technology is speed. Thousands of parallel executing cores are implemented in a GPU, whereas a CPU, the central processing unit of a

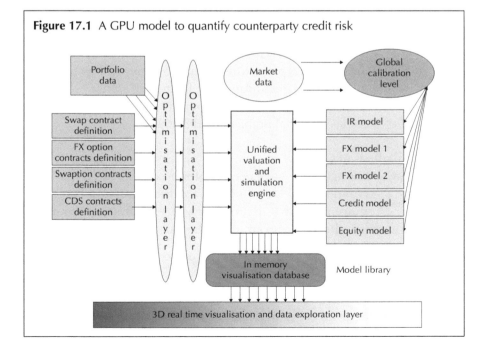

Figure 17.1 A GPU model to quantify counterparty credit risk

standard PC, has just multiple cores (as of 2018). Most software providers claim that the GPUs are 20 to 100 times faster than their rival CPUs. In addition, CPU applications and fast GPU technology have been combined in the recent past to easily implement standard CPU applications at high speed.

(b) Increasing user-friendliness: Special languages to execute financial code in the GPU framework as CUDA (compute unified device architecture) as well as OpenGL (open graphics library) and OpenCg (C stands for the computer language and g for graphics), have been developed, specifically designed for parallel computing in the GPU framework.

(c) Structural efficiency: CPU technology typically depends on a compiler, which translates the source code into an executable language. The GPU languages such as CUDA, OpenGL and OpenCg may be more difficult to program, but do not require compiling. Therefore, manipulation of the language code – for example, stress testing or optimisation – can be easily and quickly achieved.

(d) More precision? Advocates of the GPU technology claim that "you can eat the cake and have it too", meaning GPUs are faster and at the same time more accurate. The faster speed is evident. However, the question whether parallel iterative search procedures are more accurate than standard mathematical techniques as finite difference methods, vector-splitting techniques, Fourier transforms, etc to solve complex financial problems is debatable.

Limitations of GPUs

(a) Although there have been efforts to combine CPU and GPU technology, GPUs still have a different architecture and require their own distinct structure of programming and specialised programming languages such as CUDA, OpenGL and OpenCg.

(b) GPUs provide efficient and fast solutions for problems that are complex but can be represented in matrices, since matrix multiplication and manipulation is easy to execute. However, for nonlinear, path-dependent structures, GPUs may not be well suited.

Altogether, the GPU technology is a promising new approach to derive fast, real-time results for complex financial problems, for which analytical solutions are questionable or not at all available. However, one can argue that, if mathematical techniques are available, they should, although slower, have preference over brute-force, non-analytical, iterative search procedures.

NEW DEVELOPMENTS IN ARTIFICIAL INTELLIGENCE AND FINANCIAL MODELLING

We will now discuss new developments in artificial intelligence (AI) such as neural networks and genetic algorithms. We will also investigate whether related areas such as Bayesian probabilities, fuzzy logic and chaos theory are promising tools for financial modelling.

What is AI? Typically, it is not a good idea to define a term and use that same term in the definition. But let us do it anyway: AI is the attempt to create AI. Less ironical: AI is the science of creating intelligent machines. One of the most successful concepts to create AI comprises neural networks.

Neural networks

Neural networks are the most widely applied AI concept in finance. Neural networks are typically used in trading and investing, trying to forecast prices and volatilities of stocks, bonds, exchange rates etc. Several companies, such as Tradecicion and BrainMaker, offer specific neural network software to make financial predictions. Neural networks are also applied in derivatives pricing and credit risk management. Two types of neural networks currently exist.

1. Biological neural networks, consist of living systems with neurons (a nerve cell), whose electrical or chemical information is transmitted to other neurons via synapses.
2. Our interest is mainly in artificial neural networks (ANNs). An ANN is a nonliving system, which tries to mimic the functioning of the human brain, in particular the ability to learn.

The learning process in an ANN can be achieved by different methods. One of the most popular is "backpropagation", which applies weighting factors. Each weighting factor has a resistance attached to it. Numerous simulations (epochs) of different combinations of weighting factors are run. If the neural network output is close to the target value, the weighting factors are strengthened, ie, the resistance is turned down. If certain weighting factors produce bad results, the weighting factors are weakened, ie, the resistance is turned up.

Meissner and Kawano (2001) show that a neural network can improve option pricing. The applied Neural Network is the popular multilayer perceptrons (MLPs) network, which can be mathematically expressed as

$$y_{NN} = \sum_{h=1}^{H} \beta_h T \sum_{i=1}^{n} w_{ih} x_i \qquad (17.1)$$

where

y_{NN}: Output of the neural network (the option price)
β_h: Weighting factor of layer node h_j, which reflects the strength between h_j and the output y_{NN} (see Figure 17.2)
T: Transfer function, usually a simple hyperbolic function such as the tangent function. This function standardises weighted input variables to values between -1 and $+1$.
w_{ih}: Weighting factor of input x_i, which reflects the strength between input x_i and the hidden layer node h (see Figure 17.2)
x_i: Input variable i (the spot/strike S/K, option maturity T, implied volatility (and interest rate r)

Graphically, an MLP neural network can be expressed as in figure 17.2.

Using backwardation techniques together with a Garch (see Chapter 9, "Dynamic conditional correlations") produced volatility, Meissner and Kawano (2001) show that a neural network can learn to produce the volatility smile of options, which is observed in reality. Hence the neural network gives better option pricing results than the standard Black–Scholes–Merton model.

Within the ANN framework we differentiate two types of network: traditional supervised networks and unsupervised, creative, self-learning networks.

In a traditional supervised learning network, the input data is typically "labelled", ie, engineers provide the network with information about the input. For example, when trying to visually diagnose a melanoma, the engineers provide the network with

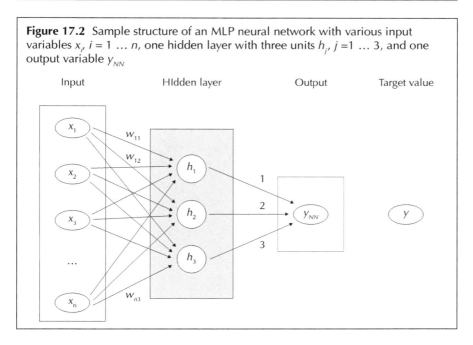

Figure 17.2 Sample structure of an MLP neural network with various input variables x_i, $i = 1 \ldots n$, one hidden layer with three units h_j, $j = 1 \ldots 3$, and one output variable y_{NN}

information such as edges, colours, size, depths, etc of a melanoma. The network then first targets the first representation in the first network layer, for example edges. After correctly identifying those, the result is fed into the second layer, which tries to identify another representation, for example colour. After successfully identifying colour, the first- and second-layer results are fed into the third layer and so on. Figure 17.3 shows the procedure.

Traditional, supervised neural networks can be powerful; however, they require human input and constant human supervision. This drawback has led to unsupervised neural networks, which resemble human learning more closely: a two-year-old child realises when it spills a cup that the liquid disseminates and Mum yells, learning on its own about physical and social processes.

Unsupervised neural networks typically work with unlabelled data, meaning they freely analyse and identify objects. For example, in medicine, largely unsupervised neural networks have been applied in diagnosis, particularly in dermatology. In a 2017 study by Esteva *et al* a dataset of 129,450 clinical images with two critical binary classifications – keratinocyte carcinomas versus benign seborrheic keratosis, and malignant melanomas versus benign nevi

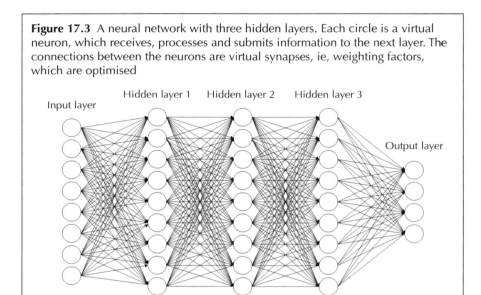

Figure 17.3 A neural network with three hidden layers. Each circle is a virtual neuron, which receives, processes and submits information to the next layer. The connections between the neurons are virtual synapses, ie, weighting factors, which are optimised

– were tested. The deep neural networks achieved performance on par with 21 board-certified dermatologists.[3]

Besides diagnosis, deep-learning networks can also help in finding causes for illnesses, since they are very capable of discovering hidden associations between variables. For example, a deep-learning network could screen millions of data of Alzheimer patients and try to find new correlations between Alzheimer's and genetic, medical, physical, environmental and social records of the patient.

In finance, deep-learning networks are applied to various problems. They try to identify whether a market downturn is a small correction or the start of a long term down trend. Similarly they try to identify if an upward move is a false breakout or the start of a long term upward trend.

Since neural networks are also very capable of finding associations, they try to find correlations between an asset price and determining factors such as fundamental factors (PE ratio, EPS, dividend yield, for instance) and technical factors (MACD (moving average convergence divergence), RSI (relative strength index), momentum etc) (Meissner, Alex and Nolte, 2003).[4]

Numerous other research on neural networks and option pricing exists such as Rubinstein (1985), Freisleben and Ripper (1997), White, Hatfield and Dorsey (1998), Yao, Yili and Tan (2000) and Gradojevic, Gencay and Kukolj (2009). However, most neural networks in finance are applied to simply forecasting stock prices, option prices, mutual fund values etc, often based on finding technical analysis patterns. For a good overview on neural networks applied in finance, although a bit outdated, see Fadlalla and Lin (2001).

Limitations of neural networks
Naturally neural networks have their drawbacks. First, they often are a "black box", ie, the mathematical or computational algorithm that derives the output can be very complex and can therefore be unknown. Hence trial-and-error methods must be applied. Second, neural networks often have quite slow convergence rates. Third, neural networks can suffer from the reproducibility problem. This means that results cannot be replicated in new simulations. Last and most important, neural networks can get stuck at local optima, not deriving the general optimum. These drawbacks have limited the usage of neural networks in reality.

To overcome these drawbacks, neural networks in the recent past have been combined with other disciplines – for example, fuzzy logic, genetic algorithms and Bayesian statistics – to improve the neural network performance.

Before we discuss those, let us have a look at a recent development, termed "financial networks".

> "Estimating systemic risk in networks of financial institutions represents, today, a major challenge in both science and financial policy making"
>
> Joseph Stiglitz *et al*

Financial networks
Financial networks display the connections and interactions between financial institutions. They are applied in modern portfolio theory (Tola 2005) and in predicting large correlated price moves (Onnela 2003, Khandani and Lo 2011). However, the main application of financial networks lies in finding default associations, in particular trying to find the contagion risk in a systemic downturns (Elliott *et al* 2014, Aldasoro *et al* 2015).

Financial networks typically apply minimum spanning trees, which have three properties:

1. all vertices (ie, nodes) are directly or indirectly connected by edges (which relate to connections between the neurons of a neural network);
2. the total edge weight is minimised; and
3. the minimum spanning tree has no cycles.[5]

Let us look at creating a minimum spanning tree with a financial example.

Example 17.1
Given are five entities, A, B, C, D, E, and their default correlations, possibly derived from historical data. We assume that there is a non-zero default correlation between all entities (see Table 17.1).

Table 17.1 Default correlation $\rho_{i,j}$ among entities A, B, C, D, and E

	A	B	C	D	E
A	1	0.55	0.3	0.1	0.65
B		1	0.5	0.6	0.58
C			1	0.25	0.35
D				1	0.4
E					1

The default correlations in Table 17.1 are now converted into metric distances via equation (17.2)

$$d_{i,j} = \sqrt{2(1-\rho_{i,j})} \qquad (17.2)$$

The derivation of equation (17.2) is in the Appendix. Applying equation (17.2) to Table 17.1, we derive the distance matrix $d_{i,j}$ as shown in Table 17.2.

Table 17.2 Matrix of distances $d_{i,j'}$ derived from Table 17.1 via equation (17.2)

	A	B	C	D	E
A	1	0.95	1.18	1.34	0.84
B		1	1.00	0.89	0.92
C			1	1.22	1.14
D				1	1.10
E					1

THE FUTURE OF CORRELATION MODELLING

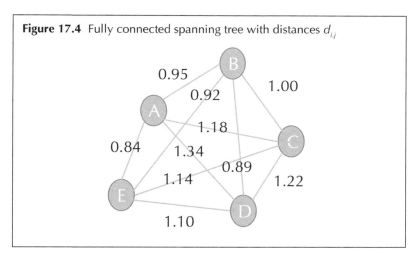

Figure 17.4 Fully connected spanning tree with distances $d_{i,j}$

We now assign the distances $d_{i,j}$ to the entity tree. Since we assumed that there is a non-zero default correlation between all entities, the tree is fully connected (see Figure 17.4).

Importantly, we now have to find the minimum spanning tree, which satisfies the properties (1) to (3) above. There are several optimisation methods to find a minimum spanning tree. One of the easiest is the Kruskal's Algorithm,[6] which consists of two steps:

Step 1: Sort the edges between the vertices in ascending order, see Table 17.3.

Table 17.3 Distances $d_{i,j}$ in ascending order

AE = 0.84
BD = 0.89
BE = 0.92
AB = 0.95
BC = 1.00
DE = 1.10
CE = 1.14
AC = 1.18
CD = 1.22
AD = 1.34

Step 2: Build the minimum spanning tree, starting from the lowest distances, however, avoiding cycles. This gives us Table 17.4.

Table 17.4 Minimum spanning tree MST

AE = 0.84
BD = 0.89
BE = 0.92
~~AB = 0.95~~ (not applied since a cycle ABE would be created)
BC = 1.00
~~DE = 1.10~~ (not necessary, since the MST is finished)
~~CE = 1.14~~ (not necessary, since the MST is finished)
~~AC = 1.18~~ (not necessary, since the MST is finished)
~~CD = 1.22~~ (not necessary, since the MST is finished)
~~AD = 1.34~~ (not necessary, since the MST is finished)

Applying the minimum spanning Table 17.4 to our tree Figure 17.4, we derive Figure 17.4a.

The solution is $S = 0.84 + 0.89 + 0.92 + 1.00 = 3.65$. This is the minimum distance that connects all vertices and avoids cycles.

How is this useful in finance? A minimum spanning tree gives us a convenient visual representation of dependencies between financial variables. In our example of default correlation, the minimum spanning tree shows the most critical default associations. Therefore, in a crisis, these associations are the ones most likely to become contagious. For the minimum spanning tree of

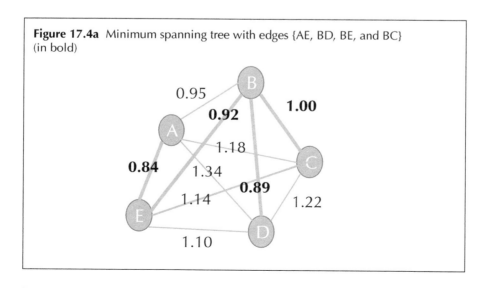

Figure 17.4a Minimum spanning tree with edges {AE, BD, BE, and BC} (in bold)

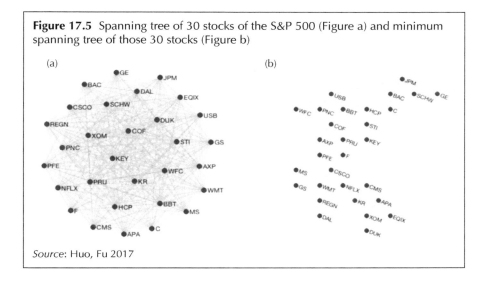

Figure 17.5 Spanning tree of 30 stocks of the S&P 500 (Figure a) and minimum spanning tree of those 30 stocks (Figure b)

Source: Huo, Fu 2017

Figure 17.4a, we can conclude that entity B has high contagion risk, since it is connected to three entities, C, D and E, whereas entity E has two connections, and entities A, C and D have only one connection, ie, lower contagion risk.

In reality, spanning trees (which show all connections) and minimum spanning trees (which show the critical connections) can become quite complex, as seen in Figure 17.5.

Building a spanning tree of all 500 S&P stocks would naturally be more complex and visually quite overwhelming. Therefore, several papers try to reduce the high-dimensional problem with financial networks; see for example Gan and Djauhari (2014) and King and Tidor (2009).

Fuzzy Logic
Fuzzy logic is an exciting field. It alters the traditional concept of reasoning. In traditional logic a statement can either be true, typically assigned with the value 1, or false, assigned with the value 0. Fuzzy logic, however, argues that there can be a "partial truth" to a statement, assigning truth values ranging between 0 and 1.

For example, a professor asks the question: What are the prime numbers between 10 and 20? The correct answer is the set {11, 13, 17, 19}. If a student gives the answer {11, 13, 17}, traditional logic would argue that the answer is false. However, fuzzy logic would argue that the answer is partially true – actually 75% true.

Fuzzy logic has some real-world applications. For example it is applied in Japan to improve the punctuality of trains. If a train is one minute late, fuzzy logic can assign a punctuality value of close to 1 (totally punctual), making no action necessary. The later a train arrives, fuzzy logic can assign gradually lower punctuality values, initiating action for low punctually values as priority access to stations to have the train catch up time. Hence fuzzy logic often applies flexible if–then statements to construct specific, flexible commands to address a problem.

Fuzzy logic can tolerate imprecise information, but lacks learning ability. Therefore, the learning ability of neural networks is often combined with fuzzy logic. In addition, genetic algorithms are often introduced, creating genetic fuzzy neural networks (GFNNs).

Genetic algorithms

Genetic algorithms are based on phenomena found in evolution, such as selection, crossover and mutation.

Each individual or element in a genetic algorithm is defined as a vector with parameters and weights. Selection can be done by various methods: (a) roulette wheel selection, where a random selection of potentially useful solutions for recombining the individuals is performed; (b) crossover method, which creates the next generation by different "crossings" (loosely speaking "combinations") of the parents' organism strings to produce a variety of child organisms. Mutation, ie, a change in the genetic property of an individual, is typically quantified as single-point mutation, meaning only a single nucleotide parameter is replaced by a new parameter. This replacement is performed at a certain mutation rate. For example if the mutation rate is specified as 30%, this means that in 30% of the simulations a mutation will take place.

Genetic fuzzy neural networks

In finance, numerous studies on GFNNs exist. They are mainly applied to forecast stock prices or support trading decisions; see Yu and Zhang (2005), Yang, Wu and Lin (2012), Li and Xiong (2006), Kuo, Chen, and Hwang (2001) or Huang (2008). After learning, most of the GFNN models were able to outperform the benchmark index.

"My book was criticised before it was published, which is a compliment"
– Benoît Mandelbrot

Chaos theory

Another interesting field with potential applications in finance is chaos theory. Chaos theory is a field that studies the behaviour of dynamic systems. It is mainly applied in meteorology to explain and forecast weather dynamics, but is also used to explain phenomena in physics, engineering, biology, economics and finance. The definition of a chaotic system is not unique. However, let us look at the five main criteria of a chaotic system are.

1. Strong dependence on initial conditions
This condition was derived in the famous 1972 paper by the mathematician and meteorologist Edward Lorenz, "Predictability: Does the Flap of a Butterfly's Wings in Brazil set off a Tornado in Texas?". Lorenz argued that a flap of a butterfly in Brazil can influence weather conditions, even cause a tornado in a region very far away. Earlier, in 1961, Lorenz had found that changes in the decimal places from three to six improved the modelling of weather predictions significantly. This strong dependence on initial conditions is one reason for the second criteria of a chaotic system.

2. Predictions are possible for only a short period of time
Clearly this condition applies to modelling weather. Weather can be predicted quite well for a short period of time, for example for 12 hours or 24 hours. However, the longer the time horizon of the prediction – for example, three days or five days – the less predictable weather becomes. For an ever-longer time horizon, for example 15 or 30 days, a reliable forecast is virtually impossible, since the weather system is chaotic in the long term, ie, it is unpredictable.

3. Self-similarity
Chaotic systems typically display self-similarity. This means that an object is similar or exactly the same as parts of the objects, viewed on a different scale. For example a coast line viewed from far often displays the same patterns as the same coastline viewed from very close. Self-similarity is a property of fractals, which were

introduced by Benoît Mandelbrot in 1975. Mandelbrot discovered fractals in many natural phenomena such as mountains, rivers and blood vessels, and also in music, paintings and architecture. Interestingly, Mandelbrot claimed to have found fractals also in stock price movements. In 2004, he published a book with Richard Hudson (Hudson and Mandelbrot 2004), in which the Gaussian distribution on stock price returns is also questioned.

4. Regime changes

Chaotic systems do not behave chaotic all the time. They can, when moving on an attractor, be somewhat predictable. An attractor is a set towards which a variable, according to a mathematical algorithm, evolves over time. Loosely speaking, an attractor attracts a variable to move towards or around the attractor. An attractor can simply be a point, a curve or a surface. Complex attractors with a fractal structure or with non-integer dimensions are called "strange attractors". Figure 17.6 shows a two-dimensional attractor.

Figure 17.6 An example of an attractor: a variable will often stay in one set of rings until a regime change occurs and the variable will move towards a new regime, ie, a different set of rings with different dynamics

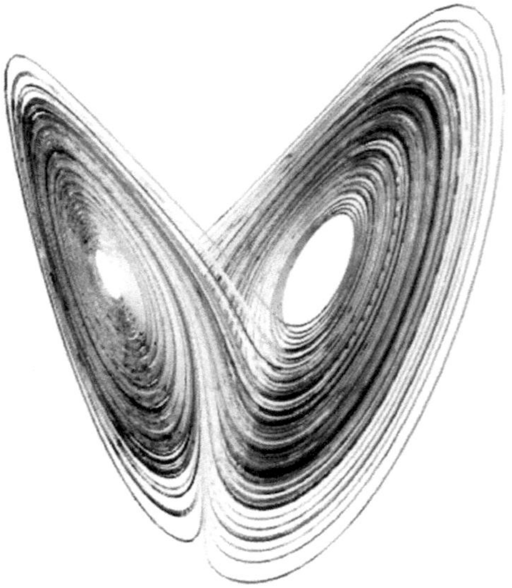

The form of a strange attractor may be close to a butterfly or the number 8 as seen in Figure 17.6.

5. Deterministic nature
A chaotic system is mathematically deterministic. It does not include random factors, such as a random drawing from a certain distribution, which is often applied in finance (compare equations (5.1) and (5.2), equations (9.33) to (9.35)). However, the deterministic nature of chaos theory is not a sufficient condition for a good predictability of the system in the long run.

Chaos theory and finance
Can chaos theory explain and predict phenomena in finance? Criterion 1 of chaos theory is the strong dependence on initial conditions. It is not critical in finance. Low levels of a stock price in t_0 do tend have higher volatilities. For example a stock price moving from 100 by 5 to 105 has a 5% increase. A stock price moving from 10 by 5 to 15, has a 50% increase. In general, though, it is of minor importance at what level the stock price, which we are trying to forecast, is in t_0.

Criterion 2, the possible predictability in the short term, but limited predictability in the long run is also not present in finance. It can even be argued that in this sense finance is "anti-chaotic". Stock market predictions in the short term, for a day or a week, are often more difficult than longer-term predictions, as for example yearly predictions. This is because longer-term stock market movements are based on long-term economic conditions as recessions or economic periods of prosperity.

Criterion 3, the self-similarity can be found in finance. For example, the performance of the Dow Jones Industrial Average (Dow) shows a similar pattern when observed by month, by weekday or intra-day.

From Figures 17.7 to 17.9, we observe the self-similarity property for the Dow performance. Especially the weekday (Figure 17.8) and intra-day performance (Figure 17.9) are similar. A strong performance in the beginning of the time period (Tuesday and 10.30–11.00) then weakens and is followed by a negative performance towards the end (Thursday and 14.00–14.30) with an uptick at the end

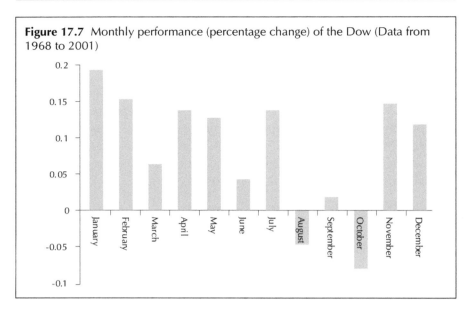

Figure 17.7 Monthly performance (percentage change) of the Dow (Data from 1968 to 2001)

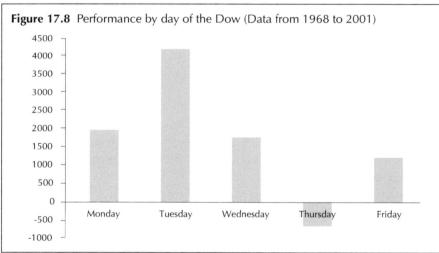

Figure 17.8 Performance by day of the Dow (Data from 1968 to 2001)

(Friday and 15.00–16.00). This is also similar to the monthly performance in Figure 17.7.

Criterion 4, the different regimes in chaos theory translate well to finance. We just call them trends. Long-term upward trends during an economic expansion or long-term downward trends in a recession exist, as well as short-term intra-day upward and

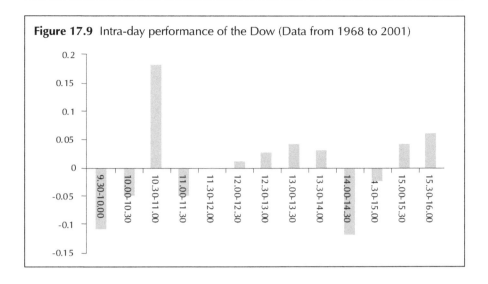

Figure 17.9 Intra-day performance of the Dow (Data from 1968 to 2001)

downward trends. These trends are exploited by traders: "the trend is your friend".

Criterion 5, the deterministic nature of chaos theory is not an adequate property for financial modelling. As mentioned numerous times in this book (see Chapter 5 and equations (5.1) and (5.2) or equations (8.33) to (8.35)), financial variables can be well modelled with a stochastic process.

Conclusion: can we apply chaos theory to model and forecast financial variables?

From our analysis, we find that chaos criteria 3 and 4, the self-similarity principle and the regime change, are also found in finance. However, in criteria 1, 2 and 5, the dependence on initial conditions, the short- but not long-term predictability and the deterministic nature of chaos theory are typically not properties in finance. The critical question is whether criteria 3 and 4 are sufficient to support financial trading decisions.

Some companies believe so. Financial Chaos Theory and Tetrahex, which sells fractal finance software, are using chaos theory to offer trade support. They apply fractal dimensions (for example, the dimension 2.5) and try to find buy-and-sell signals based on deriving technical indicators as such MACD (moving average convergence divergence, which gives buy-and-sell signals when different moving averages cross) as well as identifying trends.

Some research has shown some explanatory power for financial variables using chaotic dynamics such as Trippi (1994) and Peters (1996).

So far no attempt has been made to apply chaos theory for correlation modelling. Since only some of the chaos criteria are appropriate for financial modelling, it is questionable whether chaos theory is a useful tool for correlation modelling. But we are always happy to be proven wrong.

Bayesian probabilities
Bayesian statistics and their probabilities are a further concept with potential application to financial modelling. The Bayesian approach reinterprets and extends the classical probability reasoning. Bayesian probabilities were founded by the English mathematician Thomas Bayes in the 18th century and popularised by the French mathematician and astronomer Pierre Laplace.

At the heart of the Bayesian approach is the Bayes theorem:

$$P(A\,|\,B) = \frac{P(B\,|\,A)P(A)}{P(B)} \qquad (17.3)$$

It is important to note that the Bayesian theorem (17.3) is algebraically identical with the classical, frequentist probability theory (called "frequentist", since it draws its conclusion on the frequency of data). In fact, we had derived equation (17.3) in the Appendix of Chapter 1, in equations (A1 to A3). However, the Bayesian theory reinterprets the variables in equation (17.3).

In frequentist theory, $P(A)$ and $P(B)$ are the probabilities of events A and B, respectively. $P(A\,|\,B)$ is the probability of A, conditional on B occurring or having occurred. $P(B\,|\,A)$ is the probability of B, conditional on the probability on A having occurred. However, in Bayesian theory the variables in equation (17.3) have the following interpretation:

$P(A)$: A prior initial probability. $P(A)$ is the hypothesis before accounting for evidence. $P(A)$ can be a personal subjective belief, rather than an objectively derived probability.

$P(B)$: The probability of the evidence B, which will influence the critical outcome $P(A\,|\,B)$.

$P(A|B)$: The posterior probability. $P(A|B)$ is the probability of A given that the evidence B is observed.

$P(B|A)/P(B)$: Support that B provides for deriving $P(A|B)$.

From these definitions, two main properties follow.

1. In classical probability theory a hypothesis is a proposition, which is either true or false, so the probability of the proposition is 0 or 1. In Bayesian logic, a probability is assigned to a hypothesis (above the hypothesis $P(A)$), which can take truth values between 0 and 1. This adds flexibility to the process of deriving the conditional probabilities. It is related to fuzzy logic, which also applies the concept of partial truth (see "Fuzzy Logic" above).
2. Bayesian logic is a dynamic theory. If new evidence is found (ie, incorporating the values for $P(B)$ and $P(B|A)$), this evidence is incorporated, and a revised outcome $P(A|B)$ is derived. Hence Bayesian theory shows how a subjective belief changes in time following new evidence.

Let us look at an example of Bayesian probability.

Example 17.2
An analyst performs some approximate studies and believes that the default probability of Ford Motor Company is $P(A) = 10\%$. The economy, as in 2008, is in a severe recession and systemic risk exists (see Chapter 1, "How does correlation risk fit into the broader picture of risks in finance?"). The analyst finds new evidence that there is a positive default correlation between General Motors (GM) and Ford. In particular, the conditional default probability of GM if Ford defaults, $P(B|A) = 20\%$. In addition, the default probability of GM, $P(B) = 15\%$. What is the default probability of Ford applying this new evidence? Using Bayes equation (17.3), this new posterior probability $P(A|B)$ is

$$P(A|B) = \frac{P(B|A)P(A)}{P(B)} = \frac{0.2 \times 0.1}{0.15} = 0.13 = 13\%$$

Hence, the initially assumed default probability of 10% for Ford increases to 13% applying the new evidence applied via the Bayes theorem.

Note that, in order to apply the Bayes rule of equation (17.3), a co-dependence of A and B has to be sensible. This means that A has to be dependent on B just as B has to be dependent on A, since if $P(B\,|\,A) \geq 0$, the result $P(A\,|\,B)$ will also be non-zero (assuming $P(A)$ and $P(B)$ are also non-zero).

For example, let $P(A)$ be the default probability of company A, which issues a catastrophe bond. Let $P(B)$ be the probability of the catastrophe (for example a tsunami) occurring. $P(A\,|\,B)$ is the probability of the company default dependent on the catastrophe occurring. $P(A\,|\,B) \geq 0$, since, if the catastrophe occurs, the default probability of company A increases, since it may not be able to pay the insurance claims. However, $P(B\,|\,A) = 0$, since the probability of the catastrophe occurring does not depended on the default probability of the company. Hence in this case, the Bayes rule cannot be applied; see Burke and Meissner (2011) for the valuation of cat bonds.

Bayesian methods have been successfully applied in numerical financial applications such as financial forecasting, risk modelling and inferring financial data such as volatilities and derivatives prices; see Gamerman and Lopes (2006), Rachef et al (2008), Hore (2009), or Quintana et al (2009). While Bayesian methods are useful in fairly simple, one-parameter estimation problems, the drawback of Bayesian methods lies in its limitations to solve complex statistical problems. However, numerical approximations such as maximum entropy, transformation group analysis, reference analysis and sequential Monte Carlo simulation based on particle filtering have enhanced Bayesian methods in the past; see Hore et al (2009) for details.

So far no attempt has been made to use Bayesian methods to model or infer correlations. However, with its flexibility and assisted by advanced numerical methods, Bayesian methods should be able to enhance correlation modelling in the future.

SUMMARY

In this chapter, we discussed new developments in financial modelling, which can be applied to correlation modelling.

One new methodology to solve complex financial problems is to apply GPU (graphical processing units) technology. GPUs have their roots in the computer gaming industry, where gamers receive instant responses for their three-dimensional activities at low cost. Not surprisingly, the GPU technology has been adapted to solve complex financial problems such as evaluating the correlation credit risk of large portfolios or the sensitivities of complex derivatives. The GPU technology implies that the financial problems are solved numerically: for example, with Monte Carlo simulation without the need of mathematical solvency. Advantages of the GPU technology are speed and the special code, which does not require compiling. One of the disadvantages of the GPU technology is the difficulty to handle nonlinear processes. Some quants are generally apprehensive to solve financial problems numerically without an underlying mathematical algorithm.

Neural networks are by far the most widely applied artificial intelligence concept in finance. Neural networks try to mimic the functioning of the human brain and have therefore the ability to learn. The most popular learning technique is 'backpropagation'. If the neural network output is close to the target value, the network strengthens the algorithm that led to successful outcome by increasing weighting factors. Conversely, if an output is far away from the target value, the network weakens the algorithm.

Deep-learning networks try to learn on their own, ie, without labelled data (ie, information) from human beings. Deep-learning neural networks have been applied in finance to identify trends and find associations between an asset price and fundamental and technical data. Limitations of neural networks lie in the fact that the algorithm is hidden and that neural networks can get stuck at local but not general optima.

Financial Networks give a visual representation of the associations among financial variables. They are applied in portfolio management amd stock price forecasting, but primarily in risk management. Typically a spanning tree with all connections between variables is created. To find critical connections, often a minimum spanning tree is derived. In the area of risk management, these critical connections are the ones most likely to become contagious in a crisis.

Fuzzy logic is another interesting field with potential applications for finance. Fuzzy logic alters the traditional concept of truth, in which a statement is either entirely true or entirely false. In particular, fuzzy logic introduces the concept of partial truth. If the question is "What is the natural number set from 1 and 4, including 1 and 4?", the answer is of course the set {1, 2, 3, 4}. If the given answer is {1, 2, 3}, then this would be incorrect under traditional reasoning. However, fuzzy logic would argue that the answer is at least partially true. Fuzzy logic can handle imprecise information well, but lacks the ability to learn. Therefore, it is a good idea to combine fuzzy logic with neural networks. In addition, often generic algorithms are introduced to fuzzy neural networks.

Genetic algorithms apply phenomena found in evolution such as selection, crossover and mutation. Each of these phenomena is expressed as a mathematical algorithm. Selection can be modelled either randomly by sampling from a statistical distribution, or deterministically by applying parametric inputs. Crossover produces the next generation by different combinations of parents' organisms. Mutation, ie, the change in the genetic property, can be achieved by introducing a mutation rate. A high mutation rate parameter means a high rate of mutation from the parents to the next generation, and vice versa.

Several financial studies exist that combine genetic algorithms, fuzzy logic and neural networks, termed GFNN, models. Most GFNN models are able to outperform a benchmark index.

A further interesting field with potential applications to finance is chaos theory. It was developed in the 1960s and 1970s and is typically applied to weather modelling but has also been applied in physics, biology, economics and finance.

Chaos theory has several criteria: (1) strong dependence on initial conditions, as shown in the famous butterfly analogy: the flap of a butterfly in Brazil can potentially cause a tornado in a different continent; (2) predictions are possible for only a short period of time; (3) self-similarity, ie, patterns found when viewing a system from afar can be also found when viewing the system very close; (4) regime change; (5) deterministic nature. Investigating if these criteria apply to finance, we find that the self-similarity principle and the regime change translate well to finance. However, the high dependence on initial conditions, the short- but not long-term predictability and the deterministic nature of chaos theory, do not apply in finance. Nevertheless, some companies provide trading models based on chaos theory, applying foremost the self-similarity principle to forecast short-term and long-term stock price patterns.

Bayesian statistics and their probabilities are a further concept with potential application to financial modelling. The Bayesian approach reinterprets and extends the classical probability reasoning. Bayesian logic introduces a prior probability, which is the hypothesis before accounting for evidence. This prior probability can be based on personal beliefs. In addition, a posterior probability is derived, when additional evidence is considered. As a consequence, the probability assigned to a hypothesis can have partial truth values, just as in fuzzy logic. In addition, Bayesian logic is a dynamic theory, since the posterior probability is revised if new evidence is found. Bayesian methods have been successfully applied in financial forecasting, risk modelling and financial inference. No attempts have been made so far to apply Bayesian methods to model financial correlations.

APPENDIX: DERIVATION OF EQUATION (17.2)

$$d_{i,j} = \sqrt{2(1-\rho_{i,j})}$$

The average distance between two variables $X_{i,t} = \{x_{i,1} \ldots x_{i,n}\}$ and $X_{j,t} = \{x_{j,1} \ldots x_{j,n}\}$ is

$$d_{i,j}^2 = \frac{1}{n}\sum_{t=1}^{T}(x_{i,t} - x_{j,t})^2$$

Normalising, ie, subtracting the mean μ and dividing by the standard deviation σ, we derive

$$d_{i,j}^2 = \frac{1}{n}\sum_{t=1}^{T}\left[\frac{(x_{i,t} - \mu_i)}{\sigma_i} - \frac{(x_{j,t} - \mu_j)}{\sigma_j}\right]^2$$

Multiplying, we get

$$d_{i,j}^2 = \frac{1}{n}\sum_{t=1}^{T}\left[\left(\frac{(x_{i,t} - \mu_i)}{\sigma_i}\right)^2 + \left(\frac{(x_{j,t} - \mu_j)}{\sigma_j}\right)^2 - 2\left[\frac{(x_{i,t} - \mu_i)}{\sigma_i}\frac{(x_{j,t} - \mu_j)}{\sigma_j}\right]\right]$$

Since

$$\sigma_i^2 = \frac{1}{n}\sum_{t=1}^{T}(x_{i,t} - \mu_i)^2, \sigma_j^2 = \frac{1}{n}\sum_{t=1}^{T}(x_{i,t} - \mu_j)^2$$

and applying the covariance

$$COV_{i,j} = \frac{1}{n}\sum_{t=1}^{T}(x_{i,t} - \mu_i)(y_{i,t} - \mu_j)$$

we derive

$$d_{i,j}^2 = \frac{1}{n}\left[n + n - 2\left[\frac{nCOV_{i,j}}{\sigma_i \sigma_j}\right]\right]$$

Eliminating n, we get

$$d_{i,j}^2 = \left[1 + 1 - 2\left[\frac{COV_{i,j}}{\sigma_i \sigma_j}\right]\right]$$

Applying the correlation coefficient

$$\rho_{i,j} = \frac{COV_{i,j}}{\sigma_i \sigma_j},$$

we derive

$$d_{i,j} = \sqrt{2(1 - \rho_{i,j})} \qquad (17.2)$$

Equation (17.2) satisfies the axioms of a metric:

(a) for identical variables, there is zero distance: If $i = j \rightarrow \rho_{i,j} = 1$ and from equation (17.2) $\rightarrow d_{i,j} = 0$;
(b) distances $d_{i,j}$ are symmetrical: $d_{i,j} = d_{j,i}$; and
(c) the direct distance $d_{i,j}$ is smaller equal an indirect difference $d_{i,k}, d_{k,j}: d_{i,j} \leq d_{i,k} + d_{k,j}$. $d_{i,j} = d_{i,k} + d_{k,j}$ only if k lies on the (straight) distance $d_{i,j}$.

A simple spreadsheet displaying

$$d_{i,j} = \sqrt{2(1 - \rho_{i,j})}$$

can be found at www.dersoft.com/distance.xlsx

Questions for Chapter 17
Answers to these questions can be found at the back of this book.

1. Graphical processing units are a technology that originated in the gaming industry and has been modified to solve complex financial problems. What is the general approach of GPUs to solve financial problems?
2. What are the advantages of applying the GPU technology in finance?
3. What are the disadvantages of the GPU technology in finance?
4. What is a general concern when applying GPU technology to finance?
5. Artificial neural networks mimic the human brain and have therefore the ability to learn. How do they learn?
6. What are the limitations of neural networks?
7. Fuzzy logic is cool since it alters the traditional logic of a statement being either true or false. What logic does fuzzy logic apply?
8. Which three main concepts of evolution do genetic algorithms apply to? Explain them briefly.
9. A chaotic system has several properties; name four.
10. Which properties of chaos theory translate well to finance, which do not?
11. Which concept does Bayesian logic share with fuzzy logic with?
12. What are prior probabilities and posterior probabilities in the Bayesian theory?

---

1 In most sovereign states, legislation allows "netting" with a specific counterparty. This is the process of adding the positive PV with the negative PV of all deals with the counterparty. Only if this netted portfolio PV is positive does counterparty risk exist; see Chapter 15.
2 Multi-threading is a technology in which the processor switches between different programming instructions (threads), which allows the parallel execution of multiple commands.
3 Esteva A., B. Kuprel, R. Novoa, J. Ko, S. Swetter, H. Blau and S. Thrun, "Dermatologist-level classification of skin cancer with deep neural networks", *Nature* 542, 115–118, February 2017
4 See Meissner, G., A. Alex and K. Nolte, "A Refined MACD Indicator – Evidence against the Random Walk Hypothesis?", *ABAC Journal*, August 2001, reprinted in *Futures Magazine*, July 2002; also published in German in *Handbuch des Risk Managements*, August 2003.

5   A topological cycle means that a certain number of vertices form a closed chain. For example, in the spanning tree the dotted lines are potential connections and the non-dotted lines between the vertices ABE form a cycle. Cycles are excluded from a minimum spanning tree, since they imply unnecessary cost. For example, a telecommunication company that wants to connect all households would need more lines (edges) if its network had cycles.

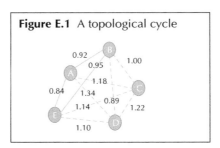

Figure E.1 A topological cycle

6   Kruskal, J. B. (1956), "On the shortest spanning subtree of a graph and the traveling salesman problem", Proceedings of the American Mathematical Society, 7: 48–50.

Answers to Questions and Problems in Correlation Risk Modelling and Management

Answers to Questions and Problems of Chapter 1: Correlation Basics: Definitions, Applications and Terminology

1. What two types of financial correlations exist?

    We differentiate (a) static financial correlations, which measure how two or more financial assets are associated within a certain time period, and (b) dynamic financial correlations, which measure how two or more financial assets move together in time.

2. What is "wrong-way correlation risk" or for short "wrong-way risk"?

    Wrong-way risk exists when there is a tendency for both the credit exposure and the credit risk to increase. For example, wrong-way risk exists if Deutsche Bank sells a put on itself. In this case the put buyer has wrong-way risk: if the Deutsche Bank stock decreases in price, the credit exposure increases (since the put is more valuable). But, if the Deutsche Bank stock decreases in price, this typically also means that the default probability of Deutsche Bank increases; hence the credit risk for the put buyer with respect to Deutsche Bank also increases.

3. Correlations can be non-monotonous. What does this mean?

    It means that the value of a variable such as a credit default swap (CDS) or a collateralised debt obligation (CDO) can increase or decrease for a continued increase or decrease of correlation values (see Figure 1.2).

4. Correlations are critical in many areas in finance. Name five.

   Financial correlations are critical in (1) investments, (2) trading, (3) risk management, (4) financial crises, (5) regulation, and more.

5. High diversification is related to low correlation. Why is this considered one of the few "free lunches" in finance?

   Following the capital asset pricing model (CAPM), it can be shown that a higher diversification leads to a higher return/risk ratio of the assets of a portfolio. This effect is enhanced with lower correlation values between the assets. This can be seen from equation (1.5),

   $$\sigma_P = \sqrt{w_X^2 \sigma_X^2 + w_Y^2 \sigma_Y^2 + 2 w_X w_Y COV_{XY}}.$$

   The lower the correlation, expressed as the covariance COV_{XY}, the lower the portfolio risk σ_P.

6. Create a numerical example and show why a lower correlation results in a higher return/risk ratio.

   The critical equations are:

   $$\mu_P = w_X \mu_X + w_Y \mu_Y \qquad (1.1)$$

   and

   $$\sigma_P = \sqrt{w_X^2 \sigma_X^2 + w_Y^2 \sigma_Y^2 + 2 w_X w_Y COV_{XY}} \qquad (1.5)$$

   From equation (1.5) we can already observe that a lower covariance (Cov) (ie, a lower correlation) leads to a lower portfolio volatility σ_P and hence a higher return/risk ratio μ_P/σ_P. Let us confirm this in a numerical example.

   Assume asset A and asset B have performed as in Table 1.

   For an equal weighting (ie, $w_x = w_y = 0.5$), from Table 1 it follows that $\mu_P = 25.30\%$. The (sample) covariance

   $$COV_{XY} = \frac{1}{n-1} \sum_{t=1}^{n} (x_t - \mu_X)(y_t - \mu_Y). = -0.1525.$$

   From equation (1.5), $\sigma_P = 15.79\%$. Hence the return/risk ratio = 25.30%/15.79% = 160.27.

Table 1

	Asset A	Asset B
2013	100.00	200.00
2014	120.00	230.00
2015	108.00	460.00
2016	194.40	414.00
2017	178.85	480.24
2018	304.05	384.19

Table 2

	Asset A	Asset B
2013	100.00	200.00
2014	120.00	230.00
2015	108.00	460.00
2016	194.40	414.00
2017	178.85	480.24
2018	350.00	384.19

In Table 2 we increased the value of asset A in 2018 to 350.00.

This results in a lower correlation expressed as the (sample) covariance of −0.1783. The portfolio return in Table 2 is slightly higher than in Table 1 and results in 27.87%. The portfolio volatility (ie, the portfolio risk) σ_p = 16.74%. Hence the return/risk ratio is 27.87%/16.74% = 166.47. The reader may look at the spreadsheet at www.dersoft.com/CAPM.xls for these results.

7. What is "correlation trading"?

Correlation trading is trying to exploit the changes in correlation between two or more financial assets.

8. What is "pairs trading"?

In pairs trading a type of statistical arbitrage is performed. Let us assume assets X and Y have moved in a highly correlated manner in time. If now asset X performs poorly with respect to Y, then asset X is bought and asset Y is sold with the expectation that the gap will narrow.

9. Name three correlation options in which a lower correlation results in a higher option price.

   Here are more than three:
   - Option on the better of two. Payoff = max(S_1, S_2)
   - Call on the maximum of two. Payoff = max[0, max(S_1, S_2) − K]
   - Exchange option (such as a convertible bond). Payoff = max(0, S_2 − S_1)
   - Spread call option. Payoff = max[0, (S_2 − S_1) − K]
   - Option on the better of two or cash. Payoff = max(S_1, S_2, cash)
   - Dual-strike call option. Payoff = max(0, S_1 − K_1, S_2 − K_2)
   - Basket options.

   $$\text{Payoff} = \left[\sum_{i=1}^{n} n_i S_i - K, 0\right],$$

   where n_i is the weight of assets i

10. Name one correlation option where a lower correlation results in a higher option price.

    Option on the worse of two with a payoff min(S_1, S_2)

11. Create a numerical example of a two-asset portfolio and show that a lower correlation coefficient leads to a lower VaR number.

    In example 1.2, we derived the 10-day VaR for a two-asset portfolio with a correlation coefficient of 0.7, daily standard deviation of returns of asset 1 of 2%, asset 2 of 1%, and US$10 million invested in asset 1 and US$5 million invested in asset 2, on a 99% confidence level. The VaR came out to US$1.7513 million.

    Let us now decrease the correlation coefficient between asset 1 and asset 2 to 0.6. The VaR then reduces to 1.7174. This can be verified with the spreadsheet at www.dersoft.com/2assetVaR.xlsx.

12. Why do correlations typically increase in a systemic market crash?

ANSWERS TO QUESTIONS AND PROBLEMS IN CORRELATION RISK MODELLING AND MANAGEMENT

In a systemic crash, typically the "herding mentality" of traders and investors sets in, resulting in panic selling. As a result many assets decrease in price simultaneously, resulting in a high price correlation of the assets.

13. In 2005, a correlation crisis with respect to CDOs occurred that led to huge losses of several hedge funds. What happened?

In 2005 General Motors was downgraded to BB and Ford was downgraded to BB+, so both companies were now in "junk" status. A downgrade to junk typically leads to a sharp bond price decline, since many mutual funds and pension funds are not allowed to hold junk bonds.

Importantly, the correlation of the bonds in CDOs that referenced investment-grade bonds decreased, since bonds of different credit qualities typically have lower correlations. This led to huge losses of hedge funds, which had put on a strategy where they were long the equity tranche of the CDO and short the mezzanine tranche of the CDO. (See Figure 1.7 for details.) Hedge funds had bought the equity tranche (0% to 3% tranche) to collect the high equity tranche spread. They had then presumably hedged the risk by going short the mezzanine tranche (3% to 7% tranche). However, this hedge was flawed since the equity tranche spread increased and the mezzanine tranche spread decreased, so the hedge funds lost on both of their positions.

14. In the global financial crisis of 2007 to 2009, many investors in the presumably safe super-senior tranches got hurt. What exactly happened?

Many investors had leveraged the super-senior tranches, termed leveraged super-senior (LSS) tranches, to receive a higher spread. This leverage was typically 10 to 20 times, meaning an investor paid US$10,000,000 but had risk exposure of US$100,000,000 to US$200,000,000. What made things technically even worse was that these LSSs came with an option for the investors to unwind the super-senior tranche if the spread had widened (increased). Therefore many investors started to sell the LSS at very low prices, realising a loss and increasing the LSS tranche spread even further.

15. What is the main objective of the Basel III accord?

    The objective of the Basel accords is to "provide incentives for banks to enhance their risk measurement and management systems" and "to contribute to a higher level of safety and soundness in the banking system" In particular, Basel III is being developed to address the deficiencies of the banking system during the financial crisis 2007 to 2009.

16. The Basel accords have no legal authority. So why do most developed countries implement them?

    About 100 countries have implemented Basel II as a regulatory requirement for their banks. The reason is mainly twofold: (1) it increases the soundness and safety of the country's banking system and (2) it results in a higher credit rating (from Standard & Poor's, Moody's, Fitch, and Dagong) of the country and its banks, which allows international trade at a lower cost of capital.

17. How is correlation risk related to market risk and credit risk?

    Correlation risk can be categorised as its own type of risk. However, correlation risk is also an integral part of market risk and credit risk. In particular, market risk is typically quantified with the value-at-risk (VaR) concept. VaR is highly sensitive to correlation between the assets in the portfolio (see Chapter 10). Arguably, correlation risk is even more critical in credit risk. Default correlation and correlated migration to a lower credit state are not only important in structured products such as collateralised debt obligations (CDOs), but also critical in the loan portfolios of mortgage lenders, for credit-card debt, and in all loan portfolios in general. A combined, correlated default or migration to a lower credit state of the debtors can lead to huge unexpected losses for the creditors.

18. How is correlation risk related to systemic risk and to concentration risk?

Systemic risk can be defined as the risk that a financial market or an entire financial system collapses. Naturally, if an entire financial market collapses, such as the mortgage market and stock market from 2007 to 2009, the correlation between the prices in decline, increases. See also Figure 1.8.

Concentration risk can be defined as the risk of financial loss due to a concentrated exposure to a particular group of counterparties. Correlation risk and concentration risk are related. The lower the concentration risk, the lower is the worst-case scenario for the creditor. Similarly, the lower the correlation between the debtors, the lower is also the worst-case scenario for the debtor. This can be seen from equation (1.11), $P(X \cap Y) = \rho_{XY}\sqrt{P_X(1-P_X)P_Y(1-P_Y)} + P_X P_Y$. The lower the correlation coefficient ρ_{XY}, the lower the probability of joint default, $P(X \cap Y)$. See also the numerical example 1.3.

19. How can we measure the joint probability of occurrence of a binomial event as default or no-default?

    We can apply the binomial correlation measure of Lucas 1995, equation (1.11):

    $$P(X \cap Y) = \rho_{XY}\sqrt{P_X(1-P_X)P_Y(1-P_Y)} + P_X P_Y \quad (1.11)$$

20. Can it be that two binomial events are negatively correlated but they have a positive probability of joint default?

    Yes. This can be seen from equation (1.11) above. A slightly negative correlation coefficient ρ_{XY} can result in a positive joint default probability $P(X \cap Y)$, if the product of the standard deviations of the binomial events $\sqrt{P_X(1-P_X)P_Y(1-P_Y)} + P_X P_Y$ is fairly low and the product of the default probabilities $P_X P_Y$ is high. For example, if the standard deviation of both entities is 30% and a default probability of both entities is 10%, together with a negative correlation coefficient of –0.1, then, following equation (1.11), this leads to a joint default probability of +0.1%.

21. What are value-at-risk (VaR) and credit value-at-risk (CVaR)? How are they related?

VaR measures the maximum loss of a portfolio with respect to a certain probability for a certain time frame with respect to (correlated) market risk. Market risk is the risk that a price or a rate in the (a) equity market, (b) interest-rate market, (c) currency market or (d) commodity market changes unfavourably.

CVaR measures the maximum loss of a portfolio of (correlated) debt with a certain probability for a certain time frame.

Hence VaR is the risk related to market risk and CVaR is the risk related to credit risk. For both VaR and CVaR, correlation is critical. For the exposure of VaR to correlation, see example 1.2, and Chapter 10.

22. Correlation risk is quite broadly defined in trading practice, referring to any co-movement of assets in time. How is the term *correlation* defined in statistics?

In statistics or financial theory, especially in recent publications, the term "correlation" is often defined only referring to the linear Pearson correlation model, as in Cherubini *et al* (2004), Nelsen (2006) or Gregory (2010).

23. What do the terms "measure of association" and "measure of dependence" refer to in statistics?

In statistics, the terms "measure of association" and "measure of dependence" typically refer to associations of variables measured by concepts other than the Pearson correlation measure.

Answers to Questions and Problems of Chapter 2: Empirical Properties of Correlation

1. In which state of the economy are equity correlations the highest?

    In an economic recession. This is because in a recession multiple stocks decrease together, resulting in high stock price correlation.

2. In which state of the economy is equity correlation volatility high?

ANSWERS TO QUESTIONS AND PROBLEMS IN CORRELATION RISK MODELLING AND MANAGEMENT

Generally, in bad economic times. However, in our study, the correlation volatility was slightly higher in normal economic periods (83.40%) than in a recession (80.48%). Correlation volatility was lowest in expansionary periods (71.17%).

3. What follows from questions 1 and 2 for risk management?

   Traders and risk managers should take the higher correlation level and higher correlation volatility in bad economic times into consideration.

4. What is mean reversion?

   Mean reversion is the tendency of a variable to be pulled back to its long-term mean.

5. How can we quantify mean reversion?

   We can start with equation (2.2), $S_t - S_{t-1} = a(\mu_S - S_{t-1})\Delta t + \sigma_S \sqrt{\Delta t}$.

   Ignoring stochasticity, equation (2.2) reduces to equation (2.4):

   $$S_t - S_{t-1} = a\mu_S - aS_{t-1}$$

   To find the mean reversion rate a, we can run a standard regression analysis of the form

   $$Y = \alpha + \beta X$$

   Following equation (2.4), we are regressing $S_t - S_{t-1}$ with respect to S_{t-1}:

   $$\underbrace{S_t - S_{t-1}}_{Y} = \underbrace{a\mu_S}_{\alpha} - \underbrace{aS_{t-1}}_{\beta X} \qquad (2.5)$$

   From equation (2.5), we observe that the regression coefficient β is equal to the negative mean reversion parameter a.

6. What is autocorrelation? Name two approaches for how to quantify autocorrelation.

   Autocorrelation is the degree of which a variable is correlated to its past values. Autocorrelation can be quantified with the Nobel Prize-awarded autoregressive conditional heteroscedasticity (ARCH) model of Robert Engle (1982) or its extension, generalised autoregressive conditional heteroscedasticity (GARCH) by Tim Bollerslev (1988); see Chapter 9 for more details. However, we can also regress the time series of a variable to its past time series values to derive autocorrelation. This is the approach taken in the book.

7. For equity correlations, we see the typical decrease of autocorrelation with respect to time lags. What does that mean?

It means that correlation levels can be better explained by more recent correlations than by correlations that existed farther back in time.

8. How are mean reversion and autocorrelation related?

Mean reversion and autocorrelation are inversely related: the higher mean reversion is (ie, the more strongly a variable is pulled back to its long-term mean); the lower is autocorrelation (ie, the degree to which a variable is correlated to its past values).

9. What is the distribution of equity correlations?

Our empirical studies showed that equity correlations are not normally or lognormally distributed. Rather they can be best approximated with the Johnson SB distribution. See the spreadsheet "Correlation Fitting" at http://www.dersoft.com/correlationfitting.docx, under "Chapter 2."

10. When modelling stocks, bonds, commodities, exchange rates, volatilities and other financial variables, we typically assume a normal or lognormal distribution. Can we do this for equity correlations?

No, as mentioned under question 9, equity correlation cannot be approximated well with a normal or lognormal distribution. One reason is that most correlations in finance are positive and increase the more positive they are, with the exception of very high correlation values. So a rather complex distribution such as the Johnson SB with four parameters can approximate equity correlations well. See Figure 2.6.

Answers to Question and Problems of Chapter 3: The Pearson Correlation Model – Work of the Devil?

1. What does the Pearson correlation coefficient measure?

    The linear strength and direction of an association.

2. What does the Pearson regression coefficient measure?

    The nature (ie, slope) and direction of a linear association.

3. The Pearson correlation model incorporates only the first two movements of distribution of the variables. What severe limitation follows from this property?

    It follows that nonlinear association cannot be evaluated with the Pearson model. For example, the function $Y = X^2$, results in a Pearson correlation coefficient of 0, although Y is dependent on X.

4. What is the Pearson correlation of $Y = X^2$? Why is it distorted?

    As just mentioned, the Pearson correlation coefficient of the function $Y = X^2$ is $\rho_{XY} = 0$. This is because only the first two moments (mean and standard deviation) are applied in the Pearson model.

5. Why does the Variance overweight outliers?

    This because in the variance equation

    $$Var(Y) = \frac{1}{n-1} \sum_{i=1}^{n} (y_i - \bar{y})^2$$

    differences between the data points y_i and the mean of y, $\bar{y}$ are squared, which means that higher differences, ie, outliers are weighted higher.

6. What is nonsense correlation?

    It is deriving a high association (for example a high Pearson correlation) between two or more variables, although these variables are not causally related. An example would be the high correlation between autism and organic-food consumption.

7. Correlation is highly time-sensitive. What follows from this property?

It follows that different time periods can lead to very different correlation results, giving the opportunity to manipulate the results.

8. Does heteroscedasticity distort the Pearson model? The regression parameters $\hat{\alpha}$ and $\hat{\beta}$ are robust with respect to heteroscedasticity. However, the conventional standard error term of the regression coefficient $\hat{\beta}$, $se(\hat{\beta})$,

$$se(\hat{\beta}) = \sqrt{\frac{\sigma_\varepsilon^2}{\sum_{i=1}^{n}(x_i - \bar{x})^2}} \tag{3.12}$$

is a function of the variance of the error term σ_ε^2, hence the standard error $se(\hat{\beta})$ is not heteroscedasticity robust. Therefore inference tests which include the standard error are non-heteroscedasticity robust and can give false results such as falsely rejecting the null hypothesis (type 1 error) or falsely accepting the null hypothesis (type 2 error).

9. Does multicollinearity distort the Pearson model?

In case of perfect multicollinearity, two or more regressors are perfectly linearly correlated, ie, have a correlation coefficient of 1. Perfect multicollinearity is extremely rare and principally occurs only when the researcher has misspecified the model, ie, has done a mistake. In case of perfect multicollinearity, the regression model will become unsolvable.

Partial collinearity exists if two or more regressors are not perfectly but highly correlated.

Partial multicollinearity does not violate any assumptions of the Pearson regression model. As a consequence, the analytical results of a regression analysis as a whole are unbiased. However, since the individual regressors are highly correlated, it is difficult to determine their individual impact. Therefore the analytical power of the individual regressors can be distorted.

10. Do you agree that "Everything that relies on Correlation is Charlatanism" (Nassim Taleb)?

The author of this book believes that this statement is something of an exaggeration. However, the Pearson model has severe limitations for finance and should be applied only if the data set is linear; sufficient data with few outliers is present; different correlation regimes have been scrutinised; and the causality has been exogenously analysed and accepted.

Answers to Questions and Problems of Chapter 4: Cointegration

1. Which two major drawbacks of the Pearson correlation model mainly sparked the creation of the Cointegration model?

    The linearity of the Pearson regression function and the lack of causality between the dependent variable (also called regressant) and the independent variables (also called regressors)

2. What is a stationary process?

    A stationary process is a process where mean and variance are constant in time (weak stationary) or all moments (strict stationary) are constant in time.

3. Is a random drawing from a standard normal distribution ε_t, =normsinv(rand()) in Excel and norminv(rand) in MATLAB a stationary process?

    Yes. A random drawing ε_t from a normal distribution is strictly stationary, since it has constant mean and variance, skewness and kurtosis, as seen in Figure 4.1

4. Why is constant autocorrelation, also called covariance-stationarity, sometimes added as a criteria of a stationary process?

    The answer is that it is "difficult to work with" variables that have varying autocorrelation. If a variable has different autocorrelation in time, there can be a positive correlation between Y and X for some time periods, but negative correlation between Y and X when X for other time periods.

5. A stationary process can be formulised as $F_X(X_{t_1+\tau}, \ldots, X_{t_k+\tau}) = F_X(X_{t_1}, \ldots, X_{t_k})$. Interpret this equation.

   In the equation the joint distribution F_X is not a function of time τ, ie, the moments of F_X do not change in time, in particular do not follow any trends.

6. What does integrated to the order d mean?

   A time series is integrated to the order d, I(d), if taking repeated differences d times, results in a stationary process.

7. What is cointegration?

   If two or more time series (eg, two stocks prices in time) are individually integrated, but some linear combination (a portfolio) of them has a lower order of integration, then the two series are said to be cointegrated.

8. What applications does the cointegration concept have in finance?

   There are three main applications: trading an Index, cost-effective hedging and pairs trading.

9. Explain the Granger–Engle two-step process to find cointegrated stocks!

   The first step is to find the nature of the possible cointegration, ie, to find the value of β in a linear regression. This is typically done with an OLS (ordinary least square) estimate.

   The second step is to test if the portfolio of stocks X and Y is really stationary. This can be done with a Dickey–Fuller test, augmented Dickey–Fuller test, Phillips–Perron test, Johnson test, or Phillips–Outliaris test.

10. What does the Dickey–Fuller test try to achieve?

    The Dickey–Fuller test is a special test for stationarity, which tests if an autoregressive process has a unit root, ie, a = 1, see Equation 4.5.

11. What does Granger causality try to achieve?

    Granger causality is a concept that attempts to find the causality between two variables by making two critical assumptions:

1. The cause happens before the effect.
2. The cause has unique information about the future values of its effect.

12. Which two key elements of the Pearson correlation model does Granger causality combine?

The critical elements of the Granger causality multiple regression function includes autoregression terms of the variable Y *and* time-lagged regressive terms of X:

$$Y_t = \underbrace{a_1 Y_{t-1} + a_2 Y_{t-2} + \ldots + a_p Y_{t-p}}_{Y \text{ autoregression term}} + \underbrace{b_1 X_{t-1} + b_2 X_{t-2} + \ldots + b_q X_{t-q}}_{\text{Time-lagged regression term}} + \varepsilon_t$$

13. Do you think Granger causality is "true causality"?

This is discussed controversially. Granger causality applies autoregressive and lagged regressive terms to derive the impact on the dependent variable. Hence it combines standard multiple Pearson regression techniques in one model. On the negative, Granger causality, being an extension of the Pearson approach, is still a linear model. So can the Granger causality concept find "true causality"? Besides this being a highly philosophical question, "nonsense correlation" is still possible in the Granger model: "A rooster crows before the sun rises. Therefore, the rooster causes the sun to rise."

14. What is the limitation of the Granger causality concept?

Granger causality, being an extension of the Pearson approach, is still a linear model. And, as mentioned in question 12, nonsense correlation is still possible.

Answers to Questions and Problems of Chapter 5: Bottom-up Approaches

1. The original Heston (1993) model correlates the Brownian motion of which two financial variables? What is the most significant result of the original Heston model?

The two variables that are correlated in the Heston model are the stock price S and the volatility σ. One of the most significant results is that the Heston model can replicate volatility skews found in reality well.

2. To create negative correlation between asset 1 and asset 2 in the Heston (1993) model, what value does the correlation coefficient α take in equation $dz_1(t) = \alpha dz_2(t) + \sqrt{1-\alpha^2} dz_3(t)$?

   The correlation coefficient α would take negative values.

3. The Heston model is one of the most widely applied correlation models in finance. Why?

   The Heston model is mathematically convenient, since by construction dz_1 is standard normal. In addition, it is dynamic and versatile since it can positively and negatively correlate the Brownian motion of variables.

4. What is the difference between the Pearson correlation model and the binomial correlation model of Lucas (1995)?

   The binomial correlation model of Lucas is a special case of the Pearson model. The Pearson model's correlation coefficient is

   $$\rho_1(X,Y) = \frac{E(XY) - E(X)E(Y)}{\sqrt{E(X^2) - (E(X))^2}\sqrt{E(Y^2) - (E(Y))^2}} \quad (3.3)$$

   whereas the binomial correlation coefficient is

   $$\rho\left(1_{\{\tau_X \leq T\}}, 1_{\{\tau_Y \leq T\}}\right) = \frac{P(XY) - P(X)P(Y)}{\sqrt{\left(P(X) - (P(X))^2\right)}\sqrt{\left(P(Y) - (P(Y))^2\right)}} \quad (5.8)$$

   By construction, equation (5.8) can model only binomial events, for example, default and no default. With respect to equation (3.3), we observe that, in equation (3.3), X and Y are sets of $i = 1, ..., n$ variates, with $i \in \mathcal{R}$. $P(X)$ and $P(Y)$ in equation (5.8), however, are scalars, for example, the default probabilities of entities X and Y for a certain time period T, respectively, $0 \leq P(X) \leq 1$, and $0 \leq P(Y) \leq 1$. Hence the binomial correlation approach of equation (5.8) is a limiting case of the Pearson correlation approach of equation (3.3).

5. What are the limitations of the binomial correlation model of Lucas (1995)?

   As in the Pearson model, the most severe limitation is that the binomial model analyses only linear relationships between variables. However, most financial relationships are nonlinear.

6. What is the basic principle of the copula correlation model?

   It joins n single-variate distributions to one (however, n-dimensional) distribution.

7. Why is the Gaussian copula model the most popular copula model in finance?

   Because of its mathematical and computational simplicity and high intuition.

8. What does "In the copula mapping process, the marginal distributions are preserved" mean?

   The statement means that the percentiles are preserved. For example, the 5th percentile of the marginal distribution (ie, the original distribution) is mapped to the 5th percentile of the new standard normal distribution; the 10th percentile of the marginal distribution is mapped to the 10th percentile of the standard normal distribution; and so on.

9. Given are the marginal 1-year default probabilities of 5% for asset 1 and 7% for asset 2. If the Gaussian correlation coefficient is 0.3, what is the joint probability of default in year 1, assuming asset 1 and asset 2 are jointly bivariately distributed?

   From equation (5.14), the joint default probability is $Q(t_{asset_1} \leq 1 \cap t_{asset_2} \leq 1) \equiv M(x_{asset_1} \leq -1.6449 \cap x_{asset_2} \leq -1.4758, \rho = 0.3) = 0.93\%$.

   See spreadsheet www.dersoft.com/2assetdefaulttime-copula.xlsm. .

10. Given are the 5-year default probability of entity i of 10% and the 6-year default probability of entity i of 13%. What is the forward default probability in year 6 and what is the default intensity in year 6?

    The forward probability, viewed at time 0, is

    $$q(0)_{5,6} = Q(6) - Q(5) = Q(13\%) - Q(10\%) = 3\%$$

The default intensity, also called hazard rate, viewed at time 5 (ie, the end of period 5 or the beginning of period 6) is

$\lambda(5)_{5,6} = (Q_6 - Q_5)/(1 - Q_5) = 13\% - 10\%/(1 - 10\%) = 3.33\%$

11. What are the limitations of the Gaussian copula for financial applications?

   a) The Gaussian copula has low tail dependence. Following a definition by Joe (1999), a bivariate copula has lower tail dependence if

   $$\lim_{y_1 \downarrow 0, y_2 \downarrow 0} P\left[\left(\tau_1 < N_1^{-1}(y_1)\right) | \left(\tau_2 < N_2^{-1}(y_2)\right)\right] > 0 \qquad (5.22)$$

   where τ_i is the default time of asset i, y_i is the marginal distribution of asset i, and N^{-1} is the inverse of the standard normal distribution. However, it can be easily shown that the Gaussian copula has no tail dependence for any correlation parameter ρ: $\lim_{y_1 \downarrow 0, y_2 \downarrow 0} P\left[\left(\tau_1 < N_1^{-1}(y_1)\right) | \left(\tau_2 < N_2^{-1}(y_2)\right)\right] = 0, \rho \in \{-1, 1\}$.

   b) Some researchers report that the one-factor version of the Gaussian copula has problems in calibrating CDO tranches. However, other studies of Hull and White (2004), Andersen and Sidenius (2004) and Burtschell et al (2008) find no problems in calibration.

   c) The Gaussian copula is principally static and consequently allows only limited risk management. In particular, there is no stochastic process for the critical underlying variables' default intensity and default correlation. However, back-testing and stress-testing the variables for different time horizons can give valuable sensitivities; see Whetten and Adelson (2004) and Meissner et al (2008b).

12. Since the Gaussian copula has low tail dependence, which other copulas seem more suitable to model financial correlations?

   Other copulas such as the Student's t or the Gumbel copula have higher tail dependence and may be more suited to model financial correlations.

ANSWERS TO QUESTIONS AND PROBLEMS IN CORRELATION RISK MODELLING AND MANAGEMENT

13. Can the copula model be blamed for the great recession of 2007 to 2009?

    The copula model is a rigorous statistical correlation model. For finance, the limitations discussed in question 11 apply. The critical problem with respect to the 2007–2009 global financial crisis was not the financial models themselves, but inadequate calibration. Benign default probabilities and default correlations from 2003 to 2006 were input into the models. It cannot be expected that models produce correct outputs if the inputs are flawed. "Garbage in, garbage out" in programming terminology.

14. What is the basic idea in contagion-correlation models?

    Contagion-correlation modelling, pioneered by Davis and Lo (1999 and 2001) and Jarrow and Yu (2001), is based on the idea that the default of one entity impacts the default intensity of another entity. Hence contagion default modelling incorporates counterparty risk (ie, the direct impact of a defaulting entity on the default intensity of another entity).

15. Name the limitations of contagion models.

    Introducing symmetric contagion among all entities creates the problem of circularity. In this case, the construction of a joint distribution is rather complex. One solution is to model "asymmetric dependence" (ie, the default of primary entities impacts the default intensity of secondary entities, but not vice versa).

    As with all financial models, the user has to be aware of the general limitations of financial models. Models can serve as an approximation of the complex financial reality, but will never exactly replicate it.

16. Derive correlated samples x_1, x_2, and x_3, from a multivariate standard normal distribution which are correlated by the matrix

$$\Sigma = \begin{bmatrix} 1 & 0.2 & 0.3 \\ 0.2 & 1 & 0.4 \\ 0.3 & 0.4 & 1 \end{bmatrix}$$

applying Cholesky decomposition (see Appendix A2 for details).

See the model www.dersoft.com/matrixprimer.xlsx sheet "Cholesky Decomposition" for the answer.

Answers to Questions and Problems of Chapter 6: Valuing CDOs with the Gaussian Copula – What Went Wrong?

1. What is the basic idea of a CDO?

   CDOs transfer credit risk from the originator to the investors.

2. Name the three main types of CDOs.

   The three main types of CDOs are cash CDOs, synthetic CDOs, and nonfunded CDOs.

3. Which are the three main players in a CDO? Why is the SPV typically AAA- rated?

   1. The originator (or protection buyer), who transfers the credit risk.
   2. The investor, who assumes the credit risk.
   3. The SPV (special purpose vehicle), which manages the CDO.

   The SPV is AAA-rated in order to reduce the credit risk for the investor.

4. Name the motives of these three players to enter into a CDO.

   The motivation for the originator is naturally to transfer the credit risk, which improves the originator's credit rating, frees credit lines, reduces regulatory capital and lowers funding cost. The motivation for the investor is to receive high yields. The motivation for the SPV is fee income.

5. Name the three financial principles that are incorporated in a CDO and explain them briefly.

   A CDO is a structured product that includes the financial principles of:

ANSWERS TO QUESTIONS AND PROBLEMS IN CORRELATION RISK MODELLING AND MANAGEMENT

1. Diversification. A skilled manager will include bonds and loans in a CDO, which have a high degree of diversification (ie, they are low or negatively correlated).
2. Subordination. This means the defaults in higher tranches are protected by defaults in lower tranches, since defaults are absorbed by lower tranches first.
3. Overcollateralisation. Typically the assets in a CDO have a higher value than the liabilities that the SPV owes to the investors. This overcollateralisation adds an additional element of protection for investors.

6. What is the default probability of an entity based on the Merton 1974 model, if the current asset value V_0 = US\$4,000,000, the debt value D = US\$3,000,000, the maturity T of the debt is in 1 year, the risk-free interest rate r is 2% and the volatility of the assets σ is 20%?

It is $N(-d_2)$ in the Merton 1974 model, which comes out to 7.53%. A simple model that derives the answer can be found at www.dersoft.com/Mertonmodel.xlsx.

7. In the Merton 1974 model, there is a closed-form solution for the default probability. What is it?

As mentioned in question 6, it is $N(-d_2)$, in the model

$$d_1 = \frac{\ln\left(\dfrac{S_0}{De^{-rT}}\right) + \dfrac{\sigma^2}{2}T}{\sigma\sqrt{T}}$$

and

$$d_2 = d_1 - \sigma\sqrt{T} \quad E = V_0 N(d_1) - De^{-rT} N(d_2)$$

8. The elegant Merton 1974 model principally serves as a basis for more realistic extensions. What are the limitations of the Merton 1974 model?

The ingenious Merton 1974 model outlines the principles of a company's default using structural properties such as assets and debt. The main limitations of the model are that only one form of debt D is modelled and that default can occur only at debt maturity T. Naturally, numerous extensions of the model have been created to bring the model in line with the complexities of reality.

9. The Merton 1974 model is the basis for all structural models. Why is the Merton model called structural?

Because it uses the structural data of a company such as assets and liabilities as inputs.

10. When valuing the default probability in a CDO, why do we map the default probability of asset i, λ_i, to standard normal via $N^{-1}(\lambda_i)$?

This is done mainly for mathematical and computational convenience. The default barrier M_n is (multivariate) standard normal, so to compare it with the default probability of asset i, λ_i, we map λ_i to standard normal via $N^{-1}(\lambda_i)$.

11. The multivariate copula function M_n serves as the default threshold. How is the default of asset i derived in the copula model?

To derive the threshold, typically the popular Gaussian copula model is applied. We derive the default threshold as

$$M_n\left[N^{-1}(u_1),\ldots,N^{-1}(u_n);\rho_M\right] \tag{5.4}$$

where M_n is the n-variate Gaussian distribution, N^{-1} is again the inverse of a standard normal distribution, and u_x is a uniform random vector $u_x \in [0,1]$, =rand() in Excel/VBA or randn() in MATLAB. ρ_M is the asset correlation matrix.

12. The credit triangle is $s \approx \lambda\,(1-R)$, where s is the credit spread, λ is the default intensity, and R is the recovery rate. When $R = 0$, we have $s \approx \lambda$. Explain the intuition of $s \approx \lambda$.

The relationship $s \approx \lambda$ is intuitive since the default probability λ is the risk that the investor takes, and the investor should be compensated for this risk by receiving a similar amount, the spread s. The relationship $s \approx \lambda\,(1-R)$ was formally derived by Lando (1998) with $R = 0$ and by Duffie and Singleton (1990) with $R \neq 0$.

ANSWERS TO QUESTIONS AND PROBLEMS IN CORRELATION RISK MODELLING AND MANAGEMENT

13. The recovery rate is often modelled as being higher, the lower the credit rating of an asset. This seems counterintuitive. But why is it rational?

    Recovery rates are often approximated using historical recovery rates of defaulted companies. Interestingly, typically rating agencies assign a lower recovery rate to higher-rated entities. The logic is that higher-rated entities will default only in a recession, in which recovery rates are lower. Lower-rated entities are assigned a higher recovery rate, since they can default even in an economic expansion.

14. Can the Gaussian copula be blamed for the global financial crisis of 2007 to 2009?

    No. The Gaussian copula is a sound statistical correlation model. Applied to finance, the limitations of slim tails, occasional calibration problems and the principally static nature are of concern. However, the main problem in 2007 and 2008, when valuing CDOs with the Gaussian copula, was inadequate calibration. Benign default probability functions were applied, and low default correlations between the assets in the CDO were input in correlation matrices. When data from non-crisis periods are input into a model, it cannot be expected that the model will produce correct outputs in a crisis!

15. What were the main reasons for the misevaluation of CDOs before and during the crisis?

    As mentioned in question 15, the main reason for the misevaluation of CDOs in 2007 and 2008 was inadequate calibration. No model can produce correct results when fed incorrect inputs.

Answers to Questions and Problems of Chapter 7: The One-factor Gaussian Copula Model – Too Simplistic?

1. Name the three strongly simplistic assumptions of the one-factor Gaussian copula (OFGC) model.

    1. The default probabilities of assets in the portfolio are assumed to be identical.

435

2. The pairwise default correlations between all assets in the portfolio are assumed to be identical.
3. The recovery rates of all assets in the portfolio are assumed to be identical.

2. For which portfolios are those assumptions justifiable?

Those assumptions are justifiable only for very homogeneous portfolios, for example for portfolios that have the same or similar credit ratings and/or that belong to the same sector.

3. The correlation concept of the OFGC is incorporated in the simple equation (7.1) $x_i = \sqrt{\rho}\, M + \sqrt{1-\rho}\, Z_i$. Explain the correlation concept with this equation.

The key property of equation (7.1) is that we do not model the default correlation between the assets i in the portfolio directly, but instead we condition defaults on M. We assume that ρ is identical for all asset pairs. Therefore, we have the same relationship between every asset i and M: if ρ is one, every asset i has a perfect correlation with M; hence all assets are perfectly correlated. If ρ is zero, all assets i depend only on their idiosyncratic factor Z_i; hence the assets are independent. For a ρ of 0.7071 (and therefore $\sqrt{\rho} = 0.5$), all x_i are determined equally by M and Z_i. Importantly, once we have determined M (by a random drawing from a standard normal distribution), the assets i are conditionally (on M) independent. Therefore we name this approach "conditionally independent default" (CID) correlation modelling.

4. Equation (7.1) applies the conditionally independent default (CID) correlation approach. Explain the term "conditionally independent"!

As mentioned under question 3, once we have drawn M and Z_i, the correlation between the assets is determined not directly, but indirectly, by conditioning x_i on M. Hence the assets are not directly dependent, but "conditionally independent".

5. Why are the variables M, Z_i and the resulting x_i in equation (7.1) called latent and frailty variables?

ANSWERS TO QUESTIONS AND PROBLEMS IN CORRELATION RISK MODELLING AND MANAGEMENT

They are called latent (meaning hidden) because they can't be observed in reality.

They are called frailty variables because the lower M, Z_i and the resulting x_i are, the earlier the default of company i.

6. In equation (7.1), the x_i are standard normally distributed. How are the x_i transformed into probabilities?

The x_i are transformed into probabilities simply by using $N(x_i) = P_i$, $0 \le P_i \le 1$, where N is the cumulative standard normal distribution function.

7. In equation (7.2), $s_i^t = 1 - P_i$, s_i^t is the survival probability of asset i at time t, and $1 - P_i$ is the default threshold, which includes the correlation. Solve equation (7.2) for the default time t of asset i.

We take the natural logarithm ln of both sides:

$\ln s_i^t = \ln(1 - P_i)$ or
$t \ln(s_i) = \ln(1 - P_i)$ or
$t = \ln(1 - P_i)/\ln(s_i)$

What is the default time of asset i if = 80% and P_i = 50%?

It is $t = \ln(0.5)/\ln(0.8) = 3.10$ years.

8. Calculate the fair equity tranche spread of a CDO for the following CDO with a 3-year maturity: the starting notional is US$2,000,000,000, with 125 equally weighted companies. Hence each asset has a notional value of US$16,000,000.

Let us assume spread payments and payouts are annually in arrears. The recovery rate for every asset is 30%. Interest rates are constant at 5%. We consider an equity tranche with a detachment point of 3%. Hence the equity tranche has a starting notional value of US$60,000,000.

Let us assume that we have derived that one asset defaults after 1.5 years and one asset defaults at 2.5 years. Hence the starting notional of US$60,000,000 reduces to US$44,000,000 for t_2 (end year 2) and to US$28,000,000 for t_3 (end of year 3).

What is the equity tranche spread derived by the OFGC?

437

From equation (7.4), the numerator is:

$e^{-0.05 \times 1} \times 0 \times 0.7 + e^{-0.1 \times 2} \times (\$60{,}000{,}000 - \$44{,}000{,}000) \times 0.7$
$+ e^{-0.05 \times 3} \times (\$44{,}000{,}000 - \$28{,}000{,}000) \times 0.7 = \$19{,}774{,}108$

From equation (7.4), the denominator is:

$e^{-0.05 \times 1} \times \$60{,}000{,}000 + e^{-0.05 \times 2} \times \$44{,}000{,}000$
$+ e^{-0.05 \times 3} \times \$28{,}000{,}000 = \$120{,}986{,}435$

Hence the fair equity tranche spread, paid annually in arrears, is:

US$19,774,108/US$120,986,435 = 16.34%.

9. The tranche spread of the equity tranche and the senior tranche behave very differently with respect to changes in the correlation of the assets in the CDO. Draw a graph showing the tranche spread–correlation dependence for the equity tranche and a senior tranche.

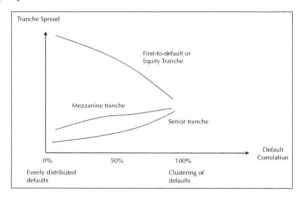

10. Explain the graph that you created in problem 9.

The negative relationship between the equity tranche spread and default correlation is intuitive: the higher the default correlation of the companies in the CDO, the higher the probability of extreme events; that is, the probability of either many or no defaults is high. The high probability of no defaults reduces the riskiness and hence reduces the equity tranche spread. The high probability of many defaults at the same time increases the riskiness of the equity tranche, which increases the equity tranche spread. However, this effect does not impact the equity tranche significantly, since the losses are capped at the detachment level.

The opposite logic applies to the senior tranche: if default correlation is high, many defaults may occur at the same time. Therefore, the senior tranche may be impacted; hence the riskiness and the spread are both high.

11. Name the main differences between the standard Gaussian copula and the OFGC.

    The core equation of the OFGC was displayed in equation (7.1).

    $$x_i = \sqrt{\rho}\, M + \sqrt{1-\rho}\, Z_i \qquad (7.1)$$

    By construction, x_i in equation (7.1) is standard normal. Therefore, we can easily create the cumulative standard normal distribution of the x_i:

    $$N(x_i) \qquad (7.1a)$$

    where N is the one-dimensional cumulative standard normal distribution. Importantly, $N(x_i)$ includes the default correlation between the $i = 1, ..., n$ assets via the correlated x_i, derived in equation (7.1).

    In comparison, the n-dimensional cumulative standard normal distribution M_n was derived in the standard Gaussian copula framework with equation (5.12):

    $$M_n\left[N^{-1}(Q_1(t)), ..., N^{-1}(Q_n(t)); \rho_M\right] \qquad (5.12)$$

    where $Q_i(t)$ is the cumulative default distribution of asset i with respect to t, and ρ_M is the correlation matrix of the assets in the portfolio.

    Let us look at the differences in the OFGC of equations (7.1) and (7.1a), and standard copula of equation (5.12).

    a) The correlations between the assets i in equation (7.1) are modelled indirectly by conditioning the auxiliary variable of asset i, x_i, on a common factor M. In contrast, equation (5.12) applies the typical correlation matrix ρ_M (for an example, see Chapter 1, Table 1.3).

b) As a consequence, in the OFGC all asset pairs in the portfolio have the same correlation. The standard Gaussian copula is richer as it can model asset pair correlation individually in the correlation matrix.
c) The cumulative normal distribution in equation (7.1a), which includes the correlation between the assets i via x_i, is conveniently one-dimensional. The cumulative normal distribution in equation (5.12) is n-dimensional.
d) The bivariate case of the standard Gaussian copula is equivalent with the OFGC: sampling from equation (7.12) is achieved by Cholesky decomposition (as explained in Appendix 5A of Chapter 5). In the bivariate case, Cholesky sampling of two correlated variables x_1 and x_2 from equation (5.12) reduces to

$$x_1 = \varepsilon_1$$
$$x_2 = \sqrt{\rho}\,\varepsilon_1 + \sqrt{1-\rho}\,\varepsilon_2$$

where ε_1 and ε_2 are independent samples from $n \sim (0,1)$. This is equivalent to samples $i = 1,2$ from equation (7.1).

12. The OFGC is a first, simplistic approach to derive the tranche spread in a CDO and the credit risk in portfolios. Name three extensions of the OFGC.

1. The OFGC is principally static (ie, it has a one-period time horizon). However, the static property of the OFGC can be relaxed, as in Hull et al (2005), who apply a dynamic OFGC model. Hence they modify equation (7.1) and model

$$dz_i(t) = \sqrt{\rho(t)}\,dM(t) + \sqrt{1-\rho(t)}\,dZ_i(t) \qquad (7.6)$$

where $dM(t)$ and $dZ_i(t)$ are $n \sim (0,1)$ and independent. It follows from equation (7.6) that $dz_i(t)$ is also $n \sim (0,1)$. The dependence on $M(t)$ again determines indirectly the correlation between assets i.

2. Furthermore, more common factors M can be modelled. In this case equation (7.1) generalises to

$$x_i = \sum_{k=1}^{m} \sqrt{p_{i,k}}\,M_k + Z_i \sum_{k=1}^{m} \sqrt{p_{i,k}}$$

and the correlation between x_i and x_j is

$$\sum_{k=1}^{m}\sqrt{p_{i,k}p_{j,k}}$$

3. A further extension of the OFGC is the popular one-factor Student-*t* copula.

$$\bar{x}_i = \sqrt{\rho}M + \sqrt{1-\rho}Z_i \qquad (7.7)$$

where M and Z_i are independent and $n \sim (0,1)$. $x_i = \bar{x}_i\sqrt{W}$ where W follows an inverse gamma distribution. It follows that the latent variable x_i is Student-*t* distributed.

13. Should we apply the OFGC to value CDOs? Should we apply the OFGC to value credit risk in portfolios?

    To answer these questions, we have to address the assumptions of the OFGC (ie, same default probability of all assets in a CDO or any other portfolio, and same correlation between all asset pairs in a CDO or another portfolio). Are these assumptions too simplistic to derive the credit risk in a CDO or other portfolios? The answer is: only in rare cases, if the assets in the portfolio are very homogeneous (ie, they have similar default probabilities and similar default correlations), is the OFGC an adequate model.

    Most portfolios of investment banks, however, are highly diversified with assets from different sectors and different geographical regions and hence have different default probabilities and default correlations. In this case the OFGC is an inappropriately simplistic model!

14. Why do "traders seem to disagree" with the OFGC?

    Traders deliberately alter the tranche correlations to derive desired tranche spreads, which violates the basic principle of the OFGC, which assumes a constant CDO-wide, tranche-nonspecific default correlation.

15. Explain the correlation smile that traders apply to derive tranche spreads. How is the correlation smile related to the volatility smile when pricing options?

Traders use a higher correlation for the equity tranche and the super-senior tranches than the mezzanine tranche, constituting the correlation smile (see Figure 7.9).

However, there is a crucial difference between the volatility smile of options and the correlation smile of CDOs. While an increase in the implied correlation increases the senior tranche spread, an increase in the implied correlation decreases the equity tranche spread. This is because the equity tranche spread has a negative dependence on implied correlation (see Figure 7.8). Hence, CDO traders arbitrarily decrease the equity tranche spread and arbitrarily increase the senior tranche spread.

Answers to Questions and Problems of Chapter 8: Financial Correlation Models – Top-Down Approaches

1. What is the difference between bottom-up and top-down correlation models?

    In the bottom-up models of Chapters 5, 6 and 7, the distribution of the portfolio intensity is an aggregate of the individual entities' default intensities. In a top-down model, the evolution of the portfolio intensity distribution is derived directly (ie, abstracting from the individual entities' default intensities).

2. For which types of portfolios are top-down correlation models appropriate?

    Top-down models are typically applied in practice if:
    a) the default intensities of the individual entities are unavailable or unreliable;
    b) the default intensities of the individual entities are unnecessary; this may be the case when valuating a homogeneous portfolio such as an index of homogeneous entities; and/or
    c) the sheer size of a portfolio makes the modelling of individual default intensities problematic.

3. Why can the one-factor Gaussian copula (OFGC) be considered a top-down model?

ANSWERS TO QUESTIONS AND PROBLEMS IN CORRELATION RISK MODELLING AND MANAGEMENT

The one-factor Gaussian copula model can be considered a top-down correlation model since it abstracts from the individual default intensities of each asset i. Rather, one default intensity is assumed for all assets in the portfolio.

4. Markov processes are "memoryless". What does this mean? Give an example.

This means that only the present information, not the past, is relevant. For example, rolling a die or playing roulette are both memoryless processes. Whatever trial result occurred, it is irrelevant for future results of trials, that result is irrelevant for future results of trials.

5. What is a transition rate?

In credit-risk modelling, transition rates are probabilities to move from one credit state to another.

6. Why does higher transition rate volatility mean higher default correlation in the Schönbucher 2006 model?

A higher transition rate volatility means higher default correlation since a higher transition rate volatility means a higher transition rate of all entities n to a lower state, hence a higher default correlation; likewise, a lower transition rate volatility means a lower transition rate of all entities n to a lower state, hence lower default correlation.

7. Why does an increase in stochastic time change mean a higher default correlation in the Hurd–Kuznetsov 2006 model?

In the Hurd–Kuznetsov 2006 model, correlation is induced by the speed of the stochastic clock τ_t. An increase in the speed of the clock increases the speed of migration of all entities and hence increases the probability of simultaneous defaults. If the stochastic clock jumps, the probability of simultaneous defaults is even higher.

8. What is the "random thinning" process in top-down models, and what does it accomplish?

Random thinning allows the allocation of the portfolio intensity to the sum of the individual entities' intensities. In addition, the name of the entity that defaults is revealed at the default time, highlighting the fact that random thinning allocates the portfolio intensity to the individual entities.

Answers to Questions and Problems of Chapter 9: Stochastic Correlation Models

1. What is a deterministic process? Name two examples.

   A deterministic process is a process with a known outcome. For example, counting numbers by one and the movement of the planets in our solar system are deterministic processes.

2. What is a stochastic or random process? Name two examples.

   A stochastic or random process is a process with an unknown outcome. The behaviour of stock prices or correlations are random processes.

3. Why does it seem like a good idea to model financial correlations as a stochastic process? Give two reasons.

   From the empirical Chapter 2, we derived that financial correlations behave somewhat erratically and randomly. In addition, many other financial variables, such as equities, bonds, commodities, exchange rates, interest rates, volatility and more, are often modelled with a stochastic process, and this stochastic modelling produces good results with respect to replicating the behaviour of these variables in reality.

4. How is stochasticity modelled in the dynamic conditional correlation (DCC) concept?

   The DCC model is a concept in the ARCH framework. Here, one of the core equations is:

   $$r_{i,t} = \sigma_{i,t} \varepsilon_{i,t} \qquad (9.7)$$

   where:

   $r_{i,t}$: Return of asset i at time t
   $\sigma_{i,t}$: Standard deviation of the return of asset i at time t (also called volatility)
   $\varepsilon_{i,t}$: Random drawing from a standard normal distribution for asset i and time t, $\varepsilon = n \sim (0,1)$.

ANSWERS TO QUESTIONS AND PROBLEMS IN CORRELATION RISK MODELLING AND MANAGEMENT

Hence, stochasticity enters the model via $\varepsilon_{i,t}$.

In addition, the variance σ^2 or the standard deviation σ in equation (9.7) is modelled with an ARCH process (or one of many extensions such as GARCH, NGARCH, EGARCH, TGARCH,[1] and more) of the form

$$\sigma_t^2 = a_0 + a_1\sigma_{t-1}^2\varepsilon_{t-1}^2 + \ldots + a_q\sigma_{t-q}^2\varepsilon_{t-q}^2 \qquad (9.8)$$

where $a_0 > 0$, $a_1 \geq 0$, so that σ^2 is positive and $q \in N$.

Stochasticity enters the model again via ε_{t-1}^2 and ε_{t-q}^2.

5. The geometric Brownian motion (GBM) is applied to model many financial variables, such as stock prices, commodities and exchange rates. What are two of the limitations of the GBM to model financial correlations?

   a) The GBM of the form

   $$\frac{d\rho}{\rho} = \mu dt + \sigma \varepsilon \sqrt{dt} \qquad (9.2)$$

   where:

   ρ: Correlation between two or more variables
   μ: Expected growth rate of ρ
   μ: Expected volatility of ρ
   ε: Random drawing from of standard normal distribution. Formally, $\varepsilon = n \sim (0,1)$. We can compute ε as =normsinv(rand()) in Excel/VBA and norminv(rand) in MATLAB

   Equation (9.2) has no mean reversion. However, we derived in Chapter 2 that financial correlations exhibit strong mean reversion.

   b) Equation (9.2) is not bounded, meaning correlation ρ can take values bigger than 1 and smaller than −1. From equation (9.2) we see that a value of $\rho > 1$ is more likely to happen when the growth rate μ is high, if the volatility σ is high, and if we have a high value of ε in a simulation. Conversely, values of $\rho < -1$ are more likely to occur for low values of μ and ε and high values of σ.

6. The Vasicek model is an improvement over the GBM to model financial correlations. Why?

    It includes mean reversion.

7. The bounded Jacobi process seems like a good choice to model financial correlations. What advantage does it have over the GBM and the Vasicek model?

    The bounded Jacobi process is:

    $$d\rho = a(m_\rho - \rho_t)dt + \sigma_\rho \sqrt{(h-\rho_t)(\rho_t - f)}\,\varepsilon_t \sqrt{dt} \qquad (9.15)$$

    where h: upper boundary level, and f: lower boundary level (ie, $h \geq \rho \geq f$).

    The bounded Jacobi process is restricted to correlation values between −1 and +1, when the boundary conditions

    $$a \geq \frac{\sigma^2(h-f)/2}{(m_\rho - f)} \qquad (9.17)$$

    for the lower bound f and

    $$a \geq \frac{\sigma^2(h-f)/2}{(h - m_\rho)} \qquad (9.18)$$

    for the lower bound f are met.

8. In the Buraschi, Porchia and Trojani 2010 stochastic correlation model, which two stochastic processes are correlated?

    As in the Heston model, the Buraschi, Porchia and Trojani 2010 stochastic correlation model correlates the relative change of the variable of interest S with the change in volatility σ:

    $$\frac{dS}{S} = \mu dt + \sigma_t dz_1 \qquad (9.22)$$

    $$d\sigma_t^2 = a(m_\sigma^2 - \sigma_t^2)dt + \xi \sigma_t dz_2 \qquad (9.23)$$

    The correlation between the stochastic processes (9.22) and (9.23) is achieved by the identity

    $$dz_1(t) = \sqrt{\rho_1}\,dz_2(t) + \sqrt{1-\rho_1}\,dz_3(t) \qquad (9.24)$$

    where $dz_2(t)$ and $dz_3(t)$ are independent, and $dz(t)$ and $dz(t')$ are independent, $t \neq t'$.

9. In the Buraschi, Porchia and Trojani 2010 model, which financial properties can be replicated? Name two.

   a) The negative relationship between returns and volatility (sometimes called "leverage") and the higher correlation in a recession (sometimes referred to as "asymmetric correlation"), which we also found in the empirical Chapter 2, can be modelled.
   b) In addition, volatility skews (ie, higher volatility when returns are negative) and the right balance between correlation persistence correlation mean-reversion can be modelled.

10. Should we model correlation with a deterministic or a stochastic process?

    Like many financial variables, financial correlations behave randomly and unpredictably, as we observed in Chapter 2. Therefore it is not a good idea to model them with a deterministic process.

    Should we model financial correlations with a stochastic process? This is mainly an empirical question: do financial correlations in the real world behave in a way that can be captured with a certain stochastic model? The research in this area has just started, but the first results are promising.

Answers to Questions and Problems of Chapter 10: Quantifying Market Correlation Risk

1. When we talk about "market risk," which four markets are typically included?

   1) equity market;
   2) fixed-income market;
   3) commodity market; and
   4) foreign exchange market.

2. Name several other markets not included in the four markets mentioned in (1).

   Other markets are the energy market, real-estate market, weather market, economic variables and the derivatives market.

3. What is market correlation risk?

   Market correlation risk is the risk that the correlations between the prices in one market or between these markets change unfavourably.

4. We can measure market correlation risk with Cora. What information does Cora give us?

   Cora measures how much a dependent variable changes if the correlation between two or more independent variables changes by an infinitesimally small amount. Formally,

   $$\text{Cora} = \frac{\partial V}{\partial \rho(x_{i=1,\ldots,n})}$$

   where V is the value of a dependent financial variable and $\rho(x_{i=1,\ldots n})$ is the correlation or correlation matrix of the independent variables $x_{i=1,\ldots n}$.

5. What is Cora mathematically?

   Cora is the first mathematical derivative of a function (such as VaR) with respect to correlation between the underlying variables (such as the assets in the VaR portfolio).

6. Name three applications of Cora in finance.

   We typically calculate Cora for a portfolio of assets. In this case dependent variable V can be:

   a) The return/risk ratio μ_p/σ_p of the portfolio. We derived Cora for the return/risk ratio μ_p/σ_p in the introductory Chapter 1 for a two-asset portfolio. This was displayed in Figure 1.3, where Cora is the slope of the μ_p/σ_p function.

   b) The risk of a portfolio, measured by the standard deviation of asset returns.

   c) The risk of a portfolio measured by the VaR concept. We already derived the Cora in Chapter 1 for a two-asset portfolio. Hence in this case V in equation (10.1) is the VaR.

7. Measuring correlation risk is not totally new. In option theory, a Vanna exists. What information does Vanna give us?

ANSWERS TO QUESTIONS AND PROBLEMS IN CORRELATION RISK MODELLING AND MANAGEMENT

Vanna tells us how much the option price V^* changes if the correlation between the future option price F and the volatility of the forward price σ changes. Formally:

$$\text{Vanna} = \frac{\partial^2 V^*}{\partial \rho(F, \sigma)} \qquad (10.6)$$

8. What is the relationship between Vanna and Cora?

Vanna is a special case of Cora, with the dependent variable being the option price V^* and the correlated variables being the forward price or rate F and the volatility of F, σ.

9. What information does Gora give us?

Gora measures how much Cora changes if the correlation between two or more independent variables changes by an infinitesimally small amount. Formally,

$$\text{Gora} = \frac{\partial \text{Cora}}{\partial \rho(x_{i=1}, \ldots ,_n)} = \frac{\partial^2 V}{\partial \rho^2(x_{i=1}, \ldots ,_n)} \qquad (10.2)$$

Variables are defined as in equation (10.1).

10. What is Gora mathematically?

Gora is the first partial derivative of the Cora function or the second partial derivative of the original function V with respect to correlation. That is, Gora measures the curvature of a function with respect to correlation.

11. OK, here is a tough one: differentiate the price function of an exchange option

$$E = S_2 e^{-q_2 T} N \left(\frac{\ln\left(\frac{S_2 e^{-q_2 T}}{S_1 e^{-q_1 T}}\right) + \frac{1}{2}\left(\sigma_1^2 + \sigma_2^2 - 2\rho\sigma_1\sigma_2\right)T}{\sqrt{\sigma_1^2 + \sigma_2^2 - 2\rho\sigma_1\sigma_2}\sqrt{T}} \right)$$

$$- S_1 e^{-q_1 T} N \left(\frac{\ln\left(\frac{S_2 e^{-q_2 T}}{S_1 e^{-q_1 T}}\right) + \frac{1}{2}\left(\sigma_1^2 + \sigma_2^2 - 2\rho\sigma_1\sigma_2\right)T}{\sqrt{\sigma_1^2 + \sigma_2^2 - 2\rho\sigma_1\sigma_2}\sqrt{T}} \right) \qquad (10.8)$$

with respect to the correlation coefficient ρ. Try doing this yourself first. After rearranging, you can just use the chain rule. If you give up, look at http://www.dersoft.com/exchangeoptioncora.docx, for the answer.

12. Arguably, the most important application of correlation risk management is in risk management. In practice, the risk of a portfolio is often measured with the VaR concept. Is VaR sensitive to changes in the correlation of the assets in the portfolio? That is, what is the Cora of VaR?

    $Cora_{VaR}$ measures how much VaR changes for an infinitesimally small change in all pairwise correlations of all asset returns in the portfolio. Formally,

    $$Cora_{VaR} = \frac{\partial(VaR)}{\partial \rho(x_{i=1,\ldots,n})} \qquad (10.15)$$

    Variables are defined as in equation (10.1).

13. What is the Gora of VaR?

    Gora for VaR measures how much Cora of VaR changes if the correlation of all assets in the portfolio changes, or what the curvature of the original VaR function is. Formally,

    $$Gora_{VaR} = \frac{\partial Cora_{VaR}}{\partial \rho(x_{i=1,\ldots,n})} = \frac{\partial^2(VaR)}{\partial \rho^2(x_{i=1,\ldots,n})} \qquad (10.18)$$

    Variables are defined as in equation (10.1).

14. Cora and Gora can be extended in many ways. Name two.

    We can derive two types of Gap-Cora.

    a) One measures the correlation exposure of VaR with respect to a change of the correlation between a single asset in the portfolio and *all* other assets; formally:

    $$GAP\text{-}Cora_{i,P} = \frac{\partial(VaR)}{\partial \rho(x_{i,j=1,\ldots,n})} \qquad (10.16)$$

    b) Another type of Gap-Cora measures the correlation exposure of VaR with respect to a change of the correlation between the correlation of just *two* assets i and j; formally:

    $$GAP\text{-}Cora_{i,j} = \frac{\partial(VaR)}{\partial \rho(x_{i,j})} \qquad (10.17)$$

We can also derive the Gap-Gora for equations (10.16) and (10.17). This would tell us how much the Gap-Coras change if the correlation changes.

Answers to Questions and Problems of Chapter 11: Quantifying Credit Correlation Risk

1. What is credit risk?

   Credit risk is the risk of financial loss due to an unfavourable change in the credit quality of a debtor.

2. Which two types of credit risk exist? What is the relationship between these two types of credit risk?

   There are principally two types of credit risk: (1) migration risk and (2) default risk. See Figure 11.1 for a graph.

   Default risk is a special case of migration risk for a migration of the debtor into the default state. Default risk exists only for a long credit position, for example being long a bond or long a tranche in a CDO.

   However, migration risk and default risk have different dynamics. For example, if a bond migrates to a lower state, for example CCC, the bond investor just suffers a paper loss and will receive the principal investment back at maturity if the bond does not default. However, if a bond defaults and stays in default, the bond investor will not receive the principal investment back, just the recovery rate of the bond.

3. What is credit correlation risk?

   Credit correlation risk is the risk that credit quality correlations between two or more counterparties change unfavourably.

4. Name three financial products that are exposed to credit correlation risk.

   All loan portfolios of financial institutions, as well as all structured products such as collateralised debt obligations (CDOs) and mortgage-backed securities (MBSs), are exposed to credit correlation risk. In addition, all portfolios that apply derivatives as a hedge also include credit correlation risk.

5. A CDS that is used as a hedge has three parties: (1) the investor (CDS buyer); (2) the counterparty (CDS seller); and (3) the underlying asset. The default correlation between which two entities is most significant for the valuation of a CDS?

Most significant is the default correlation between the counterparty c and the reference asset r.

6. For the counterparty, the default correlation between the investor and the underlying asset is also of importance. What is the worst-case scenario for the counterparty from a risk perspective?

The worst-case scenario for the counterparty is when the default correlation between the investor i and the reference entity r is *negative*, with the credit quality of the investor decreasing and the credit quality of the reference asset increasing. An increase in the credit quality of the reference entity increases the present value of the CDS for the counterparty since the counterparty is now receiving an above-market spread (this is beneficial from a profit perspective but negative from a risk perspective since a higher present value means more credit exposure). In addition, the decrease in the credit quality of the investor means higher credit risk for the counterparty with respect to the investor.

7. When valuing a CDS, we can also include the default intensity correlation of all three entities. Draw a Venn diagram that displays the default intensity correlation's properties.

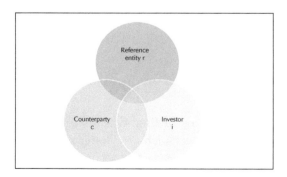

ANSWERS TO QUESTIONS AND PROBLEMS IN CORRELATION RISK MODELLING AND MANAGEMENT

8. What information does the Cora of a CDS give us?

   As defined in Chapter 11, Cora measures how much a dependent variable changes if the correlation between one or more independent variables changes. For a CDS, we have four Coras. The most critical Cora is the change in the CDS value for a change in the reference asset–counterparty default correlation:

   $$\text{CDSCora}_1 = \frac{\partial \text{CDS}}{\partial \lambda(r \cap c)} \qquad (11.11)$$

9. Since there are three entities in a CDS, there are principally three Coras. Name them and interpreted them. Which one is the most critical?

   a) As mentioned in question 8, the Cora of a CDS with respect to the credit correlation between the reference asset r and the counterparty c is most critical, meaning it has the highest impact on the CDS spread.

   Other Coras with respect to a CDS are

   b) $$\text{CDSCora}_2 = \frac{\partial \text{CDS}}{\partial \lambda(r \cap i)} \qquad (11.12)$$

   CDSCora_2 measures how much the value of the CDS changes if the default correlation between the reference asset r and the investor i, $\lambda(r \cap i)$, changes by a very small amount.

   c) $$\text{CDSCora}_3 = \frac{\partial \text{CDS}}{\partial \lambda(i \cap c)} \qquad (11.13)$$

   CDSCora_3 measures how much the value of the CDS changes if the default correlation between the investor i and the counterparty c, $\lambda(i \cap c)$, changes by a very small amount. However, CDSCora_3 is close to 0, since the effects of a change in the correlation between the investor i and the counterparty c net.

   d) $$\text{CDSCora}_4 = \frac{\partial \text{CDS}}{\partial \lambda(r \cap c \cap i)} \qquad (11.14)$$

We can also derive the sensitivity of the CDS value with a change in the joint default correlation of *all* entities in a CDS. The default intensity correlation $\lambda(r \cap c \cap i)$ can be simulated by a trivariate copula, as in Brigo and Pallavicini (2008), or can be simulated by Monte Carlo simulation. The numerical values for $CDSCora_4$ are complex and depend on the default intensity input parameter values $\lambda(r)$, $\lambda(c)$, $\lambda(i)$, the volatilities of $\lambda(r)$, $\lambda(c)$, $\lambda(i)$, and the correlation $\lambda(r \cap c \cap i)$. Different sensitivities of the CDS spread result for different combinations of the input parameters.

10. What does the Gora of a CDS tell us?

The Gora of a CDS tells us how much the Cora of a CDS changes if the correlation between the entities in question changes by an infinitesimally small amount. Since we have four different Coras for a CDS, we have four different Goras.

11. What are the two main risks in a CDO?

Credit risk and correlation risk are the two main risks in a CDO.

12. The value of a CDO and its tranches depends critically on the correlation of the assets in the CDO. Draw a graph showing the equity tranche value, mezzanine tranche value and a senior tranche value with respect to correlation.

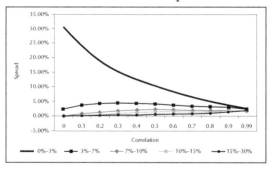

13. What does the Cora of a tranche in a CDO tell us?

It tells us how much the spread of the tranche changes if the correlation between all assets in the CDO changes by an infinitesimally small amount.

14. Which tranche in a CDO has the highest correlation risk, ie, the highest Cora?

Definitely the equity tranche (ie, the 0–3% tranche). We observe that the equity tranche spread changes strongly for a change in the correlation, since the slope of the equity function (ie, the Cora) is highly negative.

15. CDOs and their correlation properties are sometimes termed "toxic". Do you agree with this view?

Not at all. The correlation properties of the CDO as displayed in Figure 11.15 are very intuitive. In addition, the correlation risk can be quantified with Cora and Gora and hedged accordingly. CDOs are not toxic, but traders are, who overinvested in them, did not hedge the risks, and did not want to take the blame for their irresponsible, high-risk trading.

Answers to Questions and Problems of Chapter 12: Hedging Correlation Risk

1. What is hedging?

   Hedging means reducing risk, or, more precisely, hedging is entering into a second trade to reduce the risk of an original trade.

2. Name the three main ways to hedge.

   1) Eliminate the original position. So, when a bond was bought, just sell the bond.
   2) Hedge the position with a derivative such as a future, swap or option.
   3) Enter into a position that is negatively correlated with the original position. For example, if the investor bought a Greek bond, the investor can sell a Spanish bond. This is a good hedge as long as the Greek bond price and the Spanish bond price are positively correlated.

3. Name two reasons why it is more difficult to hedge correlation risk compared to equity risk or currency risk.

   a) Hedging correlation risk involves two or more assets, since the correlation is measured between at least two assets.

b) Hedging financial correlation is challenging because there is principally no underlying instrument that trades in the market and that can be bought or sold as a hedge.

4. Can it be a good idea not to hedge an exposure such as a correlation exposure?

Yes. If the correlation does not change or does not move in the unfavourable direction, it would, in retrospect, have been a good idea not to hedge.

5. In a delta hedge, the delta amount of the exposure is sold or bought. Give an example of delta hedging.

Example 12.1a:

An option trader at Goldman Sachs buys a call on IBM. The call option premium is US$10,000 (eg, the trader bought 1,000 calls with a call premium of C_0 = US$10). IBM trades at $S_0 = 100$. The trader decides to delta-hedge the IBM price risk of the option. The delta, derived from an option pricing model such as the Black–Scholes-Merton model, comes out to 60%. Formally:

$$\Delta C = \frac{\partial C}{\partial S} \approx \frac{0.6}{1} \qquad (12.1a)$$

where:

Δ_C: Delta of the call
C: Call price
S: Price of the underlying stock IBM
∂: Partial derivative operator

Equation (12.1a) reads: How much does the call price C change if S changes by an infinitesimally small amount, assuming all other variables influencing the call price are constant? For practical purposes, the change in S can be approximated by a change of 1, as done in equation (12.1a).

How much IBM stock does the option trader have to sell to stay delta-neutral, meaning the option trade has no price risk with respect to IBM?

ANSWERS TO QUESTIONS AND PROBLEMS IN CORRELATION RISK MODELLING AND MANAGEMENT

The option trader has to sell IBM stock in the delta amount, hence 60% of the option premium of US$10,000. Therefore, the option trader sells 60 shares at US$100 each and receives US$6,000. The option trader now has no IBM price risk.[2] Let us show this.

If IBM increases by 1%, following equation (12.1a) the call price increases by 0.60%. Therefore, the profit on the call is:

$$C_1 \times 1{,}000 - C_0 \,(\,1{,}000 = \text{US\$}10.060 \\ \times 1{,}000 - \text{US\$}10 \times 1{,}000 = \text{US\$}60$$

The loss on the hedge is:

$$S_1 \times 60 - S_0 \times 60 = \text{US\$}101 \times 60 - \text{US\$}100 \times 60 = \text{US\$}60$$

Hence the option trade is hedged against the price risk of IBM. What the option trader gains on the call is lost on the hedge, and vice versa.

6. Delta hedges are typically not constant. Give an example of dynamic delta hedging.

Let us assume the option trader has hedged their call option exposure as in example 12.1a in question 5. Now let us assume that the delta has increased from 0.6 to 0.7.[3] In this case the option trader has to increase their hedge to 70%; that is, they have to sell 70 shares of IBM. Now the option trader is hedged against the price risk of IBM:

Equation (12.1a) changes to:

$$\Delta C = \frac{\partial C}{\partial S} \approx \frac{0.7}{1} \qquad (12.1b)$$

If IBM increases by 1%, following equation (12.1b) the call price increases by 0.70%. Therefore the profit on the call is:

$$C_1 \times 1{,}000 - C_0 \times 1{,}000 = \text{US\$}10.070 \\ \times 1{,}000 - \text{US\$}10 \times 1{,}000 = \text{US\$}70$$

The loss on the hedge is:

$$S_1 \times 70 - S_0 \times 70 = \text{US\$}101 \times 70 - \text{US\$}100 \times 70 = \text{US\$}70$$

Hence the option trade is hedged against the price risk of IBM. What the option trader gains on the call is lost on the hedge, and vice versa.

7. Name several instruments that can hedge correlation risk.

   Principally, every instrument that can replicate the correlation risk of the original trade can serve as a hedge for correlation risk. In particular, we can use all correlation-dependent options, correlation futures, and correlation swaps.

8. How can we determine whether a certain correlation hedge is a good hedge?

   We should add the correlation exposure of the original trade and the correlation exposure of the hedge. If the sum of the correlation exposures is close to zero, it is a good correlation hedge.

9. When an investor has a perfect hedge, doesn't this mean that the profit potential is zero?

   Yes. The more the correlation exposure is hedged, the lower are both the potential profit and the potential loss from the hedged position.

10. Generally, when should we hedge with forwards, futures and swaps, and when should we hedge with options?

    The more confident an investor is that the undesirable event will occur (for example, a price decline of a bond if the bond was bought), the more appropriate it is to hedge with a future, forward or swap. In this case, no option premium is wasted.

    The less confident an investor is that the undesirable event will occur (a price decline if the bond was bought), the more appropriate it is to hedge with a put option. In this case, a put option premium has to be paid. However, if the underlying goes in the right direction (increases in price if the bond was bought), the investor participates in the bond price increase. The (put) option will expire worthless.

Answers to Questions and Problems of Chapter 13: Correlation Trading – Opportunities and Limitations

1. What is correlation trading?

   Correlation trading is the attempt to financially gain from changes in correlation between one or more assets.

ANSWERS TO QUESTIONS AND PROBLEMS IN CORRELATION RISK MODELLING AND MANAGEMENT

2. Give an example of empirical correlation trading.

   An example would be to exploit the positive correlation between international stock markets. Meissner *et al* (2018) find that the correlation between Asian markets, European markets, and the US market are highly positive. Therefore, a simple strategy of buying Europe if Asia was up, buying the US if Europe was up, and buying Asia if the US was up. The same logic applies in case of a down-markets.

3. What is pairs trading?

   Pairs trading, a type of statistical arbitrage or convergence arbitrage, was pioneered in the quant group of Morgan Stanley in the 1980s. The idea is to find two stocks, whose prices are highly correlated. Once the price correlation weakens, the stock that has increased is shorted and the stock which has declined is bought. Presumably, the spread will narrow again and a profit is realised.

4. Name the three critical elements of pairs trading.

   a) Selection of the pairs.
   b) Timing of trade execution.
   c) Timing of trade closing.

5. How can potentially successful pairs be determined?

   By applying correlation analyses, mean reversion techniques or cointegration

6. How does a quanto option work?

   A quanto option allows a domestic investor to exchange their potential payoff in a foreign currency back into their home currency at a fixed exchange rate. A quanto option therefore protects an investor against currency risk: eg, an American believes the Nikkei will increase, but is worried about a decreasing yen. The investor can buy a quanto call on the Nikkei with the yen payoff being converted into dollars at a fixed (usually the spot) exchange rate.

7. Which correlation is critical in a quanto option?

   The value of a quanto call option is highly sensitive to the correlation between the price of the underlying in foreign currency S' and the exchange rate X, $\rho(S',X)$.

8. What do Cora and Gora tell us?

   Cora measures the sensitivity of an option, a structured product such as a CDO or CMO, or any financial value as VaR (value-at-risk) or ES (expected shortfall), to correlation. In other words, it is the first partial derivative of the dependent variable V to correlation:

   $$\text{Cora} = \frac{\partial V}{\partial \rho(x_{i=1,\ldots,n})}$$

   where $x_{i=1,\ldots,n}$ are independent variables.

   The sensitivity of Cora to correlation can be quantified with Gora:

   $$\text{Gora} = \frac{\partial \text{Cora}}{\partial \rho(x_{i=1,\ldots,n})} = \frac{\partial^2 V}{\partial \rho^2(x_{i=1,\ldots,n})}$$

   Hence, Gora is the second partial derivative of the dependent variable to correlation.

9. In a CDO, why is the equity tranche investor "long correlation"?

   The equity tranche investor, (0–3% tranche), is "long correlation", since, when the correlation between the assets in the CDO increases, the equity tranche spread decreases, and the investor now receives an above market spread.

10. Is it a good idea to hedge a long equity tranche position with a short mezzanine tranche position?

    No! For low correlation levels the slope of the equity tranche and mezzanine tranche are opposite. Hence if correlation decreases, the long equity tranche investor and short mezzanine tranche investor lose on both legs; see Figure 13.2.

11. What is the main advantage of a correlation swap compared with other correlation products?

    Correlation swaps are pure correlation plays, ie, contrary to structured products (such as CDOs), or correlation options, no price or volatility components of an underlying instrument are involved.

ANSWERS TO QUESTIONS AND PROBLEMS IN CORRELATION RISK MODELLING AND MANAGEMENT

12. Why is dispersion trading correlation trading?

    Dispersion trading is trying to exploit the change in volatility of a whole index and versus the volatility of certain index components. This can be expressed with the average correlation between the assets in the portfolio, see equation (13.20).

13. What are long dispersion trading and short dispersion trading?

    Long dispersion is buying volatility on index components and selling volatility on the index. Short dispersion is selling volatility on index components and buying volatility on the index.

14. In which economic situation should a trader go "short dispersion", ie, sell straddles on individual stocks and buying a straddle on the index?

    We should go "short dispersion" when the market has a downturn, since many stocks decline jointly. We should go "long dispersion" if the market goes sideways, since the index will not change much, but individual stocks may.

15. Can correlation products be used to hedge systemic equity risk?

    Yes, going short correlation should protect against a systemic market downturn, since correlations typically increase in a downturn (and the payoff the long straddle on the index should compensate for the loss of the short straddles on individual stocks).

16. What is the advantage of variance dispersion trading?

    If dispersion trading is executed via straddles as discussed in section, the trader has to deal with the price and volatility of the underlying components and the index. If the dispersion trade is hedged, the trader has to additionally deal with the risk parameters, delta, vega, gamma, theta, vanna, volga and rho. An easier and more direct way to trade correlation is variance dispersion trading, without the hassle of having to trade and hedge the underlying options.

Answers to Questions and Problems of Chapter 14: Basel III's CVaR concept

1. What information does credit value-at-risk (CVaR) give us?

    CVaR measures the maximum loss of a portfolio due to default risk with a certain probability for a certain time frame. CVaR includes the default correlation of the assets in the portfolio.

2. Why don't we just apply the market VaR concept to value credit risk?

    First, the portfolio variance, defined in equation (1.9) $\sigma_p = \sqrt{\beta_h C \beta_v}$ would require input data as standard deviations of relative credit rating changes, and the correlation coefficient between the changes. However, this data for credit risk is rare, since credit rating changes for most entities rarely occur, often only once a year or not even at all.

    Second, the value for α in equation (1.8) $VaR = \alpha \sigma \sqrt{x}$ would assume a normal distribution of relative credit rating changes. However, credit rating changes are typically not normally distributed and depend on the current credit rating, past credit rating changes, country, sector, seniority, coupon, yield, etc. See Meissner (2005) for a further discussion.

3. Which correlation concept underlies the CVaR concept of the Basel II and III approaches?

    The simplistic one-factor Gaussian copula (OFGC).

4. In the Basel committee CVaR approach, what follows for the relationship between the CVaR value and the average probability of default, if we assume the correlation between all assets in the portfolio is zero?

    It follows that CVaR = PD(T), where PD(T) is the (identical) probability of default of all assets. So, for a 99.9% confidence level, we are 99.9% sure that we will not lose more than the average default rate PD(T). This is reasonable because there is no effect from correlation and the maximum loss is just the average default probability of the debtors.

ANSWERS TO QUESTIONS AND PROBLEMS IN CORRELATION RISK MODELLING AND MANAGEMENT

5. Deutsche has given loans to several companies in the amount of US$500,000,000. The average 1-year default probability of the companies is 2%. The copula default correlation coefficient between the companies is 3%. What is the 1-year CVaR on a 99.9% confidence level?

   Using

   $$CVaR(PD(T), \rho, X) = N\left(\frac{N^{-1}[PD(T)] + \sqrt{\rho} N^{-1}(X)}{\sqrt{1-\rho}}\right)$$

   we get 6.16%. Hence CVaR in US$ is 6.16% × US$500,000,000 = US$30,780,052.05. (See also the model www.dersoft.com/CVaR.xlsm.)

6. In the Basel committee CVaR model, the default correlation is an inverse function of the average probability of the default of the assets in the portfolio. Explain the rational for this relationship.

   It is assumed that highly rated companies with a low default probability have a higher correlation of default, since they are mostly prone to such systematic factors as a recession, in which they default together. However, companies with a high default probability are more affected by their own idiosyncratic factors and less by systematic risk, hence are assumed to be less correlated.

7. In the Basel committee approach, the required capital to be set aside for credit risk is the CVaR minus the average probability of default. Explain why.

   The rationale is that banks cover the expected loss with their own provisions as the interest rate that they charge. (Naturally low-rated debtors have to pay a higher interest rate on their loans than highly rated debtors.)

8. Which two approaches does the Basel committee allow banks to quantify double defaults?

   Substitution approach and double-default approach.

9. Which of the two approaches typically results in a lower capital requirement?

The double-default approach typically allows a lower capital charge than the substitution approach does.

10. What is the main criticism of the substitution approach?

    The substitution approach has been criticised for its lack of mathematical foundation and a lack of sensitivity to high-risk exposure (since the high-risk exposure is substituted for the guarantor's risk exposure).

Answers to Questions and Problems of Chapter 15: Basel III and XVAs

1. CVA (credit value adjustment) is an important concept of credit risk. What is CVA? Why is it important?

    CVA is an adjustment to address counterparty credit risk.

    The focus of CVA is typically defined more narrowly, referring to counterparty credit risk in a derivatives transaction. The importance of CVA is highlighted by Basel II, which reports that $2/3$ of the credit risk losses during the global financial crisis were caused by CVA volatility rather than actual defaults.

2. Why can CVA be considered a complex derivative?

    CVA is a complex derivative since it has two underlyings D^+ (the netted derivatives exposure) and PD_c (the probability of default of the counterparty), which may be correlated! This is expressed in equation (15.2):

    $$CVA_{a,c} = f\left(\underbrace{D^+_{a,c}}_{\text{Market risk}} , \underbrace{PD_c}_{\text{Credit risk}} \right) \qquad (15.2)$$

3. How can CVA without correlation between market risk and credit risk be calculated?

    We just multiply the derivatives exposure with the probability of default:

    $$CVA_{a,c} = \left(D^+_{a,c} \times PD_c\right)(1-R_c)$$

    where R_c is the recovery rate of the counterparty.

ANSWERS TO QUESTIONS AND PROBLEMS IN CORRELATION RISK MODELLING AND MANAGEMENT

4. Including the correlation between market risk and credit, the concept of wrong-way risk (WWR) arises. What is general WWR? What is specific WWR?

   General WWR exists when the probability of default of a counterparty is positively correlated with general market risk factors. Such market risk factors are interest rates, equity prices, foreign exchange rates, commodity prices, etc.

   A bank is exposed to specific WWR if future exposure to a specific counterparty is positively correlated with the counterparty's probability of default.

5. Name two examples of specific WWR.

   Specific WWR exists if there is a positive correlation between the default probability of the obligor o and the guarantor g (ie, the CDS seller). This means, the higher the default probability of the obligor PD_o, the higher is also the default probability of the guarantor PD_g (see Figure 15.5).

   Another example of specific WWR is a company selling put options on its own stock (see Figure 15.7). If the stock price declines, this means higher credit exposure (since the present values of the put increases) and higher credit risk (since a lower stock price typically means higher default risk).

6. How does the Basel committee address WWR?

   A multiplier α is applied to increase the derivatives exposure $D^+_{a,c}$. The multiplier α is set to 1.4, which means the credit exposure $D^+_{a,c}$ is increased by 40% compared with assuming credit exposure $D^+_{a,c}$ and credit risk PD_c are independent.

7. What is DVA? Should DVA be allowed to be applied in financial practice?

   DVA (debt value adjustment) adjusts the value of a derivatives portfolio by taking the entities' own default probability into consideration. DVA should not be allowed since:

   a) An entity as "a" would benefit from its own increasing default probability PD_a, since a higher default probability would increase DVA (via equation (15.18)), which

465

in turn increases the value of the derivatives portfolio (via equation (15.19))!

b) Entity "a" could realise the DVA benefit only if it actually defaults!

8. What is FVA (funding value adjustment)? Should FVA be included into the pricing of derivatives?

FVA is an adjustment to the price of a transaction due to the cost of funding for the transaction or the related hedge. Whether FVA should be included in the pricing is an ongoing debate. Professors Hull, White and Duffie argue that adding funding costs violates the risk-neutral derivatives pricing principle. It would lead to arbitrage opportunities, since the same derivative would have different prices. However, derivatives traders argue their treasury department charges them the funding cost, so FVA should be included in the pricing process.

9. Why does the Basel not require to have all derivatives centrally cleared?

The Basel accord encourages as many OTC derivatives to be cleared on exchanges as possible. However, some derivatives are so complex that a central clearing is problematic.

10. Explain why ColVA (collateral value adjustment) can increase or decrease the value of a derivatives portfolio.

If the interest rate paid by an entity A to borrow cash is lower than the interest rate that is typically paid by A, then there will be benefit from the collateralisation, ie, ColVA will be positive. If the interest rate paid by entity A to borrow cash is higher than the interest rate that is typically paid by A, then there will a loss from the collateralisation, ie, ColVA will be negative.

11. Why is KVA (regulatory capital adjustment) one of the most complex XVAs?

a) Due to changing market factors, the present value of the derivatives portfolio is constantly changing, resulting in changing KVAs.

b) The maturity of a derivative can be up to 30 years, requiring the KVA calculation going far into the future.
c) KVA has to be calculated for each counterparty since netting sets with each counterparty determine the specific counterparty KVA.
d) Regulations regarding KVA are currently evolving and can be hard to anticipate.

12. The variation margin MVA can be a source of dispute between counterparties. Why?

Variation margins are complex in nature since they depend on market variables, such as underlying derivatives price, credit quality of the counterpart, liquidity of the derivative, which constantly change. In addition, the BCBS requires all entities to exchange on a daily basis, the full amount of variation margin, which is a cost-intensive.

Answers to Questions and Problems of Chapter 16: Fundamental Review of the Trading Book (FRTB)

1. Name five key elements of the FRTB ("Fundamental Review of Trading Book").

   a) After about 20 years of applying VaR (value-at-risk) with a 99% confidence level and a 10-day horizon, now the expected shortfall on a 97.5% confidence level for different liquidity time horizons is applied.
   b) Six risk types are determined: (1) equity risk (2) interest-rate risk, (3) foreign-exchange risk (FX), (4) counterparty credit spread risk, (5) reference credit spread risk and (6) commodity risk. For each risk type ES (expected shortfall) has to be derived daily on a 97.5% one-tailed confidence level for different time horizons. ES also has to be derived for a period of significant stress.
   c) The FRTB-CVA framework addresses the credit exposure part of CVA. Future potential volatility (termed "variability") of the credit exposure is newly implemented, which is directly related to market prices.
   d) Since the increase in correlation within and between markets was highly underestimated in the 2007–8 crisis,

the FRTB includes numerous correlations within the risk type buckets, between the risk types, correlations between credit spread of a counterparty and systematic factor, and correlations between the credit spread of a counterparty and the associated hedge.

e) Hedges are recognised in the calculation of CVA, encouraging banks to hedge their credit exposure.

2. Explain the variables in $VaR_P = \sigma_P \alpha \sqrt{x}$.

VaR_P is the portfolio VaR (value at risk), α is the x-axis value representing a certain confidence level and x is time in days, σ_P is the portfolio volatility, ie, $\sigma_P = \sqrt{\beta_h C \beta_v}$, which includes the correlation between asset returns via the covariance matrix C; see Chapter 1, section "Risk Management and Correlation", as well as Chapter 10.

3. Define ES in terms of VaR.

ES (expected shortfall) is the average loss when exceeding VaR. Hence we have $ES = E(L \mid L > VaR)$, which is equation (16.1), where E : Expected value and L : Loss

4. How are α-values, ie, x-axis values for a certain confidence levels, derived?

α is the x-axis value representing a certain confidence level. It can be derived as =normsinv(confidence level) in Excel and norminv(confidence level) in MatLab.

5. In a normal distribution, how can VaR-α values be converted into ES-α values?

ES is the average loss when exceeding VaR. So to derive ES α-levels from certain VaR α-levels, we have to take all the VaR α-levels that exceed a specific significance level, and average them; see spreadsheet www.dersoft.com/VaRESconversion.xlsx.

6. Is it a good idea that the BCBS abandoned VaR in favour of ES?

ES is the expected loss, given that the loss is bigger than VaR. So, if we are interested in extreme losses in a crisis, ES is the appropriate measure. Loosely speaking, VaR tells us "How bad will it get in good times?" and ES tells us "How bad will it get in bad times?"

7. Which five risk factors does the BCBS require as inputs to calculate market risk?

   (1) Equity risk, (2) interest-rate risk, (3) credit spread risk, (4) FX risk and (5) commodity risk.

8. The BCBS applies 10-day overlapping time periods to derive ES. What is the consequence of this approach?

   Risk factor variables with a long liquidity time horizon are mathematically overweighted, since the liquidity horizon $LH_j - LH_{j-1}$ is higher. Eg, for a risk factor variable in risk category $j = 5$, $LH_j - LH_{j-1} = 250$, for a risk variable in risk category $j = 1$, $LH_j - LH_{j-1} = 10$. In addition, risk factor variables changes in risk category 5 are incorporated in all simulations (1) to (5), whereas risk factor variables in lower risk categories are not.

9. Name three critical differences between CVaR (credit value-at-risk) and CVA (credit value adjustment).

   a) CVaR derives the credit risk in standard exposures such as bonds and loans. CVA derives credit risk in a derivatives transaction.
   b) In the Basel III accord, CVA is an ES (expected shortfall)-based concept, while CVaR is derived by the VaR-based concept.
   c) In CVaR, the default correlation is derived simplistically with the one-factor Gaussian copula model. The Basel III CVA approach applies numerous Pearson correlations, such as the correlation between risk types (equity risk, interest-rate risk, FX risk, commodity risk, counterparty credit spread risk and reference asset credit spread risk) within the risk types, as well as correlations between credit spread of a counterparty and systematic factor, and correlations between the credit spread of a counterparty and the associated hedge.

10. Name three critical elements in Basel III's new calculation of the capital charge K for CVA.

   a) The incorporation of changes to market risk factors (equity risk, interest-rate risk, FX risk, credit-spread risk, and commodity risk), which drive the credit exposure volatility (termed "variability" in the accord), is a new element in the calculation of CVA.

   b) Numerous Pearson correlations between the risk types (equity risk, interest-rate risk, FX risk, commodity risk, counterparty credit spread risk and reference asset credit spread risk) within the risk types, as well as correlations between credit spread of a counterparty and systematic factor, and correlations between the credit spread of a counterparty and the associated hedge are part of the CVA capital charge.

   c) Direct hedges, indirect hedges as well as index hedges (mostly CDSs (credit default swaps)) are for the first time recognised in the CVA derivation and reduce the CVA capital charge K.

11. Which correlations are inputs to derive the capital charge K for CVA?

   As already mentioned on question (10b), the correlations are Pearson correlations between the risk types (equity risk, interest-rate risk, FX risk, commodity risk, counterparty credit spread risk and reference asset credit spread risk) within the risk types, as well as correlations between credit spread of a counterparty and systematic factor, and correlations between the credit spread of a counterparty and the associated hedge are part of the CVA capital charge.

Answers to Questions and Problems of Chapter 17: The Future of Correlation Modelling

1. GPU technology originated in the gaming industry and has been modified to solve complex financial problems. What is the general approach of graphical processing units (GPUs) to solve financial problems?

   GPU technology alters memory in a parallel execution of commands to instantaneously produce high-resolution three-dimensional images. The GPU technology was derived in the computer gaming industry, where gamers request high-resolution, instant response of their three-dimensional activities at low cost.

2. What are the advantages of applying the GPU technology in finance?

   The advantages of GPU technology are (a) speed, (b) increasing user-friendliness and (c) structural efficiency (ie, no compiling is necessary). It is debatable whether GPU technology is also more accurate than applying mathematical algorithms.

3. What are the disadvantages of the GPU technology in finance?

   a) Although there have been efforts to combine central processing unit (CPU) and GPU technology, GPUs still have a different architecture and require their own distinct structure of programming and specialised programming languages such as CUDA, OpenGL and OpenCg.
   b) GPUs provide efficient and fast solutions for problems that are complex but can be represented in matrices, since matrix multiplication and manipulation are easy to execute. However, for nonlinear, path-dependent structures, GPUs may not be well suited.

4. What is a general concern when applying GPU technology to finance?

   Altogether, the GPU technology is a promising new approach to derive fast, real-time results for complex financial problems, for which analytical solutions are questionable or not at all available. However, one can argue that if mathematical techniques are available, although slower, they should have preference over brute-force, non-analytical, iterative search procedures.

5. Artificial neural networks mimic the human brain and therefore have the ability to learn. How do they learn?

The learning process in an artificial neural network (ANN) can be achieved by different methods. One of the most popular is "backpropagation" (an abbreviation of "backward propagation of errors"), which applies weighting factors. Each weighting factor has a resistance attached to it. Numerous simulations (epochs) of different combinations of weighting factors are run. If the neural network output is close to the target value, the weighting factors are strengthened; that is, the resistance is turned down. If certain weighting factors produce bad results, the weighting factors are weakened; that is, the resistance is turned up.

6. What are the limitations of neural networks?

Naturally, neural networks have their drawbacks. First, they are so-called black boxes; that is, the mathematical algorithm, which optimises the output, is hidden. Second, neural networks often have quite a slow convergence rate. Third, and most important, neural networks can get stuck at local optima, not deriving the general optimum. These reasons have limited the usage of neural networks in reality.

7. Fuzzy logic is cool since it alters the traditional logic of a statement being either true or false. What logic does fuzzy logic apply?

Fuzzy logic alters the traditional concept of reasoning. In traditional logic a statement can either be true, typically assigned the value 1, or false, assigned the value 0. Fuzzy logic, however, argues that there can be a "partial truth" to a statement, assigning truth values ranging between 0 and 1.

For example, a professor asks the question: "What are the prime numbers between 10 and 20?" The correct answer is the set {11, 13, 17, 19}. If a student gives the answer {11, 13, 17}, traditional logic would argue that the answer is false. However, fuzzy logic would argue that the answer is partially true, actually 75% true.

8. Which three main concepts of evolution do genetic algorithms apply? Explain them briefly.

Genetic algorithms are based on phenomena found in evolution such as selection, crossover and mutation.

Each individual or element in a genetic algorithm is defined as a vector with parameters and weights. *Selection* can be done by various methods.

a) In roulette wheel selection, a random selection of potentially useful solutions for recombining the individuals is performed.
b) The crossover method creates the next generation by different "crossings" (loosely speaking, combinations) of the parents' organism strings to produce a variety of child organisms.
c) Mutation (ie, a change in the genetic property of an individual) is typically quantified as single-point mutation, meaning only a single nucleotide parameter is replaced by a new parameter. This replacement is performed at a certain mutation rate. For example, if the mutation rate is specified as 30%, this means that in 30% of the simulations a mutation will take place.

9. A chaotic system has several properties; name four.

1) Strong dependence on initial conditions.
2) Predictions possible for only a short period of time.
3) Self-similarity.
4) Regime changes.
5) Deterministic nature.

10. Which properties of chaos theory translate well to finance, and which do not?

From our analysis, we find that chaos criteria 3 and 4, the self-similarity principle and the regime changes, are also found in finance. However, criteria 1, 2 and 5, the dependence on initial conditions, the short-term but not long-term predictability, and the deterministic nature of chaos theory, are typically not properties in finance. The critical question is whether criteria 3 and 4 are sufficient to support financial trading decisions.

11. Which concept does Bayesian logic share with fuzzy logic?

The Bayesian approach reinterprets and extends classical probability reasoning. The Bayesian theorem is algebraically identical with the classical frequentist probability theory (called "frequentist" since it draws its conclusions from the frequency of data). However, the probabilities are reinterpreted. Bayesian probabilities are related to fuzzy logic, since both apply the concept of partial truth.

12. What are prior probabilities and posterior probabilities in the Bayesian theory?

A prior initial probability, $P(A)$, is the hypothesis before accounting for evidence. $P(A)$ can be a personal subjective belief, rather than an objectively derived probability. The *posterior* probability $P(A \mid B)$, is the probability of A given that the evidence B is observed.

---

1 The "N" in "NGARCH" stands for nonlinear, the "E" in "EGARCH" stands for exponential, and the "T "in "TGARCH" stands for truncated. See Bollerslev (2008) for a nice overview of all ARCH extensions.
2 This is true for small changes in the IBM price. If the IBM changes by a large amount, the delta changes and has to be adjusted.
3 An increase in the delta can happen for several reasons: (a) the price of the underlying increases; (b) the implied volatility decreases; or (c) the maturity of the option decreases.